LEGAL RESEARCH AND CITATION

CITATION EXERCISES

By

Larry L. Teply
Professor of Law
Creighton University

AMERICAN CASEBOOK SERIES®

WEST GROUP

 *TEXT IS PRINTED ON 10% POST CONSUMER RECYCLED PAPER*

PREFACE

Legal citation is an important skill used by lawyers in law practice. It plays an integral role in the writing of legal memoranda, appellate briefs, and other documents. In addition, legal citation is a fundamental element in the writing of judicial opinions in the United States.

This set of citation exercises is designed to be used with the fifth edition of the *Legal Research and Citation* text published by the West Group, with other legal research texts, or independently. If these exercises are used with the fifth edition of the *Legal Research and Citation* text or other research texts, it is strongly recommended that these exercises be assigned and completed **prior** to the coverage of the cited sources in class. In this way, students will be familiar with the sources being discussed in class. It will also avoid any overlap with additional exercises or assignments dealing with the same sources.

Like the exercises in preceding editions, the forty exercises in this set emphasize learning through the actual use and citation of legal research sources in the law library. These exercises included in this edition focus on the most important legal sources cited by law students and lawyers.

Although they may be used in conjunction with any citation system, the exercises and explanations in this edition focus primarily on the most widely accepted citation system in the United States: *The Bluebook*. This citation guide is compiled by the editors of the *Harvard Law Review, Columbia Law Review, University of Pennsylvania Law Review*, and *Yale Law Journal*. *See* Columbia Law Review et al., *The Bluebook: A Uniform System of Citation* (16th ed. 1996) [hereinafter *The Bluebook*]. However, these exercises can be adapted to other systems of citations, such as *The University of Chicago Manual of Legal Citation* (*The Maroon Book*). *See* University of Chicago Law Review & University of Chicago Legal Forum, *The University of Chicago Manual of Legal Citation* (1989).

The format of these exercises allows them to be conducted on a large scale. Each exercise contains one hundred basic problems. This format spreads the demand for books over a large number of sources. In most instances, only a few students will be seeking the same volume. This format also provides a more uniform wear and tear on library materials, and it helps to reduce problems of missing materials.

The problem number system used by these exercises also deals with the difficulty of several students having the same answers. This system is explained in detail in the "General Instructions for Students," which immediately follows this Preface. Because the combination of problem numbers shifts with each exercise, answer-sheet overlaps between any two students are minimized. As a result, students are less tempted to short-cut the learning process by finding other students who have already prepared the assignment. Furthermore, because corrected answer sheets are not readily "transferable," these exercises may be reused in subsequent years. With six hundred individual problem numbers available for each assignment, these exercises can be used for three years in a law school with the entering class of two hundred students without assigning the same problem number twice during that period.

Every effort has been made to make these exercises and teacher's answer manual as accurate as possible. Nevertheless, because of changes in legal publications, inaccuracies in typing, developments in the law, or further modifications in citation systems, errors might occur. I sincerely regret any inconvenience that results from these inaccuracies, changes in the library materials, or interim revisions (or changes in new editions) of *The Bluebook*.

In addition to the copyrighted excerpts showing case names, reporters, and digests from West Group, I would like to acknowledge Shepard's, which permitted me to reprint a portion of a page from *Shepard's United States Citations Case Edition*, © 1994 by Shepard's. In addition, I would like to recognize the prior permission of Lawyers Cooperative Publishing Co. (now part of West Group) to reproduce excerpts from *U.S. Supreme Court Resports, Lawyers' Edition 2d* and *U.S. Supreme Court Digest, Lawyers' Edition*, which is currently published by LEXIS Law Publishing, Charlottesville, VA (800) 446-3410.

I am especially indebted to Mary Hiser (Class of 1999), who has served as my research assistant for this edition of these exercises. I want to thank her for her invaluable suggestions and review of these materials. I also want to acknowledge the logistical support for this project provided by Dean Lawrence Raful and the Creighton Law School administration. I also appreciate the excellent secretarial assistance provided by Joan Hillhouse and Pat Andersen as well as the excellent copying service provided by Tianne Snell. In addition, I want to thank Law Library Director Kay Andrus, Associate Law Library Director Ann Kitchel, Legal Reference Librarian Patrick Charles, and Reference/Library Automation Librarian Ana Marie Hinman for their helpful comments, suggestions, and support. Finally, I want to express appreciation to my wife, Frannie, and my two children, Robert and Benjamin, for their support and encouragement.

L.L.T.

Omaha, Nebraska
April, 1999

GENERAL INSTRUCTIONS
FOR STUDENTS

———

You will be assigned an individual problem number (a number from one to six hundred) that will direct you to your particular assignment within each exercise. In order to complete an exercise, you should first read the introductory material and then examine the instructions at the beginning of the exercise. You then will find your individual problem number in the six columns of numbers under the heading "Problem #." For example, the instructions to the first exercise require you to use a legal dictionary to find the definition of a legal term listed with your problem number. If you were assigned problem number 397, you should look in the left-hand column of problem numbers for number 397. That entry is shown below:

PROBLEM #   **LEGAL TERM**

48 137 217 397 477 567   Trade secret

This entry directs you to find the term, trade secret, in a legal dictionary. For your answer to this exercise, you are asked to state the following information:

(a) the title of the dictionary used (*e.g.*, *Black's Law Dictionary*);

(b) the author's full name, if any is listed (*e.g.*, Brian A. Garner, David Mellinkoff, etc.);

(c) the copyright date of the dictionary that you used (*e.g.*, 1999);

(d) the edition of the dictionary if it is not the first edition (*e.g.*, 2d edition, 3d revised edition, 4th edition, etc.); and

(e) the citation of dictionary in *Bluebook* (or another designated) form.

Unless otherwise instructed, write your answers on the answer sheet provided in Part 4 of these exercises. You would use the same basic procedure to complete each subsequent exercise. If a source needed to complete a particular exercise is unavailable or a change is necessary for some other reason, you should use a different problem number for that exercise only.

Some of the commonly asked questions about the use of these library exercises and the answers to those questions include the following:

Do you retain the same problem number for all forty-two citation exercises? You should use the same assigned problem number for each of the exercises.

How should italics be indicated in answers to the exercises? Unless otherwise instructed, italics should be indicated by <u>underscoring</u>.

When a citation is required, what citation form should you use? Unless otherwise instructed, you should use *Bluebook* form.

How are problem numbers reassigned when you encounter difficulty finding a needed book or answering an exercise? Unless your instructor designates otherwise, you should use the following self-reassignment procedure. Add 105 to your problem number (or subtract 105 if you have been assigned a problem number between 495 and 600), and do that problem instead.

For example, assume that your assigned problem number is 397 and that you are unable to complete one of the exercises because a needed book is unavailable. You would add 105 to 397 and do problem number 502 for this exercise only. In this situation, you should clearly indicate on your answer sheet which problem number you used and the reason for the change.

If by adding 105 you still have trouble, you should add 1 more, and so on. In the above example, you would do problem number 503. Note that you would use this new problem number only for this exercise.

Are you permitted to work with other students on the answers to the exercises? Unless you are otherwise instructed, you may discuss the assignments with other students. The final written product, however, must reflect your own individual work. In any event, you will find that overlap of answer sheets for any given group of students will be minimal.

Should you keep a copy of your answer sheet? Unless otherwise instructed, you should retain a photocopy of your answer sheet. In case your answer sheet is misplaced, you must be able to supply your instructor with a copy of your answers.

TABLE OF CONTENTS

PART 1

CITING BOOKS, PERIODICALS, AND OTHER SECONDARY SOURCES

A. EXERCISES IN THIS PART

Part 1 focuses on citing texts, treatises, periodicals, and other secondary sources. The eight exercises in this part cover the following sources:

Citation Exercise 1. Dictionaries
Citation Exercise 2. Legal Encyclopedias (I)
Citation Exercise 3. Legal Encyclopedias (II)
Citation Exercise 4. Texts and Treatises
Citation Exercise 5. Legal Periodicals (I)
Citation Exercise 6. Legal Periodicals (II)
Citation Exercise 7. A.L.R. Annotations
Citation Exercise 8. Restatements of the Law

B. BASIC CITATION FORMS ILLUSTRATED

The following chart illustrates the basic forms for citations of various secondary sources based on the *Bluebook* rules and typeface conventions for legal memoranda and court documents:

CITING SECONDARY SOURCES IN *BLUEBOOK* FORM	
SOURCE	**BASIC CITATION FORMS**
DICTIONARIES —Usual Form —Special Forms	David Mellinkoff, *Mellinkoff's Dictionary of American Legal Usage* 345 (1992). *Black's Law Dictionary* 700 (6th ed. 1990). *Ballentine's Law Dictionary* 128 (3d ed. 1969).
LEGAL ENCYCLOPEDIAS —National —Locally Oriented	24A Am. Jur. 2d *Divorce & Separation* § 633 (1998). 11 C.J.S. *Boundaries* § 143 (1995). 18 Fla. Jur. 2d *Decedent's Property* § 274 (1997). 13 Cal. Jur. 3d *Constitutional Law* §§ 220-222 (1989).

CITING SECONDARY SOURCES IN *BLUEBOOK* FORM
(CONTINUED)

SOURCE	BASIC CITATION FORMS
TEXTS & TREATISES —With one author —With two authors —With three or more authors —Works organized by sections —Multi-volume works —Works with editors	Larry L. Teply, *Legal Negotiation in a Nutshell* 5 (1992). Frederick Pollock & Frederic W. Maitland, *The History of English Law* 55 (2d rev. ed. 1968). Helene S. Shapo et al., *Writing and Analysis in the Law* 207 (1989). Mark A. Rothstein et al., *Employment Law* § 3.36, at 171-72 (1994). 5 Charles A. Wright & Arthur R. Miller, *Federal Practice and Procedure: Civil* § 1277 (2d ed. 1990). *Industrial Concentration: The New Learning* (Harvey J. Goldschmid et al. eds., 1974).
LEGAL PERIODICALS —Articles with one author —Articles with two authors —Articles with three or more authors —Articles with the year as part of the volume designation —Student works with a named author —Student works with an unnamed author —Nonconsecutively paginated journals	Larry L. Teply, *Antitrust Immunity of State and Local Governmental Action*, 48 Tulane L. Rev. 272 (1974). Ralph H. Folsom & Larry L. Teply, *Trademarked Generic Words*, 89 Yale L.J. 1323 (1980). Griffin B. Bell et al., *Automatic Disclosure in Discovery—The Rush to Reform*, 27 Ga. L. Rev. 1 (1992). Richard Delgado et al., *Fairness and Formality: Minimizing the Risk of Prejudice in Alternative Dispute Resolution*, 1985 Wis. L. Rev. 1359. Dan Thu Thi Phan, Note, *Will Fair Use Function on the Internet?* 98 Colum. L. Rev. 169 (1998). Note, *Mens Rea in Federal Criminal Law*, 111 Harv. L. Rev. 2402 (1998). Gene H. Wood, *The Child as Witness*, 6 Fam. Advoc., Spring 1984, at 14.
A.L.R. ANNOTATIONS	Kimberly J. Winbush, Annotation, *Searches and Seizures: Reasonable Expectation of Privacy in Contents of Garbage or Trash Receptacle*, 62 A.L.R.5th 1 (1998).
RESTATEMENTS OF THE LAW	Restatement of Conflict of Laws § 113 (1934). Restatement (Second) of Conflict of Laws § 29 (1971).

CITATION EXERCISE 1
DICTIONARIES

A. INTRODUCTION

1. Dictionaries in Legal Writing

Dictionaries are useful research and reference tools. They are sometimes cited in court opinions and other types of legal writing. *See* Ellen P. Aprill, *The Law of the Word: Dictionary Shopping in the Supreme Court*, 30 Ariz. St. L.J. 275 (1998); Note, *Looking It Up: Dictionaries and Statutory Interpretation*, 107 Harv. L. Rev. 1437 (1994).

2. *Bluebook* Form for Citing Dictionaries

Most dictionaries are cited like any other book. *Bluebook* Rule 15 governs the citation form for books, pamphlets, and other nonperiodic materials. The following are the typical elements of a book citation in *Bluebook* form:

(1) the **volume number** (if more than one);

(2) the **full name of the author** as it is given in the publication, with the following technical modifications:

    (a) a designation such as "Jr." or "III" should be included; however, a comma should be inserted before such designations only when the author has done so;

    (b) a book with two authors should be cited in the order they are given in the publication, connected by an ampersand (&);

    (c) a book with three or more authors should be cited to the first author only, followed by "et al." (and others);

    (d) when a single volume of a multi-volume work is cited, only the author(s) of the volume cited should be given; and

    (e) when a book has institutional authors or editors, follow *Bluebook* Rule 15.1.3;

(3) the **main title in full** as it is given on the title page (including a serial number, if any, but omitting a subtitle unless it is particularly relevant); capitalize the title according to *Bluebook* Rule 8, *i.e.*, capitalize the initial word, the word immediately following a colon, and all other words in the title; however, do not capitalize articles, conjunctions, and prepositions of four or fewer letters;

(4) the **section, paragraph, or page** number (if a specific part of the book is cited); when a book is organized by sections or paragraphs, cite to them (*e.g.*, ¶ 22 or § 84); to facilitate finding the material within a section or paragraph, page number(s) may be added (*e.g.*, ¶ 22, at 77 or § 84, at 988) (*Bluebook* Rule 3.4);

(5) the **full name of the editor or translator**, if any (*Bluebook* Rule 15.1.2);

(6) the **edition** (if other than the first); and

(7) the **year** of publication.

Bluebook Rules 3.4, 15.1.1, 15.1.2, 15.1.3, 15.2, 15.3 & 15.4; *see also infra* Citation Exercise 4.

The following are examples of typical *Bluebook* citations of dictionaries:

[Example 1] Thomas Sheridan, *A General Dictionary of the English Language* (1796).

> In the above citation, the entire work is cited; thus, no specific page reference is given.

[Example 2] 2 Samuel Johnson, *A Dictionary of the English Language* 950 (1785).

> In the above citation, material appearing on page 950 in volume 2 of the dictionary is cited.

Some dictionaries no longer have a designated author:

[Example 3] *Webster's New International Dictionary* 1388 (2d ed. 1945).

3. Special *Bluebook* Forms for *Black's Law Dictionary* and *Ballentine's Law Dictionary*

Bluebook Rule 15.7 provides **special citation forms** for two frequently cited law dictionaries:

[Example 4] *Black's Law Dictionary* 977 (6th ed. 1990).

[Example 5] *Ballentine's Law Dictionary* 42 (3d ed. 1969).

See Bluebook Rule 15.7(a).

4. Typeface Conventions

In Examples 1-5 above, the title of the dictionary (book) appears in italics. In typewritten or handwritten material, italics can be shown by underscoring:

[Example 6] Thomas Sheridan, <u>A General Dictionary of the English Language</u> (1796).

This typeface format (italics or underscoring) is the *Bluebook* standard for court documents and legal memoranda. *See Bluebook* Practitioners' Notes P.1 & P.1(b).

In contrast, large and small capital letters have traditionally been used in citations of books in law review footnotes. Both the author's name and the book title appear in large and small capital letters. Thus, the above citation would appear as follows in a typical law review footnote:

[**Example 7**] THOMAS SHERIDAN, A GENERAL DICTIONARY OF THE ENGLISH LANGUAGE (1796).

Some law reviews vary the typeface from this convention by replacing large and small capital letters with ordinary roman type. *See Bluebook* Rules 2.1 & 2.1(b).

B. INSTRUCTIONS FOR COMPLETING THIS EXERCISE

To complete this exercise, use the sixth edition of *Black's Law Dictionary*, the third edition of *Ballentine's Law Dictionary*, or another legal dictionary (if these editions of *Black's* and *Ballentine's* are unavailable) to find the definition of the term listed with your problem number below. For your answer to this exercise, state the following information:

(a) the title of the dictionary used (*e.g.*, *Black's Law Dictionary*);

(b) the author's full name, if any is listed (*e.g.*, Brian A. Garner, David Mellinkoff, etc.);

(c) the copyright date of the dictionary that you used (*e.g.*, 1999);

(d) the edition of the dictionary if it is not the first edition (*e.g.*, 2d edition, 3d revised edition, 4th edition, etc.);

(e) the editor's full name, if any is listed (*e.g.*, William S. Anderson); and

(f) the citation of dictionary in *Bluebook* (or another designated) form; include the specific page(s) where the definition can be found; cite multiple pages by giving inclusive page numbers, separated by a hyphen (*e.g.*, 35-36); if the pages cited consist of three or more numbers, you should retain the last two digits and drop the repetitious digit(s) (*e.g.*, 173-74 or 1135-36) (*see Bluebook* Rule 3.3(d)); assume that your citation will appear in a court document or legal memorandum, not in a law review article.

Unless otherwise instructed, write your answers on the answer sheet provided in Part 4 of these exercises.

PROBLEM #	LEGAL TERM
1 190 270 350 430 520	Chattel(s)
2 191 271 351 431 521	Libel
3 192 272 352 432 522	Palm off
4 193 273 353 433 523	Fellow servant(s)
5 194 274 354 434 524	Sedition
6 195 275 355 435 525	Malfeasance
7 196 276 356 436 526	Good faith
8 197 277 357 437 527	Demise
9 198 278 358 438 528	Negligence
10 199 279 359 439 529	Battery

PROBLEM #	LEGAL TERM
11 200 280 360 440 530	Promissory estoppel
12 101 281 361 441 531	Spite fence
13 102 282 362 442 532	Undue influence
14 103 283 363 443 533	Warrant
15 104 284 364 444 534	Judgment
16 105 285 365 445 535	Execution
17 106 286 366 446 536	Writ
18 107 287 367 447 537	Creditor
19 108 288 368 448 538	Bailment
20 109 289 369 449 539	Ordinance
21 110 290 370 450 540	Surety
22 111 291 371 451 541	Habeas corpus
23 112 292 372 452 542	Scire facias
24 113 293 373 453 543	Tender
25 114 294 374 454 544	Assault
26 115 295 375 455 545	Duress
27 116 296 376 456 546	Bribery
28 117 297 377 457 547	Deficiency judgment
29 118 298 378 458 548	Laches
30 119 299 379 459 549	Heirs
31 120 300 380 460 550	Quasi contract
32 121 201 381 461 551	Municipal corporation
33 122 202 382 462 552	Sovereign immunity
34 123 203 383 463 553	Pari delicto
35 124 204 384 464 554	Demurrer
36 125 205 385 465 555	Adverse possession
37 126 206 386 466 556	Capias
38 127 207 387 467 557	Parens patriae
39 128 208 388 468 558	Derivative action
40 129 209 389 469 559	Conversion
41 130 210 390 470 560	Assumption of risk
42 131 211 391 471 561	Kidnapping
43 132 212 392 472 562	Aggravated assault
44 133 213 393 473 563	Deposition
45 134 214 394 474 564	Long-arm statutes
46 135 215 395 475 565	Police power
47 136 216 396 476 566	Summary judgment
48 137 217 397 477 567	Trade secret
49 138 218 398 478 568	Agent
50 139 219 399 479 569	Proximate cause
51 140 220 400 480 570	Summons
52 141 221 301 481 571	Transitory action
53 142 222 302 482 572	Verdict
54 143 223 303 483 573	Aleatory contract
55 144 224 304 484 574	Demand
56 145 225 305 485 575	Estoppel
57 146 226 306 486 576	Inquest
58 147 227 307 487 577	Affirmative defense
59 148 228 308 488 578	Consortium
60 149 229 309 489 579	Perjury

PROBLEM #	LEGAL TERM
61 150 230 310 490 580	Burglary
62 151 231 311 491 581	Fixture
63 152 232 312 492 582	Delivery
64 153 233 313 493 583	Immunity
65 154 234 314 494 584	Public law
66 155 235 315 495 585	Best evidence rule
67 156 236 316 496 586	Depreciation
68 157 237 317 497 587	Reformation
69 158 238 318 498 588	Trust
70 159 239 319 499 589	Felony
71 160 240 320 500 590	Easement
72 161 241 321 401 591	Attorney's lien
73 162 242 322 402 592	Veto
74 163 243 323 403 593	Attachment
75 164 244 324 404 594	Intent
76 165 245 325 405 595	Mortgage
77 166 246 326 406 596	Trover
78 167 247 327 407 597	Caveat emptor
79 168 248 328 408 598	Mandamus
80 169 249 329 409 599	Injunction
81 170 250 330 410 600	Guest statute(s)
82 171 251 331 411 501	Release
83 172 252 332 412 502	Supplemental pleading
84 173 253 333 413 503	Sequestration
85 174 254 334 414 504	Waiver
86 175 255 335 415 505	Remittitur
87 176 256 336 416 506	Inadequate remedy at law
88 177 257 337 417 507	Diversity of citizenship
89 178 258 338 418 508	Garnishment
90 179 259 339 419 509	Embezzlement
91 180 260 340 420 510	Bond
92 181 261 341 421 511	Reliance
93 182 262 342 422 512	Arrest
94 183 263 343 423 513	Fraud
95 184 264 344 424 514	Malice
96 185 265 345 425 515	Forcible entry
97 186 266 346 426 516	Nuisance
98 187 267 347 427 517	Privilege
99 188 268 348 428 518	Revocation
100 189 269 349 429 519	Additur

CITATION EXERCISE 2
LEGAL ENCYCLOPEDIAS (I)

A. INTRODUCTION

1. *American Jurisprudence Second* and *Corpus Juris Secundum*

American Jurisprudence Second (Am. Jur. 2d) and *Corpus Juris Secundum* (C.J.S.) are national legal encyclopedias. They are multi-volume sets that comprehensively treat all aspects of the law. They are alphabetically arranged by topic and kept up to date by the staff of West Group.

2. *Bluebook* Form

According to *Bluebook* Rule 15.7(a), legal encyclopedias such as *American Jurisprudence Second* and *Corpus Juris Secundum* are cited using a special form. The elements of a typical citation are as follows:
  (1) the **volume number**;
  (2) the abbreviated **name** of the encyclopedia (*e.g.*, Am. Jur. 2d, C.J.S., etc.);
  (3) the specific **topic or title** within the encyclopedia (*e.g.*, Mortgages);
  (4) the **section** number;
  (5) the **page** number(s) (when it would be helpful for finding specific material within the section) (*Bluebook* Rule 3.4); and
  (6) the copyright **date** of the volume.

The following are typical examples of citations to material in *Corpus Juris Secundum* and *American Jurisprudence Second*:

  [Example 1] 11 C.J.S. *Boundaries* § 1 (1995).
  [Example 2] 11 C.J.S. *Boundaries* § 31, at 89 (1995).
  In Example 1, only the section is cited; in Example 2, the page number is added to facilitate location of specific material within a lengthy section.
  [Example 3] 35 Am. Jur. 2d *Mortgages* § 600 (1996).

See Bluebook Rule 15.7(a).

3. Typeface Conventions

As indicated in Citation Exercise 1, italics can be shown by underscoring in typewritten or handwritten material:

[Example 4] 11 C.J.S. <u>Boundaries</u> § 1 (1995).

This typeface format (italics or underscoring) is the *Bluebook* standard for court documents and legal memoranda. *See Bluebook* Practitioners' Notes P.1 & P.1(b).

As also indicated in Citation Exercise 1, book titles in law reviews are shown in large and small capital letters. Thus, the citation given in Example 3 above would appear as follows in a law review footnote:

[Example 5] 35 AM. JUR. 2D *Mortgages* § 600 (1996).

B. INSTRUCTIONS FOR COMPLETING THIS EXERCISE

To complete this exercise, find the topic and section of *American Jurisprudence Second* listed with your problem number below. For your answer to this exercise, state the following:

(a) the volume number of the *Am. Jur. 2d* volume in which you found the topic and section;

(b) the copyright date of the *Am. Jur. 2d* volume in which you found this topic and section (*e.g.*, 1999); and

(c) the citation of the section in *Bluebook* (or another designated) form; abbreviate "and" to "&" when that word is included the name of the topic; assume that your citation will appear in a court document or legal memorandum, not in a law review article.

Unless otherwise instructed, write your answers on the answer sheet provided in Part 4 of these exercises.

PROBLEM #	AM. JUR. 2D TOPIC AND SECTION
1 155 206 322 421 533	Abandoned, Lost, & Unclaimed Property § 14
2 156 207 323 422 534	Homestead § 28
3 157 208 324 423 535	Laundries, Dyers, & Drycleaners § 7
4 158 209 325 424 536	Public Lands § 9
5 159 210 326 425 537	Replevin § 11
6 160 211 327 426 538	Landlord & Tenant § 56
7 161 212 328 427 539	Death § 556
8 162 213 329 428 540	Abstracts of Title § 7
9 163 214 330 429 541	Abuse of Process § 8
10 164 215 331 430 542	Mortgages § 15
11 165 216 332 431 543	Highways, Streets, & Bridges § 52
12 166 217 333 432 544	Evidence § 5
13 167 218 334 433 545	Carriers § 19
14 168 219 335 434 546	Landlord & Tenant § 17
15 169 220 336 435 547	Fraud & Deceit § 20
16 170 221 337 436 548	Acknowledgments § 21
17 171 222 338 437 549	Boundaries § 18
18 172 223 339 438 550	Cancellation of Instruments § 15
19 173 224 340 439 551	International Law § 14

PROBLEM #	AM. JUR. 2D TOPIC AND SECTION
20 174 225 341 440 552	Adverse Possession § 294
21 175 226 342 441 553	Labor & Labor Relations § 22
22 176 227 343 442 554	Hotels, Motels, & Restaurants § 3
23 177 228 344 443 555	Insolvency § 5
24 178 229 345 444 556	Fences § 8
25 179 230 346 445 557	Admiralty § 2
26 180 231 347 446 558	Parent & Child § 11
27 181 232 348 447 559	Adultery & Fornication § 7
28 182 233 349 448 560	Deeds § 13
29 183 234 350 449 561	Negligence § 4
30 184 235 351 450 562	Husband & Wife § 18
31 185 236 352 451 563	Banks & Financial Institutions § 34
32 186 237 353 452 564	Costs § 10
33 187 238 354 453 565	Municipal Corporations, Counties, & Other Political Subdivisions § 33
34 188 239 355 454 566	Life Tenants & Remaindermen § 11
35 189 240 356 455 567	Sales § 108
36 190 241 357 456 568	Animals § 18
37 191 242 358 457 569	Pardon & Parole § 10
38 192 243 359 458 570	Fixtures § 5
39 193 244 360 459 571	Railroads § 8
40 194 245 361 460 572	Mobs & Riots § 12
41 195 246 362 461 573	Patents § 65
42 196 247 363 462 574	Homicide § 5
43 197 248 364 463 575	Aliens & Citizens § 20
44 198 249 365 464 576	Judgments § 5
45 199 250 366 465 577	Damages § 32
46 200 251 367 466 578	Infants § 12
47 101 252 368 467 579	Ne Exeat § 4
48 102 253 369 468 580	Contribution § 8
49 103 254 370 469 581	Monopolies, Restraints of Trade, & Unfair Trade Practices § 31
50 104 255 371 470 582	Banks & Financial Institutions § 25
51 105 256 372 471 583	Bigamy § 9
52 106 257 373 472 584	Labor & Labor Relations § 82
53 107 258 374 473 585	False Pretenses § 54
54 108 259 375 474 586	Extradition § 21
55 109 260 376 475 587	Drugs & Controlled Substances § 18
56 110 261 377 476 588	Domicil § 6
57 111 262 378 477 589	Gifts § 4
58 112 263 379 478 590	Malicious Prosecution § 16
59 113 264 380 479 591	Death § 560
60 114 265 381 480 592	Insurance § 12
61 115 266 382 481 593	Mobs & Riots § 14
62 116 267 383 482 594	Irrigation § 21
63 117 268 384 483 595	Jury § 20
64 118 269 385 484 596	Cemeteries § 16
65 119 270 386 485 597	Certiorari § 11
66 120 271 387 486 598	Libel & Slander § 37
67 121 272 388 487 599	Rape § 37
68 122 273 389 488 600	Public Works & Contracts § 3
69 123 274 390 489 501	Civil Service § 3

PROBLEM #	AM. JUR. 2D TOPIC AND SECTION
70 124 275 391 490 502	Public Officers & Employees § 14
71 125 276 392 491 503	Money § 13
72 126 277 393 492 504	Interest & Usury § 53
73 127 278 394 493 505	Customs Duties & Import Regulations § 11
74 128 279 395 494 506	Pardon & Parole § 11
75 129 280 396 495 507	Improvements § 8
76 130 281 397 496 508	Extradition § 2
77 131 282 398 497 509	Copyright & Literary Property § 3
78 132 283 399 498 510	Community Property § 30
79 133 284 400 499 511	Gambling § 15
80 134 285 301 500 512	Public Utilities § 31
81 135 286 302 401 513	Conspiracy § 2
82 136 287 303 402 514	Records & Recording Laws § 47
83 137 288 304 403 515	Inheritance, Estate, & Gift Taxes § 19
84 138 289 305 404 516	Contempt § 17
85 139 290 306 405 517	Gas & Oil § 20
86 140 291 307 406 518	Contracts § 87
87 141 292 308 407 519	Licenses & Permits § 13
88 142 293 309 408 520	Markets & Marketing § 42
89 143 294 310 409 521	Mines & Minerals § 14
90 144 295 311 410 522	Fires § 7
91 145 296 312 411 523	Cotenancy & Joint Ownership § 5
92 146 297 313 412 524	Lost & Destroyed Instruments § 12
93 147 298 314 413 525	Libel & Slander § 33
94 148 299 315 414 526	New Trial § 54
95 149 300 316 415 527	Privacy § 3
96 150 201 317 416 528	Logs & Timber § 37
97 151 202 318 417 529	Name § 78
98 152 203 319 418 530	Dead Bodies § 70
99 153 204 320 419 531	Nuisances § 6
100 154 205 321 420 532	Process § 30

CITATION EXERCISE 3
LEGAL ENCYCLOPEDIAS (II)

A. INTRODUCTION

1. *Bluebook* Form and Typeface

The basic *Bluebook* form and typeface for citing legal encyclopedias are set out in Citation Exercise 2.

2. Special Note on Supplements

Like many legal research sources, legal encyclopedias are kept up to date by pocket-part supplements. When material in a supplement is cited, that fact should be indicated parenthetically. *See Bluebook* Rules 3.2(c) & 15.4(e).

[Example 1] 35 Am. Jur. 2d *Mortgages* § 1195 (Supp. 1998).
[Example 2] 101A C.J.S. *Zoning & Land Planning* § 146 (1979 & Supp. 1998).
In Example 1, only the supplement is cited; in Example 2, both the main volume and supplement are cited.

3. Locally Oriented Encyclopedias

Locally oriented legal encyclopedias are available for some jurisdictions. Examples include *Florida Jurisprudence Second*, *California Jurisprudence Third*, *New York Jurisprudence Second*, and *Ohio Jurisprudence Third*. These locally oriented encyclopedias are traditionally cited using a format similar to that of the national legal encyclopedias.

[Example 3] 42 Cal. Jur. 3d *Landlord & Tenant* § 258 (1978).
[Example 4] 30 Ohio Jur. 3d *Damages* § 130 (1995).

B. INSTRUCTIONS FOR COMPLETING THIS EXERCISE

To complete this exercise, find the title and section of *Corpus Juris Secundum* (*C.J.S.*) listed with your problem number below. For your answer to this exercise, state the following:

(a) the volume number of the *C.J.S.* volume in which you found the title and section;

(b) the copyright date of the *C.J.S.* volume in which you found the title and section (*e.g.*, 1999); and

(c) the citation of the section in *Bluebook* (or another designated) form; abbreviate "and" to "&" when that word is included the name of the title; assume that your citation will appear in a court document or legal memorandum, not in a law review article.

Unless otherwise instructed, write your answers on the answer sheet provided in Part 4 of these exercises.

PROBLEM #	C.J.S. TITLE AND SECTION
1 200 222 394 417 576	Constitutional Law § 1218
2 101 223 395 418 577	Injunctions § 217
3 102 224 396 419 578	Elections § 123
4 103 225 397 420 579	Interest & Usury § 24
5 104 226 398 421 580	Divorce § 46
6 105 227 399 422 581	Guardian & Ward § 144
7 106 228 400 423 582	International Law § 53
8 107 229 301 424 583	Intoxicating Liquors § 430
9 108 230 302 425 584	Eminent Domain § 59
10 109 231 303 426 585	Constitutional Law § 908
11 110 232 304 427 586	Divorce § 276
12 111 233 305 428 587	Constitutional Law § 655
13 112 234 306 429 588	Divorce § 608
14 113 235 307 430 589	Pardon & Parole § 75
15 114 236 308 431 590	Obstructing Justice § 22
16 115 237 309 432 591	Zoning & Land Planning § 20
17 116 238 310 433 592	Social Security § 29
18 117 239 311 434 593	Public Lands § 231
19 118 240 312 435 594	Associations § 43
20 119 241 313 436 595	Assault & Battery § 105
21 120 242 314 437 596	Aliens § 196
22 121 243 315 438 597	Agency § 387
23 122 244 316 439 598	Aeronautics & Aerospace § 287
24 123 245 317 440 599	Judgments § 44
25 124 246 318 441 600	Accord & Satisfaction § 9
26 125 247 319 442 501	Prohibition § 12
27 126 248 320 443 502	Principal & Surety § 42
28 127 249 321 444 503	Payment § 53
29 128 250 322 445 504	Motor Vehicles § 254
30 129 251 323 446 505	Landlord & Tenant § 746
31 130 252 324 447 506	Labor Relations § 823
32 131 253 325 448 507	Labor Relations § 297
33 132 254 326 449 508	Property § 12
34 133 255 327 450 509	Payment § 53
35 134 256 328 451 510	Pardon & Parole § 72
36 135 257 329 452 511	Payment § 51
37 136 258 330 453 512	Principal & Surety § 88
38 137 259 331 454 513	Labor Relations § 291
39 138 260 332 455 514	Labor Relations § 855

PROBLEM #	C.J.S. TITLE AND SECTION
40 139 261 333 456 515	Principal & Surety § 40
41 140 262 334 457 516	Prohibition § 7
42 141 263 335 458 517	Acknowledgments § 15
43 142 264 336 459 518	Agency § 98
44 143 265 337 460 519	Armed Services § 15
45 144 266 338 461 520	Assignments § 66
46 145 267 339 462 521	Attorney & Client § 256
47 146 268 340 463 522	Social Security § 17
48 147 269 341 464 523	Brokers § 133
49 148 270 342 465 524	Specific Performance § 159
50 149 271 343 466 525	Alteration of Instruments § 64
51 150 272 344 467 526	Constitutional Law § 1262
52 151 273 345 468 527	Injunctions § 250
53 152 274 346 469 528	Electricity § 29
54 153 275 347 470 529	Interest & Usury § 93
55 154 276 348 471 530	Divorce § 112
56 155 277 349 472 531	Habeas Corpus § 29
57 156 278 350 473 532	Bonds § 4
58 157 279 351 474 533	Joint Stock Companies § 41
59 158 280 352 475 534	Eminent Domain § 132
60 159 281 353 476 535	Constitutional Law § 1014
61 160 282 354 477 536	Divorce § 312
62 161 283 355 478 537	Constitutional Law § 730
63 162 284 356 479 538	Divorce § 650
64 163 285 357 480 539	Pardon & Parole § 68
65 164 286 358 481 540	Obscenity § 32
66 165 287 359 482 541	Zoning & Land Planning § 30
67 166 288 360 483 542	Social Security § 18
68 167 289 361 484 543	Public Lands § 168
69 168 290 362 485 544	Attachment § 13
70 169 291 363 486 545	Armed Services § 40
71 170 292 364 487 546	Aliens § 329
72 171 293 365 488 547	Agency § 520
73 172 294 366 489 548	Gas § 87
74 173 295 367 490 549	Searches & Seizures § 62
75 174 296 368 491 550	Abstracts of Title § 2
76 175 297 369 492 551	Prohibition § 8
77 176 298 370 493 552	Pledges § 42
78 177 299 371 494 553	Payment § 16
79 178 300 372 495 554	Motor Vehicles § 262
80 179 201 373 496 555	Landlord & Tenant § 729
81 180 202 374 497 556	Labor Relations § 822
82 181 203 375 498 557	Labor Relations § 306
83 182 204 376 499 558	Postal Service § 8
84 183 205 377 500 559	Postal Service § 7
85 184 206 378 401 560	Property § 9
86 185 207 379 402 561	Prohibition § 36
87 186 208 380 403 562	Public Administrative Law & Procedure § 145
88 187 209 381 404 563	Public Lands § 168
89 188 210 382 405 564	Motions & Orders § 49

PROBLEM #	C.J.S. TITLE AND SECTION
90 189 211 383 406 565	Motor Vehicles § 465
91 190 212 384 407 566	Payment § 15
92 191 213 385 408 567	Burglary § 30
93 192 214 386 409 568	Constitutional Law § 59
94 193 215 387 410 569	Bonds § 22
95 194 216 388 411 570	Divorce § 680
96 195 217 389 412 571	Constitutional Law § 389
97 196 218 390 413 572	Compromise & Settlement § 4
98 197 219 391 414 573	Joint Ventures § 40
99 198 220 392 415 574	Divorce § 139
100 199 221 393 416 575	Judgments § 235

CITATION EXERCISE 4
TEXTS AND TREATISES

A. INTRODUCTION

1. Texts and Treatises in Legal Writing

Texts and treatises are excellent sources for background research and commentary on the law. They are often cited in legal writing as secondary authority.

2. Citing Texts and Treatises in *Bluebook* Form

Citation Exercise 1 (Dictionaries) set out the basic rules for citing texts and treatises in *Bluebook* form. Recall that the typical elements of a book citation in *Bluebook* form include the following:

(1) the **volume number** (if more than one);

(2) the **full name of the author** as it is given in the publication, with the following technical modifications:

> (a) a designation such as "Jr." or "III" should be included; however, a comma should be inserted before such designations only when the author has done so;

> (b) a book with two authors should be cited in the order they are given in the publication, connected by an ampersand (&);

> (c) a book with three or more authors should be cited to the first author only, followed by "et al." (and others);

> (d) when a single volume of a multi-volume work is cited, only the author(s) of the volume cited should be given; and

> (e) when a book has institutional authors or editors, follow *Bluebook* Rule 15.1.3;

(3) the **main title in full** as it is given on the title page (including a serial number, if any, but omitting a subtitle unless it is particularly relevant); capitalize the title according to *Bluebook* Rule 8, *i.e.*, capitalize the initial word, the word immediately following a colon, and all other words in the title; however, do not capitalize articles, conjunctions, and prepositions of four or fewer letters;

(4) the **section, paragraph, or page** number (if a specific part of the book is cited); when a book is organized by sections or paragraphs, cite to them (e.g., ¶ 22 or § 22); to facilitate finding the material within a section or paragraph, page number(s) may be added (*e.g.*, ¶ 22, at 77 or § 84, at 988-89) (*Bluebook* Rule 3.4);

(5) the **editor or translator**, if any (*see Bluebook* Rule 15.1.2);

(5) the **edition** (if other than the first); and

(6) the **year** of publication.

Bluebook Rules 3.4, 15.1.1, 15.1.2, 15.1.3, 15.2, 15.3 & 15.4.

The following are examples of typical *Bluebook* citations of texts and treatises:

[Example 1] Larry L. Teply & Ralph U. Whitten, *Civil Procedure* 934 (1994).

[Example 2] 7 Charles A. Wright et al., *Federal Practice and Procedure: Civil* § 1701, at 485 (2d ed. 1986).

2. Typeface Conventions

As shown in Examples 1 and 2 above, the titles of books in citations in court documents and legal memoranda appears in italics. In typewritten or handwritten material, italics can be shown by underscoring:

[Example 3] Larry L. Teply & Ralph U. Whitten, <u>Civil Procedure</u> 934 (1994).

See Bluebook Practitioners' Note P.1(b). In law review footnotes, both the author's name and the book title appear in large and small capital letters:

[Example 4] LARRY L. TEPLY & RALPH U. WHITTEN, CIVIL PROCEDURE 934 (1994).

Some law reviews vary the typeface from this convention by replacing large and small capital letters with ordinary roman type. *See Bluebook* Rules 2.1 & 2.1(b).

B. INSTRUCTIONS FOR COMPLETING THIS EXERCISE

Assume that you want to cite the section or page of the text or treatise listed with your problem number below. To complete this exercise, find the section or page of the designated text or treatise in the library. **Note carefully the author(s) and edition of the text or treatise.** You may need to consult the card catalog or an online catalog to determine the call number or location of the designated text or treatise.

For your answer to this exercise, state the following:

(a) the volume number of the text or treatise (if there is more than one) (*e.g.*, 3, 9A, etc.);

(b) the full name(s) of the author(s) as stated on the title page of the text or treatise (*e.g.*, Homer H. Clark, Jr.);

(c) the title of the book (*e.g.*, The Law of Domestic Relations in the United States);

(d) the edition of the text or treatise (if other than the first) (*e.g.*, second edition);

(e) the copyright date of the text or treatise (*e.g.*, 1988); and

(f) the citation of the text or treatise in *Bluebook* (or another designated) form; **include a specific ("pinpoint") reference to the designated section or page in your citation.** Assume that your citation will appear in a court document or legal memorandum, not in a law review article (*e.g.*, Homer H. Clark, Jr., The Law of Domestic Relations in the United States § 13.6 (2d ed. 1988).

Unless otherwise instructed, write your answers on the answer sheet provided in Part 4 of these exercises.

PROBLEM #	TEXT OR TREATISE
1 128 250 301 426 551	Section 3.34 of the second edition of Scoles and Hay's *Conflict of Laws*
2 129 251 302 427 552	Section 5.13 of the second edition of Cunningham, Stoebuck, and Whitman's *The Law of Property*
3 130 252 303 428 553	Section 115 of the sixth edition of Bogert's *Trusts* text
4 131 253 304 429 554	Section 6.1 of the fourth edition of Calamari and Perillo's *The Law of Contracts*
5 132 254 305 430 555	Section 2-5 of the fourth edition of White and Summers' *Uniform Commercial Code* text
6 133 255 306 431 556	Section 15 of the second edition of Reuschlein and Gregory's *The Law of Agency and Partnership*
7 134 256 307 432 557	Section 3.1 of the third edition of Hazen's *The Law of Securities Regulation*
8 135 257 308 433 558	Section 217 of the first edition of Sullivan's *Handbook of the Law of Antitrust*
9 136 258 309 434 559	Section 6.19 of the first edition (1995) of Folsom and Gordon's *International Business Transactions* text
10 137 259 310 435 560	Section 2.15 of the first edition of Lewis' *Civil Rights and Employment Discrimination Law*
11 138 260 311 436 561	Section 2.14 of the fifth edition of Nowak and Rotunda's *Constitutional Law* text
12 139 261 312 437 562	Section 3-26 of the second edition of Tribe's *American Constitutional Law*
13 140 262 313 438 563	Section 8.4.3 of the first edition of Aman and Mayton's *Administrative Law* text
14 141 263 314 439 564	Section 2.11 of the first edition of Juergensmeyer and Roberts' *Land Use Planning and Control Law*
15 142 264 315 440 565	Section 8 of the fifth edition of Wright's *Law of Federal Courts* text
16 143 265 316 441 566	Section 3.17 of the second edition of Friedenthal, Kane, and Miller's *Civil Procedure* text
17 144 266 317 442 567	Section 2.10 of the fourth edition of James, Hazard, and Leubsdorf's *Civil Procedure*
18 145 267 318 443 568	Section 1.10 of the first edition of Mueller and Kirkpatrick's *Evidence* text
19 146 268 319 444 569	Section 3.32 of the third edition of Nelson and Whitman's *Real Estate Finance Law*

PROBLEM #	**TEXT OR TREATISE**
20 147 269 320 445 570	Page 19 of the second edition of Burke's *Personal Property in a Nutshell*
21 148 270 321 446 571	Page 27 of the first edition of Mennell's *Wills and Trusts in a Nutshell*
22 149 271 322 447 572	Section 5.02 of the fourth edition of Averill's *Uniform Probate Code in a Nutshell*
23 150 272 323 448 573	Section 8-1 of the second edition of Kionka's *Torts in a Nutshell*
24 151 273 324 449 574	Page 24 of the fifth edition of Phillips' *Products Liability in a Nutshell*
25 152 274 325 450 575	Section 8.3 of the third edition of Krause's *Family Law in a Nutshell*
26 153 275 326 451 576	Section 5.10 of the second edition of Frolik and Kaplan's *Elder Law in a Nutshell*
27 154 276 327 452 577	Section 24 of the second edition of Siegel's *Conflicts in a Nutshell*
28 155 277 328 453 578	Page 13 of the third edition of Hill's *Landlord and Tenant Law in a Nutshell*
29 156 278 329 454 579	Section 7.02 of the second edition of Thomas' *Sex Discrimination in a Nutshell*
30 157 279 330 455 580	Section 17.41 of the second edition of Scoles and Hay's *Conflict of Laws*
31 158 280 331 456 581	Section 2-3 of the fourth edition of Kane's *Civil Procedure in a Nutshell*
32 159 281 332 457 582	Page 29 of the third edition of Canby's *American Indian Law in a Nutshell*
33 160 282 333 458 583	Page 52 of the first edition of Laitos and Tomain's *Energy and Natural Resources Law in a Nutshell*
34 161 283 334 459 584	Section 12.2 of the second edition of Scoles and Hay's *Conflict of Laws*
35 162 284 335 460 585	Section 8.12 of the second edition of Cunningham, Stoebuck, and Whitman's *The Law of Property*
36 163 285 336 461 586	Section 55 of the sixth edition of Bogert's *Trusts* text
37 164 286 337 462 587	Section 11.18 of the fourth edition of Calamari and Perillo's *The Law of Contracts*
38 165 287 338 463 588	Section 6-6 of the fourth edition of White and Summers' *Uniform Commercial Code* text
39 166 288 339 464 589	Section 68 of the second edition of Reuschlein and Gregory's *The Law of Agency and Partnership*
40 167 289 340 465 590	Section 13.3 of the third edition of Hazen's *The Law of Securities Regulation*
41 168 290 341 466 591	Section 156 of the first edition of Sullivan's *Handbook of the Law of Antitrust*
42 169 291 342 467 592	Section 12.23 of the first edition (1995) of Folsom and Gordon's *International Business Transactions* text
43 170 292 343 468 593	Section 4.4 of the first edition of Lewis' *Civil Rights and Employment Discrimination Law*
44 171 293 344 469 594	Section 9.3 of the fifth edition of Nowak and Rotunda's *Constitutional Law* text

PROBLEM #	TEXT OR TREATISE
45 172 294 345 470 595	Section 5-14 of the second edition of Tribe's *American Constitutional Law*
46 173 295 346 471 596	Section 13.11.1 of the first edition of Aman and Mayton's *Administrative Law* text
47 174 296 347 472 597	Section 4.25 of the first edition of Juergensmeyer and Roberts' *Land Use Planning and Control Law*
48 175 297 348 473 598	Section 23 of the fifth edition of Wright's *Law of Federal Courts* text
49 176 298 349 474 599	Section 6.3 of the second edition of Friedenthal, Kane, and Miller's *Civil Procedure* text
50 177 299 350 475 600	Section 3.2 of the fourth edition of James, Hazard, and Leubsdorf's *Civil Procedure*
51 178 300 351 476 501	Section 3.9 of the first edition of Mueller and Kirkpatrick's *Evidence* text
52 179 201 352 477 502	Section 5.4 of the third edition of Nelson and Whitman's *Real Estate Finance Law*
53 180 202 353 478 503	Page 102 of the third edition of Lowe's *Oil and Gas Law in a Nutshell*
54 181 203 354 479 504	Page 31 of the second edition of Jarvis, Closen, Hermann, and Leonard's *AIDS Law in a Nutshell*
55 182 204 355 480 505	Page 68 of the third edition of Leslie's *Labor Law in a Nutshell*
56 183 205 356 481 506	Page 5 of the second edition of Hall, Ellman, and Strouse's *Health Care Law and Ethics in a Nutshell*
57 184 206 357 482 507	Page 218 of the fourth edition of Gellhorn's *Antitrust Law and Economics in a Nutshell*
58 185 207 358 483 508	Page 47 of the second edition of Burke's *Personal Property in a Nutshell*
59 186 208 359 484 509	Page 51 of the first edition of Mennell's *Wills and Trusts in a Nutshell*
60 187 209 360 485 510	Section 8.03 of the fourth edition of Averill's *Uniform Probate Code in a Nutshell*
61 188 210 361 486 511	Section 4-2 of the second edition of Kionka's *Torts in a Nutshell*
62 189 211 362 487 512	Page 43 of the fifth edition of Phillips' *Products Liability in a Nutshell*
63 190 212 363 488 513	Section 12.4 of the third edition of Krause's *Family Law in a Nutshell*
64 191 213 364 489 514	Section 8.2 of the second edition of Frolik and Kaplan's *Elder Law in a Nutshell*
65 192 214 365 490 515	Section 42 of the second edition of Siegel's *Conflicts in a Nutshell*
66 193 215 366 491 516	Page 81 of the third edition of Hill's *Landlord and Tenant Law in a Nutshell*
67 194 216 367 492 517	Section 10.04 of the second edition of Thomas' *Sex Discrimination in a Nutshell*
68 195 217 368 493 518	Section 9.9 of the second edition of Cunningham, Stoebuck, and Whitman's *The Law of Property*
69 196 218 369 494 519	Section 10 of the sixth edition of Bogert's *Trusts* text
70 197 219 370 495 520	Section 16.14 of the fourth edition of Calamari and Perillo's *The Law of Contracts*

PROBLEM #	TEXT OR TREATISE
71 198 220 371 496 521	Section 11-9 of the fourth edition of White and Summers' *Uniform Commercial Code* text
72 199 221 372 497 522	Section 157 of the second edition of Reuschlein and Gregory's *The Law of Agency and Partnership*
73 200 222 373 498 523	Section 14.2 of the third edition of Hazen's *The Law of Securities Regulation*
74 101 223 374 499 524	Section 15.13 of the first edition (1995) of Folsom and Gordon's *International Business Transactions* text
75 102 224 375 500 525	Section 7.1 of the first edition of Lewis' *Civil Rights and Employment Discrimination Law*
76 103 225 376 401 526	Section 11.13 of the fifth edition of Nowak and Rotunda's *Constitutional Law* text
77 104 226 377 402 527	Section 9-2 of the second edition of Tribe's *American Constitutional Law*
78 105 227 378 403 528	Section 6.2 of the first edition of Juergensmeyer and Roberts' *Land Use Planning and Control Law*
79 106 228 379 404 529	Section 50 of the fifth edition of Wright's *Law of Federal Courts* text
80 107 229 380 405 530	Section 6.10 of the second edition of Friedenthal, Kane, and Miller's *Civil Procedure* text
81 108 230 381 406 531	Section 4.8 of the fourth edition of James, Hazard, and Leubsdorf's *Civil Procedure*
82 109 231 382 407 532	Section 4.15 of the first edition of Mueller and Kirkpatrick's *Evidence* text
83 110 232 383 408 533	Section 7.15 of the third edition of Nelson and Whitman's *Real Estate Finance Law*
84 111 233 384 409 534	Section 2-15 of the fourth edition of Kane's *Civil Procedure in a Nutshell*
85 112 234 385 410 535	Page 77 of the third edition of Canby's *American Indian Law in a Nutshell*
86 113 235 386 411 536	Page 147 of the first edition of Laitos and Tomain's *Energy and Natural Resources Law in a Nutshell*
87 114 236 387 412 537	Page 271 of the third edition of Lowe's *Oil and Gas Law in a Nutshell*
88 115 237 388 413 538	Page 87 of the second edition of Jarvis, Closen, Hermann, and Leonard's *AIDS Law in a Nutshell*
89 116 238 389 414 539	Page 135 of the third edition of Leslie's *Labor Law in a Nutshell*
90 117 239 390 415 540	Page 129 of the second edition of Hall, Ellman, and Strouse's *Health Care Law and Ethics in a Nutshell*
91 118 240 391 416 541	Page 71 of the fourth edition of Gellhorn's *Antitrust Law and Economics in a Nutshell*
92 119 241 392 417 542	Section 9.6 of the third edition of Nelson and Whitman's *Real Estate Finance Law*
93 120 242 393 418 543	Section 5.12 of the first edition of Mueller and Kirkpatrick's *Evidence* text

PROBLEM #	**TEXT OR TREATISE**
94 121 243 394 419 544	Section 5.19 of the fourth edition of James, Hazard, and Leubsdorf's *Civil Procedure*
95 122 244 395 420 545	Section 11.8 of the second edition of Friedenthal, Kane, and Miller's *Civil Procedure* text
96 123 245 396 421 546	Section 68 of the fifth edition of Wright's *Law of Federal Courts* text
97 124 246 397 422 547	Section 7.16 of the first edition of Juergensmeyer and Roberts' *Land Use Planning and Control Law*
98 125 247 398 423 548	Section 12-7 of the second edition of Tribe's *American Constitutional Law*
99 126 248 399 424 549	Section 14.10 of the fifth edition of Nowak and Rotunda's *Constitutional Law* text
100 127 249 400 425 550	Section 21.12 of the first edition (1995) of Folsom and Gordon's *International Business Transactions* text

LEGAL PERIODICALS (I)

A. INTRODUCTION

1. Periodical Literature

Periodical literature is an excellent research source and has persuasive value as a secondary authority. Legal periodicals are forums for review of the law, criticism of current legal rules, and innovative suggestions.

Legal periodicals are published by law schools, bar associations, and commercial sources. Some focus on specialized areas of the law. Articles in legal periodicals typically analyze legal topics thoroughly, and the text is supported by extensive case and statutory citations. Such articles are particularly useful sources for (1) gaining perspective or background information on a legal topic, (2) finding references to primary authority, and (3) supporting arguments for a change in the law.

This exercise focuses on the required abbreviation of periodical titles in *Bluebook* citations. The next exercise examines all other elements of citing periodical literature in *Bluebook* form.

2. Periodicals Listed in *Bluebook* Table T.13

A key element in a citation of an article in a periodical is the identification of the name of the periodical. *See Bluebook* Rule 16. Specific instructions for citing the names of English language periodicals are set out in *Bluebook* Table T.13 ("Periodicals"). Abbreviations for many frequently cited periodicals are listed in Table T.13. If the periodical is included in the alphabetical listing in the table, the designation in the table should be used.

> **[Example 1]** Harvard Law Review = Harv. L. Rev.
> **[Example 2]** Law and Human Behavior = Law & Hum. Behav.

Be aware that periodical names may change over time. If any doubt exists about the name of the periodical, check the title page of the issue that is being cited. The name as it appears on that page should be used in the citation.

3. Periodicals Not Listed in *Bluebook* Table T.13

Even if a periodical is not listed in *Bluebook* Table T.13, the table provides abbreviations for various words that are commonly used in periodical names. To use the table, simply look up each word of the title. Note that geographical words in the name of the periodical should be abbreviated as provided in another *Bluebook* table (Table T.10). Follow the specific directions given at the beginning of Table T.13 for articles and prepositions appearing in the name.

[Example 3] Academ[ic, y] = Acad.
[Example 4] Alabama = Ala. [from Table T.10]

4. Spacing

When a periodical is listed in *Bluebook* Table T.13, simply·follow the spacing given for the relevant entry. When a periodical is not listed, *Bluebook* Rule 6.1(a) (which governs spacing) must be followed. Rule 6.1(a) provides that when names of periodicals are abbreviated, all adjacent single capital letters must be closed up (*i.e.*, no space between the capital letters):

[Example 5] Transp. L.J. (**not** Transp. L. J.)

However, when one or more of the capital letters in the abbreviation stands for the name of a geographic or institutional entity, *Bluebook* Rule 6.1(a) provides that the capital letters referring to that entity must be set off from other adjacent single capital letters with a space:

[Example 6] S.D. L. Rev. (**not** S.D.L. Rev.)

Note that under *Bluebook* Rule 6.1(a), single capital letters should not be closed up with longer abbreviations:

[Example 7] Fordham Urb. L.J. (**not** Fordham Urb.L.J.)

5. Typeface Conventions

In Examples 1-7, above, the abbreviated names of the periodicals appear in ordinary roman typeface, the standard typeface format for periodical names appearing in court documents and legal memoranda. *See Bluebook* Practitioners' Note P.1(b). Note that the typeface used in *Bluebook* Table T.13 is the typeface used in law review footnotes. Periodical names appear in large and small capital letters in law review citations:

[Example 8] Harvard Law Review = HARV. L. REV.
[Example 9] Law and Human Behavior = LAW & HUM. BEHAV.

B. INSTRUCTIONS FOR COMPLETING THIS EXERCISE

The purpose of this exercise is to familiarize you with required abbreviations in *Bluebook* Table T.13 ("Periodicals") and, if necessary, *Bluebook* Table T.10 ("Geographical Terms"). You may also need to refer to *Bluebook* Rule 6.1(a), which governs spacing in abbreviations.

To complete this exercise, find the names of the two periodicals listed with your problem number below. For your answer to this exercise, determine the proper abbreviation of the name of the periodicals for purposes of a *Bluebook* (or another designated) form of citation. Assume that your citation will appear in a court document or legal memorandum, not in a law review article.

Unless otherwise instructed, write your answers on the answer sheet provided in Part 4 of these exercises.

PROBLEM #	PERIODICALS
1 161 300 310 420 530	(a) William Mitchell Law Review (b) Journal of Pharmacy Law
2 162 201 311 421 531	(a) Boston College Law Review (b) Journal of Intellectual Property Law
3 163 202 312 422 532	(a) High Technology Law Journal (b) Journal of Accountancy
4 164 203 313 423 533	(a) Journal of Air Law and Commerce (b) Alabama Lawyer
5 165 204 314 424 534	(a) Oregon Law Review (b) Utah Bar Journal
6 166 205 315 425 535	(a) Pace Law Review (b) Texas Bar Journal
7 167 206 316 426 536	(a) New England Law Review (b) Maine Bar Journal
8 168 207 317 427 537	(a) Notre Dame Law Review (b) Florida Bar Journal
9 169 208 318 428 538	(a) Louisiana Law Review (b) Arizona Attorney
10 170 209 319 429 539	(a) Journal of Family Law (b) South Carolina Lawyer
11 171 210 320 430 540	(a) Drake Law Review (b) Nevada Lawyer
12 172 211 321 431 541	(a) Fordham Urban Law Journal (b) Delaware Lawyer
13 173 212 322 432 542	(a) Ocean and Coastal Law Journal (b) Michigan Bar Journal
14 174 213 323 433 543	(a) Seton Hall Constitutional Law Journal (b) Maine Bar Journal
15 175 214 324 434 544	(a) Tulane Law Review (b) Oregon State Bar Journal
16 176 215 325 435 545	(a) University of Baltimore Law Review (b) Rhode Island Bar Journal
17 177 216 326 436 546	(a) Yale Journal on Regulation (b) The Elder Law Journal
18 178 217 327 437 547	(a) Black Law Journal (b) Alabama Lawyer
19 179 218 328 438 548	(a) American University Law Review (b) Energy Law Journal
20 180 219 329 439 549	(a) Boston University Journal of Tax Law (b) Cardozo Women's Law Journal
21 181 220 330 440 550	(a) Missouri Law Review (b) American Journal of Tax Policy
22 182 221 331 441 551	(a) Osgoode Hall Law Journal (b) Federal Communications Law Journal
23 183 222 332 442 552	(a) Connecticut Probate Law Journal (b) San Diego Justice Journal
24 184 223 333 443 553	(a) Journal of Energy Law and Policy (b) Asian Law Journal
25 185 224 334 444 554	(a) Delaware Journal of Corporate Law (b) Clinical Law Review
26 186 225 335 445 555	(a) Cooley Law Review (b) Connecticut Insurance Law Journal
27 187 226 336 446 556	(a) Atomic Energy Law Journal (b) Seton Hall Journal of Sport Law
28 188 227 337 447 557	(a) Tulane Maritime Law Journal (b) The Sports Lawyers Journal
29 189 228 338 448 558	(a) Tennessee Law Review (b) Wisconsin Environmental Law Journal
30 190 229 339 449 559	(a) Journal of Law and Politics (b) Louisiana Bar Journal
31 191 230 340 450 560	(a) Loyola Law Review (New Orleans) (b) Puget Sound Law Review

PROBLEM #	**PERIODICALS**
32 192 231 341 451 561	(a) Massachusetts Law Review (b) Journal of Contemporary Law
33 193 232 342 452 562	(a) Journal of Products Liability (b) American Journal of Tax Policy
34 194 233 343 453 563	(a) Law and Society Review (b) Alabama Lawyer
35 195 234 344 454 564	(a) Berkeley Women's Law Journal (b) Arizona Attorney
36 196 235 345 455 565	(a) Santa Clara Law Review (b) Oregon State Bar Bulletin
37 197 236 346 456 566	(a) Practical Lawyer (b) Maine Bar Journal
38 198 237 347 457 567	(a) Pepperdine Law Review (b) Louisiana Bar Journal
39 199 238 348 458 568	(a) Law and Contemporary Problems (b) Orange County Lawyer
40 200 239 349 459 569	(a) Journal of Law and Health (b) Texas Bar Journal
41 101 240 350 460 570	(a) University of Florida Law Review (b) Utah Bar Journal
42 102 241 351 461 571	(a) Ecology Law Quarterly (b) Florida Bar Journal
43 103 242 352 462 572	(a) George Mason University Civil Rights Law Review (b) Rhode Island Bar Journal
44 104 243 353 463 573	(a) Kentucky Law Journal (b) Wisconsin Women's Law Journal
45 105 244 354 464 574	(a) Marquette Law Review (b) Michigan Bar Journal
46 106 245 355 465 575	(a) Trademark Reporter (b) Michigan Journal of Gender & Law
47 107 246 356 466 576	(a) Stanford Journal of International Law (b) Naval Law Review
48 108 247 357 467 577	(a) Stetson Law Review (b) Seton Hall Journal of Sport Law
49 109 248 358 468 578	(a) Transportation Law Journal (b) Delaware Lawyer
50 110 249 359 469 579	(a) Public Land Law Review (b) Rhode Island Bar Journal
51 111 250 360 470 580	(a) National Black Law Journal (b) Texas Wesleyan Law Review
52 112 251 361 471 581	(a) Journal of Law and Commerce (b) Nevada Lawyer
53 113 252 362 472 582	(a) Ohio Northern University Law Review (b) Texas Bar Journal
54 114 253 363 473 583	(a) Ohio State Law Journal (b) Duke Journal of Gender Law & Policy
55 115 254 364 474 584	(a) New York Law School Law Review (b) Journal of Accountancy
56 116 255 365 475 585	(a) Maryland Law Review (b) Florida Bar Journal
57 117 256 366 476 586	(a) Labor Law Journal (b) Texas Bar Journal
58 118 257 367 477 587	(a) Journal of Corporation Law (b) Nevada Lawyer
59 119 258 368 478 588	(a) Iowa Law Review (b) Naval Law Review
60 120 259 369 479 589	(a) Human Rights Quarterly (b) Nevada Lawyer
61 121 260 370 480 590	(a) Gonzaga Law Review (b) Alabama Lawyer
62 122 261 371 481 591	(a) Indiana Law Journal (b) Journal of International Legal Studies
63 123 262 372 482 592	(a) Golden Gate University Law Review (b) Utah Bar Journal
64 124 263 373 483 593	(a) Fordham International Law Journal (b) Naval Law Review
65 125 264 374 484 594	(a) Florida State University Law Review (b) Nevada Lawyer
66 126 265 375 485 595	(a) Creighton Law Review (b) Texas Intellectual Property Law Journal
67 127 266 376 486 596	(a) Cleveland-Marshall Law Review (b) Maine Bar Journal
68 128 267 377 487 597	(a) Idaho Law Review (b) American Journal of Tax Policy
69 129 268 378 488 598	(a) Saint Louis University Law Journal (b) Asian Law Journal
70 130 269 379 489 599	(a) William and Mary Law Review (b) Journal of Pharmacy Law
71 131 270 380 490 600	(a) University of Pittsburgh Law Review (b) Delaware Lawyer
72 132 271 381 491 501	(a) Loyola of Los Angeles Law Review (b) Florida Bar Journal
73 133 272 382 492 502	(a) Journal of Maritime Law and Commerce (b) Arizona Attorney
74 134 273 383 493 503	(a) Journal of Dispute Resolution (b) Louisiana Bar Journal
75 135 274 384 494 504	(a) California Western Law Review (b) Delaware Lawyer
76 136 275 385 495 505	(a) Cardozo Law Review (b) Wisconsin Women's Law Journal
77 137 276 386 496 506	(a) International and Comparative Law Quarterly (b) Nevada Lawyer
78 138 277 387 497 507	(a) Journal of Business Law (b) Connecticut Insurance Law Journal
79 139 278 388 498 508	(a) Columbia Journal of Transnational Law (b) Maine Bar Journal
80 140 279 389 499 509	(a) Southern Methodist University Law Review (b) Arizona Attorney

PROBLEM #	**PERIODICALS**
81 141 280 390 500 510	(a) Uniform Commercial Code Law Journal (b) Alabama Lawyer
82 142 281 391 401 511	(a) West Virginia Law Review (b) Florida Bar Journal
83 143 282 392 402 512	(a) University of Kansas Law Review (b) Orange County Lawyer
84 144 283 393 403 513	(a) Vanderbilt Law Review (b) South Carolina Lawyer
85 145 284 394 404 514	(a) Whittier Law Review (b) Oregon State Bar Journal
86 146 285 395 405 515	(a) Western New England Law Review (b) Texas Bar Journal
87 147 286 396 406 516	(a) South Dakota Law Review (b) Utah Bar Journal
88 148 287 397 407 517	(a) Quinnipiac Law Review (b) Journal of International Business Law
89 149 288 398 408 518	(a) San Diego Law Review (b) Journal of International Taxation
90 150 289 399 409 519	(a) North Carolina Law Review (b) Journal of Accountancy
91 151 290 400 410 520	(a) Ohio State Journal on Dispute Resolution (b) Maine Bar Journal
92 152 291 301 411 521	(a) New Mexico Law Review (b) Florida Bar Journal
93 153 292 302 412 522	(a) John Marshall Law Review (b) Delaware Lawyer
94 154 293 303 413 523	(a) Chicago-Kent Law Review (b) Arizona Attorney
95 155 294 304 414 524	(a) Connecticut Law Review (b) Texas Bar Journal
96 156 295 305 415 525	(a) University of Hawaii Law Review (b) Nevada Lawyer
97 157 296 306 416 526	(a) University of Toledo Law Review (b) Florida Bar Journal
98 158 297 307 417 527	(a) Washington & Lee Law Review (b) Alabama Lawyer
99 159 298 308 418 528	(a) San Fernando Valley Law Review (b) Oregon State Bar Journal
100 160 299 309 419 529	(a) Maine Law Review (b) Journal of International Law & Practice

CITATION EXERCISE 6
LEGAL PERIODICALS (II)

A. INTRODUCTION

1. *Bluebook* Form for Citing Articles in Legal Periodicals

According to *Bluebook* Rule 16, most articles in legal periodicals are cited by the following:

(1) the **full name of the author** as it is given in the publication, with the following technical modifications. Note that these rules are essentially the same as those used for authors of books (*see supra* Citation Exercises 1 and 4):

> (a) a designation such as "Jr." or "III" should be included; however, a comma should be inserted before such designations only when the author has done so;

> (b) an article with two authors should be cited in the order they are given in the publication, connected by an ampersand (&); and

> (c) an article with three or more authors should be cited to the first author only, followed by "et al." (and others);

(2) the **title of the article**; capitalize the title according to *Bluebook* Rule 8, *i.e.*, capitalize the initial word, the word immediately following a colon, and all other words in the title; however, do not capitalize articles, conjunctions, and prepositions of four or fewer letters;

(3) the **volume number** (see below);

(4) the **abbreviated periodical name** (abbreviations are listed in Tables T.13 (periodicals) and T.10 (geographic terms)) (*see supra* Citation Exercise 5);

(5) the **beginning page number** of the article (*see Bluebook* Rule 3.3(a));

(6) the specific internal page references, if any (*see Bluebook* Rule 3.3(a)); and

(7) the **date** (see below).

The following are examples of *Bluebook* citations of periodical articles complying with these rules:

[Example 1] Larry L. Teply, *Antitrust Immunity of State and Local Governmental Action*, 48 Tul. L. Rev. 272 (1974).
> This article appeared in Volume 48 of the *Tulane Law Review*; it begins on page 272.

[Example 2] Ralph H. Folsom & Larry L. Teply, *Trademarked Generic Words*, 89 Yale L.J. 1323, 1350-51 (1980).
> This article begins on page 1323, and specific material on pages 1350 and 1351 is cited.

[Example 3] Brent Nicholson & Todd Zuiderhoek, *Lender Liability Dilemma:* Fleet Factors *History and Aftermath*, 38 S.D. L. Rev. 22 (1993).

> Note that the case name reference ("Fleet Factors") in the title of the article is not italicized. *See Bluebook* Rule 2.1(a) (providing that when case names appear within a cited article title, they should not be italicized).

[Example 4] Nancy W. Perry & Larry L. Teply, *Interviewing, Counseling, and In-Court Examination of Children: Practical Approaches for Attorneys*, 18 Creighton L. Rev. 1369, 1369 & nn.2-6 (1985).

> This article begins on page 1369, and specific material on the first page of the article is cited. Footnotes 2 through 6 on page 1369 are also cited. *Bluebook* Rules 3.3(b) and (d) cover citation of footnotes.

Slightly varying forms are used for student works and book reviews. According to *Bluebook* Rule 16.5.1(a), signed and titled student works are generally cited in the same manner as other articles, except that the designation of the work (*e.g.*, Note, Comment, Commentary, Special Project, etc.) should be given before the title of the work. A work is considered signed when attribution has been given anywhere within the issue.

[Example 5] Martin Kessler & Larry Teply, Comment, *Jetport: Planning and Politics in the Big Cypress Swamp*, 25 U. Miami L. Rev. 713 (1971).

According to *Bluebook* Rule 16.5.1(b), unsigned student works should be cited by the designation given in the periodical, followed by the title of the work. A student work signed only with initials is considered to be an unsigned work. *Bluebook* Rule 16.5.1(a).

[Example 6] Note, *Designation of Defendants by Fictitious Names—Use of John Doe Complaints*, 46 Iowa L. Rev. 773 (1961).

Note that certain periodicals do not have volume numbers. If the volume is paginated consecutively throughout the entire volume, you should use the year of publication as the volume number and omit the year designation at the end of the citation. *Bluebook* Rules 3.2(a) & 16.2.

[Example 7] Comment, *Unknown Parties: The John Doe Defendant*, 1970 Law & Soc. Ord. 256.

Several periodicals paginate each *issue* separately. In this situation, you should cite the periodical by the date or period of publication and omit the year designation at the end of the citation. Note particularly how the page is cited in the example below. *See Bluebook* Rule 16.3 ("Nonconsecutively Paginated Journals and Magazines").

[**Example 8**]   Gene H. Wood, *The Child as Witness*, 6 Fam. Advoc., Spring 1984, at 14.

2. Typeface Conventions

As shown in the above examples, the title of an article should appear in italics or it should be underscored. *See Bluebook* Practitioners' Note P.1(b) (citing periodicals in documents submitted to courts and legal memoranda) & *Bluebook* Rule 2.1(b) (citing periodicals in law review footnotes). In law review footnotes, the abbreviated name of the publication would appear in large and small capital letters. *See supra* Citation Exercise 5.

B. INSTRUCTIONS FOR COMPLETING THIS EXERCISE

To complete this exercise, find the legal periodical cited with your problem number below. The following abbreviations have been used:

Harv. L. Rev. = Harvard Law Review
Yale L.J. = Yale Law Journal
Stan. L. Rev. = Stanford Law Review
Tul. L. Rev. = Tulane Law Review
Mich. L. Rev. = Michigan Law Review
Colum. L. Rev. = Columbia Law Review
Wash. L. Rev. = Washington Law Review
Minn. L. Rev. = Minnesota Law Review
Tex. L. Rev. = Texas Law Review
Va. L. Rev. = Virginia Law Review

For your answer to this exercise, cite the article in *Bluebook* (or another designated) form; assume that your citation will appear in a court document or legal memorandum, not in a law review article.

Unless otherwise instructed, write your answers on the answer sheet provided in Part 4 of these exercises.

PROBLEM #	CITED REFERENCE
1 116 211 335 450 555	110 Harv. L. Rev. 1657
2 117 212 336 451 556	86 Yale L.J. 1165
3 118 213 337 452 557	6 Stan. L. Rev. 411
4 119 214 338 453 558	37 Tul. L. Rev. 235
5 120 215 339 454 559	28 Mich. L. Rev. 485
6 121 216 340 455 560	97 Colum. L. Rev. 2255

PROBLEM #	CITED REFERENCE
7 122 217 341 456 561	51 Wash. L. Rev. 1
8 123 218 342 457 562	56 Minn. L. Rev. 159
9 124 219 343 458 563	71 Tul. L. Rev. 1389
10 125 220 344 459 564	63 Va. L. Rev. 693
11 126 221 345 460 565	108 Harv. L. Rev. 1423
12 127 222 346 461 566	87 Yale L.J. 697
13 128 223 347 462 567	7 Stan. L. Rev. 480
14 129 224 348 463 568	38 Tul. L. Rev. 469
15 130 225 349 464 569	29 Mich. L. Rev. 1
16 131 226 350 465 570	78 Colum. L. Rev. 1022
17 132 227 351 466 571	52 Wash. L. Rev. 335
18 133 228 352 467 572	59 Minn. L. Rev. 991
19 134 229 353 468 573	40 Tex. L. Rev. 509
20 135 230 354 469 574	64 Va. L. Rev. 691
21 136 231 355 470 575	90 Harv. L. Rev. 1105
22 137 232 356 471 576	88 Yale L.J. 243
23 138 233 357 472 577	50 Stan. L. Rev. 1193
24 139 234 358 473 578	40 Tul. L. Rev. 97
25 140 235 359 474 579	32 Mich. L. Rev. 289
26 141 236 360 475 580	79 Colum. L. Rev. 847
27 142 237 361 476 581	53 Wash. L. Rev. 405
28 143 238 362 477 582	63 Minn. L. Rev. 609
29 144 239 363 478 583	55 Tex. L. Rev. 371
30 145 240 364 479 584	65 Va. L. Rev. 859
31 146 241 365 480 585	91 Harv. L. Rev. 909
32 147 242 366 481 586	89 Yale L.J. 835
33 148 243 367 482 587	9 Stan. L. Rev. 433
34 149 244 368 483 588	42 Tul. L. Rev. 1
35 150 245 369 484 589	42 Mich. L. Rev. 353
36 151 246 370 485 590	80 Colum. L. Rev. 931
37 152 247 371 486 591	54 Wash. L. Rev. 239
38 153 248 372 487 592	64 Minn. L. Rev. 751
39 154 249 373 488 593	56 Tex. L. Rev. 791
40 155 250 374 489 594	83 Va. L. Rev. 1617
41 156 251 375 490 595	92 Harv. L. Rev. 963
42 157 252 376 491 596	90 Yale L.J. 473
43 158 253 377 492 597	10 Stan. L. Rev. 274
44 159 254 378 493 598	44 Tul. L. Rev. 720
45 160 255 379 494 599	43 Mich. L. Rev. 59
46 161 256 380 495 600	81 Colum. L. Rev. 960
47 162 257 381 496 501	55 Wash. L. Rev. 137
48 163 258 382 497 502	82 Minn. L. Rev. 1171
49 164 259 383 498 503	58 Tex. L. Rev. 875
50 165 260 384 499 504	67 Va. L. Rev. 887
51 166 261 385 500 505	109 Harv. L. Rev. 549
52 167 262 386 401 506	91 Yale L.J. 54
53 168 263 387 402 507	11 Stan. L. Rev. 213
54 169 264 388 403 508	50 Tul. L. Rev. 346
55 170 265 389 404 509	60 Mich. L. Rev. 269
56 171 266 390 405 510	72 Wash. L. Rev. 709

PROBLEM #	CITED REFERENCE
57 172 267 391 406 511	56 Wash. L. Rev. 51
58 173 268 392 407 512	66 Minn. L. Rev. 283
59 174 269 393 408 513	59 Tex. L. Rev. 815
60 175 270 394 409 514	68 Va. L. Rev. 63
61 176 271 395 410 515	94 Harv. L. Rev. 321
62 177 272 396 411 516	92 Yale L.J. 14
63 178 273 397 412 517	12 Stan. L. Rev. 323
64 179 274 398 413 518	52 Tul. L. Rev. 659
65 180 275 399 414 519	62 Mich. L. Rev. 753
66 181 276 400 415 520	83 Colum. L. Rev. 1121
67 182 277 301 416 521	57 Wash. L. Rev. 55
68 183 278 302 417 522	67 Minn. L. Rev. 299
69 184 279 303 418 523	60 Tex. L. Rev. 175
70 185 280 304 419 524	69 Va. L. Rev. 11
71 186 281 305 420 525	95 Harv. L. Rev. 393
72 187 282 306 421 526	93 Yale L.J. 793
73 188 283 307 422 527	13 Stan. L. Rev. 60
74 189 284 308 423 528	53 Tul. L. Rev. 135
75 190 285 309 424 529	75 Mich. L. Rev. 311
76 191 286 310 425 530	84 Colum. L. Rev. 1145
77 192 287 311 426 531	58 Wash. L. Rev. 1
78 193 288 312 427 532	68 Minn. L. Rev. 409
79 194 289 313 428 533	61 Tex. L. Rev. 595
80 195 290 314 429 534	70 Va. L. Rev. 879
81 196 291 315 430 535	96 Harv. L. Rev. 374
82 197 292 316 431 536	95 Yale L.J. 62
83 198 293 317 432 537	14 Stan. L. Rev. 284
84 199 294 318 433 538	57 Tul. L. Rev. 733
85 200 295 319 434 539	76 Mich. L. Rev. 64
86 101 296 320 435 540	85 Colum. L. Rev. 905
87 102 297 321 436 541	59 Wash. L. Rev. 141
88 103 298 322 437 542	69 Minn. L. Rev. 735
89 104 299 323 438 543	62 Tex. L. Rev. 785
90 105 300 324 439 544	71 Va. L. Rev. 65
91 106 201 325 440 545	73 Harv. L. Rev. 851
92 107 202 326 441 546	96 Yale L.J. 453
93 108 203 327 442 547	15 Stan. L. Rev. 45
94 109 204 328 443 548	59 Tul. L. Rev. 928
95 110 205 329 444 549	77 Mich. L. Rev. 12
96 111 206 330 445 550	86 Colum. L. Rev. 901
97 112 207 331 446 551	60 Wash. L. Rev. 267
98 113 208 332 447 552	70 Minn. L. Rev. 121
99 114 209 333 448 553	82 Va. L. Rev. 1753
100 115 210 334 449 554	72 Va. L. Rev. 879

CITATION EXERCISE 7
A.L.R. ANNOTATIONS

A. INTRODUCTION

1. A.L.R. Annotations

American Law Reports (A.L.R.) contains both court opinions and research articles called annotations. A textual annotation is especially useful in providing summaries of cases on the topic, defining the majority and minority rules, and providing cross-references to other sources.

A.L.R. (1st series) (1918-1947) and *A.L.R.2d* (1947-1965) have annotations on state and federal topics; *A.L.R.3d* (1965-1980) has annotations on state and federal topics until 1969 and only state topics after 1969; *A.L.R.4th* (1980 to 1991) and *A.L.R.5th* (1992 to date) have annotations on state topics; *A.L.R. Federal* (1969 to date) has annotations on federal topics.

2. *Bluebook* Form for Citing A.L.R. Annotations

Bluebook Rule 16.5.5 states that discussions in annotations such as American Law Reports should be cited by the following:

(1) the **author's full name** (*see supra Bluebook* Rule 15.1.1 and Citation Exercises 1, 4, and 6 for details);

(2) the word, **Annotation**;

(3) the **title of the annotation** in italics or underscored; capitalize the title according to *Bluebook* Rule 8, *i.e.*, capitalize the initial word, the word immediately following a colon, and all other words in the title; however, do not capitalize articles, conjunctions, and prepositions of four or fewer letters;

(4) the **volume number**;

(5) the **annotation designation** (*e.g.*, A.L.R.5th);

(6) the **page on which the annotation begins** (not the page on which the accompanying case begins); and

(7) the copyright **date** of the volume.

The following are typical *Bluebook* citations of A.L.R. Annotations:

[Example 1] John C. Claya, Annotation, *Reasonableness of Qualifications for Union Office Under § 401(e) of Labor-Management Reporting and Disclosure Act (29 U.S.C.A. § 481(e))*, 147 A.L.R. Fed. 389 (1998).

[Example 2] Jim Fraiser, Annotation, *Waiver of, or Estoppel to Assert, Failure to Give or Defects in Notice of Claim Against State or Local Political Subdivision—Modern Status*, 64 A.L.R.5th 519 (1998).

3. Typeface Conventions

As shown in Examples 1 and 2 above, titles of the annotations appear in italics or are underscored when annotations are cited in documents submitted to courts or in legal memoranda. *See Bluebook* Practitioners' Note P.1(b). In law review footnotes, the abbreviated name of the particular annotation appears in large and small capital letters:

[Example 3] John C. Claya, Annotation, *Reasonableness of Qualifications for Union Office Under § 401(e) of Labor-Management Reporting and Disclosure Act (29 U.S.C.A. § 481(e))*, 147 A.L.R. FED. 389 (1998).

B. INSTRUCTIONS FOR COMPLETING THIS EXERCISE

This exercise gives you practice in citing an A.L.R. Annotation. To complete this exercise, find the A.L.R. Annotation listed with your problem number below. Be sure to use the correct series (*A.L.R.4th*, *A.L.R.5th*, or *A.L.R. Federal*).

For your answer to this exercise, state the following:

(a) the full name of the author of the annotation, if any;

(b) the full title of the annotation exactly as it is given at the beginning of the annotation;

(c) the copyright date of the volume; and

(d) the citation of the annotation in *Bluebook* (or another designated) form; assume that your citation will appear in a court document or legal memorandum, not in a law review article.

Unless otherwise instructed, write your answers on the answer sheet provided in Part 4 of these exercises.

PROBLEM #	A.L.R. ANNOTATION
1 121 241 331 421 521	43 A.L.R.4th 71
2 122 242 332 422 522	42 A.L.R.4th 158
3 123 243 333 423 523	41 A.L.R.4th 60
4 124 244 334 424 524	40 A.L.R.4th 514
5 125 245 335 425 525	39 A.L.R.4th 399
6 126 246 336 426 526	38 A.L.R.4th 200
7 127 247 337 427 527	37 A.L.R.4th 200
8 128 248 338 428 528	36 A.L.R.4th 843
9 129 249 339 429 529	35 A.L.R.4th 947
10 130 250 340 430 530	106 A.L.R. Fed. 292
11 131 251 341 431 531	105 A.L.R. Fed. 299
12 132 252 342 432 532	32 A.L.R.4th 56
13 133 253 343 433 533	31 A.L.R.4th 623
14 134 254 344 434 534	30 A.L.R.4th 9
15 135 255 345 435 535	29 A.L.R.4th 431
16 136 256 346 436 536	28 A.L.R.4th 665

PROBLEM #	A.L.R. ANNOTATION
17 137 257 347 437 537	27 A.L.R.4th 864
18 138 258 348 438 538	26 A.L.R.4th 102
19 139 259 349 439 539	151 A.L.R. Fed. 561
20 140 260 350 440 540	24 A.L.R.4th 63
21 141 261 351 441 541	90 A.L.R.4th 298
22 142 262 352 442 542	22 A.L.R.4th 668
23 143 263 353 443 543	21 A.L.R.4th 383
24 144 264 354 444 544	20 A.L.R.4th 196
25 145 265 355 445 545	19 A.L.R.4th 639
26 146 266 356 446 546	18 A.L.R.4th 542
27 147 267 357 447 547	17 A.L.R.4th 575
28 148 268 358 448 548	16 A.L.R.4th 238
29 149 269 359 449 549	15 A.L.R.4th 824
30 150 270 360 450 550	14 A.L.R.4th 761
31 151 271 361 451 551	13 A.L.R.4th 476
32 152 272 362 452 552	12 A.L.R.4th 673
33 153 273 363 453 553	103 A.L.R. Fed. 798
34 154 274 364 454 554	10 A.L.R.4th 605
35 155 275 365 455 555	9 A.L.R.4th 633
36 156 276 366 456 556	8 A.L.R.4th 70
37 157 277 367 457 557	7 A.L.R.4th 655
38 158 278 368 458 558	6 A.L.R.4th 358
39 159 279 369 459 559	5 A.L.R.4th 574
40 160 280 370 460 560	4 A.L.R.4th 331
41 161 281 371 461 561	3 A.L.R.4th 87
42 162 282 372 462 562	2 A.L.R.4th 284
43 163 283 373 463 563	1 A.L.R.4th 144
44 164 284 374 464 564	54 A.L.R.4th 112
45 165 285 375 465 565	53 A.L.R.4th 282
46 166 286 376 466 566	52 A.L.R.4th 618
47 167 287 377 467 567	51 A.L.R.4th 565
48 168 288 378 468 568	50 A.L.R.4th 250
49 169 289 379 469 569	49 A.L.R.4th 653
50 170 290 380 470 570	48 A.L.R.4th 250
51 171 291 381 471 571	104 A.L.R. Fed. 166
52 172 292 382 472 572	3 A.L.R. Fed. 467
53 173 293 383 473 573	1 A.L.R.5th 375
54 174 294 384 474 574	5 A.L.R. Fed. 922
55 175 295 385 475 575	6 A.L.R. Fed. 317
56 176 296 386 476 576	7 A.L.R. Fed. 289
57 177 297 387 477 577	8 A.L.R. Fed. 319
58 178 298 388 478 578	9 A.L.R. Fed. 422
59 179 299 389 479 579	10 A.L.R. Fed. 511
60 180 300 390 480 580	11 A.L.R. Fed. 368
61 181 201 391 481 581	12 A.L.R. Fed. 502
62 182 202 392 482 582	13 A.L.R. Fed. 613
63 183 203 393 483 583	14 A.L.R. Fed. 473
64 184 204 394 484 584	15 A.L.R. Fed. 336
65 185 205 395 485 585	17 A.L.R. Fed. 343
66 186 206 396 486 586	18 A.L.R. Fed. 126

PROBLEM #	A.L.R. ANNOTATION
67 187 207 397 487 587	19 A.L.R. Fed. 297
68 188 208 398 488 588	20 A.L.R. Fed. 448
69 189 209 399 489 589	21 A.L.R. Fed. 314
70 190 210 400 490 590	22 A.L.R. Fed. 379
71 191 211 301 491 591	23 A.L.R. Fed. 301
72 192 212 302 492 592	24 A.L.R. Fed. 386
73 193 213 303 493 593	25 A.L.R. Fed. 179
74 194 214 304 494 594	26 A.L.R. Fed. 13
75 195 215 305 495 595	27 A.L.R. Fed. 214
76 196 216 306 496 596	28 A.L.R. Fed. 26
77 197 217 307 497 597	29 A.L.R. Fed. 906
78 198 218 308 498 598	30 A.L.R. Fed. 258
79 199 219 309 499 599	31 A.L.R. Fed. 234
80 200 220 310 500 600	32 A.L.R. Fed. 674
81 101 221 311 401 501	33 A.L.R. Fed. 403
82 102 222 312 402 502	34 A.L.R. Fed. 507
83 103 223 313 403 503	35 A.L.R. Fed. 461
84 104 224 314 404 504	36 A.L.R. Fed. 420
85 105 225 315 405 505	102 A.L.R. Fed. 575
86 106 226 316 406 506	38 A.L.R. Fed. 164
87 107 227 317 407 507	39 A.L.R. Fed. 570
88 108 228 318 408 508	40 A.L.R. Fed. 263
89 109 229 319 409 509	41 A.L.R. Fed. 146
90 110 230 320 410 510	42 A.L.R. Fed. 163
91 111 231 321 411 511	43 A.L.R. Fed. 68
92 112 232 322 412 512	44 A.L.R. Fed. 225
93 113 233 323 413 513	45 A.L.R. Fed. 185
94 114 234 324 414 514	46 A.L.R. Fed. 176
95 115 235 325 415 515	47 A.L.R. Fed. 15
96 116 236 326 416 516	48 A.L.R. Fed. 509
97 117 237 327 417 517	49 A.L.R. Fed. 16
98 118 238 328 418 518	50 A.L.R. Fed. 541
99 119 239 329 419 519	51 A.L.R. Fed. 420
100 120 240 330 420 520	52 A.L.R. Fed. 530

CITATION EXERCISE 8
RESTATEMENTS OF THE LAW

A. INTRODUCTION

1. Restatements of the Law

Restatements of the Law have been prepared under the auspices of the American Law Institute. They cover basic areas of the law, such as contracts, torts, property, and trusts. They provide a comprehensive and clear statement of legal propositions, comments, illustrations, and supporting authority. Because of the prestige of the reporters, the committees reviewing the drafts, and the American Law Institute, Restatements of the Law have been extremely persuasive secondary authorities in the courts. Subsequent revisions of the first restatements now appear as a Restatement "Second" or a Restatement "Third."

2. Citing Restatement Provisions in *Bluebook* Form

According to *Bluebook* Rule 12.8.5, restatements are cited by **section or other relevant subdivision**, not by page number. The **date** used in the citation is the date that the restatement was published. When you are citing a comment or illustration in a restatement, do not capitalize those terms in the citation (*Bluebook* Rule 3.5). Note that (1) comment, illustration, and appendix should be abbreviated cmt., illus., and app. respectively and (2) there is no comma after the section number.

The following are examples of *Bluebook* citations to a restatement:

[Example 1] Restatement of Restitution § 12 (1937).
[Example 2] Restatement (Second) of Property: Donative Transfers § 2.1 (1983).
[Example 3] Restatement of Contracts § 372(1) cmt. a (1932).
[Example 4] Restatement (Second) of Conflicts § 253 illus. 2 (1971).

3. Typeface Conventions

As shown in the above examples, restatements are cited in ordinary roman type in documents submitted to courts and in legal memoranda. *See Bluebook* Practitioners' Note P.1(h). In law review footnotes, the name of the restatement appears in large and small capital letters:

[Example 5] RESTATEMENT (SECOND) OF CONFLICTS § 253 illus. 2 (1971).

See Bluebook Rule 12.8.5.

B. INSTRUCTIONS FOR COMPLETING THIS EXERCISE

This exercise is designed to give you practice citing Restatements of the Law. To complete this exercise, find the section of the Restatement listed with your problem number. Be sure to use the **principal volume** containing the cited section. **The appendix and other volumes accompanying the Restatements should not be used.** All of the citations below are to sections appearing in a **Restatement Second**.

For your answer to this exercise, state the following:

(a) the subject with which the cited section deals (*e.g.*, the definition of an offer);

(b) the year in which the cited Restatement Second volume was published (*e.g.*, 1979); and

(c) the citation to the section listed with your problem number below in *Bluebook* (or another designated) form; assume that your citation will appear in a court document or legal memorandum, not in a law review article.

Unless otherwise instructed, write your answers on the answer sheet provided in Part 4 of these exercises.

PROBLEM #	RESTATEMENT (SECOND) OF
1 143 231 380 477 526	Contracts § 6
2 144 232 381 478 527	Agency § 3
3 145 233 382 479 528	Conflict of Laws § 2
4 146 234 383 480 529	Judgments § 3
5 147 235 384 481 530	Property: Donative Transfers § 25.1
6 148 236 385 482 531	Trusts § 3
7 149 237 386 483 532	Contracts § 25
8 150 238 387 484 533	Agency § 12
9 151 239 388 485 534	Conflict of Laws § 11
10 152 240 389 486 535	Judgments § 5
11 153 241 390 487 536	Property: Donative Transfers § 1.6
12 154 242 391 488 537	Trusts § 5
13 155 243 392 489 538	Contracts § 42
14 156 244 393 490 539	Agency § 16
15 157 245 394 491 540	Conflict of Laws § 20
16 158 246 395 492 541	Judgments § 11
17 159 247 396 493 542	Property: Donative Transfers § 13.1
18 160 248 397 494 543	Trusts § 13
19 161 249 398 495 544	Contracts § 75
20 162 250 399 496 545	Agency § 39
21 163 251 400 497 546	Conflict of Laws § 28
22 164 252 301 498 547	Judgments § 14
23 165 253 302 499 548	Property: Donative Transfers § 25.10
24 166 254 303 500 549	Trusts § 23
25 167 255 304 401 550	Contracts § 80

PROBLEM #	RESTATEMENT (SECOND) OF
26 168 256 305 402 551	Agency § 89
27 169 257 306 403 552	Conflict of Laws § 33
28 170 258 307 404 553	Judgments § 18
29 171 259 308 405 554	Property: Donative Transfers § 1.3
30 172 260 309 406 555	Trusts § 36
31 173 261 310 407 556	Contracts § 131
32 174 262 311 408 557	Agency § 146
33 175 263 312 409 558	Conflict of Laws § 41
34 176 264 313 410 559	Judgments § 19
35 177 265 314 411 560	Property: Donative Transfers § 13.7
36 178 266 315 412 561	Trusts § 48
37 179 267 316 413 562	Contracts § 193
38 180 268 317 414 563	Agency § 185
39 181 269 318 415 564	Conflict of Laws § 59
40 182 270 319 416 565	Judgments § 34
41 183 271 320 417 566	Property: Donative Transfers § 25.4
42 184 272 321 418 567	Trusts § 53
43 185 273 322 419 568	Contracts § 205
44 186 274 323 420 569	Agency § 219
45 187 275 324 421 570	Conflict of Laws § 84
46 188 276 325 422 571	Judgments § 39
47 189 277 326 423 572	Property: Donative Transfers § 1.4
48 190 278 327 424 573	Trusts § 80
49 191 279 328 425 574	Contracts § 209
50 192 280 329 426 575	Agency § 320
51 193 281 330 427 576	Conflict of Laws § 86
52 194 282 331 428 577	Judgments § 40
53 195 283 332 429 578	Torts § 508
54 196 284 333 430 579	Trusts § 274
55 197 285 334 431 580	Contracts § 224
56 198 286 335 432 581	Agency § 321
57 199 287 336 433 582	Conflict of Laws § 229
58 200 288 337 434 583	Judgments § 44
59 101 289 338 435 584	Torts § 530
60 102 290 339 436 585	Trusts § 276
61 103 291 340 437 586	Contracts § 235
62 104 292 341 438 587	Agency § 357
63 105 293 342 439 588	Conflict of Laws § 246
64 106 294 343 440 589	Judgments § 45
65 107 295 344 441 590	Torts § 586
66 108 296 345 442 591	Trusts § 307
67 109 297 346 443 592	Contracts § 244
68 110 298 347 444 493	Agency § 364
69 111 299 348 445 594	Conflict of Laws § 263
70 112 300 349 446 595	Judgments § 49
71 113 201 350 447 596	Torts § 614
72 114 202 351 448 597	Trusts § 330
73 115 203 352 449 598	Contracts § 344
74 116 204 353 450 599	Agency § 370
75 117 205 354 451 600	Conflict of Laws § 275

PROBLEM #	RESTATEMENT (SECOND) OF
76 118 206 355 452 501	Judgments § 53
77 119 207 356 453 502	Torts § 630
78 120 208 357 454 503	Trusts § 333
79 121 209 358 455 504	Contracts § 345
80 122 210 359 456 505	Agency § 386
81 123 211 360 457 506	Conflict of Laws § 278
82 124 212 361 458 507	Judgments § 63
83 125 213 362 459 508	Property: Donative Transfers § 13.4
84 126 214 363 460 509	Trusts § 339
85 127 215 364 461 510	Contracts § 352
86 128 216 365 462 511	Agency § 394
87 129 217 366 463 512	Conflict of Laws § 282
88 130 218 367 464 513	Judgments § 65
89 131 219 368 465 514	Torts § 869
90 132 220 369 466 515	Trusts § 343
91 133 221 370 467 516	Contracts § 355
92 134 222 371 468 517	Agency § 397
93 135 223 372 469 518	Conflict of Laws § 290
94 136 224 373 470 519	Judgments § 78
95 137 225 374 471 520	Torts § 892
96 138 226 375 472 521	Trusts § 376
97 139 227 376 473 522	Contracts § 367
98 140 228 377 474 523	Agency § 411
99 141 229 378 475 524	Conflict of Laws § 330
100 142 230 379 476 525	Judgments § 87

PART 2
CITING CASES

A. EXERCISES IN THIS PART

Part 2 focuses on citing cases. Some of the exercises focus exclusively on *Bluebook* rules, such as those for citing case names. Some focus on the information provided in *Bluebook* Tables concerning cases. Others focus on citing specific courts. The following is a complete listing of the twenty-two exercises contained in this part :

B. BASIC CITATION FORMS ILLUSTRATED

The following chart illustrates the basic forms for citations of various cases based on the *Bluebook* rules and typeface conventions for legal memoranda and court documents:

CITING FEDERAL COURT DECISIONS IN *BLUEBOOK* FORM

COURT	BASIC CITATION FORMS
U.S. Supreme Court —*Bluebook* citation —With parallel citations —Early (before vol. 91 of *U.S. Reports*)	*Conley v. Gibson*, 355 U.S. 41 (1957). *Conley v. Gibson*, 355 U.S. 41, 78 S. Ct. 99, 2 L. Ed. 2d 80 (1957). (NOT proper *Bluebook* form) *Capron v. Van Noorden*, 6 U.S. (2 Cranch) 126 (1804).
U.S. Court of Appeals —Numbered circuits —D.C. Circuit —Federal Circuit —Cited to WESTLAW —Cited to LEXIS	*Menowitz v. Brown*, 991 F.2d 36 (2d Cir. 1993). *Commercial Union Ins. Co. v. United States*, 999 F.2d 581 (D.C. Cir. 1993). *Young v. AGB Corp.*, 152 F.3d 1377 (Fed. Cir. 1998). *United States v. Brown*, No. 34-1139, 1996 WL 283313 (1st Cir. Mar. 4, 1996). *Shieh v. Ebershoff*, No. 93-55327, 1993 U.S. App. LEXIS 34766 (9th Cir. Dec. 30, 1993).
U.S. District Courts —Single district states —Multiple district states —District of Columbia —Cited to WESTLAW —Cited to LEXIS	*Comeau v. Rupp*, 762 F. Supp. 1434 (D. Kan. 1991). *Jordan v. Tapper*, 143 F.R.D. 575 (D.N.J. 1992). *PPS, Inc. v. Jewelry Sales Representatives, Inc.*, 392 F. Supp. 375 (S.D.N.Y. 1975). *Leisure v. Bowersox*, 990 F. Supp. 769 (E.D. Mo. 1998). *King v. Georgetown Univ. Hosp.*, 9 F. Supp. 2d 4 (D.D.C. 1998). *Doe v. Neal*, No. 94-4294, 1994 WL 702876 (E.D. Pa. Dec. 12, 1994). *Meldrum v. RPM, Inc.*, No. 1:93-CV-756, 1993 U.S. Dist. LEXIS 18880 (W.D. Mich. Dec. 3, 1993).
Early Federal Court Cases in West's *Federal Cases* Set	*The Aslesund*, 1 F. Cas. 1 (E.D.N.Y. 1877 (No. 1). *Green v. Sarmiento*, 10 F. Cas. 1117 (C.C.D. Pa. 1810) (No. 5760). *Peck v. Williamson*, 19 F. Cas. 85 (C.C.D.N.C. 1813) (No. 10,896).

CITING STATE COURT DECISIONS IN *BLUEBOOK* FORM

COURT	BASIC CITATION FORMS
Highest State Courts —Official reporter available	In documents submitted to Arkansas state courts: *Reasor-Hill Corp. v. Harrison*, 220 Ark. 521, 249 S.W.2d 994 (1952). In all other documents: *Reasor-Hill Corp. v. Harrison*, 249 S.W.2d 994 (Ark. 1952).
—Official reporter no longer published —Public domain citations	In all documents: *SDDS, Inc. v. State*, 502 N.W.2d 852 (S.D. 1993). Minimum required in all documents: *State v. Hart*, 1998 SD 93. With optional reference to the relevant West regional reporter: *State v. Hart*, 1998 SD 93, 584 N.W.2d 863.
—New York Court of Appeals	In documents submitted to New York state courts: *Szczerbiak v. Pilat*, 90 N.Y.2d 553, 686 N.E.2d 1346, 664 N.Y.S.2d 252 (1997). In all other documents: *Szczerbiak v. Pilat*, 686 N.E.2d 1346 (N.Y. 1997).
—California Supreme Court	In documents submitted to California state courts: *Davis v. KGO-T.V., Inc.*, 17 Cal. 4th 436, 950 P.2d 567, 71 Cal. Rptr. 452 (1998). In all other documents: *Davis v. KGO-T.V., Inc.*, 950 P.2d 567 (Cal. 1998).
Intermediate Appellate State Courts —Official reporter available	In documents submitted to Colorado state courts: *Bravo v. Wareham*, 43 Colo. App. 1, 605 P.2d 58 (1979). In all other documents: *Bravo v. Wareham*, 605 P.2d 58 (Colo. Ct. App. 1979).
—Official reporter no longer published —Public domain citations	In all other documents: *Nangle v. Brockman*, 972 S.W.2d 545 (Mo. Ct. App. 1998). Minimum required in all documents: *Wishnatsky v. Huey*, 1998 ND App 8. With optional reference to the relevant West regional reporter: *Wishnatsky v. Huey*, 1998 ND App 8, 584 N.W.2d 859.

CITING STATE COURT DECISIONS IN *BLUEBOOK* FORM
(CONTINUED)

COURT	BASIC CITATION FORMS
Intermediate Appellate State Courts (Continued) —Cited to WESTLAW —Cited to LEXIS —New York Supreme Court, Appellate Division —California Court of Appeal	*State v. Jones*, No. 1 CA-Cr 92-1856, 1994 WL 620653 (Ariz. Ct. App. Nov. 10, 1994). *State v. Steffen*, No. C-930351, 1994 Ohio App. LEXIS 1973 (Ohio Ct. App. May 11, 1994). In documents submitted to New York state courts: *In re Apollo*, 245 A.D.2d 699, 665 N.Y.S.2d 732 (1997). In all other documents: *In re Apollo*, 665 N.Y.S.2d 732 (App. Div. 1997). In documents submitted to California state courts: *People v. Johnson*, 62 Cal. App. 4th 608, 72 Cal. Rptr. 805 (1998). In all other documents: *People v. Johnson*, 72 Cal. Rptr. 805 (Ct. App. 1998).
State Trial Courts —New York Supreme Court —New York Family Court	In documents submitted to New York state courts: *Kitch v. Markham*, 174 Misc. 2d 611, 665 N.Y.S.2d 1019 (Sup. Ct. 1997). In all other documents: *Kitch v. Markham*, 665 N.Y.S.2d 1019 (Sup. Ct. 1997). In documents submitted to New York state courts: *In re Baby Girl S*, 174 Misc. 2d 682, 665 N.Y.S.2d 809 (Fam. Ct. 1997). In all other documents: *In re Baby Girl S*, 665 N.Y.S.2d 809 (Fam. Ct. 1997).

CITATION EXERCISE 9
CASE NAMES: REQUIRED *BLUEBOOK* ABBREVIATIONS

A. INTRODUCTION

1. Citation of Judicial Opinions

One result of litigation in appellate courts (and some trial courts) is the writing of judicial opinions. These opinions traditionally have been published in case reporters. The opinions ordinarily indicate the matters presented to the court for decision, the manner in which these matters were resolved, and the reason for that resolution. Decisions of the highest court in a jurisdiction become mandatory or controlling precedent (authority) for deciding future cases. The task of a lawyer making a legal argument will often be to demonstrate the similarity between prior cases and the desired result in the present case. However, a lawyer will sometimes attempt to demonstrate that the present case is appropriately distinguishable from a prior case to justify a different result. Occasionally, a lawyer will argue that existing precedents should be overruled and a new rule established.

Legal writers use case citation to identify relevant case law in their legal writing. Generally speaking, citations to cases (judicial opinions) in case reporters contain (up to) seven basic elements:

(1) the **case name**;

(2) the **volume number** of the reporter;

(3) the abbreviated **name of the reporter**;

(4) the **page number** on which the opinion begins (and any other pages cited in the opinion);

(5) the abbreviated **name of the court**, including its geographic jurisdiction (unless that information is clearly indicated from the reporter cited);

(6) the **year or date** of the decision; and

(7) the **subsequent history** of the case, if any.

See Bluebook Rule 10.1 ("Cases: Basic Citation Forms").

From early times, the names of the disputing parties have served as a convenient means of designating judicial proceedings. Such designations also fit well with the modern use of captions at the beginning of pleadings and other court documents. These captions designate the parties to a proceeding and their relationship (*e.g.*, plaintiff and defendant; appellant and appellee; petitioner and respondent; or intervenor). This exercise and the following two focus on the first element in a case citation: the case name. Additional exercises will then focus on the other elements listed above.

2. Case Names as They Appear in Reporters

When a judicial opinion is published in a reporter, the title of the case is given at the beginning of the case. The title of the case is sometimes referred to as the "style" of the case. Consider the following two examples showing the title or style of two reported cases.

> **BODELL CONSTRUCTION COMPANY, a Utah corporation; James Bodell; and Michael Bodell, Plaintiffs and Appellants,**
>
> v.
>
> **STEWART TITLE GUARANTY COMPANY, a Texas corporation; Vernon F. George; First Title of Utah, Inc.; Robert Elliott; Kathryn Elliott; Floyd Helm; The Property Shoppe, Inc., a Utah corporation; Kent Sundbert; Rredco Realty; Jerald Richardson; and The Rosemont Corporation, a California corporation, Defendants and Appellee.**

This case involved multiple parties. The title of the case consists of the names of the opposing parties (Plaintiffs and Defendants), separated by a *v.*—which stands for *versus*. The title provides other descriptive information, such as the fact that the Bodell Construction Co. is a Utah corporation. The title also indicates that the plaintiffs were the parties who appealed (Appellants).

> **UNITED STATES of America, Plaintiff,**
>
> v.
>
> **TWO PARCELS OF REAL PROPERTY LOCATED AT 101 NORTH LIBERTY STREET AND 105 LIBERTY STREET IN CLANTON, CHILTON COUNTY, ALABAMA, WITH ALL APPURTENANCES AND IMPROVEMENTS THEREON, Defendant.**

Sometimes, when the proceeding is in rem—technically against a res (thing) such as a piece of real property or a ship, the title of the case will be the res itself. In this example, the United States Government was seeking forfeiture of the two described parcels of property in Chilton County, Alabama.

On rare occasions, the title of the case will be the popular name (*e.g.*, the *Tea Rose* case) or simply "Judgment of" followed by the full date. *See Bluebook* Rule 10.2.1

3. *Bluebook* Citation Rules for Case Names

As illustrated by the above examples, the titles of reported cases often provide considerable detail about the parties and nature of an action. The *Bluebook* provides several conventions to make the case-name portion of the citation more manageable. The principal purpose of these *Bluebook* conventions is simply to save space. The total number of pages in an issue of a law review is limited. Similarly, lawyers often must comply with strict page limits for appellate briefs and other legal documents. *Bluebook* rules help minimize the space utilized in citing cases by providing for (1) standard omissions and deletions and (2) standard abbreviations of words used in case names.

A secondary benefit of a uniform system of abbreviations and omissions relates to electronic searching for case names in databases. Because computer programs search literally, unusual omissions or abbreviations (that are not anticipated by a researcher) might cause a case to be missed. For example, a computer researcher would find it difficult to retrieve a case involving the American Agricultural Movement, Inc. as a party if it were abbreviated to "A Ag. Mov., Inc."

4. Required *Bluebook* Abbreviations of Case Names in Textual Sentences

In making arguments or providing explanations, legal writers discuss and cite cases as legal authority. In doing so, they will often use case names or entire case citations as **grammatical parts of textual sentences**, *i.e.*, as a subject of a sentence, a direct object, an object of a preposition, etc. Consider the following two examples adapted from an appellate brief filed in the U.S. Supreme Court:

> **[Example 1]** *Phillips Petroleum Co. v. Shutts* is a textbook example of the application of this fairness principle.
>> Here, the full case name (*Phillips Petroleum Co. v. Shutts*) is used as the subject of the sentence.
>
> **[Example 2]** In his brief in opposition to the petition for certiorari, Dr. Gore argued strenuously that this Court's decision in *TXO Products Corp. v. Alliance Resources Corp.*, 509 U.S. 443 (1993), authorized the kind of extraterritorial punishment that took place here. That argument reflects a fundamental misunderstanding of *TXO.*
>> Here, the case name (*TXO Products Corp. v. Alliance Resources Corp.*) and a shortened version of it (*TXO*) are used as objects of prepositions.

When case names appear as grammatical parts of textual sentences (as in the above examples), the abbreviated form of the case name is used in three situations: (a) procedural phrases; (b) eight specified words; and (c) widely recognized initials of the full name of the party (see below).

(a) Abbreviation of Procedural Phrases

Some types of cases, such as guardianship, probate, disbarment, habeas corpus, contempt, and bankruptcy proceedings, do not have traditional adversary parties or are not contested. In these types of cases, the title of the case is often listed as "petition of," "matter of," or "application of" and the party's name. In citing such cases, these and similar expressions should be abbreviated to the Latin phrase "*In re*" (meaning "in the matter of"). *Bluebook* Rule 10.2.1(b).

> **In the Matter of Terry Anton ROBINSON.**

Cite as: *In re Robinson* (**NOT** *In the Matter of Robinson*) (Given names of the party, such as "Terry Anton," are omitted—*see* § A(2) in Exercise 10.)

In addition, some cases are brought on behalf of another person known as a "relator." For example, an action may be brought in the name of the people at the instance of a particular party who is beneficially interested in the outcome. The case title usually indicates this situation by using terms such as "on relation of," "for the use of," "on behalf of," "on the information of," or "by." These and similar expressions should be shortened to "*ex rel.*" *Bluebook* Rule 10.2.1(b). "*Ex rel.*" is the abbreviation of the Latin term "*ex relatione*," meaning "on the relation of."

> **Simon PLAMONDON, On Relation of the COWLITZ TRIBE OF INDIANS**
> **v.**
> **The UNITED STATES.**

Cite as: *Plamondon ex rel. Cowlitz Tribe of Indians v. United States* (**NOT** *Plamondon on Relation of the Cowlitz Tribe of Indians v. United States*)

(b) Abbreviation of And, Association, Brothers, Company, Corporation, Incorporated, Limited, and Number

The following eight words should be abbreviated **unless** they are the **first word** of a party's name, including a relator. *Bluebook* Rule 10.2.1(c).

And = &
Brothers = Bros.
Corporation = Corp.
Limited = Ltd.

Association = Ass'n
Company = Co.
Incorporated = Inc.
Number = No.

> **OAKES FARMING ASSOCIATION, a cooperative, Plaintiff, Appellee and Cross-Appellant,**
> **v.**
> **MARTINSON BROTHERS, a partnership, and John Martinson, Linda L. Martinson, Oscar Martinson and Susan M. Libecki, jointly and severally as individuals, Defendants, Appellants and Cross-Appellees.**

Cite as: *Oakes Farming Ass'n v. Martinson Bros.* (**NOT** *Oakes Farming Association v. Martinson Brothers*) (Terms describing a party already named, such as "a cooperative," "Plaintiff," etc. are omitted—*see* § A(1) in Exercise 10; additional parties on each side of the case, *e.g.*, "John Martinson," "Linda L. Martinson," etc., are also omitted—*see* § A(6) in Exercise 10.)

ASSOCIATION OF LITTLE FRIENDS, INC., Petitioner-Appellant, v. CITY OF ESCANABA, Respondent-Appellee.	**Cite as:** *Association of Little Friends, Inc. v. City of Escanaba* (**NOT** *Ass'n of Little Friends, Inc. v. City of Escanaba*) (Association is the **first word** of the party's name)

(c) Abbreviation of Widely Recognized Initials of the Full Name of the Party

Some governmental agencies, boards, commissions, businesses, private organizations, and similar entities are commonly referred to in spoken language by their widely recognized initials. These initials (without periods) **may** be used in case names rather than their full names (*Bluebook* Rules 10.2.1(c) & 6.1(b)). Consider the following examples:

American Broadcasting Company = ABC
American Federation of Labor = AFL
Civil Aeronautics Board = CAB
Central Intelligence Agency = CIA
Congress of Industrial Organizations = CIO
Environmental Protection Agency = EPA
Equal Employment Opportunity Commission = EEOC
Federal Communications Commission = FCC
Food and Drug Administration = FDA
Federal Deposit Insurance Corporation = FDIC
Federal Trade Commission = FTC
International Business Machines Corporation = IBM
Interstate Commerce Commission = ICC
National Association for the Advancement of Colored People = NAACP
National Broadcasting Company = NBC
National Labor Relations Board = NLRB
Securities and Exchange Commission = SEC
Tennessee Valley Authority = TVA

APPALACHIAN POWER COMPANY, et al., Petitioners, v. ENVIRONMENTAL PROTECTION AGENCY, Respondent, Public Service Electric & Gas Company, et al., Intervenors.	**Cite as:** *Appalachian Power Co. v. EPA* **or** *Appalachian Power Co. v. Environmental Protection Agency* ("Company" is abbreviated in a proper *Bluebook* citation—*see* § A(4)*(b)*, above.)

5. Required *Bluebook* Abbreviations of Case Names
in Citation Sentences and Phrases

In addition to being used as grammatical parts of textual sentences, cases are often cited as authority for propositions. When the case supports the **entire** sentence, a separate **citation sentence** is used. *Bluebook* Rule 1.1(a)(i) & Practitioners' Note P.2. Consider the following example adapted from an appellate brief filed in the U.S. Supreme Court:

> **[Example 3]** The Seventh Amendment right to a jury trial does not apply to the States. *Hardware Dealers Mut. Fire Ins. Co. v. Glidden Co.*, 284 U.S. 151, 158 (1931). Furthermore, the States have wide latitude in allocating responsibilities between judges and juries. *See, e.g.*, *Jackson v. Denno*, 378 U.S. 368, 391 n.19 (1964); *Stein v. New York*, 346 U.S. 156, 179 (1943).
>
>> Here, the case names, *Hardware Dealers Mut. Fire Ins. Co. v. Glidden Co.*, *Jackson v. Denno*, and *Stein v. New York*, are parts of separate citation sentences; they are not grammatical parts of textual sentences.

When the case supports only **part** of a sentence, a **citation clause** is inserted, separated by commas, from the textual sentence (*Bluebook* Rule 1.1(a)(ii) & Practitioners' Note P.2). Consider the following example adapted from the same appellate brief:

> **[Example 4]** Even in the much more sensitive area of capital sentencing, this Court has indicated that a judge is free to impose a more severe penalty than the jury's recommended sentence, *Harris v. Alabama*, 513 U.S. 504, 513-14 (1995), and the reviewing court may reweigh the balance of aggravating and mitigating circumstances when the jury has found and relied upon an invalid aggravating factor, *Clemons v. Mississippi*, 494 U.S. 738, 745-47 (1990).
>
>> Here, the case names are part of citation clauses inserted in the text; they are not grammatical parts of textual sentences.

When case names appear in this manner (*i.e.*, in citation sentences or clauses), the *Bluebook* provides for further abbreviation **in addition to** that already discussed for case names as grammatical parts of textual sentences. Three specific sources will need to be consulted for this purpose: (a) Table T.6 for case names (in the blue pages in the "Tables and Abbreviations" section near the end of the *Bluebook*); (b) Table T.10 for geographical terms (in the blue pages in the "Tables and Abbreviations" section near the end of the *Bluebook*); and (c) Rule 10.2.2 concerning other words of eight letters or more.

(a) Table T.6 ("Case Names")

Table T.6 ("Case Names") lists required abbreviations for approximately 120 words that typically appear in case names. These abbreviations must be used **as long as they are not the first word of the name of a party or a relator**. *Bluebook* Rules 10.2.1(c) & 10.2.2.

Consider, for example, the *Hardware Dealers Mutual Fire Insurance* case cited in Example 3, above. The title of this case, as it appears in *United States Reports*, is as follows:

HARDWARE DEALERS MUTUAL FIRE INSUR-
ANCE CO. *v.* GLIDDEN CO. ᴇᴛ ᴀʟ.

"Mutual," "Insurance," and "Company" are included on the list of required abbreviations in Table T.6. Thus, in Example 3 above, they were abbreviated in the case name, *Hardware Dealers Mut. Fire Ins. Co. v. Glidden Co.*, because the case name appears as part of a separate citation sentence.

In contrast, if this same case name had appeared as a grammatical part of a textual sentence, only "Company" would have been abbreviated (*see* § A(4)*(b)* above): "In *Hardware Dealers Mutual Fire Insurance Co. v. Glidden Co.*, 284 U.S. 151, 158 (1931), the Court held that the Seventh Amendment right to a jury trial does not apply to the States."

Plurals of words listed in Table T.6 are formed by adding the letter "s" to the abbreviation (*e.g.*, Manufacturers = Mfrs. or Administrators = Adm'rs)—**unless otherwise indicated in the table** (*e.g.*, Laborator[y, ies] = Lab.).

(b) Table T.10 ("Geographical Terms")

Table T.10 ("Geographical Terms") lists required abbreviations for U.S. states, cities, and territories, Australian states, Canadian provinces, foreign countries, and foreign regions (*e.g.*, Kansas = Kan., British Columbia = B.C., or People's Republic of China = P.R.C.). These abbreviations are used **unless the geographical unit itself is a named party**. *Bluebook* Rule 10.2.2. *Bluebook* Rule 10.2.2 also specifically states that "United States" should **not** be abbreviated.

CABLE BELT CONVEYORS, INC. and
Paul N. Howard Company, Petitioners,

v.

ALUMINA PARTNERS OF
JAMAICA, Respondent.

In a citation sentence or clause, cite as: *Cable Belt Conveyors, Inc. v. Alumina Partners of Jam.* (As indicated in Table T.10, "Jamaica" should be abbreviated as "Jam.")

<table>
<tr><td>

Dr. Robert B. COLEMAN, Appellant,

v.

DISTRICT OF COLUMBIA, Appellee.

</td></tr>
</table>

Cite as: *Coleman v. District of Columbia* (The geographical unit, the "District of Columbia," is the named party and should not be abbreviated even though Table T.10 indicates the abbreviation is "D.C.")

(c) *Rule 10.2.2 Concerning Words of Eight Letters or More*

Bluebook Rule 10.2.2 (as well as the introduction to Table T.6) indicates that words of eight letters or more **may** also be abbreviated if **substantial space** is saved and "the result is unambiguous" (*e.g.*, Condominium = Condo., Compensation = Comp., etc.)

<table>
<tr><td>

Herbert W. ABRAMSON,
et al., Appellants,

v.

BUCKLEY TOWERS CONDOMINIUM,
INC., et al., Appellees.

</td></tr>
</table>

In a citation sentence or clause, cite as: *Abramson v. Buckley Towers Condo., Inc.* **or** *Abramson v. Buckley Towers Condominium, Inc.* (Words indicating multiple parties, such as *et al.*, are omitted—*see* § A(3) in Exercise 10.)

B. INSTRUCTIONS FOR COMPLETING THIS EXERCISE

The purpose of this exercise is to familiarize you with required abbreviations in *Bluebook* Table T.6 ("Case Names"), Table T.10 ("Geographical Terms"), and Rule 10.2.1(b) ("Procedural Phrases"). Assume that the following words are included in the case names **appearing in a citation sentence or phrase**. Using the above sources in *The Bluebook*, determine the proper abbreviations of the words listed with your problem number.

Unless you are otherwise instructed, write your answers on the answer sheet provided in Part 4 of these exercises.

PROBLEM #	WORDS
1 102 203 304 405 506	(a) Road (b) Tennessee (c) Australia (d) Petition of (e) Foundations (f) Industries
2 103 204 305 406 507	(a) Brotherhood (b) Illinois (c) Turkey (d) On the relation of (e) Associates (f) Schools
3 104 205 306 407 508	(a) General (b) Rhode Island (c) Bahamas (d) Application of (e) Boards (f) Systems
4 105 206 307 408 509	(a) Federal (b) South Dakota (c) Nicaragua (d) On behalf of (e) Engineers (f) Securities
5 106 207 308 409 510	(a) Administrative (b) Texas (c) Mexico (d) For the use of (e) Services (f) Steamships

PROBLEM #	WORDS
6 107 208 309 410 511	(a) Investment (b) Colorado (c) Scotland (d) In the matter of (e) Markets (f) Systems
7 108 209 310 411 512	(a) Liability (b) Hawaii (c) Iceland (d) Petition of (e) Commissioners (f) Laboratories
8 109 210 311 412 513	(a) Committee (b) Georgia (c) England (d) On the relation of (e) Centers (f) Savings
9 110 211 312 413 514	(a) Construction (b) North Dakota (c) United Kingdom (d) Application of (e) Examiners (f) Brothers
10 111 212 313 414 515	(a) Hospital (b) Oregon (c) Denmark (d) On behalf of (e) Investments (f) Industries
11 112 213 314 415 516	(a) Engineer (b) Wyoming (c) Africa (d) For the use of (e) Directors (f) Schools
12 113 214 315 416 517	(a) Advertising (b) Delaware (c) Austria (d) Petition of (e) Committees (f) Systems
13 114 215 316 417 518	(a) Technology (b) Connecticut (c) Switzerland (d) In the matter of (e) Automobiles (f) Steamships
14 115 216 317 418 519	(a) Western (b) Arizona (c) New Zealand (d) Petition of (e) Foundations (f) Securities
15 116 217 318 419 520	(a) Regional (b) Oklahoma (c) Guatemala (d) On the relation of (e) Associates (f) Systems
16 117 218 319 420 521	(a) Public (b) Pennsylvania (c) Mexico (d) Application of (e) Technologies (f) Laboratories
17 118 219 320 421 522	(a) Municipal (b) Wisconsin (c) Angola (d) On behalf of (e) Authorities (f) Savings
18 119 220 321 422 523	(a) Social (b) Florida (c) Thailand (d) For the use of (e) Utilities (f) Brothers
19 120 221 322 423 524	(a) Exchange (b) California (c) South Africa (d) Petition of (e) Manufacturers (f) Systems
20 121 222 323 424 525	(a) Building (b) New York (c) Malaysia (d) In the matter of (e) Boards (f) Industries
21 122 223 324 425 526	(a) Center (b) Arkansas (c) Honduras (d) Petition of (e) Districts (f) Schools
22 123 224 325 426 527	(a) Automobile (b) Kentucky (c) Ethiopia (d) On the relation of (e) Distributors (f) Systems
23 124 225 326 427 528	(a) Temporary (b) Alabama (c) Canada (d) Application of (e) Cooperatives (f) Steamships
24 125 226 327 428 529	(a) Uniform (b) New Jersey (c) Venezuela (d) On behalf of (e) Federations (f) Systems
25 126 227 328 429 530	(a) Railway (b) Nevada (c) Gambia (d) For the use of (e) Enterprises (f) Systems
26 127 228 329 430 531	(a) Marketing (b) South Carolina (c) Netherlands (d) Petition of (e) Products (f) Laboratories
27 128 229 330 431 532	(a) Litigation (b) Nebraska (c) Finland (d) In the matter of (e) Associations (f) Savings
28 129 230 331 432 533	(a) Board (b) Maryland (c) Hungary (d) Petition of (e) Chemicals (f) Brothers
29 130 231 332 433 534	(a) Director (b) Virginia (c) France (d) On the relation of (e) Institutes (f) Systems
30 131 232 333 434 535	(a) International (b) Louisiana (c) Indonesia (d) Application of (e) Exchanges (f) Industries

PROBLEM #	WORDS
31 132 233 334 435 536	(a) Housing (b) Kansas (c) Afghanistan (d) On behalf of (e) Hospitals (f) Schools
32 133 234 335 436 537	(a) Indemnity (b) Indiana (c) Luxembourg (d) For the use of (e) Departments (f) Systems
33 134 235 336 437 538	(a) Commission (b) North Carolina (c) Romania (d) Petition of (e) Companies (f) Steamships
34 135 236 337 438 539	(a) Equality (b) Montana (c) Poland (d) In the matter of (e) Electronics (f) Securities
35 136 237 338 439 540	(a) Information (b) Missouri (c) Singapore (d) Petition of (e) Associates (f) Systems
36 137 238 339 440 541	(a) Telephone (b) Vermont (c) Jamaica (d) On the relation of (e) Enterprises (f) Laboratories
37 138 239 340 441 542	(a) Utility (b) Mississippi (c) Lebanon (d) Application of (e) Associations (f) Savings
38 139 240 341 442 543	(a) Publishing (b) Maine (c) Bulgaria (d) On behalf of (e) Bankruptcies (f) Brothers
39 140 241 342 443 544	(a) Manufacturer (b) Michigan (c) Albania (d) For the use of (e) Commissions (f) Systems
40 141 242 343 444 545	(a) America (b) West Virginia (c) Ireland (d) Petition of (e) Investments (f) Industries
41 142 243 344 445 546	(a) Electronic (b) Massachusetts (c) El Salvador (d) In the matter of (e) Cooperatives (f) Schools
42 143 244 345 446 547	(a) Independent (b) Minnesota (c) Barbados (d) Petition of (e) Developments (f) Systems
43 144 245 346 447 548	(a) Consolidated (b) Los Angeles (c) Nigeria (d) On the relation of (e) Directors (f) Steamships
44 145 246 347 448 549	(a) Central (b) San Francisco (c) Panama (d) Application of (e) Services (f) Securities
45 146 247 348 449 550	(a) Authority (b) Philadelphia (c) Sweden (d) On behalf of (e) Machines (f) Systems
46 147 248 349 450 551	(a) Guaranty (b) New Hampshire (c) Paraguay (d) For the use of (e) Telecommunications (f) Laboratories
47 148 249 350 451 552	(a) Society (b) New Mexico (c) Philippines (d) Petition of (e) Investments (f) Savings
48 149 250 351 452 553	(a) Refining (b) Puerto Rico (c) Israel (d) In the matter of (e) Governments (f) Brothers
49 150 251 352 453 554	(a) Railroad (b) Washington (c) Norway (d) Petition of (e) Federations (f) Systems
50 151 252 353 454 555	(a) Market (b) Virgin Islands (c) Great Britain (d) On the relation of (e) Exchanges (f) Industries
51 152 253 354 455 556	(a) Service (b) Montana (c) Senegal (d) Application of (e) Associates (f) Schools
52 153 254 355 456 557	(a) Professional (b) Oklahoma (c) North America (d) On behalf of (e) Examiners (f) Systems
53 154 255 356 457 558	(a) Transportation (b) Connecticut (c) Brazil (d) For the use of (e) Enterprises (f) Steamships
54 155 256 357 458 559	(a) Association (b) District of Columbia (c) Pakistan (d) Petition of (e) Foundations (f) Securities
55 156 257 358 459 560	(a) Enterprise (b) Georgia (c) South America (d) In the matter of (e) Commissioners (f) Systems

PROBLEM #	WORDS
56 157 258 359 460 561	(a) Cooperative (b) Wisconsin (c) Bermuda (d) Petition of (e) Indemnities (f) Laboratories
57 158 259 360 461 562	(a) Electric (b) New Jersey (c) North Korea (d) On the relation of (e) Liabilities (f) Savings
58 159 260 361 462 563	(a) Insurance (b) Kansas (c) Latvia (d) Application of (e) Associates (f) Brothers
59 160 261 362 463 564	(a) University (b) Massachusetts (c) Poland (d) For the use of (e) Subcommittees (f) Securities
60 161 262 363 464 565	(a) Telephone (b) Virginia (c) Bolivia (d) Petition of (e) Boards (f) Industries
61 162 263 364 465 566	(a) Product (b) North Dakota (c) Canada (d) In the matter of (e) Enterprises (f) Schools
62 163 264 365 466 567	(a) Mutual (b) Florida (c) Algeria (d) Application of (e) Institutes (f) Systems
63 164 265 366 467 568	(a) National (b) Minnesota (c) Argentina (d) Petition of (e) Distributors (f) Steamships
64 165 266 367 468 569	(a) Surety (b) Wyoming (c) Swaziland (d) On the relation of (e) Committees (f) Securities
65 166 267 368 469 570	(a) Atlantic (b) Rhode Island (c) Venezuela (d) Application of (e) Associations (f) Systems
66 167 268 369 470 571	(a) Division (b) South Carolina (c) Turkey (d) For the use of (e) Enterprises (f) Laboratories
67 168 269 370 471 572	(a) Business (b) New York (c) New Zealand (d) Petition of (e) Electronics (f) Savings
68 169 270 371 472 573	(a) Examiner (b) California (c) Denmark (d) In the matter of (e) Engineers (f) Brothers
69 170 271 372 473 574	(a) Casualty (b) Maine (c) Mozambique (d) Application of (e) Foundations (f) Securities
70 171 272 373 474 575	(a) Pacific (b) Vermont (c) Mexico (d) Petition of (e) Telecommunications (f) Industries
71 172 273 374 475 576	(a) Telegraph (b) Tennessee (c) Lithuania (d) On the relation of (e) Investments (f) Schools
72 173 274 375 476 577	(a) Memorial (b) Indiana (c) Portugal (d) Application of (e) Automobiles (f) Systems
73 174 275 376 477 578	(a) Southern (b) Arkansas (c) Australia (d) For the use of (e) Commissions (f) Steamships
74 175 276 377 478 579	(a) Production (b) Hawaii (c) Belgium (d) Petition of (e) Enterprises (f) Securities
75 176 277 378 479 580	(a) Manufacturing (b) Missouri (c) Panama (d) In the matter of (e) Investments (f) Systems
76 177 278 379 480 581	(a) Transcontinental (b) Nebraska (c) South America (d) Application of (e) Authorities (f) Laboratories
77 178 279 380 481 582	(a) Administratrix (b) South Dakota (c) Northern Ireland (d) Petition of (e) Commissioners (f) Savings
78 179 280 381 482 583	(a) Economy (b) Michigan (c) Brazil (d) On the relation of (e) Cooperatives (f) Brothers
79 180 281 382 483 584	(a) Industrial (b) Arizona (c) South Korea (d) Application of (e) Associations (f) Securities
80 181 282 383 484 585	(a) Department (b) Oregon (c) United Kingdom (d) For the use of (e) Executors (f) Industries

PROBLEM #	WORDS
81 182 283 384 485 586	(a) Environmental (b) New Mexico (c) Hong Kong (d) Petition of (e) Institutes (f) Schools
82 183 284 385 486 587	(a) Chemical (b) Kentucky (c) Bolivia (d) In the matter of (e) Associates (f) Systems
83 184 285 386 487 588	(a) Telecommunication (b) Louisiana (c) Nigeria (d) Application of (e) Chemicals (f) Steamships
84 185 286 387 488 589	(a) Organization (b) Mississippi (c) Senegal (d) Petition of (e) Directors (f) Securities
85 186 287 388 489 590	(a) Medical (b) Pennsylvania (c) France (d) On the relation of (e) Electronics (f) Systems
86 187 288 389 490 591	(a) Steamship (b) Texas (c) Norway (d) Application of (e) Investments (f) Laboratories
87 188 289 390 491 592	(a) Pharmaceutical (b) Delaware (c) Ireland (d) For the use of (e) Departments (f) Savings
88 189 290 391 492 593	(a) Subcommittee (b) Colorado (c) Dominican Republic (d) Petition of (e) Companies (f) Securities
89 190 291 392 493 594	(a) Securities (b) Alabama (c) England (d) In the matter of (e) Liabilities (f) Brothers
90 191 292 393 494 595	(a) Federation (b) Illinois (c) Scotland (d) Application of (e) Buildings (f) Industries
91 192 293 394 495 596	(a) Executor (b) Maryland (c) Philippines (d) Petition of (e) Authorities (f) Schools
92 193 294 395 496 597	(a) Agricultural (b) Nevada (c) Argentina (d) On the relation of (e) Associates (f) Systems
93 194 295 396 497 598	(a) Broadcasting (b) Washington (c) Guatemala (d) Application of (e) Examiners (f) Steamships
94 195 296 397 498 599	(a) Financial (b) Los Angeles (c) Portugal (d) For the use of (e) Institutes (f) Securities
95 196 297 398 499 600	(a) Government (b) Philadelphia (c) Netherlands (d) Petition of (e) Districts (f) Systems
96 197 298 399 500 501	(a) Institute (b) Puerto Rico (c) Ukraine (d) In the matter of (e) Cooperatives (f) Laboratories
97 198 299 400 401 502	(a) Laboratory (b) San Francisco (c) Singapore (d) Application of (e) Centers (f) Savings
98 199 300 301 402 503	(a) District (b) American Samoa (c) Israel (d) Petition of (e) Indemnities (f) Brothers
99 200 201 302 403 504	(a) Environment (b) District of Columbia (c) Lebanon (d) On the relation of (e) Associations (f) Securities
100 101 202 303 404 505	(a) Development (b) West Virginia (c) United Arab Emirate (d) Application of (e) Associates (f) Industries

CITATION EXERCISE 10
CASE NAMES: INCLUSIONS AND DELETIONS (I)

A. INTRODUCTION

In addition to required abbreviations (*see supra* Citation Exercise 9), the *Bluebook* establishes detailed rules governing what parts of the case name as set out in the reporter should be included or deleted for purposes of citation. This exercise focuses on the *Bluebook* rules for:

    (1) terms describing a party already named;
    (2) given names and initials of individuals;
    (3) words indicating multiple parties;
    (4) alternative names for a party;
    (5) consolidation of two or more actions;
    (6) additional parties on each side of the case;
    (7) partnership names;
    (8) business firm designations; and
    (9) Commissioner of Internal Revenue as a party.

1. Descriptive Terms

Titles of cases typically include terms describing a party already named, such as defendant, appellant, warden, superintendent, etc. Those descriptions should be omitted. *Bluebook* Rule 10.2.1(e).

MAD RIVER BOAT TRIPS, INC.,   **Appellant (Defendant),**   v.   **JACKSON HOLE WHITEWATER, INC.,**   **Appellee (Plaintiff).**

Cite as: *Mad River Boat Trips, Inc. v. Jackson Hole Whitewater, Inc.* (The terms, Appellant (Defendant) and Appellee (Plaintiff), describe parties already named.)

2. Given Names and Initials of Individuals

Traditionally, parties are cited by their surnames (last or family name), and no part of a surname consisting of more than one word should be omitted (*e.g.*, Garcilaso de la Vega, Von Der Linden, etc.).

The general rule is that given names or initials of individuals should be omitted (*e.g.*, a party listed in the reporter as "Jane S. Smith" would be cited as "Smith"). *Bluebook* Rule 10.2.1(g). However, given names and initials of individuals should be retained in the citation in three situations. First, given names and initials should be retained when the party's surname has been abbreviated in the report (*e.g.*, Jane S., J.S., or J.S.S.).

> **Robert STALNAKER, Administrator of the Public Employees' Retirement System, Appellant and Cross–Appellee,**
>
> v.
>
> **M.L.D., Appellee and Cross–Appellant.**

Cite as: *Stalnaker v. M.L.D.* (The given name "Robert" is omitted pursuant to the general rule, but the initials "M.L." are retained because M.L.'s surname has been abbreviated to "D." Again, the additional descriptive terms should be omitted.)

Second, given names or initials of individuals should be retained when they are part of the name of a business firm (*e.g.*, Jane S. Smith Construction Co.).

> **JOHN R. SEXTON & CO.**
>
> v.
>
> **Betsy Y. JUSTUS, Secretary of the North Carolina Department of Revenue.**

Cite as: *John R. Sexton & Co. v. Justus* ("John R." is retained because it is part of the name of a business firm, but "Betsy Y." is omitted because Betsy Y. Justus is an individual. The description of Justus as the Secretary of the North Carolina Department of Revenue should be omitted—*see supra* § A(1).)

Third, given names or initials of individuals should be retained when they are part of a foreign name and the name is **entirely** in a foreign language or when the given names follow a foreign surname (*e.g.*, Le Bup Thi Dao, Chom Cho Ha, etc.). *Bluebook* Rule 10.2.1(g).

> **UNITED STATES of America, Appellee,**
>
> v.
>
> **MANG SUN WONG, Chi Hong Lam and Hang Fang Ko, Defendants,**
>
> **Mang Sun Wong, Defendant–Appellant.**

Cite as: *United States v. Mang Sun Wong* (The given names should be included because they are entirely in a foreign language.)

> **James K. WONG, Plaintiff–Appellant,**
>
> v.
>
> **Henry Ho WONG and Colene Smith Wong, husband and wife, individually, and as tenants by the entirety, Defendants–Appellees.**

Cite as: *Wong v. Wong* (The given names should be included only when the name is entirely in a foreign language; in this example, they are not.)

3. Words Indicating Multiple Parties

Words indicating multiple parties should be omitted. Examples include *et al.* (and others), *et ux.* (and wife), and *et vir.* (and husband). *Bluebook* Rule 10.2.1(a).

Barry ROMM et ux. **v.** **Lawrence L. FLAX et ux.**

Cite as: *Romm v. Flax* (*Et ux.* is the abbreviation for the Latin "et uxor" (and wife) and should be omitted.)

4. Alternative Party Names

Alternative names for a party should be omitted. *Bluebook* Rule 10.2.1(a).

Richard and Susan ZEID, Appellants, **v.** **Dr. William PEARCE, d/b/a Coronado Animal Clinic, Appellee.**

Cite as: *Zeid v. Pearce* ("d/b/a" stands for "doing business as"; thus, Coronado Animal Clinic is omitted because it is an alternative name for the party already cited.)

5. Consolidated Actions

Only the first listed case should be cited when the case is a consolidation of two or more actions. *Bluebook* Rule 10.2.1(a).

SECRET DESIRES LINGERIE, INC. et al. **v.** **CITY OF ATLANTA et al.** **GAMBILL, d/b/a L & L Ltd.** **v.** **CITY OF ATLANTA.**

Cite as: *Secret Desires Lingerie, Inc. v. City of Atlanta* (The second action, *Gambill v. City of Atlanta*, was consolidated with the first listed action; the second action should not be cited; *et al.* is omitted because it is an indication of multiple parties—*see* § A(3) *supra.*)

6. Additional Parties on Each Side of the Case

All parties other than the first listed on each side of the case should be omitted, except the first-listed "relator" (*see supra* Exercise 9) should be included in the citation. *Bluebook* Rule 10.2.1(a).

Sally Inez ADAMS, on Behalf of
her niece, Jamill C. BOYSAW

v.

HERCULES, INC. and Insurance
Company of North America.

Cite as: *Adams ex rel. Boysaw v. Hercules, Inc.* ("Boysaw" is a relator and is included in the citation; "Insurance Company of North America" is omitted because it is an additional party on the defendant's side of the case; "on behalf of" becomes *ex rel.—see* § A(4)*(a)* in Exercise 9.)

7. Partnerships

No portion of a partnership name should be omitted. *Bluebook* Rule 10.2.1(a).

VERSYSS INCORPORATED,
Plaintiff, Appellant,

v.

COOPERS AND LYBRAND, ETC.,
et al., Defendants, Appellees.

Cite as: *Versyss Inc. v. Coopers & Lybrand* ("Coopers and Lybrand" is a partnership name and is retained in full; "Incorporated" is abbreviated to "Inc."; "and" is abbreviated to "&"; these latter abbreviations should be made whether the case name appears as part of a grammatical part of a textual sentence or in a citation—*see* § A(4)*(b)* in Exercise 9.)

8. Business Firm Designations

Business firm designations like Incorporated or Inc., Limited or Ltd., National Association or N.A., Federal Savings Bank or F.S.B., Socidad Anonima or S.A., Aktiengesellchaft or A.G., etc. should be omitted when "the [cited] name also contains words such as 'Ass'n,' 'Bros.,' 'Co.,' 'Corp.,' and 'R.R.,' clearly indicating that the party is a business firm." *Bluebook* Rule 10.2.1(h).

LEAD INDUSTRIES ASSOCIATION,
INC., Petitioner,

v.

ENVIRONMENTAL PROTECTION
AGENCY, Respondent,

Bunker Hill Company, Intervenor.

In a textual sentence, cite as: *Lead Industries Association v. EPA.* **In a citation sentence or clause, cite as:** *Lead Indus. Ass'n v. EPA* ("Inc." is omitted because Ass'n is already cited; Bunker Hill Co., an intervenor, is an additional party and is omitted— *see supra* § A(6); for the other abbreviations, *see supra* § A(1)*(b)* (Ass'n), § A(1)*(c)* (EPA) (optional), and § A(2)(a) (Indus.) in Exercise 9).

9. Commissioner of Internal Revenue

A special rule applies when the cited party name is "Commissioner of Internal Revenue." In that situation, only "Commissioner" should be used. *Bluebook* Rule 10.2.1(j). Commissioner of Internal Revenue, however, should be dropped entirely if it follows the actual name of the Commissioner because it describes a party already named—*see* § A(1) *supra*.

Paul F. GRAY, Jr., Petitioner-Appellant, v. **COMMISSIONER OF INTERNAL REVENUE, Respondent-Appellee.**

Cite as: *Gray v. Commissioner* (Do **NOT** cite as "Commissioner of Internal Revenue" or "C.I.R.," or any other variant.)

NATIONAL TREASURY EMPLOYEES UNION, et al., Appellants, v. **Roscoe L. EGGER, Commissioner, Internal Revenue Service, et al.**

Cite as: *National Treasury Employees Union v. Egger* (Commissioner of Internal Revenue is not the cited party; it is dropped entirely because it follows the actual name of the Commissioner; it describes a party already named—"Roscoe L. Egger.")

B. INSTRUCTIONS FOR COMPLETING THIS EXERCISE

The purpose of this exercise is to give you practice in citing case names in proper form. To complete this exercise, you must find six cases using the citations given with your problem number below. All the citations are to cases in one volume of West's *Federal Reporter Third*. The *Federal Reporter* is currently in a third series. (When a publisher begins a new series, the volume numbering of the new series begins again with one. In order to prevent confusion with the first series, a "2d" is added to the reporter citation of a case in the second series, a "3d" is added to the reporter citation of a case in the third series, etc.) For example, assume that one of the citations to which you are directed is "110 F.3d 222." You would find the case beginning on page 222 of volume 110 of the **third series** of the *Federal Reporter* (F.3d) in the library.

For your answer to this exercise, state the following for each of the cases that begin on the pages listed in (a)-(f):

(1) the full title of the case as it is stated in the reporter at the beginning of the reported case; **you should omit obviously irrelevant portions of the case title if the title is a lengthy one**;

(2) the proper citation of the case name using *Bluebook* (or another designated) form; **do not give a full citation of the case**; assume that the case name is

going to appear in a **citation sentence or clause,** not as a grammatical part of a textual sentence.

Unless otherwise instructed, write your answers on the answer sheet provided in Part 4 of these exercises.

PROBLEM #	VOL. #	PAGES WITH THAT VOLUME
1 103 204 307 409 511	1 F.3d	(a) 82 (b) 176 (c) 826 (d) 1184 (e) 1208 (f) 1478
2 104 205 308 410 512	2 F.3d	(a) 105 (b) 280 (c) 359 (d) 769 (e) 1137 (f) 1143
3 105 206 309 411 513	3 F.3d	(a) 75 (b) 131 (c) 238 (d) 329 (e) 797 (f) 1343
4 106 207 310 412 514	4 F.3d	(a) 2 (b) 237 (c) 327 (d) 567 (e) 709 (f) 875
5 107 208 311 413 515	5 F.3d	(a) 10 (b) 18 (c) 154 (d) 195 (e) 303 (f) 1178
6 108 209 312 414 516	7 F.3d	(a) 11 (b) 106 (c)180 (d) 552 (e) 774 (f) 821
7 109 210 313 415 517	9 F.3d	(a) 18 (b) 290 (c) 383 (d) 524 (e) 1174 (f) 1352
8 110 211 314 416 518	11 F.3d	(a) 17 (b) 228 (c) 381 (d) 399 (e) 534 (f) 1180
9 111 212 315 417 519	12 F.3d	(a) 75 (b) 119 (c) 166 (d) 245 (e) 381 (f) 1030
10 112 213 316 418 520	13 F.3d	(a) 40 (b) 54 (c) 58 (d) 93 (e) 310 (f) 1297
11 113 214 317 419 521	15 F.3d	(a) 82 (b) 333 (c) 432 (d) 533 (e) 790 (f) 1365
12 114 215 318 420 522	16 F.3d	(a) 38 (b) 82 (c) 99 (d) 338 (e) 590 (f) 1149
13 115 216 319 421 523	17 F.3d	(a) 119 (b) 123 (c) 209 (d) 691 (e) 883 (f) 965
14 116 217 320 422 524	18 F.3d	(a) 1 (b) 13 (c) 20 (d) 147 (e) 323 (f) 514
15 117 218 321 423 525	20 F.3d	(a) 160 (b) 173 (c) 428 (d) 745 (e) 1188 (f) 1214
16 118 219 322 424 526	21 F.3d	(a) 18 (b) 159 (c) 411 (d) 436 (e) 568 (f) 1292
17 119 220 323 425 527	22 F.3d	(a) 54 (b) 88 (c) 135 (d) 290 (e) 414 (f) 1001
18 120 221 324 426 528	23 F.3d	(a) 129 (b) 143 (c) 254 (d) 374 (e) 496 (f) 1032
19 121 222 325 427 529	24 F.3d	(a) 16 (b) 49 (c) 151 (d) 178 (e) 809 (f) 901
20 122 223 326 428 530	25 F.3d	(a) 43 (b) 109 (c) 1162 (d) 1289 (e) 1325 (f) 1437
21 123 224 327 429 531	26 F.3d	(a) 19 (b) 29 (c) 50 (d) 563 (e) 573 (f) 1139
22 124 225 328 430 532	27 F.3d	(a) 17 (b) 160 (c) 185 (d) 188 (e) 232 (f) 510
23 125 226 329 431 533	28 F.3d	(a) 19 (b) 23 (c) 51 (d) 71 (e) 279 (f) 1013
24 126 227 330 432 534	29 F.3d	(a) 28 (b) 165 (c) 211 (d) 229 (e) 245 (f) 433
25 127 228 331 433 535	30 F.3d	(a) 14 (b) 33 (c) 206 (d) 466 (e) 743 (f) 1402
26 128 229 332 434 536	31 F.3d	(a) 42 (b) 79 (c) 105 (d) 224 (e) 569 (f) 639
27 129 230 333 435 537	32 F.3d	(a) 27 (b) 139 (c) 220 (d) 315 (e) 665 (f) 1222
28 130 231 334 436 538	33 F.3d	(a) 96 (b) 134 (c) 309 (d) 818 (e) 836 (f) 1153
29 131 232 335 437 539	34 F.3d	(a) 13 (b) 188 (c) 320 (d) 932 (e) 1132 (f) 1480
30 132 233 336 438 540	36 F.3d	(a) 18 (b) 143 (c) 278 (d) 291 (e) 743 (f) 1361
31 133 234 337 439 541	37 F.3d	(a) 9 (b) 25 (c) 74 (d) 139 (e) 202 (f) 587
32 134 235 338 440 542	38 F.3d	(a) 1 (b) 67 (c) 76 (d) 232 (e) 551 (f) 1094
33 135 236 339 441 543	39 F.3d	(a) 27 (b) 222 (c) 273 (d) 370 (e) 537 (f) 658
34 136 237 340 442 544	40 F.3d	(a) 11 (b) 43 (c) 170 (d) 187 (e) 224 (f) 293
35 137 238 341 443 545	41 F.3d	(a) 9 (b) 39 (c) 73 (d) 250 (e) 553 (f) 1144
36 138 239 342 444 546	42 F.3d	(a) 53 (b) 79 (c) 106 (d) 439 (e) 972 (f) 1037
37 139 240 343 445 547	43 F.3d	(a) 11 (b) 15 (c) 29 (d) 644 (e) 788 (f) 869
38 140 241 344 446 548	45 F.3d	(a) 48 (b) 155 (c) 173 (d) 243 (e) 279 (f) 348
39 141 242 345 447 549	46 F.3d	(a) 24 (b) 37 (c) 196 (d) 705 (e) 1470 (f) 1547
40 142 243 346 448 550	47 F.3d	(a) 23 (b) 39 (c) 88 (d) 133 (e) 447 (f) 787
41 143 244 347 449 551	48 F.3d	(a) 8 (b) 142 (c) 173 (d) 179 (e) 1120 (f) 1193
42 144 245 348 450 552	49 F.3d	(a) 26 (b) 69 (c) 490 (d) 702 (e) 713 (f) 1541
43 145 246 349 451 553	51 F.3d	(a) 5 (b) 14 (c) 45 (d) 76 (e) 96 (f) 618
44 146 247 350 452 554	52 F.3d	(a) 1 (b) 15 (c) 23 (d) 94 (e) 723 (f) 734

PROBLEM #	VOL. #	PAGES WITH THAT VOLUME
45 147 248 351 453 555	53 F.3d	(a) 48 (b) 106 (c) 186 (d) 192 (e) 363 (f) 523
46 148 249 352 454 556	54 F.3d	(a) 9 (b) 21 (c) 156 (d) 177 (e) 379 (f) 432
47 149 250 353 455 557	55 F.3d	(a) 34 (b) 94 (c) 101 (d) 231 (e) 285 (f) 527
48 150 251 354 456 558	56 F.3d	(a) 39 (b) 85 (c) 441 (d) 504 (e) 878 (f) 1016
49 151 252 355 457 559	58 F.3d	(a) 27 (b) 59 (c) 176 (d) 222 (e) 557 (f) 857
50 152 253 356 458 560	59 F.3d	(a) 78 (b) 95 (c) 230 (d) 374 (e) 1249 (f) 1276
51 153 254 357 459 561	60 F.3d	(a) 8 (b) 27 (c) 83 (d) 143 (e) 350 (f) 1020
52 154 255 358 460 562	62 F.3d	(a) 29 (b) 86 (c) 209 (d) 294 (e) 408 (f) 835
53 155 256 359 461 563	63 F.3d	(a) 166 (b) 248 (c) 287 (d) 413 (e) 609 (f) 614
54 156 257 360 462 564	64 F.3d	(a) 5 (b) 83 (c) 191 (d) 264 (e) 860 (f) 1406
55 157 258 361 463 565	65 F.3d	(a) 64 (b) 102 (c) 127 (d) 144 (e) 198 (f) 335
56 158 259 362 464 566	66 F.3d	(a) 8 (b) 12 (c) 105 (d) 164 (e) 438 (f) 729
57 159 260 363 465 567	67 F.3d	(a) 7 (b) 46 (c) 97 (d) 203 (e) 435 (f) 1489
58 160 261 364 466 568	68 F.3d	(a) 14 (b) 41 (c) 197 (d) 694 (e) 840 (f) 1380
59 161 262 365 467 569	69 F.3d	(a) 1 (b) 22 (c) 64 (d) 260 (e) 337 (f) 1360
60 162 263 366 468 570	70 F.3d	(a) 12 (b) 34 (c) 150 (d) 325 (e) 422 (f) 1201
61 163 264 367 469 571	71 F.3d	(a) 1 (b) 9 (c) 129 (d) 518 (e) 720 (f) 1040
62 164 265 368 470 572	73 F.3d	(a) 30 (b) 36 (c) 224 (d) 238 (e) 279 (f) 628
63 165 266 369 471 573	77 F.3d	(a) 34 (b) 60 (c) 112 (d) 223 (e) 450 (f) 637
64 166 267 370 472 574	78 F.3d	(a) 84 (b) 117 (c) 139 (d) 266 (e) 524 (f) 1355
65 167 268 371 473 575	79 F.3d	(a) 17 (b) 26 (c) 49 (d) 241 (e) 726 (f) 731
66 168 269 372 474 576	81 F.3d	(a) 48 (b) 365 (c) 376 (d) 455 (e) 541 (f) 1274
67 169 270 373 475 577	82 F.3d	(a) 55 (b) 63 (c) 217 (d) 322 (e) 371 (f) 524
68 170 271 374 476 578	83 F.3d	(a) 27 (b) 37 (c) 118 (d) 153 (e) 649 (f) 894
69 171 272 375 477 579	85 F.3d	(a) 44 (b) 185 (c) 356 (d) 675 (e) 950 (f) 1149
70 172 273 376 478 580	86 F.3d	(a) 3 (b) 15 (c) 248 (d) 852 (e) 982 (f) 1472
71 173 274 377 479 581	87 F.3d	(a) 126 (b) 218 (c) 273 (d) 751 (e) 970 (f) 1467
72 174 275 378 480 582	158 F.3d	(a) 59 (b) 92 (c) 150 (d) 326 (e) 802 (f) 890
73 175 276 379 481 583	90 F.3d	(a) 43 (b) 82 (c) 955 (d) 1173 (e) 1372 (f) 1459
74 176 277 380 482 584	91 F.3d	(a) 75 (b) 497 (c) 670 (d) 790 (e) 914 (f) 1002
75 177 278 381 483 585	92 F.3d	(a) 81 (b) 274 (c) 702 (d) 727 (e) 957 (f) 1425
76 178 279 382 484 586	94 F.3d	(a) 71 (b) 189 (c) 499 (d) 523 (e) 914 (f) 1121
77 179 280 383 485 587	97 F.3d	(a) 39 (b) 45 (c) 200 (d) 337 (e) 347 (f) 1329
78 180 281 384 486 588	98 F.3d	(a) 22 (b) 25 (c) 33 (d) 297 (e) 366 (f) 825
79 181 282 385 487 589	99 F.3d	(a) 1 (b) 108 (c) 340 (d) 403 (e) 449 (f) 1042
80 182 283 386 488 590	100 F.3d	(a) 141 (b) 659 (c) 878 (d) 919 (e) 1150 (f) 1308
81 183 284 387 489 591	101 F.3d	(a) 23 (b) 486 (c) 495 (d) 519 (e) 546 (f) 549
82 184 285 388 490 592	102 F.3d	(a) 74 (b) 516 (c) 534 (d) 591 (e) 842 (f) 848
83 185 286 389 491 593	103 F.3d	(a) 169 (b) 243 (c) 535 (d) 627 (e) 750 (f) 948
84 186 287 390 492 594	104 F.3d	(a) 83 (b) 109 (c) 131 (d) 913 (e) 1133 (f) 1226
85 187 288 391 493 595	105 F.3d	(a) 65 (b) 137 (c) 306 (d) 343 (e) 436 (f) 583
86 188 289 392 494 596	106 F.3d	(a) 1 (b) 147 (c) 366 (d) 469 (e) 768 (f) 1445
87 189 290 393 495 597	107 F.3d	(a) 64 (b) 274 (c) 476 (d) 733 (e) 750 (f) 754
88 190 291 394 496 598	108 F.3d	(a) 173 (b) 201 (c) 231 (d) 241 (e) 244 (f) 739
89 191 292 395 497 599	110 F.3d	(a) 24 (b) 44 (c) 56 (d) 364 (e) 769 (f) 1341
90 192 293 396 498 600	111 F.3d	(a) 70 (b) 251 (c) 433 (d) 593 (e) 1427 (f) 1578
91 193 294 397 499 501	112 F.3d	(a) 50 (b) 124 (c) 226 (d) 267 (e) 311 (f) 329
92 194 295 398 500 502	113 F.3d	(a) 83 (b) 235 (c) 476 (d) 556 (e) 787 (f) 984
93 195 296 399 401 503	114 F.3d	(a) 1 (b) 145 (c) 186 (d) 446 (e) 731 (f) 955
94 196 297 400 402 504	116 F.3d	(a) 134 (b) 172 (c) 237 (d) 221 (e) 1095 (f) 1137

PROBLEM #	VOL. #	PAGES WITH THAT VOLUME
95 197 298 301 403 505	117 F.3d	(a) 1 (b) 180 (c) 309 (d) 421 (e) 519 (f) 785
96 198 299 302 404 506	118 F.3d	(a) 56 (b) 140 (c) 178 (d) 239 (e) 516 (f) 1134
97 199 300 303 405 507	121 F.3d	(a) 281 (b) 341 (c) 393 (d) 669 (e) 675 (f) 691
98 200 201 304 406 508	122 F.3d	(a) 34 (b) 58 (c) 93 (d) 363 (e) 825 (f) 835
99 101 202 305 407 509	125 F.3d	(a) 172 (b) 200 (c) 468 (d) 535 (e) 551 (f) 806
100 102 203 306 408 510	126 F.3d	(a) 1 (b) 433 (c) 679 (d) 926 (e) 1010 (f) 1420

CASE NAMES: INCLUSIONS AND DELETIONS (II)

A. INTRODUCTION

This exercise continues (from Citation Exercise 10) to examine additional rules relating to what parts of the case name as set out in the reporter should be included or deleted for purposes of a *Bluebook* citation. This exercise focuses on the *Bluebook* rules for:

(1) labor unions;

(2) geographical terms, including

    (a) "City of" and similar phrases;

    (b) "State of" and similar phrases;

    (c) "United States of America";

    (d) terms indicating national or larger geographical locations;

    (e) other prepositional phrases of location;

    (f) geographical words that are not introduced by a preposition;

(3) procedural phrases;

(4) "the";

(5) "in rem" cases;

(6) bankruptcy and similar cases; and

(7) extremely long case names.

1. Labor Unions

Labor unions are cited exactly as they appear in the official reporter, subject to the following four modifications. First, cite only the smallest unit of the union. *Bluebook* Rule 10.2.1(i)*(i)*.

SAN FRANCISCO FIRE FIGHTERS LOCAL 798, INTERNATIONAL ASSOCIATION OF FIRE FIGHTERS, AFL-CIO, Plaintiff and Respondent,

v.

CITY AND COUNTY OF SAN FRANCISCO et al., Defendants and Appellants.

Cite as: *San Francisco Fire Fighters Local 798 v. City of San Francisco* (**NOT** *San Francisco Fire Fighters Local 798, International Association of Fire Fighters, AFL-CIO v. City of San Francisco*) (County of San Francisco was omitted because only the first-listed party, the City of San Francisco, is cited—*see* § A(6) ("Additional Parties on Each Side of the Case") in Exercise 10 & *Bluebook* Rule 10.2.1(a).)

Second, omit all craft and industry designations **except the first full designation**. *Bluebook* Rule 10.2.1(i)*(ii)*.

> INTERNATIONAL UNION OF PE-
> TROLEUM & INDUSTRIAL
> WORKERS, Petitioner,
>
> v.
>
> NATIONAL LABOR RELATIONS
> BOARD, Respondent.

In a textual sentence, cite as*: International Union of Petroleum & Industrial Workers v. NLRB* **or** *International Union of Petroleum & Industrial Workers v. National Labor Relations Board* (Petroleum & Industrial Workers is the first full designation; use of "NLRB" is optional—*see* § A(4)*(c)* in Exercise 9.)

In a citation sentence or clause, cite as: *International Union of Petroleum & Indus. Workers v. NLRB* **or** *International Union of Petroleum & Indus. Workers v. National Labor Relations Bd.* ("Industr[ial]" and "Board" are listed in Table T.6—*see* § A(5)*(a)* in Exercise 9.)

> Robert B. REICH, Secretary, United
> States Department of Labor,
> Plaintiff–Appellee,
>
> v.
>
> LOCAL 396, INTERNATIONAL BROTH-
> ERHOOD OF TEAMSTERS, CHAUF-
> FEURS, WAREHOUSEMEN AND
> HELPERS OF AMERICA, AFL–CIO,
> Defendant–Appellant.

In a textual sentence, cite as: *Reich v. Local 396, International Brotherhood of Teamsters* (**NOT** *Reich v. Local 396, International Brotherhood of Teamsters, Chauffeurs, Warehousemen and Helpers of America, AFL-CIO*) (Teamsters is the first full designation.)

In a citation sentence or clause, cite as: *Reich v. Local 396, Int'l Bhd. of Teamsters*) ("International" and "Brotherhood" are listed in Table T.6—*see* § A(5)*(a)* in Exercise 9.)

Third, omit all prepositional phrases of location. *Bluebook* Rule 10.2.1(i)*(iv)*. Thus, "of America" was omitted in the above example.

Fourth, in lieu of citing the union name, a widely recognized abbreviation may be used. *Bluebook* Rule 10.2.1(i)*(iii)*. No periods are used between the letters. *Bluebook* Rules 6.1(b) & 10.2.1(c). The following are a few examples of widely recognized abbreviations of union names:

IBEW = International Brotherhood of Electrical Workers
ILGWU = International Ladies' Garment Workers Union
UMW = Mine Workers of America, United

LOCAL 827, INTERNATIONAL BROTH-ERHOOD OF ELECTRICAL WORKERS, Plaintiff–Respondent,

v.

Edna TRAD, John T. Dixon and Marjorie E. Simms, Defendants–Appellants.

In a textual sentence, cite as: *Local 827, International Brotherhood of Electrical Workers v. Trad* **or** *Local 827, IBEW v. Trad*

In a citation sentence or clause, cite as: *Local 827, Int'l Bhd. of Elec. Workers v. Trad* **or** *Local 827, IBEW v. Trad* ("International," "Brotherhood," and "Electric[al]" are listed in Table T.6—*see* § A(5)*(a)* in Exercise 9.)

2. Geographic Terms

Geographic terms frequently appear in case names. *The Bluebook* has several specialized rules that control whether a particular geographical term is included or deleted from a case citation.

(a) "City of" and Similar Phrases

"City of," "Town of," "Village of," "Borough of," "County of," and similar phrases should be omitted **except when they begin the name of a cited party**. *Bluebook* Rule 10.1(f).

James HERON, Plaintiff,

v.

CITY OF PHILADELPHIA, et al., Defendants.

Cite as: *Heron v. City of Philadelphia* ("City of" begins the name of the party; note that because the geographical unit is cited as the named party, "Philadelphia" should not be abbreviated even though Table T.10 indicates the abbreviation for "Philadelphia" is "Phil."—*see* § A(4)*(b)* in Exercise 9.)

(b) "State of" and Similar Phrases

"State of," "People of," and "Commonwealth of" should be omitted from the citation when the state, people, or commonwealth are litigating **in courts of other jurisdictions**. *Bluebook* Rule 10.2.1(f).

Commonwealth of KENTUCKY v. State of INDIANA et al. No. 81, Orig.

Cite as: *Kentucky v. Indiana* (This case was an original action in the U.S. Supreme Court and was reported in Volume 474 of *United States Reports*).

When those parties are litigating **in courts in their own respective jurisdictions**, cite only "State," "People," or "Commonwealth" as the party in the case name. *Bluebook* Rule 10.2.1(f).

STATE of Missouri, Respondent, v. **Danny C. SMITH, Appellant.**

Cite as: *State v. Smith* (This case was before the Missouri Court of Appeals and was reported in Volume 794 of *South Western Reporter Second*).

(c) "United States of America"

"Of America" should be omitted when it appears after "United States." "United States" should not be abbreviated. *Bluebook* Rules 10.2.1(f) & 10.2.

UNITED STATES of America, Appellee, v. **William R. TIBOLT, Defendant, Appellant.**

Cite as: *United States v. Tibolt* (**NOT** *United States of America v. Tibolt*)

(d) Terms Indicating National or Larger Geographical Locations

Terms indicating national or larger geographic locations should be included in the case name, except (1) when they occur in union names (*see* § A(1) above) and (2) when "of America" follows "United States" (*see* § A(2)*(c)* above). *Bluebook* Rule 10.2.1(f).

Grant R. OFFENBERG, Plaintiff, v. **UNUM LIFE INSURANCE COMPANY OF AMERICA, et al., Defendants.**

In a textual sentence, cite as: *Offenberg v. UNUM Life Insurance Co. of America*
In a citation sentence or clause, cite as: *Offenberg v. UNUM Life Ins. Co. of Am.* ("Insurance" and "America" are listed in Table T.6—*see* § A(5)*(a)* in Exercise 9.)

(e) Other Prepositional Phrases of Location

Other prepositional phrases of location (*i.e.*, those of less than national geographical areas, except when they follow "City of" or similar phrases—*see* § A(2)*(a)*, above) should be omitted **unless only one word would be left in the party's name**. *Bluebook* Rule 10.2.1(f).

<table>
<tr><td>

OTWELL, et al.

v.

FIRST NATIONAL BANK OF GAINESVILLE, et al.

</td><td>

In a textual sentence, cite as: *Otwell v. First National Bank*

In a citation sentence or clause, cite as: *Otwll v. First Nat'l Bank* ("National" is listed in Table T.6—*see* § A(5)*(a)* in Exercise 9.)

</td></tr>
</table>

(f) Geographical Words that Are Not Introduced by a Preposition

All geographical words that are not introduced by a preposition should be retained. *Bluebook* Rule 10.2.1(f).

<table>
<tr><td>

Wonda DAY, Plaintiff,

v.

NORTHERN INDIANA PUBLIC SERVICE COMPANY, Defendant.

</td><td>

In a textual sentence, cite as: *Day v. Northern Indiana Public Service Co.*

In a citation sentence or clause, cite as: *Day v. Northern Ind. Pub. Serv. Co.* ("Indiana" is listed in Table T.10—*see* § A(5)*(b)* in Exercise 9; "Public" and "Service" are listed in Table T.6; "Northern" should not be abbreviated even though Table T.6 indicates the abbreviation is "N." because it is the first word of the party's name—*see* § A(5)*(a)* in Exercise 9.)

</td></tr>
</table>

3. Procedural Phrases

Recall from § A(1)*(a)* *("Procedural Phrases")* in Exercise 9 that some cases do not have traditional adversary parties or are not contested. In these types of cases, the title is often listed as "petition of," "matter of," or "application of" and the party's name; these phrases should be abbreviated as *"In re"* in *Bluebook* citations.

In addition, recall that some cases are brought on behalf of another person known as a "relator." This fact is usually indicated by such phrases as "on relation of," "for the use of," "on behalf of," or "on the information of" in the case title. These phrases should be shortened to *"ex rel."* in *Bluebook* citations.

Another procedural phrase used in case names is *"Ex parte,"* which means done for, in behalf of, or on the application of only one party; this phrase indicates that an application has been made to the court without notice to the adverse party.

Two special rules apply to procedural phrases when

(1) adversary parties are named; and

(2) multiple procedural phrases are used in the case name in the reporter.

(a) Adversary Parties and Procedural Phrases

All procedural phrases except *ex rel.* should be omitted when adversary parties are named. *Bluebook* Rule 10.2.1(b).

<table>
<tr>
<td>

In the Matter of ELIZABETH A.D., Infant, Respondent Below, Appellant,

v.

Frederick HAMMACK, Petitioner Below, Appellee,

and

Brenda K.J. and James D., Adults, Respondents Below, Appellees.

</td>
<td>

Cite as: *Elizabeth A.D. v. Hammack* (**NOT** *In re Elizabeth A.D. v. Hammack*)

</td>
</tr>
</table>

For purposes of this rule, "Estate of," "Succession of," "Will of," "Marriage of," and similar terms are not treated as procedural phrases and must be retained in the citation. *Bluebook* Rule 10.2.1(b).

<table>
<tr>
<td>

ESTATE OF Lillian AITKEN; Albert Noecker, Norma Heyen, Etta Langill, Ruth Sharp, Thelma Turner, and American Physical Therapy Association, Plaintiffs,

v.

Donna E. SHALALA, Secretary, United States Department of Health and Human Services; and Bruce C. Vladeck, Administrator, Health Care Financing Administration, Defendants.

</td>
<td>

Cite as: *Estate of Aitken v. Shalala* (**NOT** *Aitken v. Shalala*)

</td>
</tr>
</table>

(b) Multiple Procedural Phrases

All procedural phrases after the first one should be omitted. *Bluebook* Rule 10.2.1(b).

<table>
<tr>
<td>

In re Ex parte Willie BOLDEN.

</td>
<td>

Cite as: *In re Bolden* (**NOT** *In re Ex parte Bolden*)

</td>
</tr>
</table>

Again, for purposes of this rule, "Estate of," "Succession of," "Will of," "Marriage of," and similar terms are not treated as procedural phrases and must be retained in the citation. *Bluebook* Rule 10.2.1(b).

<table>
<tr><td>

In re ESTATE OF ALEXANDER.

</td><td>

Cite as: *In re Estate of Alexander* (**NOT** *In re* Alexander)

</td></tr>
</table>

4. "The"

"The" is often the first word of the name of a party in a reporter and it should be omitted from the citation. *Bluebook* Rule 10.2.1(d).

<table>
<tr><td>

THE RIVAL COMPANY, Plaintiff,

v.

SUNBEAM CORPORATION,
et al., Defendants.

</td><td>

Cite as: *Rival Co. v. Sunbeam Corp.* (***NOT** The Rival Co. v. Sunbeam Corp.*)

</td></tr>
</table>

This rule is subject to three exceptions. First, "the" should be retained in the citation when it begins the name of the res in an "in rem" action (*e.g.*, *The Breakwater*—a ship; *see* § A(2) in Exercise 9.);

<table>
<tr><td>

Gary Alan KOPCZYNSKI,
Plaintiff-Appellee/Cross-Appellant,

v.

THE JACQUELINE, Documentation Number 519060, Her Engine, Tackle, Appurtenances, etc., In Rem; Seaward Marine Services, Inc., a California Corporation, Seaward Marine Services, Inc., a Virginia Corporation, ABC Doe Corporation, Wendy Webber, Jim Walker and Tim Orsac, individually, In Personam, Defendants-Appellants/Cross-Appellees.

</td><td>

Cite as*:*   *Kopczynski v. The Jacqueline* (NOT** *Kopczynski v. Jacqueline*)

</td></tr>
</table>

Second, "the" should be retained in the citation when "The Queen" or "The King" is the cited party.

<table>
<tr><td>

THE KING *v.* TONKS.

</td><td>

Cite as: *The King v. Tonks* (**NOT** *King v. Tongs*)

</td></tr>
</table>

Third, "the" should be retained in the citation when it begins the popular name of the case. When referring to a case by a popular name textually, however, "the" should be omitted. *Bluebook* Rule 10.2.1(d). Note the difference in treatment of "the" in a textual sentence and the supporting citation sentence in the following example (based on a footnote in a constitutional law treatise):

> The *Legal Tender Cases* recognized that the power of Congress to emit bills of credit as well as to incorporate national banks was clearly established. *See The Legal Tender Cases*, 110 U.S. 421, 444, 4 S. Ct. 122, 128, 28 L. Ed. 204, 213 (1884).

5. "In Rem" Cases

When several items are used as the title of an "in rem" action (*see* § A(2) in Exercise 9), only the first listed item or group of items should be cited. *Bluebook* Rule 10.2.1(a).

**UNITED STATES of America,
Plaintiff-Appellee,**

v.

$5,644,540.00 IN U.S. CURRENCY, 450 One-Ounce Gold Canadian Maple Leaf Coins, 500 One-Ounce Platinum Ingots, Defendants,

and

Kenneth Cory, Controller, etc., California Franchise Tax Board, Ann Smith Kamali, Nelson Garrett, Douglas Stavoe, and Pearl Lampros, Claimants-Appellants.

Cite as*:   United States v. $5,644,-540.00 in U.S. Currency* (**NOT** *United States v. $5,644,540.00 in U.S. Currency, 450 One-Ounce Gold Canadian Maple Leaf Coins, 500 One-Ounce Platinum Ingots*)

When real property is the cited party, the common street address, if available, should be used. *Bluebook* Rule 10.2.1(a).

George B. TELLEVIK, Chief, Washington State Patrol, and Gregory J. Webb, Chief, Carnation Police Department, Appellants,

v.

REAL PROPERTY KNOWN AS 31641 WEST RUTHERFORD STREET LOCATED IN the CITY OF CARNATION, WASHINGTON and All Appurtenances and Improvements Thereon, Respondents,

and

Donald W. Pearson and Janet A. Pearson, husband and wife, Respondents.

In a textual sentence, cite as*:* *Tellevik v. 31641 West Rutherford Street*
In a citation sentence or clause, cite as: *Tellevik v. 31641 W. Rutherford St.* ("West" and "Street" are listed in Table T.6—*see* § A(5)*(a)* in Exercise 9.)

6. Bankruptcy and Similar Cases

When a case name contains both adversary and non-adversary parties at the beginning of the opinion, such as in many bankruptcy cases, the adversary name should be cited first; the nonadversary name should be added parenthetically, introduced by an appropriate procedural phrases, such as "*In re*," and then followed by any other descriptive or introductory phrases, such as "Estate of " or "Interest of," if any. *Bluebook* Rule 10.2.1(a).

<table>
<tr><td>

In re GATEWAY PACIFIC CORP., Debtor.

OFFICIAL PLAN COMMITTEE, et al., Appellee,

v.

EXPEDITORS INTERNATIONAL OF WASHINGTON, INC., Appellant.

</td><td>

In a textual sentence, cite as: *Official Plan Committee v. Expeditors International, Inc. (In re Gateway Pacific Corp.)*

In a citation sentence or clause, cite as: *Official Plan Comm. v. Expeditors Int'l, Inc. (In re Gateway Pac. Corp.)* ("Committee," "International," and "Pacific" are all listed in Table T.6— see § A(5)*(a)* in Exercise 9.)

</td></tr>
</table>

Note, in general, that whenever party names or phrases will aid in identifying a case, that information may be appended parenthetically. *Bluebook* Rule 10.2.1(a). Consider the following example:

The Legal Tender Cases (Juilliard v. Greenman), 110 U.S. 421 (1884).

7. Extremely Long Case Names

When a case name remains extremely long even after applying all of the previously set out *Bluebook* rules, words that are unnecessary to identify the case should be omitted. *The Bluebook* suggests that the running head located at the top of each page in the reporter may serve as a guide for this purpose. *Bluebook* Rule 10.2.1.

B. INSTRUCTIONS FOR COMPLETING THIS EXERCISE

The purpose of this exercise is to give you further practice in citing case names in proper form. To complete this exercise, you must find in the library the volume of the *South Western Reporter Second* listed for your problem number below. **All of the volumes listed are from the second series (S.W.2d).**

For your answer to this exercise, state the following for each of the cases that begin on the pages listed in (a)-(f):

(1) the full case name as it is stated at the beginning of the reported case (*e.g.*, State of Missouri, Plaintiff-Respondent, v. Charles Bernard Jones, Defendant-Appellant); **you may omit obviously irrelevant portions of a party's name if the full name is a lengthy one**; and

(2) the proper citation of that case name using *Bluebook* (or another designated) form; **do not give the full citation of the case**; assume that the case name is going to appear in a **citation sentence or clause**, not as a grammatical part of a textual sentence.

Unless otherwise instructed, write your answers on the answer sheet provided in Part 4 of these exercises.

PROBLEM #	VOL. #	PAGES WITH THAT VOLUME
1 170 236 344 485 592	693 S.W.2d	(a) 120 (b) 285 (c) 181 (d) 621 (e) 640 (f) 914
2 171 237 345 486 593	692 S.W.2d	(a) 209 (b) 420 (c) 470 (d) 525 (e) 803 (f) 926
3 172 238 346 487 594	691 S.W.2d	(a) 423 (b) 485 (c) 498 (d) 717 (e) 784 (f) 857
4 173 239 347 488 595	690 S.W.2d	(a) 183 (b) 465 (c) 473 (d) 517 (e) 672 (f) 897
5 174 240 348 489 596	689 S.W.2d	(a) 45 (b) 87 (c) 399 (d) 556 (e) 647 (f) 830
6 175 241 349 490 597	688 S.W.2d	(a) 61 (b) 198 (c) 307 (d) 446 (e) 757 (f) 827
7 176 242 350 491 598	687 S.W.2d	(a) 268 (b) 374 (c) 410 (d) 444 (e) 560 (f) 924
8 177 243 351 492 599	686 S.W.2d	(a) 87 (b) 101 (c) 226 (d) 469 (e) 543 (f) 799
9 178 244 352 493 600	586 S.W.2d	(a) 24 (b) 33 (c) 137 (d) 229 (e) 429 (f) 934
10 179 245 353 494 501	684 S.W.2d	(a) 99 (b) 440 (c) 598 (d) 772 (e) 906 (f) 929
11 180 246 354 495 502	683 S.W.2d	(a) 61 (b) 140 (c) 307 (d) 743 (e) 763 (f) 928
12 181 247 355 496 503	682 S.W.2d	(a) 236 (b) 366 (c) 567 (d) 634 (e) 803 (f) 924
13 182 248 356 497 504	680 S.W.2d	(a) 153 (b) 315 (c) 365 (d) 420 (e) 709 (f) 949
14 183 249 357 498 505	679 S.W.2d	(a) 15 (b) 370 (c) 416 (d) 544 (e) 762 (f) 924
15 184 250 358 499 506	678 S.W.2d	(a) 45 (b) 93 (c) 225 (d) 443 (e) 661 (f) 800
16 185 251 359 500 507	677 S.W.2d	(a) 147 (b) 293 (c) 504 (d) 669 (e) 781 (f) 881
17 186 252 360 401 508	676 S.W.2d	(a) 1 (b) 159 (c) 231 (d) 375 (e) 448 (f) 693
18 187 253 361 402 509	675 S.W.2d	(a) 92 (b) 245 (c) 293 (d) 376 (e) 481 (f) 845
19 188 254 362 403 510	674 S.W.2d	(a) 139 (b) 293 (c) 437 (d) 737 (e) 781 (f) 953
20 189 255 363 404 511	673 S.W.2d	(a) 218 (b) 236 (c) 270 (d) 334 (e) 512 (f) 858
21 190 256 364 405 512	672 S.W.2d	(a) 20 (b) 394 (c) 470 (d) 769 (e) 860 (f) 922
22 191 257 365 406 513	671 S.W.2d	(a) 105 (b) 644 (c) 757 (d) 781 (e) 812 (f) 941
23 192 258 366 407 514	670 S.W.2d	(a) 319 (b) 494 (c) 828 (d) 857 (e) 882 (f) 954
24 193 259 367 408 515	669 S.W.2d	(a) 3 (b) 105 (c) 519 (d) 736 (e) 779 (f) 878
25 194 260 368 409 516	668 S.W.2d	(a) 1 (b) 37 (c) 252 (d) 533 (e) 806 (f) 828
26 195 261 369 410 517	667 S.W.2d	(a) 250 (b) 299 (c) 347 (d) 736 (e) 773 (f) 885
27 196 262 370 411 518	666 S.W.2d	(a) 11 (b) 48 (c) 61 (d) 213 (e) 416 (f) 613
28 197 263 371 412 519	665 S.W.2d	(a) 87 (b) 132 (c) 200 (d) 208 (e) 289 (f) 324
29 198 264 372 413 520	664 S.W.2d	(a) 625 (b) 698 (c) 734 (d) 805 (e) 830 (f) 851
30 199 265 373 414 521	663 S.W.2d	(a) 108 (b) 196 (c) 547 (d) 685 (e) 761 (f) 776
31 200 266 374 415 522	662 S.W.2d	(a) 129 (b) 141 (c) 396 (d) 693 (e) 709 (f) 779
32 101 267 375 416 523	661 S.W.2d	(a) 2 (b) 285 (c) 433 (d) 567 (e) 606 (f) 740
33 102 268 376 417 524	660 S.W.2d	(a) 58 (b) 144 (c) 265 (d) 404 (e) 521 (f) 584
34 103 269 377 418 525	659 S.W.2d	(a) 201 (b) 227 (c) 714 (d) 775 (e) 827 (f) 869
35 104 270 378 419 526	658 S.W.2d	(a) 17 (b) 70 (c) 186 (d) 218 (e) 323 (f) 665
36 105 271 379 420 527	657 S.W.2d	(a) 57 (b) 346 (c) 494 (d) 583 (e) 636 (f) 824
37 106 272 380 421 528	656 S.W.2d	(a) 11 (b) 470 (c) 589 (d) 612 (e) 740 (f) 859

PROBLEM #	**VOL. #**	**PAGES WITH THAT VOLUME**
38 107 273 381 422 529	655 S.W.2d	(a) 86 (b) 173 (c) 506 (d) 574 (e) 638 (f) 845
39 108 274 382 423 530	653 S.W.2d	(a) 35 (b) 93 (c) 377 (d) 436 (e) 539 (f) 703
40 109 275 383 424 531	652 S.W.2d	(a) 202 (b) 345 (c) 515 (d) 655 (e) 851 (f) 856
41 110 276 384 425 532	651 S.W.2d	(a) 31 (b) 232 (c) 525 (d) 613 (e) 616 (f) 851
42 111 277 385 426 533	650 S.W.2d	(a) 68 (b) 312 (c) 467 (d) 729 (e) 879 (f) 938
43 112 278 386 427 534	649 S.W.2d	(a) 198 (b) 456 (c) 524 (d) 561 (e) 791 (f) 812
44 113 279 387 428 535	648 S.W.2d	(a) 351 (b) 542 (c) 568 (d) 748 (e) 800 (f) 858
45 114 280 388 429 536	646 S.W.2d	(a) 17 (b) 177 (c) 246 (d) 347 (e) 717 (f) 765
46 115 281 389 430 537	645 S.W.2d	(a) 39 (b) 91 (c) 149 (d) 204 (e) 310 (f) 346
47 116 282 390 431 538	640 S.W.2d	(a) 147 (b) 222 (c) 343 (d) 362 (e) 619 (f) 781
48 117 283 391 432 539	641 S.W.2d	(a) 108 (b) 193 (c) 451 (d) 477 (e) 780 (f) 947
49 118 284 392 433 540	642 S.W.2d	(a) 15 (b) 160 (c) 336 (d) 504 (e) 820 (f) 907
50 119 285 393 434 541	643 S.W.2d	(a) 46 (b) 118 (c) 222 (d) 526 (e) 592 (f) 737
51 120 286 394 435 542	644 S.W.2d	(a) 148 (b) 292 (c) 355 (d) 533 (e) 615 (f) 815
52 121 287 395 436 543	647 S.W.2d	(a) 3 (b) 8 (c) 477 (d) 539 (e) 625 (f) 866
53 122 288 396 437 544	654 S.W.2d	(a) 31 (b) 68 (c) 367 (d) 376 (e) 835 (f) 889
54 123 289 397 438 545	639 S.W.2d	(a) 86 (b) 286 (c) 545 (d) 700 (e) 786 (f) 825
55 124 290 398 439 546	638 S.W.2d	(a) 108 (b) 218 (c) 272 (d) 557 (e) 905 (f) 908
56 125 291 399 440 547	637 S.W.2d	(a) 84 (b) 94 (c) 303 (d) 373 (e) 903 (f) 943
57 126 292 400 441 548	636 S.W.2d	(a) 94 (b) 530 (c) 648 (d) 706 (e) 828 (f) 896
58 127 293 301 442 549	635 S.W.2d	(a) 51 (b) 98 (c) 268 (d) 554 (e) 615 (f) 658
59 128 294 302 443 550	634 S.W.2d	(a) 6 (b) 153 (c) 234 (d) 249 (e) 286 (f) 815
60 129 295 303 444 551	633 S.W.2d	(a) 73 (b) 161 (c) 366 (d) 488 (e) 733 (f) 761
61 130 296 304 445 552	632 S.W.2d	(a) 6 (b) 227 (c) 234 (d) 621 (e) 885 (f) 950
62 131 297 305 446 553	631 S.W.2d	(a) 1 (b) 63 (c) 193 (d) 410 (e) 825 (f) 893
63 132 298 306 447 554	629 S.W.2d	(a) 201 (b) 324 (c) 524 (d) 645 (e) 816 (f) 943
64 133 299 307 448 555	628 S.W.2d	(a) 329 (b) 497 (c) 582 (d) 637 (e) 887 (f) 941
65 134 300 308 449 556	627 S.W.2d	(a) 166 (b) 382 (c) 567 (d) 741 (e) 868 (f) 928
66 135 201 309 450 557	626 S.W.2d	(a) 30 (b) 422 (c) 478 (d) 817 (e) 850 (f) 912
67 136 202 310 451 558	625 S.W.2d	(a) 1 (b) 151 (c) 192 (d) 581 (e) 731 (f) 874
68 137 203 311 452 559	624 S.W.2d	(a) 11 (b) 394 (c) 497 (d) 573 (e) 886 (f) 933
69 138 204 312 453 560	623 S.W.2d	(a) 448 (b) 699 (c) 745 (d) 797 (e) 843 (f) 895
70 139 205 313 454 561	622 S.W.2d	(a) 31 (b) 319 (c) 482 (d) 535 (e) 736 (f) 844
71 140 206 314 455 562	620 S.W.2d	(a) 5 (b) 157 (c) 181 (d) 362 (e) 648 (f) 732
72 141 207 315 456 563	619 S.W.2d	(a) 199 (b) 725 (c) 814 (d) 873 (e) 888 (f) 910
73 142 208 316 457 564	618 S.W.2d	(a) 229 (b) 280 (c) 288 (d) 470 (e) 543 (f) 591
74 143 209 317 458 565	617 S.W.2d	(a) 61 (b) 262 (c) 329 (d) 479 (e) 731 (f) 767
75 144 210 318 459 566	616 S.W.2d	(a) 39 (b) 373 (c) 452 (d) 587 (e) 600 (f) 679
76 145 211 319 460 567	615 S.W.2d	(a) 1 (b) 164 (c) 293 (d) 309 (e) 574 (f) 869
77 146 212 320 461 568	621 S.W.2d	(a) 7 (b) 22 (c) 451 (d) 539 (e) 731 (f) 889
78 147 213 321 462 569	614 S.W.2d	(a) 227 (b) 429 (c) 563 (d) 695 (e) 701 (f) 903
79 148 214 322 463 570	613 S.W.2d	(a) 431 (b) 440 (c) 716 (d) 793 (e) 800 (f) 833
80 149 215 323 464 571	612 S.W.2d	(a) 257 (b) 503 (c) 766 (d) 799 (e) 866 (f) 935
81 150 216 324 465 572	611 S.W.2d	(a) 1 (b) 860 (c) 869 (d) 897 (e) 911 (f) 928
82 151 217 325 466 573	610 S.W.2d	(a) 217 (b) 681 (c) 744 (d) 807 (e) 922 (f) 946
83 152 218 326 467 574	608 S.W.2d	(a) 51 (b) 374 (c) 405 (d) 576 (e) 722 (f) 819
84 153 219 327 468 575	607 S.W.2d	(a) 421 (b) 507 (c) 677 (d) 832 (e) 856 (f) 857
85 154 220 328 469 576	606 S.W.2d	(a) 169 (b) 578 (c) 696 (d) 725 (e) 732 (f) 901
86 155 221 329 470 577	605 S.W.2d	(a) 43 (b) 210 (c) 506 (d) 749 (e) 800 (f) 955
87 156 222 330 471 578	604 S.W.2d	(a) 221 (b) 396 (c) 415 (d) 511 (e) 626 (f) 791

PROBLEM #	**VOL. #**	**PAGES WITH THAT VOLUME**
88 157 223 331 472 579	603 S.W.2d	(a) 37 (b) 335 (c) 793 (d) 829 (e) 930 (f) 931
89 158 224 332 473 580	602 S.W.2d	(a) 118 (b) 150 (c) 327 (d) 400 (e) 609 (f) 874
90 159 225 333 474 581	601 S.W.2d	(a) 186 (b) 202 (c) 280 (d) 717 (e) 766 (f) 923
91 160 226 334 475 582	600 S.W.2d	(a) 358 (b) 457 (c) 601 (d) 656 (e) 695 (f) 850
92 161 227 335 476 583	599 S.W.2d	(a) 121 (b) 427 (c) 545 (d) 655 (e) 841 (f) 900
93 162 228 336 477 584	598 S.W.2d	(a) 11 (b) 503 (c) 609 (d) 640 (e) 660 (f) 783
94 163 229 337 478 585	597 S.W.2d	(a) 434 (b) 510 (c) 724 (d) 783 (e) 861 (f) 871
95 164 230 338 479 586	596 S.W.2d	(a) 150 (b) 240 (c) 379 (d) 716 (e) 796 (f) 924
96 165 231 339 480 587	594 S.W.2d	(a) 163 (b) 449 (c) 545 (d) 723 (e) 898 (f) 908
97 166 232 340 481 588	593 S.W.2d	(a) 84 (b) 193 (c) 731 (d) 749 (e) 869 (f) 923
98 167 233 341 482 589	592 S.W.2d	(a) 35 (b) 38 (c) 134 (d) 410 (e) 432 (f) 670
99 168 234 342 483 590	590 S.W.2d	(a) 173 (b) 241 (c) 563 (d) 783 (e) 878 (f) 946
100 169 235 343 484 591	588 S.W.2d	(a) 46 (b) 50 (c) 199 (d) 549 (e) 599 (f) 877

CITATION EXERCISE 12
U.S. SUPREME COURT DECISIONS (I)

A. INTRODUCTION

1. Structure of the Federal Court System

The federal court system has a hierarchical structure. At the bottom are the various federal trial courts where most actions are commenced. Above the federal trial courts are the U.S. Courts of Appeals and various specialized appellate courts, which review decisions of the trial courts. The United States Court of Appeals for the Federal Circuit and the United States Court of Military Appeals are other examples of specialized federal appellate courts. This structure is illustrated in the following chart. Note, however, that the specific organization of the federal court system has varied over time.

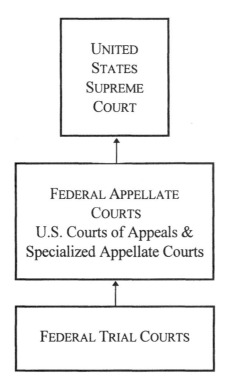

This exercise and the following four exercises focus on citing decisions of the U.S. Supreme Court. Additional exercises then focus on citing decisions of the federal appellate courts and federal trial courts.

Recall from Citation Exercise 9 that a citation to a case in a reporter contains (up to) seven basic elements:

(1) the **case name**;

(2) the **volume number** of the reporter;

(3) the abbreviated **name of the reporter**;

(4) the **page number** on which the opinion begins (and any other pages cited in the opinion);

(5) the abbreviated **name of the court**, including its geographic jurisdiction (unless that information is clearly indicated from the reporter cited);

(6) the **year or date** of the decision;

(7) the **subsequent history** of the case, if any.

The following discussion indicates how elements (2)-(6) apply to citations of U.S. Supreme Court opinions in the official reporter, *United States Reports*. Although use of unofficial reporters is widespread (*see* Exercises 13-16 below), the official reporter is technically the authoritative text.

2. Volume Number, Abbreviated Reporter Name, and Page Number

Table T.1 indicates that *United States Reports* is the preferred reporter to cite if a U.S. Supreme Court opinion has appeared in that reporter. Table T.1 also indicates that the abbreviation of that reporter is "U.S." Thus, if a U.S. Supreme Court opinion begins on page 147 of Volume 440 in *United States Reports*, a *Bluebook* citation to that opinion would refer to the volume number, the reporter, and page number as follows:

[**Example 1**] *Montana v. United States*, **440 U.S. 147** (1979).

See Bluebook Rule 10.3.2.

3. Abbreviated Name of the Court and Year or Date of Decision

The above citation contains only the year of decision in the parenthetical. The following is a step-by-step explanation of how *The Bluebook* arrived at omitting the abbreviated name of the court, including its geographical jurisdiction (*i.e.*, why "U.S. Sup. Ct." was omitted from the parenthetical containing the year of decision).

First, *Bluebook* Rule 10.4 requires that every case citation identify the court that decided the case, including its geographical jurisdiction (element (5), above). The information should be abbreviated as indicated in the appropriate *Bluebook* table(s). Table T.1 ("United States Jurisdictions") indicates the geographical jurisdiction is "U.S." Table T.7 ("Court Names") provides a list of abbreviations for courts names for use in conjunction with *Bluebook* Rule 10.4. The usual abbreviation for Supreme Court is "Sup. Ct." Applying these rules to the above case, the citation would appear as follows:

[Example 2] *Montana v. United States*, 440 U.S. 147 (**U.S. Sup. Ct.** 1979).

Second, when the highest court in a jurisdiction is being cited, the abbreviated name of the court is not given in the parenthetical. Since the U.S. Supreme Court is the highest court in the federal court system, that information should be eliminated:

[Example 3] *Montana v. United States*, 440 U.S. 147 (**U.S.** 1979).

Third, when the geographic jurisdiction is unambiguously indicated by the reporter, the geographic jurisdiction should be omitted from the parenthetical. In this instance, the cited reporter (*United States Reports*) clearly indicates the geographical jurisdiction. Thus, "U.S." should be eliminated from the parenthetical.

[Example 4] *Montana v. United States*, 440 U.S. 147 (1979).

By way of contrast, if the above case was cited to *United States Law Week*, a looseleaf service, "U.S." must be included in the parenthetical because *United States Law Week* does not exclusively report cases from the U.S. Supreme Court—the name of the reporter does not unambiguously identify the court. *See Bluebook* Rule 10.4(a).

Furthermore, when a decision is published in a reporter (such as *United States Reports*), the year of decision is placed in the parentheses. *Bluebook* Rule 10.5(a). When cases are cited to a looseleaf service, the exact date must be given. *Bluebook* Rule 10.5(b). The abbreviations for the months are listed in Table T.12 ("Months"). Thus, if the above case were cited to *United States Law Week* (U.S.L.W.) instead of *United States Reports*, the citation would appear as follows:

[Example 5] *Montana v. United States*, 47 U.S.L.W. 4190 (U.S. Feb. 22, 1979).

4. Special Note on Early U.S. Supreme Court Decisions

Up to the late nineteenth century, reporters were ordinarily designated by the last name of the individual(s) who prepared the volume. The early "nominative" reporters of U.S. Supreme Court decisions were Dallas, Cranch, Wheaton, Peters, Howard, Black, and Wallace. Later, their reports, like most other nominative reports, were incorporated into the jurisdiction-named (or court-named) reporter series—in this instance, into *United States Reports*. Despite their incorporation into *United States Reports*, however, *The Bluebook* still requires the original volume and last name of these first seven reporters be included in citations to the first ninety volumes of *United States Reports*. For example, the famous case of *Marbury v. Madison* would be cited as follows:

[Example 6] *Marbury v. Madison*, 5 U.S. (1 Cranch) 137 (1803).

See Bluebook Rules 10.3.2 & Table T.1 (indicating required abbreviations for some of the original nominative reporters).

5. Typeface Conventions

As shown in the above examples, case names (and any procedural phrases) are italicized or underscored in documents submitted to courts and in legal memoranda. *See Bluebook* Practitioners' Note P.1(a). In law review footnotes, case names that are part of full citations appear in ordinary roman type:

[Example 7] Marbury v. Madison, 5 U.S. (1 Cranch) 137 (1803).

Procedural phrases, however, are italicized (*see supra* Citation Exercises 9 & 11). *Bluebook* Rule 2.1(a).

B. INSTRUCTIONS FOR COMPLETING THIS EXERCISE

The purpose of this exercise is to give you practice in citing U.S. Supreme Court cases. To complete this exercise, find the case that begins on the page listed with your problem below in the designated volume of *United States Reports* (U.S.). **The volume of *United States Reports* used to complete this exercise is also used to complete the next exercise.**

For your answer to this exercise, state the following:

(a) the full case name as it is stated in the reporter at the beginning of the opinion (*e.g.*, Montana et al. v. United States); **you may omit obviously irrelevant portions of a party's name if the full name is a lengthy one;**

(b) the exact date of decision (*e.g.*, Feb. 22, 1979);

(c) the proper citation of that case in *Bluebook* (or another designated) form; assume that the case name is going to appear in a **citation sentence or clause**, not as a part of a grammatical part of a textual sentence, in a **legal memorandum**; **cite the case to only *United States Reports*.**

Unless otherwise instructed, write your answers on the answer sheet provided in Part 4 of these exercises.

PROBLEM #	CITATION
1 131 201 305 404 503	135 U.S. 342
2 132 202 306 405 504	343 U.S. 214
3 133 203 307 406 505	333 U.S. 591
4 134 204 308 407 506	346 U.S. 119
5 135 205 309 408 507	434 U.S. 159
6 136 206 310 409 508	322 U.S. 238
7 137 207 311 410 509	252 U.S. 308

PROBLEM #	**CITATION**
8 138 208 312 411 510	379 U.S. 378
9 139 209 313 412 511	336 U.S. 176
10 140 210 314 413 512	334 U.S. 314
11 141 211 315 414 513	378 U.S. 1
12 142 212 316 415 514	257 U.S. 308
13 143 213 317 416 515	297 U.S. 288
14 144 214 318 417 516	317 U.S. 217
15 145 215 319 418 517	328 U.S. 293
16 146 216 320 419 518	247 U.S. 231
17 147 217 321 420 519	219 U.S. 121
18 148 218 322 421 520	299 U.S. 248
19 149 219 323 422 521	332 U.S. 407
20 150 220 324 423 522	146 U.S. 102
21 151 221 325 424 523	251 U.S. 233
22 152 222 326 425 524	351 U.S. 105
23 153 223 327 426 525	385 U.S. 276
24 154 224 328 427 526	149 U.S. 273
25 155 225 329 428 527	301 U.S. 402
26 156 226 330 429 528	312 U.S. 410
27 157 227 331 430 529	258 U.S. 483
28 158 228 332 431 530	297 U.S. 629
29 159 229 333 432 531	411 U.S. 182
30 160 230 334 433 532	349 U.S. 1
31 161 231 335 434 533	118 U.S. 271
32 162 232 336 435 534	282 U.S. 481
33 163 233 337 436 535	314 U.S. 212
34 164 234 338 437 536	243 U.S. 210
35 165 235 339 438 537	367 U.S. 687
36 166 236 340 439 538	333 U.S. 683
37 167 237 341 440 539	380 U.S. 300
38 168 238 342 441 540	369 U.S. 404
39 169 239 343 442 541	206 U.S. 158
40 170 240 344 443 542	210 U.S. 339
41 171 241 345 444 543	382 U.S. 323
42 172 242 346 445 544	373 U.S. 221
43 173 243 347 446 545	365 U.S. 624
44 174 244 348 447 546	317 U.S. 217
45 175 245 349 448 547	296 U.S. 459
46 176 246 350 449 548	345 U.S. 427
47 177 247 351 450 549	340 U.S. 474
48 178 248 352 451 550	358 U.S. 242
49 179 249 353 452 551	359 U.S. 187
50 180 250 354 453 552	234 U.S. 245
51 181 251 355 454 553	272 U.S. 321
52 182 252 356 455 554	362 U.S. 482
53 183 253 357 456 555	257 U.S. 85
54 184 254 358 457 556	359 U.S. 231
55 185 255 359 458 557	250 U.S. 153
56 186 256 360 459 558	252 U.S. 538
57 187 257 361 460 559	467 U.S. 104

PROBLEM #	CITATION
58 188 258 362 461 560	220 U.S. 428
59 189 259 363 462 561	334 U.S. 624
60 190 260 364 463 562	175 U.S. 178
61 191 261 365 464 563	303 U.S. 283
62 192 262 366 465 564	244 U.S. 332
63 193 263 367 466 565	336 U.S. 220
64 194 264 368 467 566	383 U.S. 715
65 195 265 369 468 567	343 U.S. 90
66 196 266 370 469 568	262 U.S. 361
67 197 267 371 470 569	321 U.S. 126
68 198 268 372 471 570	339 U.S. 186
69 199 269 373 472 571	310 U.S. 354
70 200 270 374 473 572	288 U.S. 152
71 101 271 375 474 573	273 U.S. 83
72 102 272 376 475 574	263 U.S. 1
73 103 273 377 476 575	270 U.S. 59
74 104 274 378 477 576	332 U.S. 194
75 105 275 379 478 577	171 U.S. 220
76 106 276 380 479 578	133 U.S. 67
77 107 277 381 480 579	322 U.S. 31
78 108 278 382 481 580	308 U.S. 256
79 109 279 383 482 581	263 U.S. 103
80 110 280 384 483 582	342 U.S. 437
81 111 281 385 484 583	258 U.S. 365
82 112 282 386 485 584	166 U.S. 601
83 113 283 387 486 585	330 U.S. 545
84 114 284 388 487 586	276 U.S. 467
85 115 285 389 488 587	266 U.S. 503
86 116 286 390 489 588	312 U.S. 195
87 117 287 391 490 589	253 U.S. 300
88 118 288 392 491 590	261 U.S. 140
89 119 289 393 492 591	295 U.S. 295
90 120 290 394 493 592	291 U.S. 227
91 121 291 395 494 593	316 U.S. 4
92 122 292 396 495 594	302 U.S. 556
93 123 293 397 496 595	355 U.S. 587
94 124 294 398 497 596	308 U.S. 241
95 125 295 399 498 597	277 U.S. 258
96 126 296 400 499 598	251 U.S. 108
97 127 297 301 500 599	201 U.S. 344
98 128 298 302 401 600	267 U.S. 233
99 129 299 303 402 501	408 U.S. 204
100 130 300 304 403 502	376 U.S. 86

CITATION EXERCISE 13
U.S. SUPREME COURT DECISIONS (II)

A. INTRODUCTION

1. Parallel Citation of U.S. Supreme Court Decisions

As noted in the preceding exercise, *Bluebook* Table T.1 indicates that *United States Reports* is the preferred reporter to cite if a U.S. Supreme Court opinion is in that reporter. In practice, this rule is probably the most widely "violated" *Bluebook* rule. Many lawyers use the unofficial, commercial Supreme Court reports, West's *Supreme Court Reporter* (S. Ct.) and *United States Supreme Court Reports, Lawyers' Edition* (L. Ed. and L. Ed. 2d) (currently published by LEXIS Law Publishing and formerly by Lawyers Cooperative Publishing) in the daily practice of law rather than *United States Reports*. Despite the *Bluebook* requirement to cite only to *United States Reports*, many lawyers include references where the opinion can also be found in all three reporters (*i.e.*, "parallel citations") for convenience of the reader. By tradition, a citation to all three reporters would appear as follows:

> **[Example 1]** *Montana v. United States*, 440 U.S. 147, 99 S. Ct. 970, 59 L. Ed. 2d 210 (1979).

By consulting any one of the three reporters, the text of the *Montana* case can be found. Note carefully the spacing in the abbreviations. Both "S. Ct." and "L. Ed. 2d" have spaces; "U.S." does not. Note also that the traditional order in which the reporters are cited: *United States Reports*, then the *Supreme Court Reporter*, followed by the *Lawyers' Edition*.

2. Finding Parallel Citations for U.S. Supreme Court Decisions

Several different methods can be used to find parallel citations for U.S. Supreme Court decisions. For purposes of the exercise below, you will be asked to use one of the following two methods: (a) consulting *Shepard's United States Citations Case Edition*; or (b) consulting a table of cases in a digest.

(a) Shepard's Citations

One function performed by *Shepard's Citations* is to provide parallel citations for cases. Other functions include tracing the judicial history of a case, verifying the current status of a case, and finding later cases and other sources that have cited a case.

To use *Shepard's Citations* to find parallel citations, (1) you will need to locate *Shepard's United States Citations Case Edition* in the library collection.

This *Shepard's* set has several bound volumes and paper-covered supplements. It has entries (divisions) for citations from all three Supreme Court Reporters (*i.e.*, one part for *United States Reports* citations, one part for West's *Supreme Court Reporter* citations, and one part for *United States Supreme Court Reports, Lawyers' Edition* citations.) In the exercise below, you will know the citation to *United States Reports* (*e.g.*, 440 U.S. 147). To find parallel citations for this citation, you will need to find the divisions or parts within the *Shepard's* set covering *United States Reports* citations. (2) Examine the bindings to determine the appropriate part (division). UNITED STATES REPORTS will be the running head in these volumes.

(3) You will then need to find the appropriate entry in the **first** *Shepard's Citations* volume covering the decision. The volume numbers of *United States Reports* are shown at the top of the page and the beginning page number of each case is shown in bold print in the columns. Under the entry for the case, the parallel citations are given in parentheses. Parallel citations are given **only once** in the first *Shepard's* entry for the case; they are **not** repeated in subsequent supplementary volumes or pamphlets. If you find an entry for your case, but no parallel citations are given, you are probably using a subsequent supplementary volume. Check again for the correct volume. The entry for the above example (440 U.S. 147) is shown the figure below.

UNITED STATES REPORTS					Vol. 440
657F2d779	e 711F2d242		d 646FS859	697FS767	519FS1255
715F2d228	732F2d948	Wis	656FS1083	f 699FS1034	522FS548
727F2d473	747F2d769	101Wis2d321	667FS43	702FS956	547FS867
762F2d1282	769F2d790	166Wis2d984	749FS330	f 717FS205	f 548FS13
521FS1350	775F2d1197	304NW725	749FS331	718FS188	548FS1362
598FS108	818F2d960	481NW302	821FS70	f 720FS1066	551FS168
Cir. 6	828F2d838	79CR1245	18BRW450	f 720FS1075	552FS700
681F2d467	831F2d1077	82CR932	23BRW739	722FS995	562FS1279
j 747F2d1057	498FS656	75NwL980	52BRW1013	722FS997	570FS559
838F2d838	610FS1496	83NwL221	62BRW861	722FS1008	576FS1184
498FS114	740FS14	131PaL1256	111BRW373	750FS606	587FS1489
506FS136	Cir. Fed.	101YLJ445	Cir. 2	754FS34	590FS701
620FS130	769F2d1564	101YLJ1011	671F2d68	764FS870	603FS563
644FS254	CtCl		684F2d197	798FS759	615FS444
696FS260	677F2d868	—147—	704F2d665	802FS953	633FS47
Cir. 7	230CCL498		713F2d950	811FS91	648FS898
636F2d171	79TCt824	Montana v	718F2d543	817FS1094	654FS1431
676F2d281	132MCC837	United States	763F2d83	825FS611	656FS207
687F2d1056	Calif	1979	826F2d1189	826FS733	664FS937
j 743F2d470	33C3d831		869F2d110	f 826FS734	675FS187
789F2d478	38C3d936	(59LE210)	873F2d638	834FS641	715FS663
515FS1314	186CA3d655	(99SC970)	878F2d643	106FRD19	721FS599
535FS1044	193CA3d288	s 437FS354	906F2d833	6BRW359	722FS1196
e 537FS1239	213CA3d1332	cc 161Mt140	922F2d168	6BRW812	f 743FS1132
551FS136	191CaR467	cc 166Mt260	931F2d185	12BRW563	771FS1400
564FS885	216CaR361	cc 505P2d102	942F2d156	14BRW901	782FS978
624FS948	230CaR914	cc 531P2d1327	f 963F2d564	15BRW787	790FS79
640FS856	238CaR235	442US131	963F2d566	15BRW876	810FS163
726FS694	262CaR413	e 449US94	969F2d1356	17BRW364	814FS1202
Cir. 8	662P2d925	j 449US113	j 969F2d1372	28BRW444	95FRD177
622F2d978	702P2d519	456US467	970F2d1054	31BRW448	121FRD49
670F2d96	Idaho	460US619	970F2d1055	40BRW116	5BRW689
506FS39	114Ida46	462US313	990F2d719	49BRW933	8BRW562
Cir. 9	753P2d257	463US129	468FS589	52BRW115	17BRW642

(b) Digest Table of Cases

Digests provide subject access to chronologically published cases by organizing headnotes of the cases by topic. One function of the Table of Cases volumes accompanying digests is to provide parallel citations for the cases listed in the table. Two digests are devoted to U.S. Supreme Court opinions: West's *U.S. Supreme Court Digest* and *U.S. Supreme Court Digest, Lawyers' Edition*. Digests are used by looking up the case name in the Table of Cases. If two or more different cases with the same name or the same case have been reported more than once in the reporters covering the U.S. Supreme Court, you will need to check to see which one has the relevant citation. The relevant entry for the *Montana* case in West's *U.S. Supreme Court Digest* is shown below:

> **Montana** v. U S, Mont, 99 SCt 970, 440
> US 147, 59 LEd2d 210—Judgm 828(3.-
> 32, 3.49).

Similarly, the relevant entry in *U.S. Supreme Court Digest, Lawyers' Edition* indicates the same parallel citations:

> **Montana v United States,** 440 US 147, 59 L Ed 2d
> 210, 99 S Ct 970—cts § 757; judgt §§ 76, 79, 80,
> 81, 82, 89, 187, 198, 205

B. INSTRUCTIONS FOR COMPLETING THIS EXERCISE

This exercise gives you practice in citing U.S. Supreme Court cases using parallel citations. To complete this exercise, find the case that begins on the page listed below in the designated volume of *United States Reports* (U.S.). The citation below is to a *different* page in the same volume used to complete the preceding exercise.

For your answer to this exercise, state the following:

(a) the full case name as it is stated in the reporter at the beginning of the opinion (*e.g.*, Montana et al. v. United States); **you may omit obviously irrelevant portions of a party's name if the full name is a lengthy one**;

(b) the exact date of decision (*e.g.*, Feb. 22, 1979);

(c) the citation of that case. **For purposes of this exercise only, cite the case to *United States Reports*,** West's ***Supreme Court Reporter*, and the *Lawyers' Edition* (in that order)** (*e.g.*, *Montana v. United States*, 440 U.S. 147, 99 S. Ct. 970, 59 L. Ed. 2d 210 (1979).). Use the appropriate volume of *Shepard's* or the "Table of Cases" in one of the U.S. Supreme Court digests to find the parallel citations. Assume that the case name is going to appear in a **citation sentence or clause**, not as a part of a grammatical part of a textual sentence, in a **legal memorandum**.

Unless otherwise instructed, write your answers on the answer sheet provided in Part 4 of these exercises.

PROBLEM #	**CITATION**
1 131 201 305 404 503	135 U.S. 100
2 132 202 306 405 504	343 U.S. 579
3 133 203 307 406 505	333 U.S. 364
4 134 204 308 407 506	346 U.S. 441
5 135 205 309 408 507	434 U.S. 246
6 136 206 310 409 508	322 U.S. 137
7 137 207 311 410 509	252 U.S. 416
8 138 208 312 411 510	379 U.S. 294
9 139 209 313 412 511	336 U.S. 695
10 140 210 314 413 512	334 U.S. 653
11 141 211 315 414 513	378 U.S. 158
12 142 212 316 415 514	257 U.S. 377
13 143 213 317 416 515	297 U.S. 537
14 144 214 318 417 516	317 U.S. 341
15 145 215 319 418 517	328 U.S. 408
16 146 216 320 419 518	247 U.S. 251
17 147 217 321 420 519	219 U.S. 346
18 148 218 322 421 520	299 U.S. 304
19 149 219 323 422 521	332 U.S. 689
20 150 220 324 423 522	146 U.S. 183
21 151 221 325 424 523	251 U.S. 417
22 152 222 326 425 524	351 U.S. 345
23 153 223 327 426 525	385 U.S. 493
24 154 224 328 427 526	149 U.S. 481
25 155 225 329 428 527	301 U.S. 548
26 156 226 330 429 528	312 U.S. 100
27 157 227 331 430 529	258 U.S. 495
28 158 228 332 431 530	297 U.S. 1
29 159 229 333 432 531	411 U.S. 677
30 160 230 334 433 532	349 U.S. 294
31 161 231 335 434 533	118 U.S. 356
32 162 232 336 435 534	282 U.S. 555
33 163 233 337 436 535	314 U.S. 488
34 164 234 338 437 536	243 U.S. 502
35 165 235 339 438 537	367 U.S. 497
36 166 236 340 439 538	333 U.S. 287
37 167 237 341 440 539	380 U.S. 479
38 168 238 342 441 540	369 U.S. 186
39 169 239 343 442 541	206 U.S. 46
40 170 240 344 443 542	210 U.S. 405
41 171 241 345 444 543	382 U.S. 172
42 172 242 346 445 544	373 U.S. 341
43 173 243 347 446 545	365 U.S. 320
44 174 244 348 447 546	317 U.S. 111
45 175 245 349 448 547	296 U.S. 287
46 176 246 350 449 548	345 U.S. 22

PROBLEM #	CITATION
47 177 247 351 450 549	340 U.S. 349
48 178 248 352 451 550	358 U.S. 534
49 179 249 353 452 551	359 U.S. 207
50 180 250 354 453 552	234 U.S. 600
51 181 251 355 454 553	272 U.S. 476
52 182 252 356 455 554	362 U.S. 29
53 183 253 357 456 555	257 U.S. 441
54 184 254 358 457 556	359 U.S. 520
55 185 255 359 458 557	250 U.S. 300
56 186 256 360 459 558	252 U.S. 286
57 187 257 361 460 559	467 U.S. 752
58 188 258 362 461 560	220 U.S. 373
59 189 259 363 462 561	334 U.S. 495
60 190 260 364 463 562	175 U.S. 211
61 191 261 365 464 563	303 U.S. 177
62 192 262 366 465 564	244 U.S. 305
63 193 263 367 466 565	336 U.S. 460
64 194 264 368 467 566	383 U.S. 190
65 195 265 369 468 567	343 U.S. 306
66 196 266 370 469 568	262 U.S. 390
67 197 267 371 470 569	321 U.S. 573
68 198 268 372 471 570	339 U.S. 485
69 199 269 373 472 571	310 U.S. 150
70 200 270 374 473 572	288 U.S. 344
71 101 271 375 474 573	273 U.S. 392
72 102 272 376 475 574	263 U.S. 255
73 103 273 377 476 575	270 U.S. 593
74 104 274 378 477 576	332 U.S. 392
75 105 275 379 478 577	171 U.S. 604
76 106 276 380 479 578	133 U.S. 375
77 107 277 381 480 579	322 U.S. 607
78 108 278 382 481 580	308 U.S. 188
79 109 279 383 482 581	263 U.S. 444
80 110 280 384 483 582	342 U.S. 371
81 111 281 385 484 583	258 U.S. 451
82 112 282 386 485 584	166 U.S. 489
83 113 283 387 486 585	330 U.S. 743
84 114 284 388 487 586	276 U.S. 311
85 115 285 389 488 587	266 U.S. 17
86 116 286 390 489 588	312 U.S. 600
87 117 287 391 490 589	253 U.S. 421
88 118 288 392 491 590	261 U.S. 252
89 119 289 393 492 591	295 U.S. 555
90 120 290 394 493 592	291 U.S. 491
91 121 291 395 494 593	316 U.S. 114
92 122 292 396 495 594	302 U.S. 379
93 123 293 397 496 595	355 U.S. 96
94 124 294 398 497 596	308 U.S. 321
95 125 295 399 498 597	277 U.S. 438
96 126 296 400 499 598	251 U.S. 385

PROBLEM #	**CITATION**
97 127 297 301 500 599	201 U.S. 43
98 128 298 302 401 600	267 U.S. 132
99 129 299 303 402 501	408 U.S. 169
100 130 300 304 403 502	376 U.S. 254

CITATION EXERCISE 14
U.S. SUPREME COURT DECISIONS (III)

A. INTRODUCTION

1. West's *Supreme Court Reporter*

West's *Supreme Court Reporter* is one of the unofficial reporters covering the U.S. Supreme Court. It reports decisions of the U.S. Supreme Court, beginning with the October Term of 1882. The first volume of West's *Supreme Court Reporter* corresponds with Volume 106 of *United States Reports*. West's *Supreme Court Reporter* is part of West's National Reporter System.

2. Using References Provided at the Beginning of the Case in the Reporter Volume to Determine the *United States Reports* Citation

West's *Supreme Court Reporter* ordinarily provides cross-references to the *United States Reports* citation for each case at the beginning of the case. Consider the following example showing the parallel citations at the beginning of the *Montana* case:

970	99 SUPREME COURT REPORTER	440 U.S. 147

440 U.S. 147, 59 L.Ed.2d 210

State of MONTANA et al., Appellants,

v.

UNITED STATES.

No. 77–1134.

Argued Dec. 4, 1978.

Decided Feb. 22, 1979.

A government contractor, at the direction of the United States, filed suit in Montana courts attacking the constitutionality of Montana's imposition of a one percent gross receipts tax upon contractors of public, but not private, construction projects. After the Montana Supreme Court upheld the tax, and at the Solicitor General's direction, the contractor abandoned its request for review by the United States Supreme Court. Thereafter, in an-

as amicus in state Supreme Court, directed filing of notice of appeal to United States Supreme Court, and effected contractor's abandonment of appeal on advice of solicitor general, United States had sufficient "laboring oar" in conduct of state court litigation to actuate principles of estoppel when suit raising same issues was later instituted by contractor in federal district court at Government's direction.

2. Judgment ⬿828(3.49)

United States, as party which had sponsored prior suit in state court by government construction contractor attacking constitutionality of Montana gross receipts tax on public contractors, was collaterally estopped, in separate action brought by contractor at its behest in federal district court, from relitigating constitutionality of such gross receipts tax where issues

89

B. INSTRUCTIONS FOR COMPLETING THIS EXERCISE

This exercise is designed to familiarize you with West's *Supreme Court Reporter* and to give you further practice in citing United States Supreme Court decisions. To complete this exercise, find the case that begins on the page of the *Supreme Court Reporter* volume cited with your problem number below.

For your answer to this exercise, state the following:

(a) the full case name as it is stated in the reporter at the beginning of the opinion (*e.g.*, Montana et al. v. United States); **you may omit obviously irrelevant portions of a party's name if the full name is a lengthy one**;

(b) the exact date of decision (*e.g.*, Feb. 22, 1979); and

(c) the citation of that case in *Bluebook* (or another designated) form. **Cite only to *United States Reports*** using the parallel citation to *United States Reports* provided at the beginning of the opinion in the *Supreme Court Reporter*. Assume that the case name is going to appear in a **citation sentence or clause**, not as a part of a grammatical part of a textual sentence in a **legal memorandum**.

Unless otherwise instructed, write your answers on the answer sheet provided in Part 4 of these exercises.

PROBLEM #	CITATION
1 155 206 322 421 533	2 S. Ct. 569
2 156 207 323 422 534	101 S. Ct. 715
3 157 208 324 423 535	3 S. Ct. 202
4 158 209 325 424 536	100 S. Ct. 647
5 159 210 326 425 537	4 S. Ct. 333
6 160 211 327 426 538	99 S. Ct. 919
7 161 212 328 42? 539	5 S. Ct. 56
8 162 213 329 428 540	103 S. Ct. 1319
9 163 214 330 429 541	6 S. Ct. 265
10 164 215 331 430 542	7 S. Ct. 296
11 165 216 332 431 543	98 S. Ct. 909
12 166 217 333 432 544	9 S. Ct. 1
13 167 218 334 433 545	10 S. Ct. 47
14 168 219 335 434 546	11 S. Ct. 191
15 169 220 336 435 547	12 S. Ct. 488
16 170 221 337 436 548	13 S. Ct. 512
17 171 222 338 437 549	14 S. Ct. 334
18 172 223 339 438 550	15 S. Ct. 249
19 173 224 340 439 551	16 S. Ct. 725
20 174 225 341 440 552	17 S. Ct. 532
21 175 226 342 441 553	18 S. Ct. 38
22 176 227 343 442 554	103 S. Ct. 1134
23 177 228 344 443 555	20 S. Ct. 906
24 178 229 345 444 556	21 S. Ct. 418
25 179 230 346 445 557	102 S. Ct. 805
26 180 231 347 446 558	102 S. Ct. 2355
27 181 232 348 447 559	24 S. Ct. 253

PROBLEM #	CITATION
28 182 233 349 448 560	25 S. Ct. 462
29 183 234 350 449 561	26 S. Ct. 408
30 184 235 351 450 562	27 S. Ct. 391
31 185 236 352 451 563	28 S. Ct. 475
32 186 237 353 452 564	101 S. Ct. 2510
33 187 238 354 453 565	30 S. Ct. 415
34 188 239 355 454 566	31 S. Ct. 452
35 189 240 356 455 567	32 S. Ct. 364
36 190 241 357 456 568	33 S. Ct. 806
37 191 242 358 457 569	103 S. Ct. 3319
38 192 243 359 458 570	101 S. Ct. 633
39 193 244 360 459 571	36 S. Ct. 477
40 194 245 361 460 572	37 S. Ct. 227
41 195 246 362 461 573	38 S. Ct. 214
42 196 247 363 462 574	39 S. Ct. 316
43 197 248 364 463 575	40 S. Ct. 364
44 198 249 365 464 576	41 S. Ct. 492
45 199 250 366 465 577	96 S. Ct. 584
46 200 251 367 466 578	43 S. Ct. 445
47 101 252 368 467 579	100 S. Ct. 328
48 102 253 369 468 580	45 S. Ct. 551
49 103 254 370 469 581	46 S. Ct. 122
50 104 255 371 470 582	97 S. Ct. 1197
51 105 256 372 471 583	48 S. Ct. 380
52 106 257 373 472 584	49 S. Ct. 150
53 107 258 374 473 585	50 S. Ct. 94
54 108 259 375 474 586	52 S. Ct. 166
55 109 260 376 475 587	53 S. Ct. 451
56 110 261 377 476 588	54 S. Ct. 551
57 111 262 378 477 589	55 S. Ct. 179
58 112 263 379 478 590	51 S. Ct. 170
59 113 264 380 479 591	56 S. Ct. 450
60 114 265 381 480 592	57 S. Ct. 515
61 115 266 382 481 593	58 S. Ct. 785
62 116 267 383 482 594	59 S. Ct. 528
63 117 268 384 483 595	60 S. Ct. 431
64 118 269 385 484 596	61 S. Ct. 343
65 119 270 386 485 597	62 S. Ct. 1008
66 120 271 387 486 598	63 S. Ct. 1284
67 121 272 388 487 599	64 S. Ct. 438
68 122 273 389 488 600	65 S. Ct. 781
69 123 274 390 489 501	66 S. Ct. 1029
70 124 275 391 490 502	67 S. Ct. 1493
71 125 276 392 491 503	68 S. Ct. 1349
72 126 277 393 492 504	69 S. Ct. 726
73 127 278 394 493 505	70 S. Ct. 918
74 128 279 395 494 506	71 S. Ct. 508
75 129 280 396 495 507	72 S. Ct. 502
76 130 281 397 496 508	73 S. Ct. 1041
77 131 282 398 497 509	74 S. Ct. 381

PROBLEM #	CITATION
78 132 283 399 498 510	75 S. Ct. 832
79 133 284 400 499 511	76 S. Ct. 600
80 134 285 301 500 512	77 S. Ct. 1203
81 135 286 302 401 513	78 S. Ct. 1079
82 136 287 303 402 514	79 S. Ct. 714
83 137 288 304 403 515	80 S. Ct. 215
84 138 289 305 404 516	80 S. Ct. 1190
85 139 290 306 405 517	97 S. Ct. 1349
86 140 291 307 406 518	82 S. Ct. 248
87 141 292 308 407 519	82 S. Ct. 1386
88 142 293 309 408 520	83 S. Ct. 232
89 143 294 310 409 521	83 S. Ct. 1773
90 144 295 311 410 522	84 S. Ct. 1758
91 145 296 312 411 523	85 S. Ct. 348
92 146 297 313 412 524	88 S. Ct. 904
93 147 298 314 413 525	89 S. Ct. 501
94 148 299 315 414 526	89 S. Ct. 1835
95 149 300 316 415 527	92 S. Ct. 630
96 150 201 317 416 528	94 S. Ct. 1494
97 151 202 318 417 529	94 S. Ct. 2788
98 152 203 319 418 530	95 S. Ct. 1066
99 153 204 320 419 531	104 S. Ct. 871
100 154 205 321 420 532	104 S. Ct. 3026

CITATION EXERCISE 15
U.S. SUPREME COURT DECISIONS (IV)

A. INTRODUCTION

1. *United States Supreme Courts, Lawyer's Edition*

United States Supreme Court Reports, Lawyers' Edition unofficially reports all U.S. Supreme Court decisions. Like *West's Supreme Court Reporter*, it also reports the Chamber Opinions of individual Supreme Court Justices, which did not appear in *United States Reports* prior to 1970. (Each Justice supervises one or more of the federal judicial circuits and handles petitions from that circuit when the Court is not in session. Chamber opinions are written in response to these petitions.)

2. Using References Provided at the Beginning of the Case in the Reporter Volume to Determine the *United States Reports* Citation

The same approach described and used in Citation Exercise 14 can be used to determine the *United States Reports* citations for cases appearing in the *Lawyers' Edition*. Examine the parallel citations given at the beginning of the *Montana* case in the *Lawyers' Edition*.

[440 US 147]
STATE OF MONTANA et al., Appellants,

v

UNITED STATES

440 US 147, 59 L Ed 2d 210, 99 S Ct 970

[No. 77–1134]

Argued December 4, 1978. Decided February 22, 1979.

Decision: United States held collaterally estopped from federal court challenge to constitutionality of Montana tax on public contractors by decision in prior state litigation which government directed and financed.

SUMMARY

A contractor on a federal project in Montana instituted an action in a Montana state court, alleging that Montana's one percent gross receipts tax upon contractors of public, but not private, construction projects violated

---

B. INSTRUCTIONS FOR COMPLETING THIS EXERCISE

This exercise is designed to familiarize you with *United States Supreme Court Reports, Lawyers' Edition* and to give you further practice in citing U.S. Supreme Court decisions. To complete this exercise, find the case that begins on the page of the volume cited with your problem number below in *United States Supreme Court Reports, Lawyers' Edition*. All of the citations are to the second edition of the *Lawyers' Edition* (L. Ed. 2d). **The volume of the *Lawyers' Edition* used to complete this exercise is also used to complete the next exercise.**

For your answer to this exercise, state the following:

(a) the full case name as it is stated in the reporter at the beginning of the opinion (*e.g.*, Montana et al. v. United States); **you may omit obviously irrelevant portions of a party's name if the full name is a lengthy one**;

(b) the exact date of decision (*e.g.*, Feb. 22, 1979); and

(c) the citation of that case. **For purposes of this exercise only, cite the case to *United States Reports*, West's *Supreme Court Reporter*, and the *Lawyers' Edition* (in that order) using the parallel citations provided at the beginning of the opinion in the *Lawyers' Edition*.** Assume that the case name is going to appear in a **citation sentence or clause**, not as a part of a grammatical part of a textual sentence, in a **legal memorandum**.

Unless otherwise instructed, write your answers on the answer sheet provided in Part 4 of these Exercises.

PROBLEM #	CITATION
1 142 220 365 409 517	1 L. Ed. 2d 726
2 143 221 366 410 518	1 L. Ed. 2d 480
3 144 222 367 411 519	2 L. Ed. 2d 1126
4 145 223 368 412 520	2 L. Ed. 2d 470
5 146 224 369 413 521	3 L. Ed. 2d 667
6 147 225 370 414 522	3 L. Ed. 2d 30
7 148 226 371 415 523	4 L. Ed. 2d 724
8 149 277 372 416 524	4 L. Ed. 2d 1
9 150 228 373 417 525	5 L. Ed. 2d 592
10 151 229 374 418 526	5 L. Ed. 2d 1
11 152 230 375 419 527	6 L. Ed. 2d 1109
12 153 231 376 420 528	6 L. Ed. 2d 45
13 154 232 377 421 529	7 L. Ed. 2d 326
14 155 233 378 422 530	7 L. Ed. 2d 629
15 156 234 379 423 531	8 L. Ed. 2d 734
16 157 235 380 424 532	8 L. Ed. 2d 187
17 158 236 381 425 533	9 L. Ed. 2d 633
18 159 237 382 426 534	9 L. Ed. 2d 561
19 160 238 383 427 535	10 L. Ed. 2d 770
20 161 239 384 428 536	10 L. Ed. 2d 288
21 162 240 385 429 537	11 L. Ed. 2d 293
22 163 241 386 430 538	11 L. Ed. 2d 590

PROBLEM #	CITATION
23 164 242 387 431 539	12 L. Ed. 2d 775
24 165 243 388 432 540	12 L. Ed. 2d 678
25 166 244 389 433 541	13 L. Ed. 2d 904
26 167 245 390 434 542	13 L. Ed. 2d 855
27 168 246 391 435 543	14 L. Ed. 2d 116
28 169 247 392 436 544	14 L. Ed. 2d 239
29 170 248 393 437 545	15 L. Ed. 2d 637
30 171 249 394 438 546	15 L. Ed. 2d 294
31 172 250 395 439 547	16 L. Ed. 2d 908
32 173 251 396 440 548	16 L. Ed. 2d 239
33 174 252 397 441 549	17 L. Ed. 2d 374
34 175 253 398 442 550	17 L. Ed. 2d 249
35 176 254 399 443 551	55 L. Ed. 2d 443
36 177 255 400 444 552	18 L. Ed. 2d 830
37 178 256 301 445 553	19 L. Ed. 2d 787
38 179 257 302 446 554	19 L. Ed. 2d 438
39 180 258 303 447 555	20 L. Ed. 2d 448
40 181 259 304 448 556	20 L. Ed. 2d 569
41 182 260 305 449 557	21 L. Ed. 2d 474
42 183 261 306 450 558	21 L. Ed. 2d 344
43 184 262 307 451 559	22 L. Ed. 2d 709
44 185 263 308 452 560	22 L. Ed. 2d 542
45 186 264 309 453 561	23 L. Ed. 2d 360
46 187 265 310 454 562	23 L. Ed. 2d 57
47 188 266 311 455 563	24 L. Ed. 2d 700
48 189 267 312 456 564	24 L. Ed. 2d 258
49 190 268 313 457 565	25 L. Ed. 2d 368
50 191 269 314 458 566	25 L. Ed. 2d 577
51 192 270 315 459 567	26 L. Ed. 2d 586
52 193 271 316 460 568	26 L. Ed. 2d 300
53 194 272 317 461 569	27 L. Ed. 2d 741
54 195 273 318 462 570	27 L. Ed. 2d 657
55 196 274 319 463 571	28 L. Ed. 2d 256
56 197 275 320 464 572	28 L. Ed. 2d 367
57 198 276 321 465 573	29 L. Ed. 2d 74
58 199 277 322 466 574	29 L. Ed. 2d 519
59 200 278 323 467 575	30 L. Ed. 2d 575
60 101 279 324 468 576	30 L. Ed. 2d 716
61 102 280 325 469 577	31 L. Ed. 2d 768
62 103 281 326 470 578	31 L. Ed. 2d 612
63 104 282 327 471 579	32 L. Ed. 2d 257
64 105 283 328 472 580	32 L. Ed. 2d 693
65 106 284 329 473 581	33 L. Ed. 2d 346
66 107 285 330 474 582	33 L. Ed. 2d 122
67 108 286 331 475 583	34 L. Ed. 2d 525
68 109 287 332 476 584 ·	34 L. Ed. 2d 422
69 110 288 333 477 585	35 L. Ed. 2d 223
70 111 289 334 478 586	35 L. Ed. 2d 297
71 112 290 335 479 587	61 L. Ed. 2d 541
72 113 291 336 480 588	36 L. Ed. 2d 656

PROBLEM #	CITATION
73 114 292 337 481 589	37 L. Ed. 2d 30
74 115 293 338 482 590	37 L. Ed. 2d 446
75 116 294 339 483 591	38 L. Ed. 2d 511
76 117 295 340 484 592	38 L. Ed. 2d 427
77 118 296 341 485 593	54 L. Ed. 2d 238
78 119 297 342 486 594	39 L. Ed. 2d 505
79 120 298 343 487 595	40 L. Ed. 2d 628
80 121 299 344 488 596	53 L. Ed. 2d 786
81 122 300 345 489 597	41 L. Ed. 2d 256
82 123 201 346 490 598	42 L. Ed. 2d 378
83 124 202 347 491 599	42 L. Ed. 2d 610
84 125 203 348 492 600	42 L. Ed. 2d 399
85 126 204 349 493 501	43 L. Ed. 2d 328
86 127 205 350 494 502	43 L. Ed. 2d 171
87 128 206 351 495 503	44 L. Ed. 2d 263
88 129 207 352 496 504	44 L. Ed. 2d 643
89 130 208 353 497 505	45 L. Ed. 2d 177
90 131 209 354 498 506	45 L. Ed. 2d 374
91 132 210 355 499 507	46 L. Ed. 2d 542
92 133 211 356 500 508	46 L. Ed. 2d 561
93 134 212 357 401 509	47 L. Ed. 2d 278
94 135 213 358 402 510	47 L. Ed. 2d 444
95 136 214 359 403 511	71 L. Ed. 2d 170
96 137 215 360 404 512	72 L. Ed. 2d 249
97 138 216 361 405 513	87 L. Ed. 2d 441
98 139 217 362 406 514	74 L. Ed. 2d 646
99 140 218 363 407 515	75 L. Ed. 2d 521
100 141 219 364 408 516	76 L. Ed. 2d 638

CITATION EXERCISE 16
U.S. SUPREME COURT DECISIONS (V)

A. INTRODUCTION

1. Star Paging

Star paging indicates the original paging in any reprinted or unofficial report. Stars, brackets, indented page numbers, or similar devices in the text of the opinion are used for this purpose. This star paging feature is especially useful because "pinpoint" citations are required when referring to specific discussion within cases (*i.e.*, the page where the opinion begins and the page(s) where the specific discussion occurs within the opinion). *Bluebook* Rule 3.3(a).

By using the star paging in the unofficial reporters for U.S. Supreme Court decisions (*Supreme Court Reporter* and *United States Supreme Court Reports, Lawyers' Edition*), one can cite to the official reporter, *United States Reports*, without actually consulting it. The following excerpt illustrates star paging in the *Lawyers' Edition*. Shown below is a portion of page 223 in Volume 59 of the *Lawyers' Edition*.

MONTANA v UNITED STATES
440 US 147, 59 L Ed 2d 210, 99 S Ct 970

(Second) of Judgments § 68.1, Reporter's Note, pp 43–44 (Tent Draft No. 4, Apr. 15, 1977); 1B Moore ¶ 0.448, p 4235; Scott, 56 Harv L Rev, at 10. This exception

[440 US 163]

is of particular importance in constitutional adjudication. Unreflective invocation of collateral estoppel against parties with an ongoing interest in constitutional issues could freeze doctrine in areas of the law where responsiveness to changing patterns of conduct or social mores is critical. To be sure, the scope of the Moser exception may be difficult to delineate, particularly where there is partial congruence in the subject matter of successive disputes. But the instant case poses no such conceptual difficulties. Rather, as the preceding discussion indicates, the legal "demands" of this litigation are closely aligned in time and sub-

claims." England v Medical Examiners, 375 US 411, 415, 11 L Ed 2d 440, 84 S Ct 461 (1964) (footnote omitted). As we held in England, abstention doctrine may not serve as a vehicle for depriving individuals of an otherwise cognizable right to have federal courts make factual determinations essential to the resolution of federal questions. Id., at 417, 11 L Ed 2d 440, 84 S Ct 461. See NAACP v Button, 371 US 415, 427, 9 L Ed 2d 405, 83 S Ct 328 (1963). However here, as in England, a party has "freely and without reservation submit[ted] his federal claims for decision by the state courts . . . and ha[d] them decided there . . . ." England v Medical Examiners, supra, at 419, 11 L Ed 2d 440, 84 S Ct 461.[10] Considerations of comity as well as repose militate against redetermination of issues in a federal

---

Star paging would thus allow you to quote from the opinion in the *Lawyers'* *Edition* and to give a pinpoint citation to *United States Reports*:

> **[Example 1]** The Court pointedly observed that "[u]nreflective invocation of collateral estoppel against parties with an ongoing interest in constitutional issues could freeze doctrine in areas of the law where responsiveness to changing patterns of conduct or social mores is critical." *Montana v. United States*, 440 U.S. 147, 163 (1979).

2. Citing Multiple Pages

When the quoted portion of the case extends over more than one page in *United States Reports*, use inclusive page numbers covering the quotation, separated by a hyphen; retain the last two digits and delete other repetitious digit(s) (*e.g.*, 748-49, **not** 748-749). *Bluebook* Rule 3.3(d). Consider the following example (again drawn from the portion of the page from the *Lawyers' Edition* above):

> **[Example 2]** The Court noted that "[t]his exception is of particular importance in constitutional adjudication." *Montana v. United States*, 440 U.S. 147, 162-63 (1979).

B. INSTRUCTIONS FOR COMPLETING THIS EXERCISE

This exercise gives you practice in using star paging to cite quoted material within a source. It also gives you practice in citing multiple pages. The volume of the *Lawyers' Edition* used to complete this exercise is the same one used to complete the immediately preceding exercise. To complete this exercise, find the page (or pages) listed below in the designated volume of *Lawyers' Edition of United States Reports*. Assume you have quoted the language given with your problem number below on that page.

For your answer to this exercise, state the following:

(a) the full case name as it is stated in the reporter at the beginning of the opinion (*e.g.*, Montana et al. v. United States); **you may omit obviously irrelevant portions of a party's name if the full name is a lengthy one**;

(b) the exact date of decision (*e.g.*, Feb. 22, 1979); and

(c) the citation of the case and the quotation in *Bluebook* (or another designated) form; **cite the case only to *United States Reports*** based on the star paging in the *Lawyers' Edition*. **Do not give parallel citations.** Assume that the case name is going to appear in a **citation sentence or clause**, not as a part of a grammatical part of a textual sentence, in a **legal memorandum**.

Unless otherwise instructed, write your answers on the answer sheet provided in Part 4 of these exercises.

PROBLEM #	CITATION	QUOTED MATERIAL

1 142 220 365 409 517   1 L. Ed. 2d 489   "In short, Congress in § 2 was referring to a group of unions already defined and constituted under the § 3 procedures."

2 143 221 366 410 518   1 L. Ed. 2d 742   "No special threat to appellees arises from the . . . assertion of Commission jurisdiction to regulate Allegheny."

3 144 222 367 411 519   2 L. Ed. 2d 477   "There the question, much mooted, was whether the federal policy conflicted with the state policy fixing the price of milk which the United States purchased."

4 145 223 368 412 520   2 L. Ed. 2d 1129   "[W]e find it unnecessary to decide whether the respondent was a transferee within the meaning of § 311 because we hold that the Kentucky statutes govern the question of the beneficiary's liability."

5 146 224 369 413 521   3 L. Ed. 2d 32   "[T]he taxpayers in this case have met those conditions and should be allowed the claimed deductions. The meaning of 'home' was expressly left undecided in *Flowers*."

6 147 225 370 414 522   3 L. Ed. 2d 670   "[I]t is quite clear, generally, that accrued salaries are property and rights to property subject to levy."

7 148 226 371 415 523   4 L. Ed. 2d 8   "The equipment then had to be moved for a similar operation on the second car."

8 149 227 372 416 524   4 L. Ed. 2d 725   "The State in which the respondent is incorporated prohibits unfair or deceptive practices in the insurance business there or 'in any other state.' "

9 150 228 373 417 525   5 L. Ed. 2d 4   "[T]he United States instituted proceedings to redeem the property pursuant to . . . 28 U.S.C. § 2410(c)."

10 151 229 374 418 526   5 L. Ed..2d 600-01   "Congress did not want patentees to be barred from prosecuting their claims for direct infringement."

11 152 230 375 419 527   6 L. Ed. 2d 53   "The highest court of Delaware has thus construed this legislative enactment as authorizing discriminatory classifications based exclusively on color."

12 153 231 376 420 528   6 L. Ed. 2d 1115   "To interpret its careful consideration of the problem otherwise is to accuse the Congress of engaging in sciamachy."

13 154 232 377 421 529   7 L. Ed. 2d 631   "[T]he Court issued a writ of mandamus ordering a district judge to issue a bench warrant which he had refused to do, in the purported exercise of his discretion, for a person under an indictment returned by a properly constituted grand jury."

14 155 233 378 422 530   7 L. Ed. 2d 329   "[T]he term 'reorganization' means 'the acquisition by one corporation, in exchange solely for all or a part of its voting stock, of at least 80[%] of the . . . stock of another corporation.' "

15 156 234 379 423 531   8 L. Ed. 2d 190   "The Court of Appeals for the Second Circuit affirmed the Tax Court's orders sustaining the Commissioner's deficiency determination."

16 157 235 380 424 532   8 L. Ed. 2d 740   "Petitioner voluntarily chose this attorney as his representative in the action, and he cannot now avoid the consequences of the acts or omissions of this freely selected agent."

17 158 236 381 425 533   9 L. Ed. 2d 567   "The charge in the indictment was in the exact language of the statute, and, in specifying the conduct covered by the charge, the indictment did nothing more than state the price the defendant was alleged to have collected."

18 159 237 382 426 534   9 L. Ed. 2d 640   "The Government's theories would force upon an accrual-basis taxpayer a cash basis for advance payments in disregard of the federal statute which explicitly authorizes income tax returns to be based upon sound accrual accounting methods."

PROBLEM #	CITATION	QUOTED MATERIAL
19 160 238 383 427 535	10 L. Ed. 2d 293	"Congress restricted the full deduction under § 23(k) to bad debts incurred in the taxpayer's trade or business and provided that 'nonbusiness' bad debts were to be deducted as short-term capital losses."
20 161 239 384 428 536	10 L. Ed. 2d 775	"[T]he state law creditor, asserting that the assignment under which he claimed was a mortgage within the predecessor to § 6323, insisted upon priority over the federal lien."
21 162 240 385 429 537	11 L. Ed. 2d 593	"Under the labor agreement, however, the 'upgraded' helper does not immediately acquire permanent seniority as a journeyman."
22 163 241 386 430 538	11 L. Ed. 2d 297	"The Courts of Appeals of two Circuits have applied the doctrine, despite state law, to the collection of federal tax liens."
23 164 242 387 431 539	12 L. Ed. 2d 694	"We hold that the constitutional privilege against self-incrimination protects a state witness against incrimination under federal as well as state law."
24 165 243 388 432 540	12 L. Ed. 2d 784	"This is the first case reaching this Court . . . that directly involves the validity under § 7 of the joint participation of two corporations in the creation of a third as a new domestic producing organization."
25 166 244 389 433 541	13 L. Ed. 2d 861	"No one would deny that an employer is free to shut down his enterprise temporarily for reasons of renovation or lack of profitable work unrelated to his collective bargaining situation."
26 167 245 390 434 542	13 L. Ed. 2d 915	"The Commission, on the other hand, submits that the misrepresentation of any fact so long as it materially induces a purchaser's decision to buy is a deception prohibited by § 5."
27 168 246 391 435 543	14 L. Ed. 2d 245	"[T]he more compelling inference is that Congress intended the inquiry into the project's effect on commerce to include, but not be limited to, effect on downstream navigability."
28 169 247 392 436 544	14 L. Ed. 2d 129	"The regulation thus indicates that the question to be asked is whether the mine operators have a significant investment in the coal in place."
29 170 248 393 437 545	15 L. Ed. 2d 298	"It established that the term 'connecting lines' extends beyond physical connection to encompass lines participating in a through route."
30 171 249 394 438 546	15 L. Ed. 2d 643	"Without reference to the statute, it must be noted that petitioners' presence in the library was unquestionably lawful. It was a public facility, open to the public."
31 172 250 395 439 547	16 L. Ed. 2d 243-44	The defendants moved to dismiss the indictment on the ground it did not charge an offense under the laws of the United States."
32 173 251 396 440 548	16 L. Ed. 2d 917	"The question is squarely presented therefore, whether the chemical analysis introduced in evidence in this case should have been excluded as the product of an unconstitutional search and seizure."
33 174 252 397 441 549	17 L. Ed. 2d 255	"This unreliability in turn undermines the security of the prime contractor's performance."
34 175 253 398 442 550	17 L. Ed. 2d 379	"He was also under a federal indictment for embezzling union funds."
35 176 254 399 443 551	55 L. Ed. 2d 237	"After a jury of 5 persons had been selected and sworn, petitioner moved that the court impanel a jury of 12 persons."
36 177 255 400 444 552	18 L. Ed. 2d 1050	"New York's statute lacks this particularization. It merely says that a warrant may issue on reasonable ground to believe that evidence of crime may be obtained by eavesdrop."
37 178 256 301 445 553	19 L. Ed. 2d 443	"In holding that this Florida law . . . conflicts with the Supremacy Clause of the Constitution we but follow the unbroken rule that has come down through the years."

PROBLEM #	CITATION	QUOTED MATERIAL
38 179 257 302 446 554	19 L. Ed. 2d 793	"Several bills were then introduced combining the grant of borrowing power with various provisions to prohibit territorial expansion, and one of these bills was eventually enacted as the TVA amendments of 1959."
39 180 258 303 447 555	20 L. Ed. 2d 584	"[C]ounsel's affidavit pointed to the following evidence as tending to show a participation by Cities in the alleged conspiracy to boycott his attempts to resell the Iranian oil to which he allegedly had access under his contract."
40 181 259 304 448 556	20 L. Ed. 2d 453	"[T]he Internal Revenue Service had ruled that shareholders who sold rights would realize ordinary income in the amount of the sales price."
41 182 260 305 449 557	21 L. Ed. 2d 352	"Since in all relevant aspects the transactions here were American, not Korean, we hold that they are not 'export trade' within the meaning of the Webb-Pomerene Act."
42 183 261 306 450 558	21 L. Ed. 2d 482	"If HUD's power is not so limited, the Authority argues, HUD would be free to impair its contractual obligations to the Authority through unilateral action."
43 184 262 307 451 559	22 L. Ed. 2d 550	"To some, this may be a noble purpose, but it is wholly inconsistent with the philosophy of the First Amendment."
44 185 263 308 452 560	22 L. Ed. 2d 715	"They generally provide a guide to action that the agency may be expected to take in future cases."
45 186 264 309 453 561	23 L. Ed. 2d 76	"The text and legislative history of the Marihuana Tax Act plainly disclose a similar congressional purpose."
46 187 265 310 454 562	23 L. Ed. 2d 363	"The state statute would have allowed recovery for additional elements of damage."
47 188 266 311 455 563	24 L. Ed. 2d 261	"The experts . . . testified that they had been doubtful that radiant heat would solve the problem of the cold joint."
48 189 267 312 456 564	24 L. Ed. 2d 727	"[T]he provisions of the charter of Northern Pacific Railroad Company which are urged to bar this merger were directed only to the operations of the federal corporation, not to the operation of the railroad."
49 190 268 313 457 565	25 L. Ed. 2d 583	"This is not such a borderline case."
50 191 269 314 458 566	25 L. Ed. 2d 376	"[C]ivil labels and good intentions do not themselves obviate the need for criminal due process safeguards in juvenile courts."
51 192 270 315 459 567	26 L. Ed. 2d 305	"The *Brantley* case presented a situation where a defendant's appeal from a conviction for a lesser included offense ultimately led to retrial and conviction on the greater offense."
52 193 271 316 460 568	26 L. Ed. 2d 590	"[T]he effect of the sentence imposed here required appellant to be confined for 101 days beyond the maximum period of confinement fixed by the statute."
53 194 272 317 461 569	27 L. Ed. 2d 663	"Nor may the State penalize petitioner solely because he personally, as the committee suggests, 'espouses illegal aims.' "
54 195 273 318 462 570	27 L. Ed. 2d 747	"The principle of prudent restraint we invoke today is nothing new."
55 196 274 319 463 571	28 L. Ed. 2d 376	"It is settled that courts should give great weight to any reasonable construction of a regulatory statute adopted by the agency charged with the enforcement of that statute."
56 197 275 320 464 572	28 L. Ed. 2d 262	"[I]t is a time-honored maxim of the Anglo-American common-law tradition that a court possessed of jurisdiction generally must exercise it."
57 198 276 321 465 573	29 L. Ed. 2d 527	"The payment was made during the taxable year."

PROBLEM #	CITATION	QUOTED MATERIAL

58 199 277 322 466 574   29 L. Ed. 2d 82   "[T]he Commission concluded that no standby charge should be imposed on either party to the interconnection."

59 200 278 323 467 575   30 L. Ed. 2d 719   "The court did not . . . consider the constitutionality of § 501(c)(3) 'as a whole.' "

60 101 279 324 468 576   30 L. Ed. 2d 580   " '[O]wnership of this quantity of stock suffices to provide access to inside information.' "

61 102 280 325 469 577   31 L. Ed. 2d 619   "Petitioner . . . asserted a claim against an additional party that had virtually no relationship to the claim or relief sought."

62 103 281 326 470 578   31 L. Ed. 2d 779   "Courts are powerless to prevent the social opprobrium suffered by these hapless children, but the Equal Protection Clause does enable us to strike down discriminatory laws relating to status of birth."

63 104 282 327 471 579   32 L. Ed. 2d 701   "[T]he cause is remanded to the Special Master for further proceedings."

64 105 283 328 472 580   32 L. Ed. 2d 264   "They also contend that the Michigan statute conflicts with or is preempted by federal law."

65 106 284 329 473 581   33 L. Ed. 2d 127   "The Board ordered the company to rescind its no-distribution rule."

66 107 285 330 474 582   33 L. Ed. 2d 353   "The words 'cruel and unusual' certainly include penalties that are barbaric."

67 108 286 331 475 583   34 L. Ed. 2d 429   "[T]he policy of § 7 would not be frustrated by a holding that an employee could . . . knowingly waive his § 7 right to resign from the union and to return to work without sanction."

68 109 287 332 476 584   34 L. Ed. 2d 535   "We declined to hold that Congress intended to oust completely the antitrust laws and supplant them with the self-regulatory scheme authorized by the Exchange Act."

69 110 288 333 477 585   35 L. Ed. 2d 305   "At trial, he endeavored to develop two grounds of defense."

70 111 289 334 478 586   35 L. Ed. 2d 240   "Charges are fixed that nonowning railroads must pay owning railroads for boxcars of the latter that are on the tracks of the former."

71 112 290 335 479 587   61 L. Ed. 2d 421   "The court concluded that the investigations and the speech were clearly within the ambit of the Clause."

72 113 291 336 480 588   36 L. Ed. 2d 573   " 'Congress did not, however, intend criminal penalties for people who failed to comply with a non-existent regulatory program.' "

73 114 292 337 481 589   37 L. Ed. 2d 453   "The two films in question, 'Magic Mirror' and 'It All Comes Out in the End,' depict sexual conduct characterized by the Georgia Supreme Court as 'hard core pornography' leaving 'little to the imagination.' "

74 115 293 338 482 590   37 L. Ed. 2d 41   "The judgment of the Court of Claims on this issue is reversed and the case is remanded for further proceedings."

75 116 294 339 483 591   38 L. Ed. 2d 432   "It was assumed by the Court of Appeals, and is conceded by the respondent here, that Jenks had probable cause to arrest respondent, and that he effected a full-custody arrest."

76 117 295 340 484 592   38 L. Ed. 2d 514   "From the outset, Congress has provided that suits between citizens of different States are maintainable in the district courts only if the 'matter in controversy' exceeds the statutory minimum, now set at $10,000."

77 118 296 341 485 593   54 L. Ed. 2d 264   "However, the House and Senate initially differed on the significance that should be given the convenience-of-the-employer doctrine for purposes of § 119."

78 119 297 342 486 594   39 L. Ed. 2d 585   "After hearing, the trial court declared the recoupment regulation contrary to the Social Security Act and HEW regulations and enjoined its implementation or enforcement."

PROBLEM #	CITATION	QUOTED MATERIAL

79 120 298 343 487 595   40 L. Ed. 2d 220   "We do not suggest that where there is doubt as to local law and where the certification procedure is available, resort to it is obligatory."

80 121 299 344 488 596   53 L. Ed. 2d 413   "Indeed, the one-year statute of limitations . . . could under some circumstances directly conflict with the timetable for administrative action expressly established in the 1972 Act."

81 122 300 345 489 597   41 L. Ed. 2d 543   "There is no disagreement as to the allocation of depreciation between construction and maintenance."

82 123 201 346 490 598   42 L. Ed. 2d 390   "Since passage of the Act, this Court's decisions have read Congress' power under the Commerce Clause more expansively, extending it beyond the flow of commerce to all activities having a substantial effect on interstate commerce."

83 124 202 347 491 599   42 L. Ed. 2d 405   "Petitioners therefore are able to state that the requirements . . . are satisfied."

84 125 203 348 492 600   42 L. Ed. 2d 615   "[A] basic 'up or out' philosophy was devel oped to maintain effective leadership by heightening competition for the higher ranks while providing junior officers with incentive and opportunity for promotion."

85 126 204 349 493 501   43 L. Ed. 2d 181   "A single employee confronted by an employer investigating whether certain conduct deserves discipline may be too fearful or inarticulate to relate accurately the incident being investigated, or too ignorant to raise extenuating factors."

86 127 205 350 494 502   43 L. Ed. 2d 349   "[E]ven the prevailing law of invasion of privacy generally recognizes that the interests in privacy fade when the information involved already appears on the public record."

87 128 206 351 495 503   44 L. Ed. 2d 649   "This phrase might also merely mean . . . that the time limit established by this provision . . . runs from the date of the last voluntary payment."

88 129 207 352 496 504   44 L. Ed. 2d 271   "Even failing those alternatives, a firm may be able to liquidate under supervision of one of the self-regulatory organizations, or the district court, without danger of loss to customers."

89 130 208 353 497 505   45 L. Ed. 2d 379   "Despite the conceded illegality of the search under the Almeida-Sanchez standard, the Government contends that the exclusionary rule should not be mechanically applied in the case now before us because the policies underlying the rule do not justify its retroactive application to pre-Almeida-Sanchez searches."

90 131 209 354 498 506   45 L. Ed. 2d 189   "The District Court, therefore, properly concluded that the acquisition and merger in this case were not within the coverage of § 7 of the Clayton Act."

91 132 210 355 499 507   46 L. Ed. 2d 567   "This mistreatment was said to have been directed against minority citizens in particular and against all Philadelphia residents in general."

92 133 211 356 500 508   46 L. Ed. 2d 550   "Neither the propriety of the removal nor the jurisdiction of the court was questioned by respondent in the slightest."

93 134 212 357 401 509   47 L. Ed. 2d 456   "Embodied in the words 'cases' and 'controversies' are two complementary but somewhat different limitations."

94 135 213 358 402 510   47 L. Ed. 2d 291   "Here the Government seized respondent's property and contends that it has absolutely no obligation to prove that the seizure has any basis in fact no matter how severe or irreparable the injury."

95 136 214 359 403 511   71 L. Ed. 2d 415   "[T]he court [of appeals] correctly noted that the certificate of deposit is not expressly excluded from the definition since it is not currency and it has a maturity exceeding nine months."

Problem #	**Citation**	**Quoted Material**

96 137 215 360 404 512   72 L. Ed. 2d 801   "These arguments do not apply with the same force to classifications imposing disabilities on the minor children of such illegal entrants."

97 138 216 361 405 513   87 L. Ed. 2d 8   "By the time the Federal Rules of Civil Procedure were adopted in 1938, federal statutes had authorized and defined awards of costs to prevailing parties for more than 85 years."

98 139 217 362 406 514   74 L. Ed. 2d 304   "Given the broad powers of states under the Twenty-first Amendment, judicial deference to the legislative exercise of zoning powers by a city council or other legislative zoning body is especially appropriate in the area of liquor regulation."

99 140 218 363 407 515   75 L. Ed. 2d 153   "As long as the payment itself was not negated by a refund to the corporation, the change in character of the funds in the hands of the State does not require the corporation to recognize income."

100 141 219 364 408 516   76 L. Ed. 2d 537   "The State never, however, raised or addressed the question whether the federal exclusionary rule should be modified in any respect, and none of the opinions of the Illinois courts give any indication that the question was considered."

CITATION EXERCISE 17
U.S. COURT OF APPEALS DECISIONS AND OTHER SPECIALIZED FEDERAL APPELLATE COURTS

A. INTRODUCTION

1. West's *Federal Reporter*

West's *Federal Reporter* is the principal current reporter for federal court appellate opinions (other than U.S. Supreme Court opinions). These include opinions from the U.S. Courts of Appeals (previously the Circuit Courts of Appeals) and the Court of Appeals for the District of Columbia. It also reports opinions issued by the various specialized federal appellate courts (*e.g.*, U.S. Court of Appeals for the Federal Circuit, the Temporary Emergency Court of Appeals, etc.). The first series of the *Federal Reporter* (F.) ended with volume 300. It has been followed by a second series (*Federal Reporter Second*) (F.2d), which ended with volume 999, and now a third series (*Federal Reporter Third*) (F.3d). This latter reporter was used in conjunction with Citation Exercise 10.

2. Court References in *Bluebook* Citations

The abbreviation for the U.S. Courts of Appeal is "Cir." *Bluebook* Table T.7. The numbered circuits are cited as "1st Cir.," "2d Cir.," "3d Cir.," "4th Cir.," etc. The U.S. Court of Appeals for the District of Columbia Circuit (and its predecessors) is always cited as "D.C. Cir." The U.S. Court of Appeals for the Federal Circuit is always cited as "Fed. Cir." *Bluebook* Rule 10.4(a). For abbreviations of other specialized federal appellate courts (and preferred reporters), consult *Bluebook* Table T.1. The following are some typical citations to these courts:

> **[Example 1]** *Fort Hood Barbers Ass'n v. Herman*, 137 F.3d 302 (5th Cir. 1998).
> **[Example 2]** *Alamo v. Clay*, 137 F.3d 1366 (D.C. Cir. 1998).
> **[Example 3]** *Exxon Chem. Patents, Inc. v. Lubrizol Corp.*, 137 F.3d 1475 (Fed. Cir. 1998).

B. INSTRUCTIONS FOR COMPLETING THIS EXERCISE

This exercise gives you practice in citing federal appellate court opinions. To complete this exercise, find the case that begins on the page listed with your problem number below in the designated volume of the *Federal Reporter Second*. For your answer to this exercise, state the following:

(a) the full case name as it is stated in the reporter at the beginning of the opinion (*e.g.*, Robert L. Butler, Petitioner-Appellant, v. John C. Burke, Warden, Wisconsin State Prison); **you may omit obviously irrelevant portions of a party's name if the full name is a lengthy one;**

(b) the complete reference to the court exactly as it is indicated at the beginning of the opinion (*e.g.*, United States Court of Appeals, Seventh Circuit);

(c) the exact date of decision (*e.g.*, April 15, 1966); and

(d) the citation of that case in *Bluebook* (or another designated) form. Assume that the case name is going to appear in a **citation sentence or clause**, not as a part of a grammatical part of a textual sentence, in a **legal memorandum**. For purposes of this exercise, do not indicate any subsequent history in the citation.

Unless otherwise instructed, write your answers on the answer sheet provided in Part 4 of these exercises.

PROBLEM #	CITATION
1 150 235 311 460 525	816 F.2d 583
2 151 236 312 461 526	421 F.2d 602
3 152 237 313 462 527	151 F.2d 392
4 153 238 314 463 528	205 F.2d 13
5 154 239 315 464 529	176 F.2d 498
6 155 240 316 465 530	304 F.2d 623
7 156 241 317 466 531	261 F.2d 631
8 157 242 318 467 532	322 F.2d 397
9 158 243 319 468 533	81 F.2d 198
10 159 244 320 469 534	149 F.2d 770
11 160 245 321 470 535	164 F.2d 481
12 161 246 322 471 536	110 F.2d 566
13 162 247 323 472 537	416 F.2d 949
14 163 248 324 473 538	208 F.2d 457
15 164 249 325 474 539	118 F.2d 7
16 165 250 326 475 540	275 F.2d 166
17 166 251 327 476 541	427 F.2d 131
18 167 252 328 477 542	241 F.2d 661
19 168 253 329 478 543	170 F.2d 606
20 169 254 330 479 544	421 F.2d 1065
21 170 255 331 480 545	402 F.2d 62
22 171 256 332 481 546	379 F.2d 329
23 172 257 333 482 547	347 F.2d 96
24 173 258 334 483 548	361 F.2d 903
25 174 259 335 484 549	222 F.2d 508
26 175 260 336 485 550	336 F.2d 425
27 176 261 337 486 551	333 F.2d 363
28 177 262 338 487 552	106 F.2d 598
29 178 263 339 488 553	91 F.2d 12
30 179 264 340 489 554	374 F.2d 550
31 180 265 341 490 555	403 F.2d 687

PROBLEM #	CITATION
32 181 266 342 491 556	119 F.2d 204
33 182 267 343 492 557	427 F.2d 1322
34 183 268 344 493 558	584 F.2d 48
35 184 269 345 494 559	174 F.2d 89
36 185 270 346 495 560	236 F.2d 412
37 186 271 347 496 561	61 F.2d 889
38 187 272 348 497 562	375 F.2d 889
39 188 273 349 498 563	413 F.2d 256
40 189 274 350 499 564	396 F.2d 438
41 190 275 351 500 565	282 F.2d 913
42 191 276 352 401 566	235 F.2d 860
43 192 277 353 402 567	19 F.2d 357
44 193 278 354 403 568	202 F.2d 180
45 194 279 355 404 569	181 F.2d 100
46 195 280 356 405 570	268 F.2d 391
47 196 281 357 406 571	346 F.2d 82
48 197 282 358 407 572	199 F.2d 460
49 198 283 359 408 573	112 F.2d 119
50 199 284 360 409 574	355 F.2d 849
51 200 285 361 410 575	290 F.2d 666
52 101 286 362 411 576	817 F.2d 674
53 102 287 363 412 577	132 F.2d 790
54 103 288 364 413 578	295 F.2d 698
55 104 289 365 414 579	159 F.2d 330
56 105 290 366 415 580	180 F.2d 220
57 106 291 367 416 581	426 F.2d 1388
58 107 292 368 417 582	317 F.2d 47
59 108 293 369 418 583	351 F.2d 905
60 109 294 370 419 584	341 F.2d 908
61 110 295 371 420 585	340 F.2d 227
62 111 296 372 421 586	261 F.2d 952
63 112 297 373 422 587	384 F.2d 886
64 113 298 374 423 588	257 F.2d 22
65 114 299 375 424 589	175 F.2d 626
66 115 300 376 425 590	115 F.2d 873
67 116 201 377 426 591	406 F.2d 1035
68 117 202 378 427 592	261 F.2d 233
69 118 203 379 428 593	245 F.2d 317
70 119 204 380 429 594	168 F.2d 305
71 120 205 381 430 595	171 F.2d 696
72 121 206 382 431 596	219 F.2d 271
73 122 207 383 432 597	225 F.2d 235
74 123 208 384 433 598	200 F.2d 614
75 124 209 385 434 599	198 F.2d 550
76 125 210 386 435 600	342 F.2d 754
77 126 211 387 436 501	375 F.2d 742
78 127 212 388 437 502	818 F.2d 1148
79 128 213 389 438 503	88 F.2d 177
80 129 214 390 439 504	377 F.2d 864
81 130 215 391 440 505	143 F.2d 907

PROBLEM #	**CITATION**
82 131 216 392 441 506	122 F.2d 852
83 132 217 393 442 507	152 F.2d 422
84 133 218 394 443 508	186 F.2d 297
85 134 219 395 444 509	107 F.2d 26
86 135 220 396 445 510	423 F.2d 32
87 136 221 397 446 511	123 F.2d 962
88 137 222 398 447 512	287 F.2d 687
89 138 223 399 448 513	242 F.2d 828
90 139 224 400 449 514	247 F.2d 604
91 140 225 301 450 515	627 F.2d 1032
92 141 226 302 451 516	411 F.2d 565
93 142 227 303 452 517	221 F.2d 264
94 143 228 304 453 518	13 F.2d 588
95 144 229 305 454 519	255 F.2d 246
96 145 230 306 455 520	355 F.2d 485
97 146 231 307 456 521	102 F.2d 703
98 147 232 308 457 522	266 F.2d 52
99 148 233 309 458 523	255 F.2d 118
100 149 234 310 459 524	625 F.2d 1291

CITATION EXERCISE 18
FEDERAL TRIAL COURT
DECISIONS (I)

A. INTRODUCTION

1. West's *Federal Supplement*

The principal trial courts in the federal system are the U.S. District Courts. Selected decisions from those courts are published in West's *Federal Supplement* (F. Supp. and F. Supp. 2d), which began in 1932. Between 1880 and 1932, selected U.S. District Court decisions appeared in the *Federal Reporter* (see Citation Exercise 17). Reporting of earlier federal trial court decisions is discussed in Citation Exercise 21.

The following chart summarizes the basic pattern of reporting lower federal trial court opinions:

Federal Cases 1789-1879— Reprints U.S. Circuit and District Court opinions	*Federal Reporter* 1879 to date— Includes U.S. District Court opinions until 1932	*Federal Supplement* 1932 to date— Reports selected U.S. District Court opinions	Specialized reporters such as *Federal Rules Decisions* publish selected U.S. District Court opinions

2. Court References in *Bluebook* Citations

When U.S. District Court decisions are cited, the district (but not the division within the district) and the state should be indicated parenthetically in addition to the date. *Bluebook* Rule 10.4(a) & Table T.1. The appropriate abbreviation for the state, if any, is listed in *Bluebook* Table T.10 ("Geographic Terms: United States states, cities, and territories"). *See supra* Citation Exercise 9.

In states having only one district, the district is indicated by "D." (*e.g.*, D. Neb. for the District of Nebraska). When the state has more than one district, the district must be specifically indicated (*e.g.*, W.D.N.Y. for the Western District of New York). Adjacent capitals should be closed up (W.D.N.Y.), but single capitals should not be closed up with longer abbreviations (D. Neb.). The same is true for reporter abbreviations (*e.g.*, F. Supp.). Individual numbers consisting of both numerals and ordinals (*e.g.*, 3d) are treated as single capitals (F.3d). *Bluebook* Rule 6.1(a).

The following are some examples of typical citations of U.S. District Court decisions in West's *Federal Supplement*:

[Example 1] *Violissi v. City of Middletown*, 990 F. Supp. 93 (D. Conn. 1998).

[Example 2] *Nelson v. G.C. Murphy Co.*, 245 F. Supp. 846 (N.D. Ala. 1965).

[Example 3] *Romey v. Vanyur*, 9 F. Supp. 2d 565 (E.D.N.C. 1998).

B. INSTRUCTIONS FOR COMPLETING THIS EXERCISE

This exercise is designed to familiarize you with West's *Federal Supplement* and to give you practice in citing federal district court opinions appearing in that reporter. Find the opinion that begins on the page of the designated volume of the *Federal Supplement* (1st series) listed with your problem number below.

For your answer to this exercise, state the following:

(a) the full case name as it is stated in the reporter at the beginning of the opinion (*e.g.*, A. Shepard Titcomb, Plaintiff, v. Norton Company, Defendant); **you may omit obviously irrelevant portions of a party's name if the full name is a lengthy one**;

(b) the complete reference to the court exactly as it is indicated at the beginning of the opinion (*e.g.*, United States District Court, D. Connecticut);

(c) the exact date of decision (*e.g.*, Oct. 9, 1959); and

(d) the citation of that case in *Bluebook* (or another designated) form. Assume that the case name is going to appear in a **citation sentence or clause**, not as a part of a grammatical part of a textual sentence, in a **legal memorandum**. For purposes of this exercise, do not indicate any subsequent history in the citation.

Unless otherwise instructed, write your answers on the answer sheet provided in Part 4 of these exercises.

PROBLEM #	CITATION
1 177 262 385 498 509	480 F. Supp. 947
2 178 263 386 499 510	481 F. Supp. 651
3 179 264 387 500 511	482 F. Supp. 406
4 180 265 388 401 512	483 F. Supp. 883
5 181 266 389 402 513	476 F. Supp. 1101
6 182 267 390 403 514	478 F. Supp. 5
7 183 268 391 404 515	477 F. Supp. 1051
8 184 269 392 405 516	493 F. Supp. 1304
9 185 270 393 406 517	494 F. Supp. 151
10 186 271 394 407 518	490 F. Supp. 788
11 187 272 395 408 519	491 F. Supp. 222

PROBLEM #	CITATION
12 188 273 396 409 520	492 F. Supp. 1211
13 189 274 397 410 521	475 F. Supp. 1103
14 190 275 398 411 522	474 F. Supp. 1141
15 191 276 399 412 523	473 F. Supp. 675
16 192 277 400 413 524	479 F. Supp. 863
17 193 278 301 414 525	484 F. Supp. 101
18 194 279 302 415 526	486 F. Supp. 550
19 195 280 303 416 527	487 F. Supp. 52
20 196 281 304 417 528	488 F. Supp. 267
21 197 282 305 418 529	489 F. Supp. 678
22 198 283 306 419 530	501 F. Supp. 124
23 199 284 307 420 531	502 F. Supp. 600
24 200 285 308 421 532	503 F. Supp. 1
25 101 286 309 422 533	504 F. Supp. 78
26 102 287 310 423 534	495 F. Supp. 399
27 103 288 311 424 535	496 F. Supp. 462
28 104 289 312 425 536	497 F. Supp. 604
29 105 290 313 426 537	498 F. Supp. 389
30 106 291 314 427 538	499 F. Supp. 749
31 107 292 315 428 539	543 F. Supp. 686
32 108 293 316 429 540	544 F. Supp. 68
33 109 294 317 430 541	525 F. Supp. 867
34 110 295 318 431 542	526 F. Supp. 851
35 111 296 319 432 543	527 F. Supp. 426
36 112 297 320 433 544	528 F. Supp. 646
37 113 298 321 434 545	529 F. Supp. 1
38 114 299 322 435 546	520 F. Supp. 1059
39 115 300 323 436 547	521 F. Supp. 753
40 116 201 324 437 548	522 F. Supp. 604
41 117 202 325 438 549	523 F. Supp. 625
42 118 203 326 439 550	524 F. Supp. 427
43 119 204 327 440 551	530 F. Supp. 274
44 120 205 328 441 552	534 F. Supp. 791
45 121 206 329 442 553	531 F. Supp. 784
46 122 207 330 443 554	532 F. Supp. 639
47 123 208 331 444 555	533 F. Supp. 233
48 124 209 332 445 556	551 F. Supp. 53
49 125 210 333 446 557	552 F. Supp. 589
50 126 211 334 447 558	553 F. Supp. 845
51 127 212 335 448 559	554 F. Supp. 831
52 128 213 336 449 560	555 F. Supp. 1273
53 129 214 337 450 561	565 F. Supp. 44
54 130 215 338 451 562	564 F. Supp. 780
55 131 216 339 452 563	563 F. Supp. 836
56 132 217 340 453 564	562 F. Supp. 443
57 133 218 341 454 565	561 F. Supp. 83
58 134 219 342 455 566	515 F. Supp. 613
59 135 220 343 456 567	516 F. Supp. 961
60 136 221 344 457 568	517 F. Supp. 787
61 137 222 345 458 569	518 F. Supp. 687

PROBLEM #	CITATION
62 138 223 346 459 570	519 F. Supp. 1059
63 139 224 347 460 571	505 F. Supp. 172
64 140 225 348 461 572	506 F. Supp. 473
65 141 226 349 462 573	507 F. Supp. 566
66 142 227 350 463 574	508 F. Supp. 1044
67 143 228 351 464 575	509 F. Supp. 1111
68 144 229 352 465 576	510 F. Supp. 1039
69 145 230 353 466 577	511 F. Supp. 670
70 146 231 354 467 578	512 F. Supp. 293
71 147 232 355 468 579	513 F. Supp. 691
72 148 233 356 469 580	514 F. Supp. 712
73 149 234 357 470 581	500 F. Supp. 935
74 150 235 358 471 582	568 F. Supp. 860
75 151 236 359 472 583	567 F. Supp. 1087
76 152 237 360 473 584	566 F. Supp. 1452
77 153 238 361 474 585	535 F. Supp. 673
78 154 239 362 475 586	536 F. Supp. 356
79 155 240 363 476 587	537 F. Supp. 983
80 156 241 364 477 588	538 F. Supp. 523
81 157 242 365 478 589	539 F. Supp. 621
82 158 243 366 479 590	546 F. Supp. 324
83 159 244 367 480 591	547 F. Supp. 348
84 160 245 368 481 592	548 F. Supp. 75
85 161 246 369 482 593	549 F. Supp. 494
86 162 247 370 483 594	550 F. Supp. 81
87 163 248 371 484 595	556 F. Supp. 108
88 164 249 372 485 596	557 F. Supp. 74
89 165 250 373 486 597	558 F. Supp. 188
90 166 251 374 487 598	559 F. Supp. 229
91 167 252 375 488 599	560 F. Supp. 110
92 168 253 376 489 600	570 F. Supp. 654
93 169 254 377 490 501	569 F. Supp. 256
94 170 255 378 491 502	540 F. Supp. 1243
95 171 256 379 492 503	541 F. Supp. 534
96 172 257 380 493 504	542 F. Supp. 725
97 173 258 381 494 505	451 F. Supp. 73
98 174 259 382 495 506	452 F. Supp. 622
99 175 260 383 496 507	453 F. Supp. 272
100 176 261 384 497 508	454 F. Supp. 505

CITATION EXERCISE 19
FEDERAL TRIAL COURT
DECISIONS (II)

A. INTRODUCTION

1. Tables of Cases

Sometimes you will know that a case has been reported in a particular volume, but you will not know the exact page on which it begins. An editorial feature common to reporters is a "Table of Cases Reported." This table is an alphabetical listing of the cases contained in the volume. In reporters in West's National Reporter System, this table is located at the front of the volume.

2. Other Editorial Features in West's Reporters

Other editorial features in reporters that are part of West's National Reporter System include synopses (case summaries), headnotes (abstracts of each point of law in the case), and topics and key numbers (which provide links to other cases dealing with the same points of law).

B. INSTRUCTIONS FOR COMPLETING THIS EXERCISE

This exercise is designed to give you practice citing federal district court opinions appearing in the *Federal Supplement*. Find the volume of the *Federal Supplement* listed with your problem number below. Use the "Table of Cases Reported" to find the case listed with your problem number. For your answer to this exercise, state the following:

(a) the full case name as it is stated in the reporter at the beginning of the opinion (*e.g.*, A. Shepard Titcomb, Plaintiff, v. Norton Company, Defendant); **you may omit obviously irrelevant portions of a party's name if the full name is a lengthy one**;

(b) the complete reference to the court exactly as it is indicated at the beginning of the opinion (*e.g.*, United States District Court, D. Connecticut);

(c) the exact date of decision (*e.g.*, Oct. 9, 1959); and

(d) the citation of that case in *Bluebook* (or another designated) form. Assume that the case name is going to appear in a **citation sentence or clause**, not as a part of a grammatical part of a textual sentence, in a **legal memorandum**. For purposes of this exercise, do not indicate any subsequent history in the citation.

Unless otherwise instructed, write your answers on the answer sheet provided in Part 4 of these exercises.

PROBLEM #	F. SUPP. VOL.	CASE NAME
1 177 262 385 498 509	480 F. Supp.	Medley v. United States
2 178 263 386 499 510	481 F. Supp.	Goldwater v. Carter
3 179 264 387 500 511	482 F. Supp.	Hluchan v. Fauver
4 180 265 388 401 512	483 F. Supp.	Troyer v. Town of Babylon
5 181 266 389 402 513	476 F. Supp.	Troyer v. Karcagi
6 182 267 390 403 514	478 F. Supp.	Zaccagnini v. Morris
7 183 268 391 404 515	477 F. Supp.	Taylor v. Perini
8 184 269 392 405 516	493 F. Supp.	United States v. Reminga
9 185 270 393 406 517	494 F. Supp.	United States v. Noe
10 186 271 394 407 518	490 F. Supp.	United States v. Ochs
11 187 272 395 408 519	491 F. Supp.	United States v. State of South Dakota
12 188 273 396 409 520	492 F. Supp.	Draisma v. United States
13 189 274 397 410 521	475 F. Supp.	Cockrum v. Califano
14 190 275 398 411 522	474 F. Supp.	Loney v. Scurr
15 191 276 399 412 523	473 F. Supp.	Lavash v. Kountze
16 192 277 400 413 524	479 F. Supp.	Groover v. West Coast Shipping
17 193 278 301 414 525	484 F. Supp.	Schenck v. Bear, Stearns & Co.
18 194 279 302 415 526	486 F. Supp.	Tunnell v. Robinson
19 195 280 303 416 527	487 F. Supp.	Johnson v. Bell
20 196 281 304 417 528	488 F. Supp.	Melton v. United States
21 197 282 305 418 529	489 F. Supp.	Laurido v. Simon
22 198 283 306 419 530	501 F. Supp.	Landesman v. City of New York
23 199 284 307 420 531	502 F. Supp.	United States v. Upton
24 200 285 308 421 532	503 F. Supp.	LeBoeuf v. Ramsey
25 101 286 309 422 533	504 F. Supp.	Nelson v. Smith
26 102 287 310 423 534	495 F. Supp.	Ambrosio v. Price
27 103 288 311 424 535	496 F. Supp.	Langley v. Monumental Corp.
28 104 289 312 425 536	497 F. Supp.	Young v. Klutznick
29 105 290 313 426 537	498 F. Supp.	United States v. Place
30 106 291 314 427 538	499 F. Supp.	Begay v. Kerr-McGee Corp.
31 107 292 315 428 539	543 F. Supp.	Feller v. United States
32 108 293 316 429 540	544 F. Supp.	United States v. Sullivan
33 109 294 317 430 541	525 F. Supp.	United States v. Hinckley
34 110 295 318 431 542	526 F. Supp.	Gantlin v. Westvaco Corp.
35 111 296 319 432 543	527 F. Supp.	Medtronic, Inc. v. Gibbons
36 112 297 320 433 544	528 F. Supp.	United States v. Collins
37 113 298 321 434 545	529 F. Supp.	Berry v. Mintzes
38 114 299 322 435 546	520 F. Supp.	United States v. Finazzo
39 115 300 323 436 547	521 F. Supp.	Parker v. Rockefeller
40 116 201 324 437 548	522 F. Supp.	Fleming v. Abrams
41 117 202 325 438 549	523 F. Supp.	Davis v. Edgemere Finance
42 118 203 326 439 550	524 F. Supp.	Onnen v. United States
43 119 204 327 440 551	530 F. Supp.	Cassesse v. People of the State of New York
44 120 205 328 441 552	534 F. Supp.	Neale v. Dillon
45 121 206 329 442 553	531 F. Supp.	United States ex rel. Herring v. Fenton
46 122 207 330 443 554	532 F. Supp.	Emil J. Lauter Co. v. Brunswick Corp.
47 123 208 331 444 555	533 F. Supp.	Buckhanon v. Percy
48 124 209 332 445 556	551 F. Supp.	Mercantile Financial Corp. v. UPA Productions
49 125 210 333 446 557	552 F. Supp.	Kelly v. Stratton
50 126 211 334 447 558	553 F. Supp.	Keele v. Oxford Shipping Co.

PROBLEM #	F. SUPP. VOL.	CASE NAME
51 127 212 335 448 559	554 F. Supp.	Martin Ice Cream Co. v. Chipwich, Inc.
52 128 213 336 449 560	555 F. Supp.	Thompson v. Schweiker
53 129 214 337 450 561	565 F. Supp.	United States v. Wilson
54 130 215 338 451 562	564 F. Supp.	Hamilton v. United States
55 131 216 339 452 563	563 F. Supp.	Johnson v. Scully
56 132 217 340 453 564	562 F. Supp.	Guerrero v. Reeves Brothers
57 133 218 341 454 565	561 F. Supp.	Martin v. Foti
58 134 219 342 455 566	515 F. Supp.	Schmid v. Frosch
59 135 220 343 456 567	516 F. Supp.	Best v. Boswell
60 136 221 344 457 568	517 F. Supp.	Overstreet v. United States
61 137 222 345 458 569	518 F. Supp.	United States v. Demjanjuk
62 138 223 346 459 570	519 F. Supp.	GAF Corp. v. Eastman Kodak
63 139 224 347 460 571	505 F. Supp.	United States v. Bethea
64 140 225 348 461 572	506 F. Supp.	Davis v. Hubbard
65 141 226 349 462 573	507 F. Supp.	Piepenburg v. Cutler
66 142 227 350 463 574	508 F. Supp.	Wentworth v. Kawasaki, Inc.
67 143 228 351 464 575	509 F. Supp.	Honneus v. United States
68 144 229 352 465 576	510 F. Supp.	Zilker v. Klein
69 145 230 353 466 577	511 F. Supp.	Gallimore v. Harris
70 146 231 354 467 578	512 F. Supp.	Estes v. Harris
71 147 232 355 468 579	513 F. Supp.	Deavors v. Burnham
72 148 233 356 469 580	514 F. Supp.	Shoults v. Fields
73 149 234 357 470 581	500 F. Supp.	United States v. Mierzwicki
74 150 235 358 471 582	568 F. Supp.	Jacoby v. Schuman
75 151 236 359 472 583	567 F. Supp.	Beall v. United States
76 152 237 360 473 584	566 F. Supp.	Pizzeria Uno Corp. v. Temple
77 153 238 361 474 585	535 F. Supp.	United States v. Baylin
78 154 239 362 475 586	536 F. Supp.	Hallman v. Pennsylvania Life Insurance Co.
79 155 240 363 476 587	537 F. Supp.	Giorgi v. Doody
80 156 241 364 477 588	538 F. Supp.	Silver v. Woolf
81 157 242 365 478 589	539 F. Supp.	Kaufman v. Magid
82 158 243 366 479 590	546 F. Supp.	Georges v. Carney
83 159 244 367 480 591	547 F. Supp.	Gilday v. Quinn
84 160 245 368 481 592	548 F. Supp.	Santiago v. Schweiker
85 161 246 369 482 593	549 F. Supp.	United States v. Outboard Marine
86 162 247 370 483 594	550 F. Supp.	United States v. Richmond
87 163 248 371 484 595	556 F. Supp.	Turner v. Israel
88 164 249 372 485 596	557 F. Supp.	United States v. Gregg
89 165 250 373 486 597	558 F. Supp.	Association for Reduction of Violence v. Hall
90 166 251 374 487 598	559 F. Supp.	Downey v. Vernitron Corp.
91 167 252 375 488 599	560 F. Supp.	United States v. Crooksville Coal Co.
92 168 253 376 489 600	570 F. Supp.	Pennwalt Corp. v. Akzona Inc.
93 169 254 377 490 501	569 F. Supp.	Trujillo v. Heckler
94 170 255 378 491 502	540 F. Supp.	Ocasio v. Schweiker
95 171 256 379 492 503	541 F. Supp.	Medina v. United States
96 172 257 380 493 504	542 F. Supp.	Young v. United States
97 173 258 381 494 505	451 F. Supp.	Feeney v. Commonwealth of Massachusetts
98 174 259 382 495 506	452 F. Supp.	United States v. Augspurger
99 175 260 383 496 507	453 F. Supp.	Louis Marx & Co. v. Buddy L Corp.
100 176 261 384 497 508	454 F. Supp.	Smith v. Cooper

FEDERAL TRIAL COURT DECISIONS (III)

A. INTRODUCTION

1. West's *Federal Rules Decisions*

West's *Federal Rules Decisions* reports selected federal district court opinions that are not designated for publication in the *Federal Supplement*. These opinions either involve the Federal Rules of Civil Procedure (since 1939) or the Federal Rules of Criminal Procedure (since 1946). The following are typical *Bluebook* citations to cases in West's *Federal Rules Decisions*:

> **[Example 1]** *United States v. Skeddle*, 176 F.R.D. 263 (N.D. Ohio 1997).
> **[Example 2]** *Kelly v. United Airlines, Inc.*, 176 F.R.D. 422 (D. Mass. 1997).

See Bluebook Table T.1.

2. Special Note on West's *Bankruptcy Reporter, Federal Claims Reporter*, and Other Specialized Reporters

West has several other specialized reporters, including West's *Bankruptcy Reporter* and West's *Federal Claims Reporter*. Its *Bankruptcy Reporter* began in 1980. It reports cases from the U.S. Bankruptcy Courts as well as cases from the U.S. District Courts dealing with bankruptcy matters that are no longer reported in the *Federal Supplement*. The *Bankruptcy Reporter* also reprints bankruptcy cases appearing in West's *Federal Reporter* (*Second* and *Third*) and West's *Supreme Court Reporter* (retaining the original page numbering in those reporters). *See Bluebook* Table T.1.

West's *Federal Claims Reporter* is a continuation of the *United States Claims Court Reporter*, which began in 1983 as a reporter of cases from the U.S. Court of Claims. When the name of the U.S. Court of Claims was changed to the U.S. Court of Federal Claims in 1992, West renamed the *United States Claims Court Reporter* as the *Federal Claims Reporter* (beginning with Volume 27). Like the *Bankruptcy Reporter*, West's *Federal Claims Reporter* reprints cases arising in the U.S. Court of Federal Claims that have been reviewed in cases appearing in West's *Federal Reporter* (*Second* and *Third*) and West's *Supreme Court Reporter* (retaining the original page numbering in those reporters). *See Bluebook* Table T.1.

Another specialized federal court is the United States Court of International Trade, created in 1980. It succeeded the United States Customs Court. *See Bluebook* Table T.1.

B. INSTRUCTIONS FOR COMPLETING THIS EXERCISE

This exercise familiarizes you with West's *Federal Rules Decisions* and gives you practice citing federal district court cases in that reporter. Find the volume of the *Federal Rules Decisions* listed with your problem number below.

For your answer to this exercise, state the following:

(a) the full case name as it is stated in the reporter at the beginning of the opinion (*e.g.*, A. Shepard Titcomb, Plaintiff, v. Norton Company, Defendant); **you may omit obviously irrelevant portions of a party's name if the full name is a lengthy one;**

(b) the complete reference to the court exactly as it is indicated at the beginning of the opinion (*e.g.*, United States District Court, D. Connecticut);

(c) the exact date of decision (*e.g.*, Oct. 9, 1959); and

(d) the citation of that case in *Bluebook* (or another designated) form. Assume that the case name is going to appear in a **citation sentence or clause**, not as a part of a grammatical part of a textual sentence, in a **legal memorandum**. For purposes of this exercise, do not indicate any subsequent history in the citation.

Unless otherwise instructed, write your answers on the answer sheet provided in Part 4 of these exercises.

PROBLEM #	CITATION
1 112 225 304 488 519	1 F.R.D. 679
2 113 226 305 489 520	115 F.R.D. 233
3 114 227 306 490 521	2 F.R.D. 405
4 115 228 307 491 522	80 F.R.D. 449
5 116 229 308 492 523	81 F.R.D. 490
6 117 230 309 493 524	114 F.R.D. 69
7 118 231 310 494 525	5 F.R.D. 126
8 119 232 311 495 526	6 F.R.D. 340
9 120 233 312 496 527	7 F.R.D. 239
10 121 234 313 497 528	113 F.R.D. 121
11 122 235 314 498 529	9 F.R.D. 590
12 123 236 315 499 530	10 F.R.D. 381
13 124 237 316 500 531	105 F.R.D. 83
14 125 238 317 401 532	112 F.R.D. 342
15 126 239 318 402 533	12 F.R.D. 346
16 127 240 319 403 534	13 F.R.D. 96
17 128 241 320 404 535	14 F.R.D. 351
18 129 242 321 405 536	111 F.R.D. 56
19 130 243 322 406 537	16 F.R.D. 472
20 131 244 323 407 538	107 F.R.D. 215
21 132 245 324 408 539	17 F.R.D. 277
22 133 246 325 409 540	18 F.R.D. 347
23 134 247 326 410 541	19 F.R.D. 115
24 135 248 327 411 542	110 F.R.D. 414
25 136 249 328 412 543	21 F.R.D. 372
26 137 250 329 413 544	22 F.R.D. 238

PROBLEM #	CITATION
27 138 251 330 414 545	23 F.R.D. 281
28 139 252 331 415 546	24 F.R.D. 205
29 140 253 332 416 547	79 F.R.D. 98
30 141 254 333 417 548	26 F.R.D. 113
31 142 255 334 418 549	109 F.R.D. 81
32 143 256 335 419 550	27 F.R.D. 243
33 144 257 336 420 551	28 F.R.D. 368
34 145 258 337 421 552	29 F.R.D. 138
35 146 259 338 422 553	82 F.R.D. 122
36 147 260 339 423 554	31 F.R.D. 256
37 148 261 340 424 555	32 F.R.D. 365
38 149 262 341 425 556	32 F.R.D. 335
39 150 263 342 426 557	108 F.R.D. 403
40 151 264 343 427 558	106 F.R.D. 255
41 152 265 344 428 559	102 F.R.D. 466
42 153 266 345 429 560	37 F.R.D. 51
43 154 267 346 430 561	38 F.R.D. 482
44 155 268 347 431 562	39 F.R.D. 309
45 156 269 348 432 563	4 F.R.D. 257
46 157 270 349 433 564	181 F.R.D. 582
47 158 271 350 434 565	42 F.R.D. 398
48 159 272 351 435 566	8 F.R.D. 226
49 160 273 352 436 567	11 F.R.D. 367
50 161 274 353 437 568	15 F.R.D. 194
51 162 275 354 438 569	45 F.R.D. 375
52 163 276 355 439 570	46 F.R.D. 465
53 164 277 356 440 571	47 F.R.D. 278
54 165 278 357 441 572	48 F.R.D. 404
55 166 279 358 442 573	83 F.R.D. 556
56 167 280 359 443 574	49 F.R.D. 271
57 168 281 360 444 575	20 F.R.D. 223
58 169 282 361 445 576	51 F.R.D. 512
59 170 283 362 446 577	52 F.R.D. 139
60 171 284 363 447 578	33 F.R.D. 11
61 172 285 364 448 579	84 F.R.D. 46
62 173 286 365 449 580	85 F.R.D. 597
63 174 287 366 450 581	54 F.R.D. 524
64 175 288 367 451 582	55 F.R.D. 475
65 176 289 368 452 583	35 F.R.D. 227
66 177 290 369 453 584	56 F.R.D. 21
67 178 291 370 454 585	57 F.R.D. 503
68 179 292 371 455 586	36 F.R.D. 18
69 180 293 372 456 587	40 F.R.D. 27
70 181 294 373 457 588	91 F.R.D. 267
71 182 295 374 458 589	59 F.R.D. 577
72 183 296 375 459 590	92 F.R.D. 375
73 184 297 376 460 591	60 F.R.D. 671
74 185 298 377 461 592	88 F.R.D. 351
75 186 299 378 462 593	94 F.R.D. 584
76 187 300 379 463 594	61 F.R.D. 427

PROBLEM #	CITATION
77 188 201 380 464 595	62 F.R.D. 480
78 189 202 381 465 596	98 F.R.D. 569
79 190 203 382 466 597	100 F.R.D. 255
80 191 204 383 467 598	86 F.R.D. 324
81 192 205 384 468 599	99 F.R.D. 279
82 193 206 385 469 600	101 F.R.D. 405
83 194 207 386 470 501	64 F.R.D. 690
84 195 208 387 471 502	65 F.R.D. 375
85 196 209 388 472 503	75 F.R.D. 511
86 197 210 389 473 504	63 F.R.D. 374
87 198 211 390 474 505	66 F.R.D. 105
88 199 212 391 475 506	97 F.R.D. 427
89 200 213 392 476 507	78 F.R.D. 190
90 101 214 393 477 508	79 F.R.D. 671
91 102 215 394 478 509	69 F.R.D. 69
92 103 216 395 479 510	104 F.R.D. 42
93 104 217 396 480 511	103 F.R.D. 421
94 105 218 397 481 512	68 F.R.D. 583
95 106 219 398 482 513	96 F.R.D. 227
96 107 220 399 483 514	72 F.R.D. 564
97 108 221 400 484 515	95 F.R.D. 332
98 109 222 301 485 516	71 F.R.D. 652
99 110 223 302 486 517	93 F.R.D. 512
100 111 224 303 487 518	77 F.R.D. 430

CITATION EXERCISE 21
FEDERAL TRIAL COURT
DECISIONS (IV)

A. INTRODUCTION

1. Early Federal Trial Court Decisions

Prior to 1891, original jurisdiction of the lower federal courts was divided between federal district courts and federal circuit courts. The circuit courts also had a limited appellate jurisdiction over certain district court cases. West's *Federal Cases* makes available in thirty volumes over 18,000 federal district and circuit court opinions that had been previously published in over 230 different nominative reporters. The cases are arranged alphabetically (except for 91 cases added to the last volume). West has assigned an arbitrary number to each case. West's *Federal Cases* connects with West's *Federal Reporter*, which began publishing lower federal court opinions in January, 1880 (see chart at the beginning of Citation Exercise 18).

2. Special *Bluebook* Rule for Cases in West's *Federal Cases*

In citing cases in West's *Federal Cases* in *Bluebook* form, the Federal Case Number must be indicated at the end of the citation in a separate parenthetical:

[Example 1] *The Aslesund*, 1 F. Cas. 1 (E.D.N.Y. 1877) (No. 1).
[Example 2] *M'Grath v. Candalero*, 16 F. Cas. 128 (D.S.C. 1794) (No. 8180).
[Example 3] *Wilson v. Rousseau*, 30 F. Cas. 162 (C.C.N.D.N.Y. 1845) (No. 17,832).

See Bluebook Rule 10.4(a) & Table T.1.

B. INSTRUCTIONS FOR COMPLETING THIS EXERCISE

This exercise is designed to familiarize you with federal trial court opinions reprinted in West's *Federal Cases* and to give you practice citing them in *Bluebook* form. To complete this exercise, find the case listed with your problem number in West's *Federal Cases*. **Note carefully the Federal Case Number because sometimes two or more cases with the same name have been published.** For your answer to this exercise, state the following:

(a) the full case name as it is stated in the reporter at the beginning of the opinion (*e.g.*, Backus v. The Marengo); **you may omit obviously irrelevant portions of a party's name if the full name is a lengthy one**;

(b) the complete reference to the court exactly as it is indicated at the beginning of the opinion (*e.g.*, United States District Court, D. Connecticut or Circuit Court, E.D. Wisconsin);

(c) the exact date of decision (*e.g.*, July 11, 1849, May 1878, or June Term, 1857); and

(d) the citation of that case in *Bluebook* (or another designated) form. Assume that the case name is going to appear in a **citation sentence or clause**, not as a part of a grammatical part of a textual sentence, in a **legal memorandum**. For purposes of this exercise, do not indicate any subsequent history in the citation.

Unless otherwise instructed, write your answers on the answer sheet provided in Part 4 of these exercises.

PROBLEM #	CASE	FEDERAL CASE NO.
1 161 300 310 420 530	Abbe	6
2 162 201 311 421 531	Acker	26
3 163 202 312 422 532	Ada	38
4 164 203 313 423 533	Babbitt	695
5 165 204 314 424 534	Backus	713
6 166 205 315 425 535	Bates	1102
7 167 206 316 426 536	Bishop	1439
8 168 207 317 427 537	B.J. Willard	1454
9 169 208 318 428 538	Berry	1358a
10 170 209 319 429 539	Brown	2026
11 171 210 320 430 540	Brown	2033
12 172 211 321 431 541	Burke	2157
13 173 212 322 432 542	Clover	2908
14 174 213 323 433 543	Cayuga	2537
15 175 214 324 434 544	Chacon	2568
16 176 215 325 435 545	Cooke	3170
17 177 216 326 436 546	Cooke	3181
18 178 217 327 437 547	Corcoran	3227
19 179 218 328 438 548	Delhi	3770
20 180 219 329 439 549	Delight	3772
21 181 220 330 440 550	Delta	3778
22 182 221 331 441 551	Evans	4571
23 183 222 332 442 552	Fagan	4605
24 184 223 333 443 553	Fairchild	4610
25 185 224 334 444 554	Flower	4891
26 186 225 335 445 555	Focke	4894
27 187 226 336 446 556	Fowler	4997
28 188 227 337 447 557	Geib	5297
29 189 228 338 448 558	Gay	5281
30 190 229 339 449 559	Georgetown	5342
31 191 230 340 450 560	Hall	5919
32 192 231 341 451 561	Green	5761

PROBLEM #	CASE	FEDERAL CASE NO.
33 193 232 342 452 562	Greene	5765
34 194 233 343 453 563	Henry	6384
35 195 234 344 454 564	Hill	6498
36 196 235 345 455 565	Hinds	6516
37 197 236 346 456 566	Jewett	7307
38 198 237 347 457 567	Janeway	7208
39 199 238 348 458 568	Johnson	7416
40 200 239 349 459 569	Kennedy	7708
41 101 240 350 460 570	Keys	7747
42 102 241 351 461 571	Kingston	7822
43 103 242 352 462 572	Laski	8098
44 104 243 353 463 573	Kohlsaat	7918
45 105 244 354 464 574	Lowerre	8577
46 106 245 355 465 575	Maud Webster	9302
47 107 246 356 466 576	Marsh	9120
48 108 247 357 467 577	Marsh	9117
49 109 248 358 468 578	Napoleon	10,011
50 110 249 359 469 579	Narragansett	10,020
51 111 250 360 470 580	Neidlinger	10,086
52 112 251 361 471 581	Parker	10,733
53 113 252 362 472 582	Osprey	10,606
54 114 253 363 473 583	Odorless Rubber Co.	10,438
55 115 254 364 474 584	Phelps	11,073
56 116 255 365 475 585	Philips	11,092
57 117 256 366 476 586	Plastic Slate-Roofing	11,209
58 118 257 367 477 587	Pusey	11,477
59 119 258 368 478 588	Richmond	11,796
60 120 259 369 479 589	Ready Roofing	11,613
61 121 260 370 480 590	Siler Moon	12,856
62 122 261 371 481 591	Stansfield	13,294
63 123 262 372 482 592	Smythe	13,134
64 124 263 373 483 593	Taylor	13,803
65 125 264 374 484 594	Swearinger	13,683
66 126 265 375 485 595	Thorp	14,003
67 127 266 376 486 596	Tong Duck Chung	14,093
68 128 267 377 487 597	Trigg	14,173
69 129 268 378 488 598	Towanda	14,109
70 130 269 379 489 599	U.S. (v. Faw)	15,077
71 131 270 380 490 600	U.S. (v. Fossat)	15,137
72 132 271 381 491 501	U.S. (v. Gadsby)	15,180
73 133 272 382 492 502	U.S. (v. Keen)	15,511
74 134 273 383 493 503	U.S. (v. Hare)	15,304
75 135 274 384 494 504	U.S. (v. Horn)	15,389
76 136 275 385 495 505	U.S. (v. Queen)	16,109
77 137 276 386 496 506	U.S. (v. Reagan)	16,128
78 138 277 387 497 507	U.S. (v. Ringgold)	16,167
79 139 278 388 498 508	U.S. (v. Thompkins)	16,483
80 140 279 389 499 509	U.S. (v. Two Horses)	16,578
81 141 280 390 500 510	U.S. (v. Whiskey)	16,671
82 142 281 391 401 511	Warner	17,180

PROBLEM #	CASE	FEDERAL CASE NO.
83 143 282 392 402 512	Wall	17,093
84 144 283 393 403 513	Watson	17,286
85 145 284 394 404 514	Winans	17,861
86 146 285 395 405 515	Works	18,046
87 147 286 396 406 516	Winthrop	17,900
88 148 288 397 407 517	Einstein	4320
89 149 288 398 408 518	Hattie	6216
90 150 289 399 409 519	Lowe	8565
91 151 290 400 410 520	Parker	10,751
92 152 291 301 411 521	Russell	12,165
93 153 292 302 412 522	Tallman	13,739
94 154 293 303 413 523	U.S. (v. The Good Friends)	15,227
95 155 294 304 414 524	U.S. (v. Stott)	16,408
96 156 295 305 415 525	Whitcomb	17,529
97 157 296 306 416 526	Whipple	17,513
98 158 297 307 417 527	Zenobia	18,209
99 159 298 308 418 528	Thompson	13,938
100 160 299 309 419 529	Steam Stone Cutter	13,334

CITATION EXERCISE 22
STATE COURT DECISIONS (I)

A. INTRODUCTION

1. Structure of State Court Systems

The structure of the fifty state court systems is similar to the federal system described in the preceding exercises. There will always be various trial courts and an appellate court of highest authority. In many jurisdictions, there will be an intermediate court of appeals. The names of the courts and their authority varies substantially from state to state. However, the most common name for the highest court of a state is the supreme court.

2. Reporting State Court Cases

The reporting of state court decisions emphasizes appellate court opinions that review alleged errors committed by lower state courts. Decisions of the highest appellate court of each state are reported. In addition, some states have reporter series covering decisions of their intermediate appellate courts as well as those of their trial courts.

The two principal sources for state court opinions are (1) official reporters (for example, *Maine Reports*) and (2) West's unofficial regional reporters (for example, *Atlantic Reporter*). West's regional reporters divide the fifty states into seven geographic regions that are part of West's "National Reporter System." Beginning in 1879, West Publishing Co. began to unofficially report opinions. This reporting soon was expanded to cover all court systems in the United States and is now known as West's "National Reporter System." This system has the advantage of common editorial features and of publishing opinions much more rapidly than official reporters.

Although use of unofficial reporters is widespread, the official reporter is technically the authoritative text. Some states, however, have ceased publishing their official reports; thus, unofficial reporters are the only published sources for judicial opinions in those states. Today, most reporters are designated by: (1) the court (e.g., *California Appellate Reports*); (2) the geographic jurisdiction (e.g., *Nebraska Reports*); or (3) the geographic region (e.g., *Pacific Reporter*). Up to the late nineteenth century, however, reporters ordinarily were designated by the last name of the individual who prepared the volume. These "nominative" reports for the most part have been incorporated into the court-named or jurisdiction-named reporter series. In spite of their subsequent inclusion in these series, however, the nominative reports nonetheless must be referenced in certain case citations (using *Bluebook* form).

3. *Bluebook* Table T.1

Bluebook Table T.1 ("United States Jurisdictions") is an excellent resource in understanding the structures of the state court systems. It also provides information about the available reporters for each state. You should be aware that in-state citation conventions and abbreviations may differ from those listed in Table T.1

B. INSTRUCTIONS FOR COMPLETING THIS EXERCISE

To complete this exercise, you will need to consult *Bluebook* Table T.1. For your answer to this exercise, state the following:

(a) the name of the highest court in the jurisdiction listed with your problem number in (a) below (*e.g.*, Supreme Court);

(b) the name and the *Bluebook* abbreviation of the modern jurisdiction-named reports for the highest court in the jurisdiction listed with your problem number in (b) below and the date, if any, those reports ceased to be published (*e.g.*, Alabama Reports, Ala., ceased 1976; Arizona Reports, Ariz., to date; Iowa Reports, Iowa (no abbreviation), ceased 1968; etc.);

(c) the name and *Bluebook* abbreviation of the West regional reporter covering the jurisdiction listed with your problem number in (c) below (*e.g.*, Southern Reporter, So., So. 2d;); and

(d) the name and the *Bluebook* abbreviation, if any, of the **earliest nominative reporter** of the highest court for the jurisdiction listed with your problem number in (d) below (*e.g.*, Coleman's Cases, Cole. Cas.; Harrington, 1 Del. (1 Harr.); Kirby, not abbreviated, etc.).

Unless otherwise instructed, write your answers on the answer sheet provided in Part 4 of these exercises.

PROBLEM #	**JURISDICTIONS**
1 146 230 308 427 529	(a) Maine (b) Alabama (c) Wisconsin (d) Connecticut
2 147 231 309 428 530	(a) Maryland (b) Colorado (c) Virginia (d) Alabama
3 148 232 310 429 531	(a) Massachusetts (b) Delaware (c) Washington (d) Illinois
4 149 233 311 430 532	(a) New York (b) Florida (c) Vermont (d) Indiana
5 150 234 312 431 533	(a) West Virginia (b) Indiana (c) South Carolina (d) Iowa
6 151 235 313 432 534	(a) Maine (b) Iowa (c) Pennsylvania (d) Kentucky
7 152 236 314 433 535	(a) Maryland (b) Kentucky (c) Oregon (d) Massachusetts
8 153 237 315 434 536	(a) Massachusetts (b) Louisiana (c) Ohio (d) Maryland
9 154 238 316 435 537	(a) New York (b) Maine (c) North Carolina (d) Mississippi
10 155 239 317 436 538	(a) West Virginia (b) Minnesota (c) New Mexico (d) North Carolina
11 156 240 318 437 539	(a) Maine (b) Mississippi (c) New Jersey (d) Pennsylvania
12 157 241 319 438 540	(a) Maryland (b) Missouri (c) New Hampshire (d) Tennessee
13 158 242 320 439 541	(a) Massachusetts (b) North Dakota (c) Nevada (d) Virginia
14 159 243 321 440 542	(a) New York (b) Oklahoma (c) Nebraska (d) Wisconsin
15 160 244 322 441 543	(a) West Virginia (b) Rhode Island (c) Montana (d) Alabama
16 161 245 323 442 544	(a) Maine (b) South Dakota (c) Michigan (d) Connecticut
17 162 246 324 443 545	(a) Maryland (b) Tennessee (c) Kentucky (d) Illinois

PROBLEM #	JURISDICTIONS
18 163 247 325 444 546	(a) Massachusetts (b) Texas (c) Kansas (d) Indiana
19 164 248 326 445 547	(a) New York (b) Utah (c) Illinois (d) Iowa
20 165 249 327 446 548	(a) West Virginia (b) Wyoming (c) Idaho (d) Kentucky
21 166 250 328 447 549	(a) Maine (b) Alabama (c) Hawaii (d) Maryland
22 167 251 329 448 550	(a) Maryland (b) Colorado (c) Georgia (d) Massachusetts
23 168 252 330 449 551	(a) Massachusetts (b) Delaware (c) Connecticut (d) Illinois
24 169 253 331 450 552	(a) New York (b) Florida (c) Arkansas (d) Indiana
25 170 254 332 451 553	(a) West Virginia (b) Indiana (c) Arizona (d) Iowa
26 171 255 333 452 554	(a) Maine (b) Iowa (c) Wisconsin (d) Kentucky
27 172 256 334 453 555	(a) Maryland (b) Kentucky (c) Virginia (d) Massachusetts
28 173 257 335 454 556	(a) Massachusetts (b) Louisiana (c) Washington (d) Mississippi
29 174 258 336 455 557	(a) New York (b) Maine (c) Vermont (d) North Carolina
30 175 259 337 456 558	(a) West Virginia (b) Minnesota (c) South Carolina (d) Virginia
31 176 260 338 457 559	(a) Maine (b) Mississippi (c) Pennsylvania (d) Wisconsin
32 177 261 339 458 560	(a) Maryland (b) Missouri (c) Oregon (d) Alabama
33 178 262 340 459 561	(a) Massachusetts (b) North Dakota (c) Ohio (d) Connecticut
34 179 263 341 460 562	(a) New York (b) Oklahoma (c) North Carolina (d) Illinois
35 180 264 342 461 563	(a) West Virginia (b) Rhode Island (c) New Mexico (d) Indiana
36 181 265 343 462 564	(a) Maine (b) South Dakota (c) New Jersey (d) Iowa
37 182 266 344 463 565	(a) Maryland (b) Tennessee (c) New Hampshire (d) Kentucky
38 183 267 345 464 566	(a) Massachusetts (b) Texas (c) Nevada (d) Maryland
39 184 268 346 465 567	(a) New York (b) Utah (c) Nebraska (d) Massachusetts
40 185 269 347 466 568	(a) West Virginia (b) Wyoming (c) Montana (d) Mississippi
41 186 270 348 467 569	(a) Maine (b) Alabama (c) Michigan (d) North Carolina
42 187 271 349 468 570	(a) Maryland (b) Colorado (c) Kentucky (d) Pennsylvania
43 188 272 350 469 571	(a) Massachusetts (b) Delaware (c) Kansas (d) Tennessee
44 189 273 351 470 572	(a) New York (b) Florida (c) Illinois (d) Virginia
45 190 274 352 471 573	(a) West Virginia (b) Indiana (c) Idaho (d) Wisconsin
46 191 275 353 472 574	(a) Maine (b) Iowa (c) Hawaii (d) Alabama
47 192 276 354 473 575	(a) Maryland (b) Kentucky (c) Georgia (d) Connecticut
48 193 277 355 474 576	(a) Massachusetts (b) Louisiana (c) Connecticut (d) Illinois
49 194 278 356 475 577	(a) New York (b) Maine (c) Arkansas (d) Indiana
50 195 279 357 476 578	(a) West Virginia (b) Minnesota (c) Arizona (d) Iowa
51 196 280 358 477 579	(a) Maine (b) Mississippi (c) Wisconsin (d) Kentucky
52 197 281 359 478 580	(a) Maryland (b) Missouri (c) Virginia (d) Massachusetts
53 198 282 360 479 581	(a) Massachusetts (b) North Dakota (c) Washington (d) Kentucky
54 199 283 361 480 582	(a) New York (b) Oklahoma (c) Vermont (d) Mississippi
55 200 284 362 481 583	(a) West Virginia (b) Rhode Island (c) South Carolina (d) Virginia
56 101 285 363 482 584	(a) Maine (b) South Dakota (c) Pennsylvania (d) North Carolina
57 102 286 364 483 585	(a) Maryland (b) Tennessee (c) Oregon (d) Pennsylvania
58 103 287 365 484 586	(a) New York (b) Texas (c) Ohio (d) Wisconsin
59 104 288 366 485 587	(a) West Virginia (b) Utah (c) North Carolina (d) Alabama
60 105 289 367 486 588	(a) Maine (b) Wyoming (c) New Mexico (d) Connecticut
61 106 290 368 487 589	(a) Maryland (b) Alabama (c) New Jersey (d) Illinois
62 107 291 369 488 590	(a) New York (b) Colorado (c) New Hampshire (d) Indiana
63 108 292 370 489 591	(a) West Virginia (b) Delaware (c) Nevada (d) Iowa
64 109 293 371 490 592	(a) Maine (b) Florida (c) Nebraska (d) Kentucky
65 110 294 372 491 593	(a) Maryland (b) Indiana (c) Montana (d) Massachusetts
66 111 295 373 492 594	(a) New York (b) Iowa (c) Michigan (d) Maryland
67 112 296 374 493 595	(a) West Virginia (b) Kentucky (c) Kansas (d) Mississippi

PROBLEM #	JURISDICTIONS
68 113 297 375 494 596	(a) Maine (b) Louisiana (c) Kentucky (d) North Carolina
69 114 298 376 495 597	(a) Maryland (b) Maine (c) Illinois (d) Pennsylvania
70 115 299 377 496 598	(a) New York (b) Minnesota (c) Idaho (d) Tennessee
71 116 300 378 497 599	(a) West Virginia (b) Mississippi (c) Hawaii (d) Virginia
72 117 201 379 498 600	(a) Maine (b) Missouri (c) Georgia (d) Wisconsin
73 118 202 380 499 501	(a) Maryland (b) North Dakota (c) Connecticut (d) Alabama
74 119 203 381 500 502	(a) Massachusetts (b) Oklahoma (c) Arkansas (d) Connecticut
75 120 204 382 401 503	(a) New York (b) Rhode Island (c) Arizona (d) Illinois
76 121 205 383 402 504	(a) West Virginia (b) South Dakota (c) Wisconsin (d) Indiana
77 122 206 384 403 505	(a) Maine (b) Tennessee (c) Virginia (d) Iowa
78 123 207 385 404 506	(a) Maryland (b) Texas (c) Washington (d) Kentucky
79 124 208 386 405 507	(a) Massachusetts (b) Utah (c) Vermont (d) Maryland
80 125 209 387 406 508	(a) New York (b) Wyoming (c) South Carolina (d) Massachusetts
81 126 210 388 407 509	(a) West Virginia (b) Alabama (c) Pennsylvania (d) Mississippi
82 127 211 389 408 510	(a) Maine (b) Colorado (c) Oregon (d) North Carolina
83 128 212 390 409 511	(a) Maryland (b) Delaware (c) Ohio (d) Pennsylvania
84 129 213 391 410 512	(a) Massachusetts (b) Indiana (c)North Carolina (d) Tennessee
85 130 214 392 411 513	(a) New York (b) Iowa (c) New Mexico (d) Virginia
86 131 215 393 412 514	(a) West Virginia (b) Kentucky (c) New Jersey (d) Wisconsin
87 132 216 394 413 515	(a) Maine (b) Louisiana (c) New Hampshire (d) Alabama
88 133 217 395 414 516	(a) Maryland (b) Maine (c) Nevada (d) Connecticut
89 134 218 396 415 517	(a) Massachusetts (b) Minnesota (c) Nebraska (d) Illinois
90 135 219 397 416 518	(a) New York (b) Mississippi (c) Montana (d) Indiana
91 136 220 398 417 519	(a) West Virginia (b) Missouri (c) Michigan (d) Iowa
92 137 221 399 418 520	(a) Maine (b) North Dakota (c) Kentucky (d) Kentucky
93 138 222 400 419 521	(a) Maryland (b) Oklahoma (c) Kansas (d) Massachusetts
94 139 223 301 420 522	(a) Massachusetts (b) Rhode Island (c) Illinois (d) Maryland
95 140 224 302 421 523	(a) New York (b) South Dakota (c) Idaho (d) Mississippi
96 141 225 303 422 524	(a) West Virginia (b) Tennessee (c) Hawaii (d) North Carolina
97 142 226 304 423 525	(a) Maine (b) Texas (c) Georgia (d) Pennsylvania
98 143 227 305 424 526	(a) Maryland (b) Utah (c) Connecticut (d) Tennessee
99 144 228 306 425 527	(a) Massachusetts (b) Wyoming (c) Arkansas (d) Virginia
100 145 229 307 426 528	(a) New York (b) Colorado (c) Arizona (d) Wisconsin

CITATION EXERCISE 23
STATE COURT DECISIONS (II)

A. INTRODUCTION

1. West Regional Reporters

In 1879, West Publishing Co. began reporting state court decisions in its *North Western Reporter*. By 1887, the entire nation was covered by seven regional reporters. In the jurisdictions in which the state has ceased publishing its official reporter, West's regional reporters are the source for state court opinions. *See supra* Citation Exercise 22.

2. Official Reporters and Parallel Citations

As described in Citation Exercise 12, official reporters are technically the authoritative text for court opinions. The traditional rule has been that when state court decisions appear in both an official reporter and unofficial West reporter(s), a reference to both the official and preferred unofficial reporter(s) (known as "parallel citations") had to be included in the citation of the case.

Beginning with the fifteenth edition of the *Bluebook*, the parallel citation of state court reporters is required in only one situation. In documents submitted to a state court, all citations to cases decided by the courts of that state (but not other states) must include a citation to the official state reporter, if available, and West reporters. In all other situations, only the relevant regional reporter should be cited (assuming the case is reported therein). *See Bluebook* Rule 10.3.1 & Practitioners' Note P.3. Consider the following examples:

> **[Example 1]** *Hincks Coal Co. v. Milan*, 134 Me. 208, 183 A. 756 (1936).
>> The above citation illustrates the proper *Bluebook* form for citation of this case in documents submitted to Maine state courts.
>
> **[Example 2]** *Hincks Coal Co. v. Milan*, 183 A. 756 (Me. 1936).
>> The above citation illustrates the proper *Bluebook* form for all other situations.

Recall from Citation Exercise 12 that **the abbreviated name of the court, including its geographic jurisdiction**, should be included in the parenthetical with the date. You can determine the abbreviation of the geographic jurisdiction and the court (if any) by consulting the appropriate entry in *Bluebook* Table T.1. This information appears immediately after the name of the court (*e.g.*, **Supreme Judicial**

Court (Me.)). However, when the highest court of a jurisdiction is cited, the abbreviated name of the court may be omitted; thus, it is omitted from the *Bluebook* entry above. Furthermore, when the abbreviated name of the reporter (*e.g.*, Me.) unambiguously indicates the geographic jurisdiction, the geographic jurisdiction may also be omitted (*see* Example 1 above). Note that the geographic jurisdiction must be included in the parenthetical in Example 2 because the citation to the *Atlantic Reporter* does not clearly indicate the jurisdiction (the *Atlantic Reporter* covers several jurisdictions).

3. Finding Parallel Citations

(a) When the Unofficial Reporter Citation Is Known

Several different methods can be used to find parallel citations for state court decisions. As discussed in Citation Exercise 13, one function performed by *Shepard's Citations* is to provide parallel citations for cases. To use *Shepard's Citations* to find parallel citations, you will need to locate the appropriate *Shepard's Citations* volume covering the unofficial reporter in the library collection. These *Shepard's* sets will usually have several bound volumes and paper-covered supplements. You will then need to find the appropriate entry in the **first** *Shepard's Citations* volume covering the decision.

The volume numbers are shown at the top of the page and the beginning page number of each case is shown in bold print in the columns. Under the entry for the case, the parallel citations are given in parentheses. Remember that parallel citations are given **only once** in the first *Shepard's* entry for the case; they are **not** repeated in subsequent supplementary volumes or pamphlets. If you find an entry for your case, but no parallel citations are given, you are probably using a subsequent supplementary volume. Check again for the correct volume.

One function of the Table of Cases volumes accompanying digests is to provide parallel citations for the cases listed in the table. Digests are used by finding the appropriate digest covering the jurisdiction and simply looking up the case name in the Table of Cases. *See supra* Citation Exercise 13.

(b) When the Official Reporter Citation Is Known

When the official reporter citation is known and you want to find the parallel West reporter citation, you can use the *National Reporter Blue Book.* The *National Reporter Blue Book* consists of a series of volumes that provide the parallel citations from the official reporter to the West Report. The approximate years of coverage are Vol. 1, years to 1928; Vol. 2, 1929 to 1936; Vol. 3, 1937 to 1948; Vol. 4, 1949 to 1960; Vol. 5, 1961 to 1970; Vol. 6, 1971 to 1980; Vol. 7, 1981 to 1990, and Cumulative Paper-Covered Supplements, 1991 to date. After selecting the appropriate volume, you simply use the tables provided.

Another means of finding the unofficial reporter citation of a case when its official citation is known is to use the appropriate *state* edition of *Shepard's Citations* (*e.g.*, *Shepard's Wisconsin Citations*). The West citation is given in parentheses immediately after the page number. If the name of the case is known, the unofficial citation can also be found by consulting the "Table of Cases" in the appropriate West regional (*e.g.*, *North Western Digest*) or state digest (*e.g.*, *Massachusetts Digest*). *See supra* subsection (a) and Citation Exercise 13.

B. INSTRUCTIONS FOR COMPLETING THIS EXERCISE

This exercise gives you practice in citing cases in West's regional reporters. For your answer to this exercise, state the following:

(a) the full name of the case as it is stated in the reporter at the beginning of the opinion (*e.g.*, Kenneth Lee Benoit, Appellant, v. Commonwealth of Kentucky, Appellee); **you may omit obviously irrelevant portions of a party's name if the full name is a lengthy one**;

(b) the full designation of the court as it is stated in the reporter at the beginning of the opinion (*e.g.*, Court of Appeals of Kentucky);

(c) the exact date of decision (*e.g.*, May 6, 1966); and

(d) the citation of that case in *Bluebook* (or another designated) form. Assume that the case name is going to appear in a **citation sentence or clause**, not as a part of a grammatical part of a textual sentence, in a **legal memorandum**. For purposes of this exercise, do not indicate any subsequent history in the citation. **Also assume that you are citing the case in a document that WILL be submitted to a state court in the jurisdiction from which the case arises.**

Unless otherwise instructed, write your answers on the answer sheet provided in Part 4 of these exercises.

PROBLEM #	CITATION
1 121 241 331 421 521	11 S.E.2d 631
2 122 242 332 422 522	10 S.E.2d 506
3 123 243 333 423 523	7 S.E.2d 394
4 124 244 334 424 524	99 A.2d 860
5 125 245 335 425 525	146 S.E.2d 257
6 126 246 336 426 526	148 S.E.2d 149
7 127 247 337 427 527	188 S.W.2d 564
8 128 248 338 428 528	100 A.2d 630
9 129 249 339 429 529	190 S.W.2d 450
10 130 250 340 430 530	252 S.W.2d 809
11 131 251 341 431 531	255 S.W.2d 970
12 132 252 342 432 532	250 S.W.2d 549
13 133 253 343 433 533	168 N.W.2d 710
14 134 254 344 434 534	167 N.W.2d 587
15 135 255 345 435 535	179 N.W.2d 641
16 136 256 346 436 536	388 P.2d 637

PROBLEM #	CITATION
17 137 257 347 437 537	387 P.2d 319
18 138 258 348 438 538	386 P.2d 249
19 139 259 349 439 539	98 A.2d 55
20 140 260 350 440 540	384 P.2d 256
21 141 261 351 441 541	91 N.E.2d 401
22 142 262 352 442 542	93 N.E.2d 5
23 143 263 353 443 543	90 N.E.2d 908
24 144 264 354 444 544	96 N.E.2d 739
25 145 265 355 445 545	95 N.E.2d 685
26 146 266 356 446 546	190 So. 2d 334
27 147 267 357 447 547	179 So. 2d 324
28 148 268 358 448 548	44 So. 2d 748
29 149 269 359 449 549	43 So. 2d 763
30 150 270 360 450 550	30 N.W.2d 484
31 151 271 361 451 551	29 N.W.2d 891
32 152 272 362 452 552	28 N.W.2d 363
33 153 273 363 453 553	31 N.W.2d 170
34 154 274 364 454 554	63 P.2d 693
35 155 275 365 455 555	62 P.2d 445
36 156 276 366 456 556	61 P.2d 559
37 157 277 367 457 557	59 P.2d 771
38 158 278 368 458 558	131 P. 843
39 159 279 369 459 559	132 P. 1170
40 160 280 370 460 560	133 P. 118
41 161 281 371 461 561	134 P. 807
42 162 282 372 462 562	45 N.E.2d 280
43 163 283 373 463 563	42 N.E.2d 627
44 164 284 374 464 564	39 N.E.2d 734
45 165 285 375 465 565	33 N.E.2d 282
46 166 286 376 466 566	36 N.E.2d 760
47 167 287 377 467 567	236 A.2d 737
48 168 288 378 468 568	234 A.2d 334
49 169 289 379 469 569	233 A.2d 891
50 170 290 380 470 570	231 A.2d 740
51 171 291 381 471 571	237 A.2d 320
52 172 292 382 472 572	239 A.2d 640
53 173 293 383 473 573	240 A.2d 60
54 174 294 384 474 574	146 A.2d 676
55 175 295 385 475 575	92 A.2d 554
56 176 296 386 476 576	93 A.2d 462
57 177 297 387 477 577	94 A.2d 385
58 178 298 388 478 578	95 A.2d 689
59 179 299 389 479 579	96 A.2d 246
60 180 300 390 480 580	97 A.2d 540
61 181 201 391 481 581	36 N.W.2d 507
62 182 202 392 482 582	37 N.W.2d 473
63 183 203 393 483 583	38 N.W.2d 863
64 184 204 394 484 584	39 N.W.2d 468
65 185 205 395 485 585	40 N.W.2d 252
66 186 206 396 486 586	201 P. 1029

PROBLEM #	CITATION
67 187 207 397 487 587	202 P. 316
68 188 208 398 488 588	203 P. 920
69 189 209 399 489 589	204 P. 754
70 190 210 400 490 590	206 P. 587
71 191 211 301 491 591	103 N.W.2d 527
72 192 212 302 492 592	104 N.E.2d 669
73 193 213 303 493 593	105 N.E.2d 99
74 194 214 304 494 594	106 N.E.2d 350
75 195 215 305 495 595	107 N.E.2d 3
76 196 216 306 496 596	21 So. 2d 44
77 197 217 307 497 597	22 So. 2d 417
78 198 218 308 498 598	8 So. 2d 689
79 199 219 309 499 599	24 So. 2d 525
80 200 220 310 500 600	25 So. 2d 625
81 101 221 311 401 501	343 S.W.2d 869
82 102 222 312 402 502	344 S.W.2d 153
83 103 223 313 403 503	516 S.W.2d 610
84 104 224 314 404 504	559 S.W.2d 12
85 105 225 315 405 505	535 S.W.2d 819
86 106 226 316 406 506	509 S.W.2d 311
87 107 227 317 407 507	606 S.W.2d 56
88 108 228 318 408 508	625 S.W.2d 477
89 109 229 319 409 509	132 S.E.2d 263
90 110 230 320 410 510	133 S.E.2d 122
91 111 231 321 411 511	134 S.E.2d 889
92 112 232 322 412 512	135 S.E.2d 205
93 113 233 323 413 513	137 S.E.2d 319
94 114 234 324 414 514	136 S.E.2d 404
95 115 235 325 415 515	160 A.2d 694
96 116 236 326 416 516	161 A.2d 843
97 117 237 327 417 517	162 A.2d 854
98 118 238 328 418 518	83 A.2d 491
99 119 239 329 419 519	84 A.2d 511
100 120 240 330 420 520	85 A.2d 102

CITATION EXERCISE 24
STATE COURT DECISIONS (III)

A. INTRODUCTION

All information necessary to complete this exercise is given in Citation Exercise 23 above.

B. INSTRUCTIONS FOR COMPLETING THIS EXERCISE

This exercise gives you further practice in citing cases in West's regional reporters. For your answer to this exercise, state the following:

(a) the full name of the case as it is stated in the reporter at the beginning of the opinion (*e.g.*, Kenneth Lee Benoit, Appellant, v. Commonwealth of Kentucky, Appellee); **you may omit obviously irrelevant portions of a party's name if the full name is a lengthy one;**

(b) the full designation of the court as it is stated in the reporter at the beginning of the opinion (*e.g.*, Court of Appeals of Kentucky);

(c) the exact date of decision (*e.g.*, May 6, 1966); and

(d) the citation of that case in *Bluebook* (or another designated) form. Assume that the case name is going to appear in a **citation sentence or clause**, not as a part of a grammatical part of a textual sentence, in a **legal memorandum**. For purposes of this exercise, do not indicate any subsequent history in the citation. **Also assume that you are citing the case in a document that will NOT be submitted to a state court in the jurisdiction from which the case arises.**

Unless otherwise instructed, write your answers on the answer sheet provided in Part 4 of these exercises.

PROBLEM #	CITATION
1 121 241 331 421 521	300 S.E.2d 295
2 122 242 332 422 522	301 S.E.2d 580
3 123 243 333 423 523	302 S.E.2d 78
4 124 244 334 424 524	262 A.2d 359
5 125 245 335 425 525	298 S.E.2d 246
6 126 246 336 426 526	299 S.E.2d 3
7 127 247 337 427 527	510 S.W.2d 77
8 128 248 338 428 528	480 A.2d 398
9 129 249 339 429 529	476 S.W.2d 556
10 130 250 340 430 530	504 S.W.2d 776
11 131 251 341 431 531	404 S.W.2d 449
12 132 252 342 432 532	453 S.W.2d 759
13 133 253 343 433 533	352 N.W.2d 384
14 134 254 344 434 534	351 N.W.2d 352
15 135 255 345 435 535	358 N.W.2d 793

PROBLEM #	CITATION
16 136 256 346 436 536	681 P.2d 763
17 137 257 347 437 537	559 P.2d 958
18 138 258 348 438 538	684 P.2d 812
19 139 259 349 439 539	285 A.2d 847
20 140 260 350 440 540	460 P.2d 415
21 141 261 351 441 541	459 N.E.2d 1186
22 142 262 352 442 542	462 N.E.2d 1299
23 143 263 353 443 543	461 N.E.2d 1123
24 144 264 354 444 544	460 N.E.2d 506
25 145 265 355 445 545	463 N.E.2d 477
26 146 266 356 446 546	406 So. 2d 191
27 147 267 357 447 547	221 So. 2d 129
28 148 268 358 448 548	222 So. 2d 418
29 149 269 359 449 549	219 So. 2d 425
30 150 270 360 450 550	353 N.W.2d 502
31 151 271 361 451 551	329 N.W.2d 673
32 152 272 362 452 552	328 N.W.2d 709
33 153 273 363 453 553	326 N.W.2d 720
34 154 274 364 454 554	675 P.2d 1145
35 155 275 365 455 555	676 P.2d 1156
36 156 276 366 456 556	677 P.2d 310
37 157 277 367 457 557	678 P.2d 990
38 158 278 368 458 558	654 P.2d 733
39 159 279 369 459 559	605 P.2d 765
40 160 280 370 460 560	563 P.2d 799
41 161 281 371 461 561	607 P.2d 816
42 162 282 372 462 562	450 N.E.2d 992
43 163 283 373 463 563	451 N.E.2d 1080
44 164 284 374 464 564	452 N.E.2d 985
45 165 285 375 465 565	453 N.E.2d 1011
46 166 286 376 466 566	454 N.E.2d 860
47 167 287 377 467 567	427 A.2d 956
48 168 288 378 468 568	424 A.2d 717
49 169 289 379 469 569	275 A.2d 815
50 170 290 380 470 570	477 A.2d 67
51 171 291 381 471 571	478 A.2d 964
52 172 292 382 472 572	479 A.2d 702
53 173 293 383 473 573	481 A.2d 388
54 174 294 384 474 574	372 A.2d 1019
55 175 295 385 475 575	370 A.2d 249
56 176 296 386 476 576	320 A.2d 668
57 177 297 387 477 577	313 A.2d 439
58 178 298 388 478 578	272 A.2d 736
59 179 299 389 479 579	265 A.2d 489
60 180 300 390 480 580	263 A.2d 713
61 181 201 391 481 581	325 N.W.2d 740
62 182 202 392 482 582	290 N.W.2d 479
63 183 203 393 483 583	280 N.W.2d 393
64 184 204 394 484 584	273 N.W.2d 749

PROBLEM #	CITATION
65 185 205 395 485 585	346 N.W.2d 616
66 186 206 396 486 586	322 P.2d 406
67 187 207 397 487 587	312 P.2d 488
68 188 208 398 488 588	308 P.2d 651
69 189 209 399 489 589	307 P.2d 841
70 190 210 400 490 590	328 P.2d 420
71 191 211 301 491 591	458 N.E.2d 229
72 192 212 302 492 592	455 N.E.2d 905
73 193 213 303 493 593	456 N.E.2d 1025
74 194 214 304 494 594	457 N.E.2d 1088
75 195 215 305 495 595	324 N.W.2d 409
76 196 216 306 496 596	407 So. 2d 685
77 197 217 307 497 597	180 So. 2d 335
78 198 218 308 498 598	179 So. 2d 852
79 199 219 309 499 599	403 So. 2d 877
80 200 220 310 500 600	402 So. 2d 945
81 101 221 311 401 501	506 S.W.2d 424
82 102 222 312 402 502	517 S.W.2d 191
83 103 223 313 403 503	495 S.W.2d 658
84 104 224 314 404 504	414 S.W.2d 315
85 105 225 315 405 505	512 S.W.2d 509
86 106 226 316 406 506	392 S.W.2d 662
87 107 227 317 407 507	520 S.W.2d 321
88 108 228 318 408 508	479 S.W.2d 449
89 109 229 319 409 509	286 S.E.2d 924
90 110 230 320 410 510	287 S.E.2d 497
91 111 231 321 411 511	288 S.E.2d 519
92 112 232 322 412 512	293 S.E.2d 442
93 113 233 323 413 513	294 S.E.2d 189
94 114 234 324 414 514	295 S.E.2d 16
95 115 235 325 415 515	264 A.2d 8
96 116 236 326 416 516	400 S.W.2d 885
97 117 237 327 417 517	289 N.W.2d 469
98 118 238 328 418 518	306 So. 2d 513
99 119 239 329 419 519	290 S.E.2d 260
100 120 240 330 420 520	401 S.W.2d 460

STATE COURT DECISIONS (IV)

A. INTRODUCTION

1. Public Domain Citations

Some states have developed a vendor and medium neutral citation format in the form of an official "public domain citation." In this format, pinpoint citations would be to paragraph numbers assigned by the court instead of page numbers.

2. *Bluebook* Rules

In recognition of the actual and potential development of public domain citations, the sixteenth edition of *The Bluebook* now requires an official public domain citation to be used if the decision is available in that form. The following are examples of public domain citations:

> **[Example 1]** *State v. Knecht*, 1997 SD 53.
> **[Example 2]** *State v. Knecht*, 1997 SD 53 ¶ 21.

The above citations of a South Dakota Supreme Court opinion (*State v. Knecht*) consists of the year in which the court's opinion was issued (1997), the abbreviated name of the jurisdiction (SD for South Dakota), the opinion number as designated by the court (53). Example 2 shows a pinpoint citation to a specific paragraph in the opinion (¶ 21). In addition, according to *The Bluebook*, a parallel citation to the regional reporter may be given:

> **[Example 3]** *State v. Knecht*, 1997 SD 53, 563 N.W.2d 413.
> **[Example 4]** *State v. Knecht*, 1997 SD 53 ¶ 21, 563 N.W.2d 413, 420-21.

Note that the jurisdiction (South Dakota) is identified by the public domain citation (SD) in Examples 3 and 4; thus, the jurisdiction is omitted from the parenthetical that normally appears at the end of a citation. The court is also omitted from the parenthetical that normally appears at the end of a citation because it is assumed that the court of decision is the highest court in the state. In addition, the year is omitted from the parenthetical that normally appears at the end of the citation because it is included in the reporter designation. *See Bluebook* Rule 10.3.1(b).

B. INSTRUCTIONS FOR COMPLETING THIS EXERCISE

This exercise gives you practice in citing cases with public domain citations. For your answer to this exercise, state the following:

(a) the full name of the case as it is stated in the reporter at the beginning of the opinion (*e.g.*, State of North Dakota, Plaintiff and Appellant, v. Leonard Wayne Burckhard, Defendant and Appellee); **you may omit obviously irrelevant portions of a party's name if the full name is a lengthy one**;

(b) the full designation of the court as it is stated in the reporter at the beginning of the opinion (*e.g.*, Supreme Court of North Dakota);

(c) the public domain citation (*e.g.*, 1998 ND App 8); and

(d) the full citation of that case in *Bluebook* (or another designated) form, **including the parallel West citation.** Assume that the case name is going to appear in a **citation sentence or clause**, not as a part of a grammatical part of a textual sentence, in a **legal memorandum**. For purposes of this exercise, do not indicate any subsequent history in the citation.

Unless otherwise instructed, write your answers on the answer sheet provided in Part 4 of these exercises.

PROBLEM #	CITATION
1 146 230 308 427 529	555 N.W.2d 90
2 147 231 309 428 530	556 N.W.2d 669
3 148 232 310 429 531	558 N.W.2d 617
4 149 233 311 430 532	559 N.W.2d 841
5 150 234 312 431 533	560 N.W.2d 239
6 151 235 313 432 534	561 N.W.2d 309
7 152 236 314 433 535	562 N.W.2d 105
8 153 237 315 434 536	563 N.W.2d 391
9 154 238 316 435 537	564 N.W.2d 291
10 155 239 317 436 538	570 N.W.2d 221
11 156 240 318 437 539	569 N.W.2d 16
12 157 241 319 438 540	568 N.W.2d 477
13 158 242 320 439 541	567 N.W.2d 189
14 159 243 321 440 542	566 N.W.2d 125
15 160 244 322 441 543	565 N.W.2d 61
16 161 245 323 442 544	573 N.W.2d 515
17 162 246 324 443 545	578 N.W.2d 145
18 163 247 325 444 546	574 N.W.2d 561
19 164 248 326 445 547	575 N.W.2d 211
20 165 249 327 446 548	576 N.W.2d 15
21 166 250 328 447 549	571 N.W.2d 142
22 167 251 329 448 550	572 N.W.2d 113
23 168 252 330 449 551	565 N.W.2d 79
24 169 253 331 450 552	567 N.W.2d 387
25 170 254 332 451 553	555 N.W.2d 365
26 171 255 333 452 554	557 N.W.2d 389
27 172 256 334 453 555	559 N.W.2d 251

PROBLEM #	CITATION
28 173 257 335 454 556	584 N.W.2d 515
29 174 258 336 455 557	561 N.W.2d 1
30 175 259 337 456 558	561 N.W.2d 599
31 176 260 338 457 559	562 N.W.2d 113
32 177 261 339 458 560	563 N.W.2d 413
33 178 262 340 459 561	564 N.W.2d 315
34 179 263 341 460 562	570 N.W.2d 550
35 180 264 342 461 563	569 N.W.2d 289
36 181 265 343 462 564	568 N.W.2d 607
37 182 266 344 463 565	567 N.W.2d 216
38 183 267 345 464 566	566 N.W.2d 418
39 184 268 346 465 567	565 N.W.2d 752
40 185 269 347 466 568	572 N.W.2d 426
41 186 270 348 467 569	571 N.W.2d 155
42 187 271 349 468 570	576 N.W.2d 215
43 188 272 350 469 571	575 N.W.2d 225
44 189 273 351 470 572	574 N.W.2d 633
45 190 274 352 471 573	579 N.W.2d 184
46 191 275 353 472 574	578 N.W.2d 154
47 192 276 354 473 575	577 N.W.2d 590
48 193 277 355 474 576	579 N.W.2d 599
49 194 278 356 475 577	571 N.W.2d 653
50 195 279 357 476 578	555 N.W.2d 613
51 196 280 358 477 579	557 N.W.2d 764
52 197 281 359 478 580	559 N.W.2d 538
53 198 282 360 479 581	560 N.W.2d 213
54 199 283 361 480 582	561 N.W.2d 263
55 200 284 362 481 583	562 N.W.2d 83
56 101 285 363 482 584	569 N.W.2d 563
57 102 286 364 483 585	563 N.W.2d 849
58 103 287 365 484 586	564 N.W.2d 651
59 104 288 366 485 587	570 N.W.2d 719
60 105 289 367 486 588	562 N.W.2d 395
61 106 290 368 487 589	568 N.W.2d 627
62 107 291 369 488 590	567 N.W.2d 377
63 108 292 370 489 591	566 N.W.2d 431
64 109 293 371 490 592	565 N.W.2d 789
65 110 294 372 491 593	585 N.W.2d 129
66 111 295 373 492 594	575 N.W.2d 240
67 112 296 374 493 595	574 N.W.2d 644
68 113 297 375 494 596	578 N.W.2d 583
69 114 298 376 495 597	577 N.W.2d 782
70 115 299 377 496 598	579 N.W.2d 165
71 116 300 378 497 599	556 N.W.2d 73
72 117 201 379 498 600	571 N.W.2d 358
73 118 202 380 499 501	572 N.W.2d 439
74 119 203 381 500 502	573 N.W.2d 167
75 120 204 382 401 503	579 N.W.2d 189
76 121 205 383 402 504	558 N.W.2d 317
77 122 206 384 403 505	559 N.W.2d 802

PROBLEM #	CITATION
77 122 206 384 403 505	559 N.W.2d 802
78 123 207 385 404 506	560 N.W.2d 225
79 124 208 386 405 507	561 N.W.2d 273
80 125 209 387 406 508	562 N.W.2d 91
81 126 210 388 407 509	563 N.W.2d 377
82 127 211 389 408 510	564 N.W.2d 283
83 128 212 390 409 511	570 N.W.2d 195
84 129 213 391 410 512	569 N.W.2d 1
85 130 214 392 411 513	568 N.W.2d 280
86 131 215 393 412 514	568 N.W.2d 741
87 132 216 394 413 515	583 N.W.2d 804
88 133 217 395 414 516	566 N.W.2d 439
89 134 218 396 415 517	573 N.W.2d 176
90 135 219 397 416 518	572 N.W.2d 445
91 136 220 398 417 519	571 N.W.2d 372
92 137 221 399 418 520	576 N.W.2d 518
93 138 222 400 419 521	574 N.W.2d 556
94 139 223 301 420 522	578 N.W.2d 121
95 140 224 302 421 523	575 N.W.2d 203
96 141 225 303 422 524	580 N.W.2d 139
97 142 226 304 423 525	578 N.W.2d 589
98 143 227 305 424 526	578 N.W.2d 128
99 144 228 306 425 527	577 N.W.2d 575
100 145 229 307 426 528	582 N.W.2d 682

STATE COURT DECISIONS (V)

A. INTRODUCTION

1. West's *New York Supplement*

The New York Court of Appeals is the highest state court in New York. The intermediate appellate court in New York is the Appellate Division of the Supreme Court. The basic trial court in New York is called the Supreme Court. In some instances, the trial judges of the New York Supreme Court hear appeals from other New York courts of limited jurisdiction during the "Appellate Term of the New York Supreme Court." In those cases, the judges of the Supreme Court are acting as appellate judges.

West's *New York Supplement* started in 1887. It reports decisions of the New York Court of Appeals, the Appellate Division of the Supreme Court, and opinions from other lower courts of record in New York. The official reporter for decisions of the New York Court of Appeals is *New York Reports* (N.Y., N.Y.2d). In addition to appearing in West's *New York Supplement* (N.Y.S.2d), decisions of the New York Court of Appeals also appear in the relevant West regional reporter, the *North Eastern Reporter* (N.E., N.E.2d). The official reporter for the Appellate Division of the Supreme Court is *New York Appellate Division Reports* (A.D., A.D.2d). The official reporter for other lower New York court decisions, such as the New York Supreme Court, is *New York Miscellaneous Reports* (Misc., Misc. 2d).

2. *Bluebook* Citations of New York Cases

In documents submitted to New York state courts, New York Court of Appeals cases should be cited to three reporters: (1) the official *New York Reports*; (2) the West regional reporter, the *North Eastern Reporter*; and (3) West's *New York Supplement*, beginning with the second series of *New York Reports* in 1956 (in that order). Note that prior to 1956, the *New York Supplement* simply reprinted the first series of *New York Reports* without separate pagination; thus, a parallel citation to the *New York Supplement* should not be given when citing a case that appears in the first series of *New York Reports* (1847-1955); *see Bluebook* Table T.1 ("United States Jurisdictions, New York"). In all other documents, New York Court of Appeals decisions should be cited to the *North Eastern Reporter* (if therein).

Consider the following examples of citations of New York Court of Appeals cases in documents submitted to New York state courts:

[Example 1] *People v. Ramos*, 90 N.Y.2d 490, 685 N.E.2d 492, 662 N.Y.S.2d 739 (1997).

[Example 2] *Kingland v. Erie County*, 289 N.Y. 409, 84 N.E.2d 38 (1949).

Note that in Example 2 no parallel citation is given to West's *New York Supplement* because this case was decided prior to 1956. The *New York Supplement* only began separate pagination of New York Court of Appeals decisions when the second series of the official *New York Reports* began (see above). If these same cases were cited in any other documents, they would be cited as follows:

[Example 3] *People v. Ramos*, 685 N.E.2d 492 (N.Y. 1997).

[Example 4] *Kingland v. Erie County*, 84 N.E.2d 38 (N.Y. 1949).

In documents submitted to New York state courts, Appellate Division of the Supreme Court cases should be cited to two reporters: (1) the official *Appellate Division Reports*; and (2) West's *New York Supplement* (in that order). In all other documents, Appellate Division of the Supreme Court decisions should be cited to West's *New York Supplement* (if therein). *See Bluebook* Table T.1 ("United States Jurisdictions, New York").

Consider the following example of a citation of a case decided by the New York Appellate Division of Supreme Court in a document submitted to a New York state court:

[Example 5] *Martin v. Pitcher*, 243 A.D. 1023, 663 N.Y.S. 437 (1997).

If this same case were cited in any other document, it would be cited as follows:

[Example 6] *Martin v. Pitcher*, 663 N.Y.S. 437 (App. Div. 1997).

Other lower New York court decisions, such as decisions of the New York Supreme Court, should be cited to two reporters in documents submitted to New York state courts: (1) *New York Miscellaneous Reports*; and (2) West's *New York Supplement* (in that order) (if therein). In all other documents, only the *New York Supplement* should be cited, if therein. *See Bluebook* Table T.1 ("United States Jurisdictions, New York").

Consider the following examples of citations of cases decided by the New York Supreme Court in a document submitted to a New York state court:

[Example 7] *City of New York v. Mor*, 173 Misc. 2d 971, 662 N.Y.S.2d 687 (Sup. Ct. 1997).

[**Example 8**] *B.M. v. Z.S.*, 174 Misc. 2d 205, 663 N.Y.S.2d 774 (Fam. Ct. 1997).

If these same cases were cited in any other document, they would be cited as follows:

[**Example 9**] *City of New York v. Mor*, 662 N.Y.S.2d 687 (Sup. Ct. 1997).

[**Example 10**] *B.M. v. Z.S.*, 663 N.Y.S.2d 774 (Fam. Ct. 1997).

B. INSTRUCTIONS FOR COMPLETING THIS EXERCISE

This exercise gives you practice in citing New York court decisions. Find the three cases in the cited volume of West's *New York Supplement* that begin on the pages listed ((a), (b), and (c)) with your problem number below. For your answer to this exercise, state the following:

(a) the full name of each case as it is stated in the reporter at the beginning of the opinion (*e.g.*, Ashland Oil & Refining Company, Appellant, v. State of New York, Respondent); **you may omit obviously irrelevant portions of a party's name if the full name is a lengthy one**;

(b) the full designation of the court for each case as it is stated in the reporter at the beginning of the opinion (*e.g.*, New York Court of Appeals);

(c) the exact date of decision for each case (*e.g.*, April 23, 1970); and

(d) the citations of the cases in *Bluebook* (or another designated) form, **assuming that you are citing the cases in a document that WILL be submitted to a New York state court**. Assume also that the case names are going to appear in a **citation sentence or clause**, not as a part of a grammatical part of a textual sentence, in a **legal memorandum**. For purposes of this exercise, do not indicate any subsequent history in the citation; and

(e) the citations of the cases in *Bluebook* (or another designated) form, but **assuming that you are citing the cases in a document that will NOT be submitted to a New York state court.**. Assume also that the case names are going to appear in a **citation sentence or clause**, not as a part of a grammatical part of a textual sentence. For purposes of this exercise, do not indicate any subsequent history in the citation.

Unless otherwise instructed, write your answers on the answer sheet provided in Part 4 of these exercises.

PROBLEM #	CITATIONS			
1 119 209 375 470 584	497 N.Y.S.2d	(a) 618	(b) 959	(c) 285
2 120 210 376 471 585	496 N.Y.S.2d	(a) 401	(b) 854	(c) 605
3 121 211 377 472 586	495 N.Y.S.2d	(a) 955	(b) 723	(c) 886
4 122 212 378 473 587	494 N.Y.S.2d	(a) 95	(b) 741	(c) 933
5 123 213 379 474 588	500 N.Y.S.2d	(a) 635	(b) 787	(c) 944

PROBLEM #	**CITATIONS**			
6 124 214 380 475 589	498 N.Y.S.2d	(a) 782	(b) 891	(c) 703
7 125 215 381 476 590	499 N.Y.S.2d	(a) 665	(b) 945	(c) 351
8 126 216 382 477 591	506 N.Y.S.2d	(a) 855	(b) 904	(c) 629
9 127 217 383 478 592	507 N.Y.S.2d	(a) 844	(b) 935	(c) 129
10 128 218 384 479 593	505 N.Y.S.2d	(a) 849	(b) 624	(c) 782
11 129 219 385 480 594	504 N.Y.S.2d	(a) 87	(b) 925	(c) 993
12 130 220 386 481 595	503 N.Y.S.2d	(a) 313	(b) 869	(c) 977
13 131 221 387 482 596	402 N.Y.S.2d	(a) 382	(b) 829	(c) 751
14 132 222 388 483 597	404 N.Y.S.2d	(a) 76	(b) 853	(c) 954
15 133 223 389 484 598	451 N.Y.S.2d	(a) 682	(b) 497	(c) 591
16 134 224 390 485 599	421 N.Y.S.2d	(a) 850	(b) 896	(c) 770
17 135 225 391 486 600	415 N.Y.S.2d	(a) 797	(b) 541	(c) 738
18 136 226 392 487 501	502 N.Y.S.2d	(a) 715	(b) 877	(c) 604
19 137 227 393 488 502	392 N.Y.S.2d	(a) 606	(b) 946	(c) 568
20 138 228 394 489 503	501 N.Y.S.2d	(a) 810	(b) 938	(c) 576
21 139 229 395 490 504	398 N.Y.S.2d	(a) 877	(b) 901	(c) 789
22 140 230 396 491 505	458 N.Y.S.2d	(a) 530	(b) 743	(c) 463
23 141 231 397 492 506	412 N.Y.S.2d	(a) 833	(b) 657	(c) 325
24 142 232 398 493 507	411 N.Y.S.2d	(a) 224	(b) 637	(c) 970
25 143 233 399 494 508	447 N.Y.S.2d	(a) 893	(b) 787	(c) 601
26 144 234 400 495 509	410 N.Y.S.2d	(a) 801	(b) 726	(c) 226
27 145 235 301 496 510	407 N.Y.S.2d	(a) 660	(b) 901	(c) 373
28 146 236 302 497 511	408 N.Y.S.2d	(a) 463	(b) 806	(c) 279
29 147 237 303 498 512	430 N.Y.S.2d	(a) 578	(b) 847	(c) 231
30 148 238 304 499 513	432 N.Y.S.2d	(a) 689	(b) 535	(c) 348
31 149 239 305 500 514	434 N.Y.S.2d	(a) 916	(b) 815	(c) 325
32 150 240 306 401 515	433 N.Y.S.2d	(a) 71	(b) 941	(c) 974
33 151 241 307 402 516	448 N.Y.S.2d	(a) 135	(b) 799	(c) 117
34 152 242 308 403 517	445 N.Y.S.2d	(a) 420	(b) 841	(c) 885
35 153 243 309 404 518	414 N.Y.S.2d	(a) 889	(b) 298	(c) 977
36 154 244 310 405 519	413 N.Y.S.2d	(a) 295	(b) 515	(c) 859
37 155 245 311 406 520	446 N.Y.S.2d	(a) 255	(b) 773	(c) 969
38 156 246 312 407 521	444 N.Y.S.2d	(a) 604	(b) 725	(c) 405
39 157 247 313 408 522	442 N.Y.S.2d	(a) 774	(b) 803	(c) 670
40 158 248 314 409 523	439 N.Y.S.2d	(a) 863	(b) 966	(c) 818
41 159 249 315 410 524	441 N.Y.S.2d	(a) 644	(b) 841	(c) 575
42 160 250 316 411 525	443 N.Y.S.2d	(a) 648	(b) 783	(c) 678
43 161 251 317 412 526	457 N.Y.S.2d	(a) 763	(b) 1010	(c) 401
44 162 252 318 413 527	459 N.Y.S.2d	(a) 572	(b) 938	(c) 684
45 163 253 319 414 528	461 N.Y.S.2d	(a) 746	(b) 838	(c) 193
46 164 254 320 415 529	460 N.Y.S.2d	(a) 918	(b) 799	(c) 479
47 165 255 321 416 530	462 N.Y.S.2d	(a) 817	(b) 297	(c) 744
48 166 256 322 417 531	436 N.Y.S.2d	(a) 251	(b) 783	(c) 577
49 167 257 323 418 532	435 N.Y.S.2d	(a) 556	(b) 739	(c) 523
50 168 258 324 419 533	438 N.Y.S.2d	(a) 741	(b) 880	(c) 438
51 169 259 325 420 534	437 N.Y.S.2d	(a) 272	(b) 733	(c) 1016
52 170 260 326 421 535	440 N.Y.S.2d	(a) 927	(b) 708	(c) 477
53 171 261 327 422 536	394 N.Y.S.2d	(a) 849	(b) 913	(c) 371
54 172 262 328 423 537	391 N.Y.S.2d	(a) 540	(b) 921	(c) 953
55 173 263 329 424 538	390 N.Y.S.2d	(a) 393	(b) 693	(c) 976

Problem #	**Citations**			
56 174 264 330 425 539	388 N.Y.S.2d	(a) 876	(b) 960	(c) 80
57 175 265 331 426 540	387 N.Y.S.2d	(a) 821	(b) 854	(c) 346
58 176 266 332 427 541	386 N.Y.S.2d	(a) 703	(b) 588	(c) 326
59 177 267 333 428 542	385 N.Y.S.2d	(a) 28	(b) 992	(c) 487
60 178 268 334 429 543	384 N.Y.S.2d	(a) 733	(b) 843	(c) 610
61 179 269 335 430 544	383 N.Y.S.2d	(a) 271	(b) 900	(c) 943
62 180 270 336 431 545	382 N.Y.S.2d	(a) 28	(b) 781	(c) 938
63 181 271 337 432 546	381 N.Y.S.2d	(a) 855	(b) 924	(c) 775
64 182 272 338 433 547	508 N.Y.S.2d	(a) 923	(b) 744	(c) 880
65 183 273 339 434 548	509 N.Y.S.2d	(a) 796	(b) 928	(c) 751
66 184 274 340 435 549	465 N.Y.S.2d	(a) 857	(b) 781	(c) 665
67 185 275 341 436 550	466 N.Y.S.2d	(a) 953	(b) 860	(c) 553
68 186 276 342 437 551	467 N.Y.S.2d	(a) 191	(b) 903	(c) 975
69 187 277 343 438 552	468 N.Y.S.2d	(a) 601	(b) 943	(c) 995
70 188 278 344 439 553	406 N.Y.S.2d	(a) 732	(b) 602	(c) 650
71 189 279 345 440 554	405 N.Y.S.2d	(a) 671	(b) 865	(c) 229
72 190 280 346 441 555	420 N.Y.S.2d	(a) 371	(b) 892	(c) 859
73 191 281 347 442 556	419 N.Y.S.2d	(a) 487	(b) 757	(c) 799
74 192 282 348 443 557	418 N.Y.S.2d	(a) 565	(b) 815	(c) 537
75 193 283 349 444 558	417 N.Y.S.2d	(a) 251	(b) 514	(c) 410
76 194 284 350 445 559	416 N.Y.S.2d	(a) 778	(b) 826	(c) 173
77 195 285 351 446 560	455 N.Y.S.2d	(a) 570	(b) 653	(c) 469
78 196 286 352 447 561	397 N.Y.S.2d	(a) 376	(b) 271	(c) 541
79 197 287 353 448 562	396 N.Y.S.2d	(a) 641	(b) 949	(c) 962
80 198 288 354 449 563	395 N.Y.S.2d	(a) 627	(b) 773	(c) 889
81 199 289 355 450 564	422 N.Y.S.2d	(a) 660	(b) 963	(c) 350
82 200 290 356 451 565	423 N.Y.S.2d	(a) 625	(b) 739	(c) 417
83 101 291 357 452 566	425 N.Y.S.2d	(a) 552	(b) 861	(c) 951
84 102 292 358 453 567	424 N.Y.S.2d	(a) 402	(b) 941	(c) 862
85 103 293 359 454 568	427 N.Y.S.2d	(a) 595	(b) 525	(c) 701
86 104 294 360 455 569	426 N.Y.S.2d	(a) 463	(b) 855	(c) 701
87 105 295 361 456 570	429 N.Y.S.2d	(a) 574	(b) 732	(c) 351
88 106 296 362 457 571	428 N.Y.S.2d	(a) 902	(b) 972	(c) 428
89 107 297 363 458 572	431 N.Y.S.2d	(a) 694	(b) 824	(c) 967
90 108 298 364 459 573	449 N.Y.S.2d	(a) 168	(b) 268	(c) 623
91 109 299 365 460 574	448 N.Y.S.2d	(a) 467	(b) 597	(c) 1001
92 110 300 366 461 575	450 N.Y.S.2d	(a) 776	(b) 866	(c) 687
93 111 201 367 462 576	452 N.Y.S.2d	(a) 373	(b) 471	(c) 774
94 112 202 368 463 577	454 N.Y.S.2d	(a) 705	(b) 849	(c) 785
95 113 203 369 464 578	453 N.Y.S.2d	(a) 639	(b) 925	(c) 343
96 114 204 370 465 579	456 N.Y.S.2d	(a) 733	(b) 876	(c) 629
97 115 205 371 466 580	400 N.Y.S.2d	(a) 801	(b) 899	(c) 442
98 116 206 372 467 581	399 N.Y.S.2d	(a) 203	(b) 833	(c) 556
99 117 207 373 468 582	403 N.Y.S.2d	(a) 490	(b) 587	(c) 637
100 118 208 374 469 583	401 N.Y.S.2d	(a) 462	(b) 831	(c) 952

CITATION EXERCISE 27
STATE COURT DECISIONS (VI)

A. INTRODUCTION

1. West's *California Reporter*

The official reporter for California Supreme Court decisions is *California Reports* (Cal., Cal. 2d, Cal. 3d, Cal. 4th). California Supreme Court decisions also appear in the relevant West regional reporter: *Pacific Reporter* (P., P.2d).

The official reporter for California Court of Appeal decisions is *California Appellate Reports* (Cal. App., Cal. App. 2d, Cal. App. 3d, Cal. App. 4th). Between 1905 and 1959, California Court of Appeals decisions also appeared in West's *Pacific Reporter*.

Beginning in 1960, West began special treatment for California cases. West's *California Reporter* (Cal. Rptr., Cal. Rptr. 2d) covers California Supreme Court decisions and California Court of Appeal decisions. It also covers decisions of the Appellate Departments of the Superior Court (which are published officially in *California Appellate Reports Supplement*, bound with *California Appellate Reports*).

2. *Bluebook* Citations of California Cases

In documents submitted to California state courts, California Supreme Court cases should be cited to three reporters: (1) the official *California Reports*; (2) the West regional reporter, the *Pacific Reporter*; and (3) West's *California Reporter* (if therein) (in that order). In all other documents, California Supreme Court decisions should be cited to only the *Pacific Reporter* (if therein). *See Bluebook* Table T.1 ("United States Jurisdictions, California").

Consider the following examples of citations of California Supreme Court cases in a document submitted to a California state court:

[**Example 1**] *People v. Francis*, 42 Cal. 2d 335, 267 P.2d 8 (1954).
[**Example 2**] *Agins v. City of Tiburon*, 24 Cal. 3d 266, 598 P.2d 25, 157 Cal. Rptr. 372 (1979).

If these same cases were cited in any other document, they would be cited as follows:

[**Example 3**] *People v. Francis*, 267 P.2d 8 (Cal. 1954).
[**Example 4**] *Agins v. City of Tiburon*, 598 P.2d 25 (Cal. 1979).

In documents submitted to California state courts, California Court of Appeal cases should be cited to two reporters: (1) the official *California Appellate Reports*; and (2) West regional reporter, the *Pacific Reporter* (before 1960) or West's *California Reporter* (after 1959) (in that order). In all other documents, California Court of Appeal decisions should be cited to the *Pacific Reporter* (before 1960) or West's *California Reporter* (after 1959) (if therein). *See Bluebook* Table T.1 ("United States Jurisdictions, California").

Consider the following examples of citations of California Court of Appeal cases in a document submitted to a California state court:

> **[Example 5]** *India Paint & Lacquer Co. v. United Steel Prods. Corp.*, 123 Cal. App. 2d 597, 267 P.2d 408 (1954).
>
> **[Example 6]** *Biltoft v. Wootten*, 96 Cal. App. 3d 58, 157 Cal. Rptr. 581 (1979).

If these same cases were cited in any other document, they would be cited as follows:

> **[Example 7]** *India Paint & Lacquer Co. v. United Steel Prods. Corp.*, 267 P.2d 408 (Cal. Ct. App. 1954).
>
> **[Example 8]** *Biltoft v. Wootten*, 157 Cal. Rptr. 581 (Ct. App. 1979).

Note that "Cal." is included in the parenthetical in the case citation in Example 7 because the abbreviated name of the reporter (P.2d) does not clearly identify the geographic jurisdiction; in contrast, "Cal." is omitted from the case citation in Example 8 because "Cal. Rptr." clearly identifies the geographic jurisdiction.

B. INSTRUCTIONS FOR COMPLETING THIS EXERCISE

This exercise gives you practice in citing California court decisions. Find the two cases in the cited volume of West's *California Reporter* that begin on the pages listed ((a) and (b)) with your problem number below. For your answer to this exercise, state the following:

(a) the full name of each of the cases as they are stated in the reporter at the beginning of the opinion (*e.g.*, Opan M. Hansford, Plaintiff, Cross-Defendant and Appellant, v. Ben Lassar, Defendant, Cross-Complainant and Respondent); **you may omit obviously irrelevant portions of a party's name if the full name is a lengthy one;**

(b) the full designation of the court for each case as it is stated in the reporter at the beginning of the opinion (*e.g.*, California Supreme Court);

(c) the exact date of decision for each case (*e.g.*, Dec. 1, 1975);

(d) the citations of the cases in *Bluebook* (or another designated) form. **Assume that you are citing the cases in a document that WILL be submitted to a**

California state court. Assume also that the case names are going to appear in a **citation sentence or clause**, not as a part of a grammatical part of a textual sentence. For purposes of this exercise, do not indicate any subsequent history in the citation; and

(e) the citations of the cases in *Bluebook* (or another designated) form. **However, assume that you are citing the cases in a document that WILL NOT be submitted to a California state court..** Assume also that the case names are going to appear in a **citation sentence or clause**, not as a part of a grammatical part of a textual sentence. For purposes of this exercise, do not indicate any subsequent history in the citation.

Unless otherwise instructed, write your answers on the answer sheet provided in Part 4 of these exercises.

PROBLEM #	CITATIONS		
1 143 231 380 477 526	121 Cal. Rptr.	(a) 611	(b) 420
2 144 232 381 478 527	122 Cal. Rptr.	(a) 745	(b) 891
3 145 233 382 479 528	123 Cal. Rptr.	(a) 649	(b) 704
4 146 234 383 480 529	124 Cal. Rptr.	(a) 536	(b) 773
5 147 235 384 481 530	126 Cal. Rptr.	(a) 239	(b) 666
6 148 236 385 482 531	127 Cal. Rptr.	(a) 629	(b) 561
7 149 237 386 483 532	128 Cal. Rptr.	(a) 655	(b) 733
8 150 238 387 484 533	129 Cal. Rptr.	(a) 438	(b) 603
9 151 239 388 485 534	130 Cal. Rptr.	(a) 515	(b) 387
10 152 240 389 486 535	131 Cal. Rptr.	(a) 381	(b) 697
11 153 241 390 487 536	132 Cal. Rptr.	(a) 657	(b) 725
12 154 242 391 488 537	133 Cal. Rptr.	(a) 520	(b) 775
13 155 243 392 489 538	134 Cal. Rptr.	(a) 650	(b) 436
14 156 244 393 490 539	135 Cal. Rptr.	(a) 411	(b) 754
15 157 245 394 491 540	136 Cal. Rptr.	(a) 854	(b) 783
16 158 246 395 492 541	137 Cal. Rptr.	(a) 447	(b) 804
17 159 247 396 493 542	138 Cal. Rptr.	(a) 696	(b) 419
18 160 248 397 494 543	139 Cal. Rptr.	(a) 861	(b) 830
19 161 249 398 495 544	140 Cal. Rptr.	(a) 651	(b) 677
20 162 250 399 496 545	164 Cal. Rptr.	(a) 539	(b) 485
21 163 251 400 497 546	171 Cal. Rptr.	(a) 721	(b) 274
22 164 252 301 498 547	150 Cal. Rptr.	(a) 435	(b) 589
23 165 253 302 499 548	145 Cal. Rptr.	(a) 517	(b) 334
24 166 254 303 500 549	147 Cal. Rptr.	(a) 639	(b) 795
25 167 255 304 401 550	146 Cal. Rptr.	(a) 732	(b) 653
26 168 256 305 402 551	142 Cal. Rptr.	(a) 443	(b) 825
27 169 257 306 403 552	144 Cal. Rptr.	(a) 758	(b) 23
28 170 258 307 404 553	154 Cal. Rptr.	(a) 524	(b) 243
29 171 259 308 405 554	143 Cal. Rptr.	(a) 225	(b) 755
30 172 260 309 406 555	153 Cal. Rptr.	(a) 836	(b) 683
31 173 261 310 407 556	152 Cal. Rptr.	(a) 710	(b) 765
32 174 262 311 408 557	111 Cal. Rptr.	(a) 704	(b) 53
33 175 263 312 409 558	148 Cal. Rptr.	(a) 605	(b) 430
34 176 264 313 410 559	149 Cal. Rptr.	(a) 360	(b) 499
35 177 265 314 411 560	184 Cal. Rptr.	(a) 728	(b) 471

CITING CASES

PROBLEM #	**CITATIONS**		
36 178 266 315 412 561	175 Cal. Rptr.	(a) 604	(b) 732
37 179 267 316 413 562	182 Cal. Rptr.	(a) 617	(b) 790
38 180 268 317 414 563	174 Cal. Rptr.	(a) 684	(b) 711
39 181 269 318 415 564	185 Cal. Rptr.	(a) 654	(b) 532
40 182 270 319 416 565	183 Cal. Rptr.	(a) 810	(b) 878
41 183 271 320 417 566	173 Cal. Rptr.	(a) 846	(b) 685
42 184 272 321 418 567	169 Cal. Rptr.	(a) 706	(b) 570
43 185 273 322 419 568	177 Cal. Rptr.	(a) 861	(b) 605
44 186 274 323 420 569	168 Cal. Rptr.	(a) 667	(b) 816
45 187 275 324 421 570	178 Cal. Rptr.	(a) 630	(b) 642
46 188 276 325 422 571	179 Cal. Rptr.	(a) 443	(b) 847
47 189 277 326 423 572	170 Cal. Rptr.	(a) 629	(b) 433
48 190 278 327 424 573	180 Cal. Rptr.	(a) 617	(b) 786
49 191 279 328 425 574	181 Cal. Rptr.	(a) 903	(b) 661
50 192 280 329 426 575	172 Cal. Rptr.	(a) 696	(b) 783
51 193 281 330 427 576	166 Cal. Rptr.	(a) 859	(b) 192
52 194 282 331 428 577	176 Cal. Rptr.	(a) 780	(b) 687
53 195 283 332 429 578	167 Cal. Rptr.	(a) 876	(b) 538
54 196 284 333 430 579	156 Cal. Rptr.	(a) 450	(b) 687
55 197 285 334 431 580	157 Cal. Rptr.	(a) 392	(b) 602
56 198 286 335 432 581	158 Cal. Rptr.	(a) 662	(b) 562
57 199 287 336 433 582	159 Cal. Rptr.	(a) 684	(b) 381
58 200 288 337 434 583	160 Cal. Rptr.	(a) 323	(b) 577
59 101 289 338 435 584	161 Cal. Rptr.	(a) 87	(b) 738
60 102 290 339 436 585	162 Cal. Rptr.	(a) 431	(b) 126
61 103 291 340 437 586	163 Cal. Rptr.	(a) 619	(b) 767
62 104 292 341 438 587	165 Cal. Rptr.	(a) 440	(b) 697
63 105 293 342 439 588	205 Cal. Rptr.	(a) 643	(b) 561
64 106 294 343 440 589	206 Cal. Rptr.	(a) 545	(b) 585
65 107 295 344 441 590	208 Cal. Rptr.	(a) 547	(b) 790
66 108 296 345 442 591	207 Cal. Rptr.	(a) 549	(b) 903
67 109 297 346 443 592	209 Cal. Rptr.	(a) 682	(b) 771
68 110 298 347 444 493	200 Cal. Rptr.	(a) 440	(b) 77
69 111 299 348 445 594	201 Cal. Rptr.	(a) 807	(b) 555
70 112 300 349 446 595	195 Cal. Rptr.	(a) 503	(b) 737
71 113 201 350 447 596	196 Cal. Rptr.	(a) 841	(b) 834
72 114 202 351 448 597	197 Cal. Rptr.	(a) 590	(b) 749
73 115 203 352 449 598	198 Cal. Rptr.	(a) 779	(b) 720
74 116 204 353 450 599	199 Cal. Rptr.	(a) 60	(b) 796
75 117 205 354 451 600	193 Cal. Rptr.	(a) 692	(b) 760
76 118 206 355 452 501	192 Cal. Rptr.	(a) 743	(b) 833
77 119 207 356 453 502	190 Cal. Rptr.	(a) 355	(b) 785
78 120 208 357 454 503	202 Cal. Rptr.	(a) 826	(b) 729
79 121 209 358 455 504	203 Cal. Rptr.	(a) 433	(b) 685
80 122 210 359 456 505	204 Cal. Rptr.	(a) 435	(b) 846
81 123 211 360 457 506	227 Cal. Rptr.	(a) 817	(b) 528
82 124 212 361 458 507	228 Cal. Rptr.	(a) 509	(b) 807
83 125 213 362 459 508	229 Cal. Rptr.	(a) 789	(b) 789
84 126 214 363 460 509	230 Cal. Rptr.	(a) 834	(b) 351
85 127 215 364 461 510	231 Cal. Rptr.	(a) 738	(b) 446

PROBLEM #	**CITATIONS**		
86 128 216 365 462 511	232 Cal. Rptr.	(a) 132	(b) 619
87 129 217 366 463 512	226 Cal. Rptr.	(a) 558	(b) 855
88 130 218 367 464 513	224 Cal. Rptr.	(a) 705	(b) 865
89 131 219 368 465 514	222 Cal. Rptr.	(a) 127	(b) 746
90 132 220 369 466 515	221 Cal. Rptr.	(a) 779	(b) 292
91 133 221 370 467 516	214 Cal. Rptr.	(a) 832	(b) 567
92 134 222 371 468 517	213 Cal. Rptr.	(a) 236	(b) 825
93 135 223 372 469 518	216 Cal. Rptr.	(a) 760	(b) 575
94 136 224 373 470 519	217 Cal. Rptr.	(a) 423	(b) 783
95 137 225 374 471 520	212 Cal. Rptr.	(a) 466	(b) 737
96 138 226 375 472 521	218 Cal. Rptr.	(a) 324	(b) 585
97 139 227 376 473 522	219 Cal. Rptr.	(a) 170	(b) 773
98 140 228 377 474 523	210 Cal. Rptr.	(a) 762	(b) 271
99 141 229 378 475 524	211 Cal. Rptr.	(a) 719	(b) 22
100 142 230 379 476 525	220 Cal. Rptr.	(a) 807	(b) 621

CITATION EXERCISE 28
UNREPORTED CASES AVAILABLE ON ELECTRONIC DATABASES: WESTLAW

A. INTRODUCTION

1. Electronic Databases

Online legal computer research involves the retrieval of relevant material from the databases stored in a computer memory at a remote location. Two systems currently dominate online legal research: WESTLAW and LEXIS. These systems provide access to cases before they are published in print form. In addition, they also provide access to otherwise unreported cases that are available online through their respective databases.

Note that both state and federal court-imposed restrictions may exist on citing unreported cases. *See* Howard Slavitt, *Selling the Integrity of the System of Precedent: Selective Publication, Depublication, and Vacatur*, 30 Harv. C.R.-C.L. L. Rev. 103 (1995); Robert J. Martineau, *Restrictions on Publication and Citation of Judicial Opinions: A Reassessment*, 25 U. Mich. J.L. Ref. 119 (1994).

2. Citing Cases Available on WESTLAW

Bluebook Rule 10.8.1 provides the basic rules governing the citation of unreported cases available on electronic databases. In general, the following are the elements of these citations:

(1) the **name of the case** (*see supra* Citation Exercises 9-11);

(2) the **docket number** of the case (*e.g.*, No. 86 CIV. 2792 (CSH));

(3) the **database identifier**, including any codes or numbers that uniquely identify the case sufficiently to allow a reader to find the case (*e.g.*, 1994 WL 48854); consult *Bluebook* Rule 10.8.1 for citing early cases that have not been assigned a unique database identifier;

(4) the **screen or page number** cited, if any, preceded by an asterisk (*e.g.*, *18);

(5) the **name of the court** (based on the general rules for identifying the court, including its geographic jurisdiction) (*e.g.*, S.D.N.Y. or Cal. Ct. App.); and

(6) the **full date** of the most recent major disposition of the action (usually the date of decision) but abbreviating the month pursuant to *Bluebook* Table T.12.

Note that when a case is available in a published form such as a West reporter, the West reporter should be cited even if the case was found or obtained by means of searching electronic databases on WESTLAW or LEXIS.

Consider the following examples of citations to cases available on WESTLAW:

[Example 1] *Doyle v. Turner*, No. 86 CIV. 2792 (CSH), 1994 WL 48854 (S.D.N.Y. Feb. 16, 1994).

[Example 2] *United States v. Brown*, No. 34-1139, 1996 WL 283313 (1st Cir. Mar. 4, 1996).

[Example 3] *State v. Jones*, No. 1 CA-Cr 92-1856, 1994 WL 620653 (Ariz. Ct. App. Nov. 10, 1994).

3. Typeface Conventions

The typeface conventions for cases cited in electronic databases use the same typeface conventions as those used for cases in any other source. *See supra* Citation Exercise 12. Thus, in a law review footnote, the case name would appear in ordinary roman typeface:

[Example 4] Doyle v. Turner, No. 86 CIV. 2792 (CSH), 1994 WL 48854 (S.D.N.Y. Feb. 16, 1994).

B. INSTRUCTIONS FOR COMPLETING THIS EXERCISE

This exercise is designed to familiarize you with cases available on WESTLAW and gives you practice in citing those cases in proper form. To complete this exercise, retrieve the case listed with your problem number below on WESTLAW.

For your answer to this exercise, state the following:

(a) the full name of the case as it is stated at the beginning of the opinion (*e.g.*, Michael W. Stout, Plaintiff, v. Louis W. Sullivan, M.D., Secretary of the Department of Health and Human Services, Defendant); **you may omit obviously irrelevant portions of a party's name if the full name is a lengthy one;**

(b) the docket number(s) exactly as listed (*e.g.*, No. 89-0828-CV-W-3);

(c) the complete reference to the court exactly as it is indicated at the beginning of the opinion (*e.g.*, United States District Court, W.D. Missouri, Western Division);

(d) the exact date of the most recent major disposition (*e.g.*, April 16, 1990); and

(e) the citation of the case in *Bluebook* (or another designated) form. Assume that the case name is going to appear in a **citation sentence or clause**, not as a part of a grammatical part of a textual sentence, in a **legal memorandum**. For purposes of this exercise, do not indicate any subsequent history in the citation.

Unless otherwise instructed, write your answers on the answer sheet provided in Part 4 of these exercises.

PROBLEM #	**CITATION**
1 200 222 394 417 576	1992 WL 165840
2 101 223 395 418 577	1987 WL 10817
3 102 224 396 419 578	1991 WL 350042
4 103 225 397 420 579	1990 WL 484414
5 104 226 398 421 580	1987 WL 14927
6 105 227 399 422 581	1996 WL 875565
7 106 228 400 423 582	1997 WL 685352
8 107 229 301 424 583	1998 WL 320268
9 108 230 302 425 584	1997 WL 309460
10 109 231 303 426 585	1993 WL 245521
11 110 232 304 427 586	1996 WL 18840
12 111 233 305 428 587	1991 WL 102511
13 112 234 306 429 588	1996 WL 47304
14 113 235 307 430 589	1996 WL 515088
15 114 236 308 431 590	1997 WL 309464
16 115 237 309 432 591	1996 WL 18840
17 116 238 310 433 592	1987 WL 288146
18 117 239 311 434 593	1993 WL 497967
19 118 240 312 435 594	1994 WL 738835
20 119 241 313 436 595	1996 WL 6560
21 120 242 314 437 596	1987 WL 10817
22 121 243 315 438 597	1996 WL 641642
23 122 244 316 439 598	1994 WL 68222
24 123 245 317 440 599	1990 WL 119688
25 124 246 318 441 600	1990 WL 134899
26 125 247 319 442 501	1985 WL 1359
27 126 248 320 443 502	1984 WL 1275
28 127 249 321 444 503	1995 WL 542432
29 128 250 322 445 504	1991 WL 716758
30 129 251 323 446 505	1989 WL 118750
31 130 252 324 447 506	1992 WL 58854
32 131 253 325 448 507	1992 WL 110731
33 132 254 326 449 508	1990 WL 142404
34 133 255 327 450 509	1993 WL 390384
35 134 256 328 451 510	1997 WL 33016
36 135 257 329 452 511	1993 WL 153204
37 136 258 330 453 512	1996 WL 76165
38 137 259 331 454 513	1996 WL 663161
39 138 260 332 455 514	1997 WL 263739
40 139 261 333 456 515	1996 WL 328203
41 140 262 334 457 516	1993 WL 816526
42 141 263 335 458 517	1991 WL 175819
43 142 264 336 459 518	1993 WL 565341
44 143 265 337 460 519	1996 WL 42131

PROBLEM #	CITATION
45 144 266 338 461 520	1995 WL 164502
46 145 267 339 462 521	1993 WL 437670
47 146 268 340 463 522	1995 WL 222059
48 147 269 341 464 523	1993 WL 330093
49 148 270 342 465 524	1997 WL 205335
50 149 271 343 466 525	1993 WL 205857
51 150 272 344 467 526	1996 WL 537217
52 151 273 345 468 527	1994 WL 406548
53 152 274 346 469 528	1996 WL 442798
54 153 275 347 470 529	1994 WL 406548
55 154 276 348 471 530	1992 WL 96350
56 155 277 349 472 531	1989 WL 47369
57 156 278 350 473 532	1992 WL 541251
58 157 279 351 474 533	1997 WL 714236
59 158 280 352 475 534	1997 WL 279870
60 159 281 353 476 535	1994 WL 37001
61 160 282 354 477 536	1993 WL 313112
62 161 283 355 478 537	1989 WL 151919
63 162 284 356 479 538	1990 WL 92484
64 163 285 357 480 539	1993 WL 352809
65 164 286 358 481 540	1992 WL 176597
66 165 287 359 482 541	1987 WL 6856
67 166 288 360 483 542	1996 WL 478686
68 167 289 361 484 543	1990 WL 303126
69 168 290 362 485 544	1994 WL 285039
70 169 291 363 486 545	1997 WL 746455
71 170 292 364 487 546	1996 WL 107107
72 171 293 365 488 547	1994 WL 129573
73 172 294 366 489 548	1995 WL 464909
74 173 295 367 490 549	1991 WL 220380
75 174 296 368 491 550	1987 WL 10817
76 175 297 369 492 551	1989 WL 6489
77 176 298 370 493 552	1996 WL 526780
78 177 299 371 494 553	1992 WL 370238
79 178 300 372 495 554	1996 WL 5067
80 179 201 373 496 555	1997 WL 543068
81 180 202 374 497 556	1995 WL 121519
82 181 203 375 498 557	1994 WL 721589
83 182 204 376 499 558	1993 WL 414668
84 183 205 377 500 559	1987 WL 9402
85 184 206 378 401 560	1997 WL 305222
86 185 207 379 402 561	1996 WL 748051
87 186 208 380 403 562	1992 WL 672982
88 187 209 381 404 563	1995 WL 110355
89 188 210 382 405 564	1989 WL 8043
90 189 211 383 406 565	1991 WL 180104
91 190 212 384 407 566	1992 WL 159803
92 191 213 385 408 567	1995 WL 791937
93 192 214 386 409 568	1994 WL 682620
94 193 215 387 410 569	1994 WL 714252

PROBLEM #	CITATION
95 194 216 388 411 570	1995 WL 261981
96 195 217 389 412 571	1994 WL 481759
97 196 218 390 413 572	1994 WL 562591
98 197 219 391 414 573	1994 WL 779761
99 198 220 392 415 574	1995 WL 444414
100 199 221 393 416 575	1994 WL 67630

CITATION EXERCISE 29
UNREPORTED CASES AVAILABLE ON ELECTRONIC DATABASES: LEXIS

A. INTRODUCTION

1. Electrolic Databases

See supra Citation Exercise 28 for a brief introduction to WESTLAW and LEXIS.

2. Citing Cases Available on LEXIS

As indicated in Citation Exercise 28, *Bluebook* Rule 10.8.1 provides the basis rules governing the citation of unreported cases available on electronic databases. In general, the following are the elements of these citations:

(1) the **name of the case** (*see supra* Citation Exercises 9-11);

(2) the **docket number** of the case (*e.g.*, No. 86 CIV. 2792 (CSH));

(3) the **database identifier**, including any codes or numbers that uniquely identify the case sufficient to allow a reader to find the case (*e.g.*, 1992 U.S. Dist. LEXIS 16736); consult *Bluebook* Rule 10.8.1 for citing early cases that have not been assigned a unique database identifier;

(4) the **screen or page number** cited, if any, preceded by an asterisk (*e.g.*, *18);

(5) the **name of the court** (based on the general rules for identifying the court, including its geographic jurisdiction) (*e.g.*, S.D.N.Y. or Cal. Ct. App.); and

(6) the **full date** of the most recent major disposition of the action (usually the date of decision) but abbreviating the month pursuant to *Bluebook* Table T.12.

Note that when a case is available in a published form such as a West reporter, the West reporter should be cited even if the case was found or obtained by means of searching electronic databases on WESTLAW or LEXIS.

Consider the following examples of citations to cases available on LEXIS:

[**Example 1**] *Tyus v. Robin Constr. Corp.*, No. 92 C 2423, 1992 U.S. Dist. LEXIS 16736 (N.D. Ill. Nov. 2, 1992).

[**Example 2**] *Shieh v. Ebershoff*, No. 93-55327, 1993 U.S. App. LEXIS 34766 (9th Cir. Dec. 30, 1993).

[**Example 3**] *State v. Steffen*, No. C-930351, 1994 Ohio App. LEXIS 1973 (Ohio Ct. App. May 11, 1994).

B. INSTRUCTIONS FOR COMPLETING THIS EXERCISE

This exercise is designed to familiarize you with cases available on LEXIS and gives you practice in citing those cases in proper form. To complete this exercise, retrieve the case listed with your problem number below on LEXIS.

For your answer to this exercise, state the following:

(a) the full name of the case as it is stated at the beginning of the opinion (*e.g.*, Michael W. Stout, Plaintiff, v. Louis W. Sullivan, M.D., Secretary of the Department of Health and Human Services, Defendant); **you may omit obviously irrelevant portions of a party's name if the full name is a lengthy one**;

(b) the docket number(s) exactly as listed (*e.g.*, No. 89-0828-CV-W-3);

(c) the complete reference to the court exactly as it is indicated at the beginning of the opinion (*e.g.*, United States District Court for the Northern District of Illinois, Eastern Division);

(d) the full date of the most recent major disposition of the action (usually the date of decision) (*e.g.*, November 2, 1992); and

(e) the citation of the case in *Bluebook* (or another designated) form. Assume that the case name is going to appear in a **citation sentence or clause**, not as a part of a grammatical part of a textual sentence. For purposes of this exercise, do not indicate any subsequent history in the citation. When necessary, abbreviate "versus," "vs." or "against" to "v." in the case name.

Unless otherwise instructed, write your answers on the answer sheet provided in Part 4 of these exercises.

PROBLEM #	CITATION
1 177 262 385 498 509	1987 U.S. Dist. LEXIS 526
2 178 263 386 499 510	1994 U.S. Dist. LEXIS 62
3 179 264 387 500 511	1987 U.S. Dist. LEXIS 7157
4 180 265 388 401 512	1991 U.S. Dist. LEXIS 19159
5 181 266 389 402 513	1989 U.S. Dist. LEXIS 8276
6 182 267 390 403 514	1992 U.S. Dist. LEXIS 13521
7 183 268 391 404 515	1993 U.S. Dist. LEXIS 310
8 184 269 392 405 516	1997 U.S. Dist. LEXIS 4946
9 185 270 393 406 517	1992 U.S. Dist. LEXIS 7083
10 186 271 394 407 518	1992 U.S. Dist. LEXIS 16203
11 187 272 395 408 519	1995 U.S. Dist. LEXIS 4162
12 188 273 396 409 520	1994 U.S. Dist. LEXIS 17709
13 189 274 397 410 521	1994 U.S. Dist. LEXIS 5827
14 190 275 398 411 522	1994 U.S. Dist. LEXIS 1907
15 191 276 399 412 523	1994 U.S. Dist. LEXIS 1994
16 192 277 400 413 524	1993 U.S. Dist. LEXIS 17731
17 193 278 301 414 525	1993 U.S. Dist. LEXIS 18896
18 194 279 302 415 526	1994 U.S. Dist. LEXIS 767
19 195 280 303 416 527	1994 U.S. Dist. LEXIS 9776
20 196 281 304 417 528	1989 U.S. Dist. LEXIS 10785
21 197 282 305 418 529	1993 U.S. Dist. LEXIS 20309

PROBLEM #	CITATION
22 198 283 306 419 530	1995 U.S. Dist. LEXIS 13625
23 199 284 307 420 531	1995 U.S. Dist. LEXIS 15620
24 200 285 308 421 532	1991 U.S. Dist. LEXIS 697
25 101 286 309 422 533	1992 U.S. Dist. LEXIS 1320
26 102 287 310 423 534	1992 U.S. Dist. LEXIS 1522
27 103 288 311 424 535	1992 U.S. Dist. LEXIS 1320
28 104 289 312 425 536	1992 U.S. Dist. LEXIS 1522
29 105 290 313 426 537	1993 U.S. Dist. LEXIS 9004
30 106 291 314 427 538	1992 U.S. Dist. LEXIS 12978
31 107 292 315 428 539	1987 U.S. Dist. LEXIS 8831
32 108 293 316 429 540	1991 U.S. Dist. LEXIS 13669
33 109 294 317 430 541	1989 U.S. Dist. LEXIS 5089
34 110 295 318 431 542	1990 U.S. Dist. LEXIS 5541
35 111 296 319 432 543	1992 U.S. Dist. LEXIS 17178
36 112 297 320 433 544	1989 U.S. Dist. LEXIS 8916
37 113 298 321 434 545	1991 U.S. Dist. LEXIS 2523
38 114 299 322 435 546	1990 U.S. Dist. LEXIS 5541
39 115 300 323 436 547	1991 U.S. Dist. LEXIS 8195
40 116 201 324 437 548	1991 U.S. Dist. LEXIS 6773
41 117 202 325 438 549	1990 U.S. Dist. LEXIS 10952
42 118 203 326 439 550	1988 U.S. Dist. LEXIS 12546
43 119 204 327 440 551	1991 U.S. Dist. LEXIS 11891
44 120 205 328 441 552	1988 U.S. Dist. LEXIS 3105
45 121 206 329 442 553	1990 U.S. Dist. LEXIS 10952
46 122 207 330 443 554	1990 U.S. Dist. LEXIS 17411
47 123 208 331 444 555	1990 U.S. Dist. LEXIS 1999
48 124 209 332 445 556	1989 U.S. Dist. LEXIS 9296
49 125 210 333 446 557	1993 U.S. Dist. LEXIS 431
50 126 211 334 447 558	1988 U.S. Dist. LEXIS 14684
51 127 212 335 448 559	1994 U.S. Dist. LEXIS 13104
52 128 213 336 449 560	1993 U.S. Dist. LEXIS 18386
53 129 214 337 450 561	1995 U.S. Dist. LEXIS 2191
54 130 215 338 451 562	1994 U.S. Dist. LEXIS 767
55 131 216 339 452 563	1994 U.S. Dist. LEXIS 16349
56 132 217 340 453 564	1995 U.S. Dist. LEXIS 3701
57 133 218 341 454 565	1990 U.S. Dist. LEXIS 13934
58 134 219 342 455 566	1996 U.S. Dist. LEXIS 8274
59 135 220 343 456 567	1995 U.S. Dist. LEXIS 16607
60 136 221 344 457 568	1994 U.S. Dist. LEXIS 3623
61 137 222 345 458 569	1992 U.S. Dist. LEXIS 17230
62 138 223 346 459 570	1994 U.S. Dist. LEXIS 7459
63 139 224 347 460 571	1988 U.S. Dist. LEXIS 17340
64 140 225 348 461 572	1993 U.S. Dist. LEXIS 8643
65 141 226 349 462 573	1994 U.S. Dist. LEXIS 335
66 142 227 350 463 574	1992 U.S. Dist. LEXIS 17506
67 143 228 351 464 575	1993 U.S. Dist. LEXIS 9020
68 144 229 352 465 576	1994 U.S. Dist. LEXIS 19416
69 145 230 353 466 577	1995 U.S. Dist. LEXIS 4958
70 146 231 354 467 578	1994 U.S. Dist. LEXIS 2712
71 147 232 355 468 579	1994 U.S. Dist. LEXIS 19042

PROBLEM #	CITATION
72 148 233 356 469 580	1989 U.S. Dist. LEXIS 9389
73 149 234 357 470 581	1997 U.S. Dist. LEXIS 7426
74 150 235 358 471 582	1994 U.S. Dist. LEXIS 15590
75 151 236 359 472 583	1994 U.S. Dist. LEXIS 4764
76 152 237 360 473 584	1994 U.S. Dist. LEXIS 5816
77 153 238 361 474 585	1995 U.S. Dist. LEXIS 8585
78 154 239 362 475 586	1997 U.S. Dist. LEXIS 1815
79 155 240 363 476 587	1991 U.S. Dist. LEXIS 21163
80 156 241 364 477 588	1992 U.S. Dist. LEXIS 6622
81 157 242 365 478 589	1997 U.S. Dist. LEXIS 4863
82 158 243 366 479 590	1997 U.S. Dist. LEXIS 4945
83 159 244 367 480 591	1994 U.S. Dist. LEXIS 11154
84 160 245 368 481 592	1988 U.S. Dist. LEXIS 12546
85 161 246 369 482 593	1997 U.S. Dist. LEXIS 7426
86 162 247 370 483 594	1994 U.S. Dist. LEXIS 9761
87 163 248 371 484 595	1991 U.S. Dist. LEXIS 8195
88 164 249 372 485 596	1989 U.S. Dist. LEXIS 9389
89 165 250 373 486 597	1991 U.S. Dist. LEXIS 21139
90 166 251 374 487 598	1995 U.S. Dist. LEXIS 8585
91 167 252 375 488 599	1994 U.S. Dist. LEXIS 19416
92 168 253 376 489 600	1993 U.S. Dist. LEXIS 9020
93 169 254 377 490 501	1990 U.S. Dist. LEXIS 5541
94 170 255 378 491 502	1988 U.S. Dist. LEXIS 11275
95 171 256 379 492 503	1994 U.S. Dist. LEXIS 11396
96 172 257 380 493 504	1994 U.S. Dist. LEXIS 16349
97 173 258 381 494 505	1995 U.S. Dist. LEXIS 11316
98 174 259 382 495 506	1993 U.S. Dist. LEXIS 20309
99 175 260 383 496 507	1989 U.S. Dist. LEXIS 10785
100 176 261 384 497 508	1997 U.S. Dist. LEXIS 4946

CITATION EXERCISE 30
SUBSEQUENT HISTORY IN CASE CITATIONS

A. INTRODUCTION

1. Subsequent History

Recall from Citation Exercise 9 that citations to cases in case reporters typically contain (up to) seven basic elements:

(1) the **case name**;

(2) the **volume number** of the reporter;

(3) the abbreviated **name of the reporter**;

(4) the **page number** on which the opinion begins (and any other pages cited in the opinion);

(5) the abbreviated **name of the court**, including its geographic jurisdiction (unless that information is clearly indicated from the reporter cited);

(6) the **year or date** of the decision; and

(7) the **subsequent history** of the case, if any.

See Bluebook Rule 10.1 ("Cases: Basic Citation Forms"). This exercise focuses on the last of these elements: the subsequent history of the case.

Subsequent history refers to later proceedings relative to a reported opinion. The traditional source for finding subsequent history of a case is *Shepard's Citations*. It provides the subsequent (and prior) history of a case immediately after the parallel citation is given (if there is one). A table in *Shepard's* provides a listing of *Shepard's* symbols and their meanings. As part of noting the subsequent treatment of a case, *Shepard's Citations* also indicates when a case has been expressly overruled (using the symbol "o" in front of the subsequent citation).

2. Subsequent History in *Bluebook* Citations

Several *Bluebook* rules regulate when subsequent history of a cited opinion should be included in a citation of an opinion. In general, subsequent history must be shown when a case is cited in full. However, the sixteenth edition of the *Bluebook* now provides that denials of certiorari or similar discretionary denials of review should be omitted "unless the decision is less than two years old or the denial is particularly relevant." In addition, the history of a case on remand and any denial of a rehearing should be omitted unless it is particularly relevant. Any disposition withdrawn by the deciding authority, such an affirmance followed by a reversal on rehearing, should also be omitted. *Bluebook* Rule 10.7.

The most frequently used phrases for indicating subsequent history in *Bluebook* citations are as follows:

Bluebook Abbreviation	*Shepard's* Abbreviation	**Meaning**
aff'd,	a	Affirmed
appeal dismissed,	D	Appeal dismissed
modified,	m	Modified on appeal
rev'd,	r	Reversed on appeal
vacated,	v	Vacated on appeal
cert. denied,	cert den	Certiorari denied
cert. dismissed,	cert dis	Certiorari dismissed
overruled by	o	Overruled

See Bluebook Table T.9 ("Explanatory Phrases"). Note that these phrases are italicized (single underscored) and that most of them have a comma after them, but some do not.

The year of decision is included only with the *last* cited decision when a case with several decisions in the *same* year is cited. However, if the exact date of decision is required for either case by *Bluebook* Rule 10.5 (for all unreported cases, all cases cited to newspapers, periodicals, and looseleaf services), you should include both dates. *Bluebook* Rule 10.5(c).

When the name of a case differs in prior or subsequent history, both case names must be given in the citation; however, the second name should not be given when the parties' names are merely reversed or when the difference occurs in a citation to a denial of review by writ of certiorari or a rehearing. *Bluebook* Rule 10.7.2. A different name in subsequent history is introduced by "*sub nom.*"

The following examples illustrate how subsequent history is shown in *Bluebook* citations of cases:

> **[Example 1]** *Caminetti v. Pacific Mut. Life Ins. Co.,* 139 P.2d 908 (Cal.), *cert. denied,* 320 U.S. 802 (1943).
>
> The year of decision is included only with the *last* cited decision when a case with several decisions in the *same* year is cited. In this example, the year of decision of the California Supreme Court and the year that the U.S. Supreme Court denied certiorari were the same (1943); thus, the date was omitted from the *Pacific Reporter Second* part of the citation. Note also the sixteenth edition of the *Bluebook* provides that denials of certiorari or similar discretionary denials of review should be omitted "unless the decision is less than two years old or the denial is particularly relevant." In this instance, the subsequent history is shown because it presumably is of particular relevance for purposes of the citation.

[Example 2] *A.G. Becker, Inc. v. Board of Governors*, 693 F.2d 136 (D.C. Cir. 1982), *rev'd sub nom. Securities Indus. Ass'n v. Board of Governors*, 468 U.S. 137 (1984).

> The year of decision has been included with both cited decisions because they were decided in *different* years; when the name of a case differs in prior or subsequent history, both case names must be given in the citation; in this instance, the names differ—with the second name introduced by the phrase "*sub nom.*"

[Example 3] *Winn v. Trans World Airlines*, 75 Pa. Commw. 366, 462 A.2d 301, *aff'd by an equally divided court*, 506 Pa. 138, 484 A.2d 392 (1983).

> *Bluebook* Table T.9 provides abbreviations for subsequent and prior history in the form of explanatory phrases, such as "affirmed by an equally divided court"; note that a comma is sometimes used after the phrase (as above), but not always; the comma is not italicized (underscored); a comma is not used when what follows is a direct object.

[Example 4] *United States v. Central Nat'l Bank*, 429 F.2d 5 (8th Cir. 1970).

> No subsequent history is shown in the above example because the only subsequent history is a denial of certiorari; denials of certiorari or similar discretionary denials of review should be omitted "unless the decision is less than two years old or the denial is particularly relevant." *Bluebook* Rule 10.7.

[Example 5] *United States v. Central Nat'l Bank*, 429 F.2d 5 (8th Cir.), *cert. denied*, 400 U.S. 910 (1970).

> In this instance, the subsequent history is shown because it presumably is of particular relevance for purposes of the citation; note also that even though certiorari was denied under the name of "*Watkins v. United States*," this second name is not be given when the parties' names are merely reversed or when the difference occurs in a citation to a denial of review by writ of certiorari or a rehearing. *Bluebook* Rule 10.7.2.

3. Special Note on Prior History in *Bluebook* Citations

Prior history of a case refers to earlier proceedings in the case relative to an opinion, such as an earlier appeal. According to *Bluebook* Rule 10.7, prior history of a case generally is not indicated in a citation. It should be given "only if significant to the point for which the case is cited or if the disposition cited does not intelligibly describe the issues in the case." Prior history is indicated by an explanatory phrase (*aff'g, modifying, rev'g, enforcing*, etc.). *Bluebook* Rule 10.7 & Table T.9.

B. INSTRUCTIONS FOR COMPLETING THIS EXERCISE

To complete this exercise, find the case listed with your problem number below in the cited reporter. Then find the appropriate volume of *Shepard's Case Citations* and determine the subsequent history of that case.

For your answer to this exercise, state the following:

(a) the full case name of the case that you are shepardizing, as it is stated in the reporter at the beginning of the opinion (*e.g.*, The State, Respondent, v. Russell Collins, Appellant); **you may omit obviously irrelevant portions of a party's name if the full name is a lengthy one**;

(b) the complete reference to the court exactly as it is indicated at the beginning of the opinion (*e.g.*, Supreme Court of South Carolina);

(c) the exact date of decision (*e.g.*, Jan. 5, 1998);

(d) the entry in *Shepard's Citations* indicating the subsequent history (*e.g.*, US cert den in 383 US 952, v134 CaR 774, r528 F2d 745) for the case that you are shepardizing; do not, however, include the history on remand or a denial of a rehearing); if there is no subsequent history, answer "none";

(e) for entry listed in (d), if any, (i) the full case name as it is stated in the reporter at the beginning of the opinion; **you may omit obviously irrelevant portions of a party's name if the full name is a lengthy one**; and (ii) the exact date of decision; **(you will need to consult the case or entry in the reporter indicated in (d) to find this information)**; and

(f) the citation of the case in *Bluebook* (or another designated) form. Indicate any relevant subsequent history in the citation. For purposes of this exercise, do not show the history on remand or a denial of a rehearing in the citation; **however, do show denials and dismissals of certiorari.** Unless otherwise instructed, if you are citing a state court case, assume that you are citing it in a document that **WILL** be submitted to a state court in the jurisdiction from which the case arises. When necessary, use *Shepard's Citations* to find any missing parallel citations. **For U.S. Supreme Court actions (e.g., denials of certiorari, etc.), cite only *United States Reports* (when relevant).**

Unless otherwise instructed, write your answers on the answer sheet provided in Part 4 of these exercises.

PROBLEM #	CITATION
1 190 270 350 430 520	269 A.2d 737
2 191 271 351 431 521	276 A.2d 18
3 192 272 352 432 522	329 A.2d 376
4 193 273 353 433 523	239 A.2d 409
5 194 274 354 434 524	315 A.2d 501
6 195 275 355 435 525	284 A.2d 700
7 196 276 356 436 526	352 A.2d 4
8 197 277 357 437 527	356 A.2d 897
9 198 278 358 438 528	288 A.2d 863
10 199 279 359 439 529	273 A.2d 361

PROBLEM #	CITATION
11 200 280 360 440 530	420 P.2d 693
12 101 281 361 441 531	450 P.2d 364
13 102 282 362 442 532	455 P.2d 34
14 103 283 263 443 533	455 P.2d 395
15 104 284 364 444 534	524 P.2d 97
16 105 285 365 445 535	503 P.2d 1322
17 106 286 366 446 536	408 P.2d 116
18 107 287 367 447 537	466 P.2d 961
19 108 288 368 448 538	435 P.2d 692
20 109 289 369 449 539	213 N.E.2d 438
21 110 290 370 450 540	218 N.E.2d 428
22 111 291 371 451 541	219 N.E.2d 194
23 112 292 372 452 542	241 N.E.2d 419
24 113 293 373 453 543	244 N.E.2d 89
25 114 294 374 454 544	245 N.E.2d 771
26 115 295 375 455 545	193 N.E.2d 449
27 116 296 376 456 546	190 N.E.2d 719
28 117 297 377 457 547	134 N.E.2d 914
29 118 298 378 458 548	256 So. 2d 98
30 119 299 379 459 549	241 So. 2d 390
31 120 300 380 460 550	197 So. 2d 241
32 121 201 381 461 551	123 F. 817
33 122 202 382 462 552	128 F. 527
34 123 203 383 463 553	374 F. Supp. 301
35 124 204 384 464 554	239 F.2d 97
36 125 205 385 465 555	262 F.2d 501
37 126 206 386 466 556	281 F.2d 59
38 127 207 387 467 557	240 N.W.2d 729
39 128 208 388 468 558	221 N.W.2d 357
40 129 209 389 469 559	219 N.W.2d 920
41 130 210 390 470 560	377 F. Supp. 1065
42 131 211 391 471 561	211 N.W.2d 642
43 132 212 392 472 562	199 N.W.2d 480
44 133 213 393 473 563	182 N.W.2d 887
45 134 214 394 474 564	174 N.W.2d 504
46 135 215 395 475 565	149 N.W.2d 557
47 136 216 396 476 566	163 S.E.2d 589
48 137 217 397 477 567	197 S.E.2d 502
49 138 218 398 478 568	176 S.E.2d 818
50 139 219 399 479 569	199 S.E.2d 183
51 140 220 400 480 570	188 S.E.2d 296
52 141 221 301 481 571	236 S.E.2d 353
53 142 222 302 482 572	216 S.E.2d 608
54 143 223 303 483 573	215 S.E.2d 540
55 144 224 304 484 574	214 S.E.2d 742
56 145 225 305 485 575	307 S.W.2d 385
57 146 226 306 486 576	389 S.W.2d 774
58 147 227 307 487 577	481 S.W.2d 473
59 148 228 308 488 578	277 S.W.2d 125
60 149 229 309 489 579	278 S.W.2d 398

PROBLEM #	CITATION
61 150 230 310 490 580	418 S.W.2d 708
62 151 231 311 491 581	362 S.W.2d 695
63 152 232 312 492 582	518 S.W.2d 207
64 153 233 313 493 583	520 S.W.2d 424
65 154 234 314 494 584	337 F.2d 891
66 155 235 315 495 585	335 F.2d 1021
67 156 236 316 496 586	431 F.2d 1282
68 157 237 317 497 587	500 F.2d 144
69 158 238 318 498 588	505 F.2d 426
70 159 239 319 499 589	320 F.2d 285
71 160 240 320 500 590	317 F.2d 838
72 161 241 321 401 591	251 F.2d 69
73 162 242 322 402 592	236 F.2d 708
74 163 243 323 403 593	65 F. Supp. 130
75 164 244 324 404 594	76 F. Supp. 604
76 165 245 325 405 595	99 F. Supp. 81
77 166 246 326 406 596	100 F. Supp. 198
78 167 247 327 407 597	88 F. Supp. 64
79 168 248 328 408 598	98 F. Supp. 455
80 169 249 329 409 599	111 F. Supp. 912
81 170 250 330 410 600	116 F. Supp. 15
82 171 251 331 411 501	119 F. Supp. 295
83 172 252 332 412 502	100 Cal. Rptr. 618
84 173 253 333 413 503	549 F.2d 89
85 174 254 334 414 504	125 Cal. Rptr. 265
86 175 255 335 415 505	384 F. Supp. 1231
87 176 256 336 416 506	442 F. Supp. 1000
88 177 257 337 417 507	82 Cal. Rptr. 473
89 178 258 338 418 508	67 Cal. Rptr. 409
90 179 259 339 419 509	90 Cal. Rptr. 15
91 180 260 340 420 510	42 Cal. Rptr. 169
92 181 261 341 421 511	258 N.Y.S.2d 109
93 182 262 342 422 512	175 N.Y.S.2d 794
94 183 263 343 423 513	264 N.Y.S.2d 557
95 184 264 344 424 514	265 N.Y.S.2d 899
96 185 265 345 425 515	386 N.Y.S.2d 691
97 186 266 346 426 516	383 N.Y.S.2d 573
98 187 267 347 427 517	255 N.Y.S.2d 833
99 188 268 348 428 518	228 N.Y.S.2d 641
100 189 269 349 429 519	282 N.Y.S.2d 491

PART 3

CITING LEGISLATIVE AND OTHER SOURCES

A. EXERCISES IN THIS PART

Part 3 focuses on citing federal and state statutes; constitutions; treaties and other international agreements to which the United States is a party; legislative history; and administrative regulations. The following ten exercises are included in this part:

Citation Exercise 31. Federal Statutes (I)
Citation Exercise 32. Federal Statutes (II)
Citation Exercise 33. State Statutes (I)
Citation Exercise 34. State Statutes (II)
Citation Exercise 35. State Statutes (III)
Citation Exercise 36. Constitutions
Citation Exercise 37. Treaties
Citation Exercise 38. Legislative History
Citation Exercise 39. Administrative Regulations (I)
Citation Exercise 40. Administrative Regulations (II)

B. BASIC CITATION FORMS ILLUSTRATED

The following chart illustrates the basic forms for citations of various legislative and other sources based on the *Bluebook* rules and typeface conventions for legal memoranda and court documents:

CITING LEGISLATIVE AND OTHER SOURCES IN *BLUEBOOK* FORM	
SOURCE	**BASIC CITATION FORMS**
FEDERAL STATUTES —Session Law (entire law cited) —Session Law (specific part of the law cited)	Hatch Act Reform Amendments of 1993, Pub. L. No. 103-94, 107 Stat. 1001. Hatch Act Reform Amendments of 1993, Pub. L. No. 103-94, § 2, 107 Stat. 1001, 1001-04.

CITING LEGISLATIVE AND OTHER SOURCES IN *BLUEBOOK* FORM (CONTINUED)	
SOURCE	**BASIC CITATION FORMS**
FEDERAL STATUTES (CONTINUED) —Session Law (prior to 1957 with a chapter no.)	Judiciary Act of 1789, ch. 20, § 17, 1 Stat. 73, 83.
—Session Law (with no official or popular name)	Act of June 1, 1872, ch. 255, § 5, 17 Stat. 196, 197.
—Session Law (enacted in a different year than the year given in the name)	National Environmental Policy Act of 1969, Pub. L. No. 91-190, 83 Stat. 852 (1970).
—Session Law (indicating where the law will be or is codified)	Rules Enabling Act of 1934, ch. 651, 48 Stat. 1064 (codified as amended at 28 U.S.C. § 2072-2074 (1994)).
—Codified law in the official *U.S. Code*	28 U.S.C. § 1404(a) (1994).
—Codified law in the *U.S. Code Annotated*	Asbestos School Hazard Detection Act of 1980, 20 U.S.C.A. §§ 3601-3611 (West 1990).
—Codified law in the *U.S. Code Service*	Hatch Reform Act Amendments of 1993, § 4, 18 U.S.C.S. § 602 (Law.-Coop. 1996).
—Codified law in a supplement of an annotated code	Hatch Reform Act Amendments of 1993, § 4, 18 U.S.C.A. § 602 (West Supp. 1998).
STATE STATUTES —Session Laws	Act of Nov. 15, 1989, ch. 516, 1989 Mass. Acts 796. 1904 Ky. Acts 181.
—Cited to a Typical State Code	Neb. Rev. Stat. § 8-320 (1997). Wyo. Stat. Ann. § 1-1-122(a) (Michie 1997). Okla. Stat. Ann. tit. 2, § 9-202 (West 1997).
—Cited to a Typical State Subject-Matter Code	Cal. Penal Code § 667(c)(1) (West Supp. 1998).
CONSTITUTIONS —U.S. Constitution	U.S. Const. art. I, § 8.
—Amendments to the U.S. Constitution	U.S. Const. amend. IX.
—State Constitutions	W. Va. Const. art. 7, § 4.

CITING LEGISLATIVE AND OTHER SOURCES IN *BLUEBOOK* FORM (CONTINUED)	
SOURCE	**BASIC CITATION FORMS**
TREATIES —Bilateral, with the U.S. as a party —Multilateral, with the U.S. as a party	Extradition Treaty, May 4, 1978, U.S.-Mex., art. 5, 31 U.S.T. 5061, 5063-64. Treaty of Friendship, Commerce and Consular Rights, Feb. 13, 1934, U.S.-Fin., 49 Stat. 2659. Convention on the High Seas, Apr. 29, 1958, 13 U.S.T. 2312, 450 U.N.T.S. 82.
LEGISLATIVE HISTORY —Federal Bills —Federal Hearings —Federal Committee Reports —Congressional debates	H.R. 956, 104th Cong., 1st Sess. (1995). *The Preference System: Hearing Before the Subcomm. on Immigration and Refugee Policy of the Senate Comm. on the Judiciary*, 97th Cong. 59 (1982) (responses submitted by Labor Department to questions posed by the Senate Subcommittee on Immigration and Refugee Policy). S. Rep. No. 103-57, at 9-10 (1993), *reprinted in* 1993 U.S.C.A.A.N. 1802, 1810-11. 111 Cong. Rec. 19,379 (1965). 136 Cong. Rec. H10959 (daily ed. Oct. 22, 1990) (remarks of Rep. Dingell).
ADMINISTRATIVE REGULATIONS —Cited to the *Federal Register* —Cited to the *Code of Federal Regulations*	50 Fed. Reg. 52,170 (1985). Cuban Assets Control Regulations, 28 Fed. Reg. 6974 (1963) (codified as amended at 31 C.F.R. §§ 515.101-.809 (1998)). 31 C.F.R. § 515.101 (1998). S.E.C. Rule 13e-1, 17 C.F.R. § 240.13e-4(f)(3) (1984).
ADMINISTRATIVE DECISIONS —Cited to the official reporter	*Middle Atl. Conference*, 310 I.C.C. 609 (1960).

CITING LEGISLATIVE AND OTHER SOURCES IN *BLUEBOOK* FORM (CONTINUED)	
SOURCE	**BASIC CITATION FORMS**
RULES OF EVIDENCE, PRACTICE, PROCEDURE, AND ETHICS —Federal Rules of Civil Procedure	Fed. R. Civ. P. 11.
—Federal Rules of Criminal Procedure	Fed. R. Crim. P. 12.
—Federal Rules of Appellate Procedure	Fed. R. App. P. 28
—Federal Rules of Evidence	Fed. R. Evid. 902.
—State Rules of Procedure	Ky. R. Crim. P. 9.38.
—Codes of Ethics	Model Rules of Professional Conduct Rule 1.2(d) (1983). Model Code of Professional Responsibility DR 7-102(A)(7) (1969).

CITATION EXERCISE 31
FEDERAL STATUTES (I)

A. INTRODUCTION

1. Federal Slip and Session Laws

Federal statutes are published officially (by the federal government) in two ways: (1) slip and session laws (chronologically); and (2) a statutory code (organized by subject).

Initially, each recently enacted statute is published in a pamphlet form known as a slip law. After each session of Congress, all laws enacted during that session (along with Presidential proclamations, reorganization plans, interstate compacts approved by Congress, and concurrent resolutions) are officially published in order of enactment in the *United States Statutes at Large* (Stat.).

2. Citing *United States Statutes at Large*

According to *Bluebook* Rule 12.4, citations to statutes in the *United States Statutes at Large* (Stat.) should include the following:

(1) the official or popular **name** of the statute (or both) (*e.g.*, Employee Polygraph Protection Act of 1988); if a statute does not have an official or popular name, use the full date of enactment (*e.g.*, Act of Aug. 12, 1958); *see Bluebook* Rule 12.4(a); abbreviate months according to *Bluebook* Table T.12;

(2) the **chapter number** before 1957 (*e.g.*, ch. 42) **or public law number** thereafter (*e.g.*, Pub. L. No. 85-623); *see Bluebook* Table T.1;

(3) the particular **section**(s), if any specific sections are cited (*e.g.*, § 7);

(4) the **volume number** of *United States Statutes at Large* (*e.g.*, 100);

(5) **Stat.**—the abbreviated designation for the *United States Statutes at Large*; *see Bluebook* Table T.1;

(6) the **page number on which the act begins** in the volume (*e.g.*, 646);

(7) the **page or inclusive pages on which the relevant section or sections appear** (*e.g.*, 652 or 648-50); *see Bluebook* Rule 12.4(b); cite multiple pages by giving inclusive page numbers, separated by a hyphen or a dash (*e.g.*, 35-36); if the pages cited consist of three or more numbers, you should retain the last two digits and drop the repetitious digit(s) (*e.g.*, 173-74 or 1135-36); *see Bluebook* Rule 3.3(d);

(8) the **year** of enactment (*e.g.*, 1998); however, the year of enactment should be omitted when it appears as part of the name of the statute; *see Bluebook* Rule 12.4(d); and

(9) **the location where the statutory provision cited has been or will be codified** in the *United States Code* (if that information is known and the provisions

169

are not too widely scattered to be usefully indicated) (*e.g.*, to be codified at 15 U.S.C. § 1242); *see Bluebook* Rule 12.4(e).

The following are typical examples of citations to statutes in *United States Statutes at Large*:

> **[Example 1]** Employee Polygraph Protection Act of 1988, Pub. L. No. 100-347, § 7, 102 Stat. 646, 648-50.
> **[Example 2]** Act of Aug. 12, 1958, Pub. L. No. 85-623, 72 Stat. 562.
> **[Example 3]** Rules of Decision Act, ch. 20, § 34, 1 Stat. 73, 92 (1789) (codified as amended at 28 U.S.C. § 1652).

3. Typeface Conventions

Citations of session laws in court documents, legal memoranda, and law review articles all have the same roman typeface, as illustrated above.

B. INSTRUCTIONS FOR COMPLETING THIS EXERCISE

To complete this exercise, find the federal statute (session law) listed with your problem number below in the appropriate volume of *United States Statutes at Large* (Stat.). For your answer to this exercise, cite the statute in *Bluebook* (or another designated) form. However, for purposes of this exercise, you should **omit** any reference to the location where the statutory provision has been codified in the *United States Code*. If you have difficulty finding the needed volume of the *United States Statutes at Large*, you can try locating the statute in the "statutes section" of West's *U.S. Code Congressional and Administrative News*, which reproduces statutes exactly as they appear in the *United States Statutes at Large*.

Unless otherwise instructed, write your answers on the answer sheet provided in Part 4 of these exercises.

PROBLEM #	CITATION
1 158 255 328 453 572	78 Stat. 769
2 159 256 329 454 573	80 Stat. 372
3 160 257 330 455 574	81 Stat. 602
4 161 258 331 456 575	78 Stat. 890
5 162 259 332 457 576	83 Stat. 838
6 163 260 333 458 577	84 Stat. 1018
7 164 261 334 459 578	85 Stat. 497
8 165 262 335 460 579	92 Stat. 1607
9 166 263 336 461 580	86 Stat. 1074
10 167 264 337 462 581	87 Stat. 839
11 168 265 338 463 582	80 Stat. 795
12 169 266 339 464 583	88 Stat. 829

PROBLEM #	CITATION
13 170 267 340 465 584	89 Stat. 773
14 171 268 341 466 585	81 Stat. 613
15 172 269 342 467 586	90 Stat. 2541
16 173 270 343 468 587	82 Stat. 476
17 174 271 344 469 588	91 Stat. 533
18 175 272 345 470 589	92 Stat. 2402
19 176 273 346 571 590	83 Stat. 284
20 177 274 347 472 591	93 Stat. 387
21 178 275 348 473 592	93 Stat. 698
22 179 276 349 474 593	84 Stat. 466
23 180 277 350 475 594	93 Stat. 76
24 181 278 351 476 595	92 Stat. 1774
25 182 279 352 477 596	85 Stat. 178
26 183 280 353 478 597	91 Stat. 553
27 184 281 354 479 598	91 Stat. 319
28 185 282 355 480 599	86 Stat. 424
29 186 283 356 481 600	79 Stat. 437
30 187 284 357 482 501	93 Stat. 1067
31 188 285 358 483 502	86 Stat. 1207
32 189 286 359 484 503	71 Stat. 308
33 190 287 360 485 504	74 Stat. 362
34 191 288 361 486 505	87 Stat. 91
35 192 289 362 487 506	73 Stat. 457
36 193 290 363 488 507	72 Stat. 171
37 194 291 364 489 508	88 Stat. 266
38 195 292 365 490 509	76 Stat. 23
39 196 293 366 491 510	77 Stat. 92
40 197 294 367 492 511	89 Stat. 871
41 198 295 368 493 512	93 Stat. 1053
42 199 296 369 494 513	93 Stat. 989
43 200 297 370 495 514	90 Stat. 1260
44 101 298 371 496 515	93 Stat. 503
45 102 299 372 497 516	93 Stat. 327
46 103 300 373 498 517	91 Stat. 262
47 104 201 374 499 518	92 Stat. 499
48 105 202 375 500 519	92 Stat. 1705
49 106 203 376 401 520	92 Stat. 1325
50 107 204 377 402 521	92 Stat. 2463
51 108 205 378 403 522	71 Stat. 307
52 109 206 379 404 523	92 Stat. 808
53 110 207 380 405 524	74 Stat. 372
54 111 208 381 406 525	73 Stat. 519
55 112 209 382 407 526	78 Stat. 908
56 113 210 383 408 527	78 Stat. 908
57 114 211 384 409 528	76 Stat. 23
58 115 212 385 410 529	79 Stat. 845
59 116 213 386 411 530	77 Stat. 361
60 117 214 387 412 531	92 Stat. 3097
61 118 215 388 413 532	92 Stat. 33
62 119 216 389 414 533	78 Stat. 158

PROBLEM #	CITATION
63 120 217 390 415 534	79 Stat. 5
64 121 218 391 416 535	79 Stat. 5
65 122 219 392 417 536	79 Stat. 27
66 123 220 393 418 537	79 Stat. 136
67 124 221 394 419 538	80 Stat. 94
68 125 222 395 420 539	80 Stat. 107
69 126 223 396 421 540	80 Stat. 132
70 127 224 397 422 541	80 Stat. 203
71 128 225 398 423 542	80 Stat. 214
72 129 226 399 424 543	81 Stat. 78
73 130 227 400 425 544	81 Stat. 100
74 131 228 301 426 545	81 Stat. 79
75 132 229 302 427 546	81 Stat. 145
76 133 230 303 428 547	82 Stat. 197
77 134 231 304 429 548	82 Stat. 292
78 135 232 305 430 549	82 Stat. 395
79 136 233 306 431 550	83 Stat. 103
80 137 234 307 432 551	83 Stat. 141
81 138 235 308 433 552	83 Stat. 146
82 139 236 309 434 553	83 Stat. 283
83 140 237 310 435 554	84 Stat. 1620
84 141 238 311 436 555	84 Stat. 1674
85 142 239 312 437 556	84 Stat. 1676
86 143 240 313 438 557	84 Stat. 1713
87 144 241 314 439 558	93 Stat. 749
88 145 242 315 440 559	85 Stat. 101
89 146 243 316 441 560	85 Stat. 157
90 147 244 317 442 561	85 Stat. 178
91 148 245 318 443 562	85 Stat. 191
92 149 246 319 444 563	86 Stat. 235
93 150 247 320 445 564	86 Stat. 503
94 151 248 321 446 565	86 Stat. 532
95 152 249 322 447 566	87 Stat. 27
96 153 250 323 448 567	87 Stat. 12
97 154 251 324 449 568	87 Stat. 30
98 155 252 325 450 569	87 Stat. 197
99 156 253 326 451 570	87 Stat. 907
100 157 254 327 452 571	87 Stat. 906

CITATION EXERCISE 32
FEDERAL STATUTES (II)

A. INTRODUCTION

1. Codifications of Federal Statutes

The *United States Code* (U.S.C.) is the official subject compilation of federal statutes. It is printed and sold by the U.S. Government Printing Office. For most research purposes, however, lawyers use one of the unofficial, annotated versions of the *Code*: West's *United States Code Annotated* and LEXIS Law Publishing's (formerly Lawyers Cooperative Publishing's) *United States Code Service*.

2. Citing the *United States Code* and Its Annotated Versions

Table T.1 indicates that the official version of the *United States Code* should be cited if the provision appears therein. As a matter of convenience, however, many lawyers cite one of the annotated versions of the *Code*.

According to *Bluebook* Rule 12, provisions in the *United States Code* should be cited as follows:

(1) Cite the *United States Code* (U.S.C.) by **title number, section number,** and **edition or supplement date**. Include the **supplement number** of the official version of the *Code* if you are citing it. Include the **publisher's name** (West, Law. Co-op., LEXIS, or Gould) if you are citing an unofficial version. *See Bluebook* Table T.1. Give the **name** and **original section number** only if the statute is commonly cited in that manner or if the information would otherwise help in identifying the provision. *Bluebook* Rules 12.2 & 12.3.

(2) Cite **statutes no longer in force** to the current *Code* if they still appear therein. Otherwise, cite them to the *United States Statutes at Large* or another secondary source. *Bluebook* Rule 12.2.1(b). In any event, indicate parenthetically that they are no longer in force (*e.g.*, repealed 1998) or add a full citation to the repealing statutes, introduced by "*repealed by.*" *Bluebook* Rule 12.6.1.

(3) Cite **consecutive sections or subsections** of a statute by inclusive numbers. Identical digits or letters may be omitted when they are preceded by a punctuation mark "unless doing so would create confusion"; all other digits should be retained. *Bluebook* Rule 3.4(b) (discussing the citation of multiple sections and subsections).

(4) The **current Internal Revenue Code** (I.R.C.) is often cited as a separate codification even though it does appear in Title 26 of the *United States Code*. In memoranda and briefs, citations to the current Internal Revenue Code may omit the date and the publisher's name. *See Bluebook* Rule 12.8.1 & Practitioners' Notes P.5.

The following are typical citations to the *United States Code* and its unofficial annotated versions:

[**Example 1**]　Lanham Act § 14(c), 15 U.S.C. § 1054(c) (1994).
[**Example 2**]　33 U.S.C.A. § 1507 (West 1986).
[**Example 3**]　15 U.S.C.S. § 26 (Law. Co-op. 1991).
[**Example 4**]　Resource Conservation and Recovery Act, 42 U.S.C.A. §§ 6901-6992k (West 1995).

3. Special Note on Statutory Supplements and Pocket Parts

The official *United States Code* was first published in 1926. It is now reissued every six years by the U.S. Government Printing Office. It is also supplemented by annual cumulative supplement volumes. The supplement volumes are cited as follows:

[**Example 5**]　15 U.S.C. §§ 6301-6312 (Supp. II 1996).

The *United States Code Annotated* and the *United States Code Service* are kept up to date by pocket parts and replacement volumes. The supplementary material in these publications is cited as follows:

[**Example 6**]　35 U.S.C.A. § 42 (West 1994 & Supp. 1998),
[**Example 7**]　22 U.S.C.A. § 6321 (West Supp. 1998).

B.　INSTRUCTIONS FOR COMPLETING THIS EXERCISE

To complete this exercise, find the cited federal statutory provision listed with your problem number below in West's *United States Code Annotated* (U.S.C.A.). If the provision is no longer included in the *Code*, complete a different problem.

For your answer to this exercise, state the following:

(a) the copyright date of the volume of West's *United States Code Annotated* that you used (located on the page following the title page of the volume); and

(b) the citation of the code section in *Bluebook* (or another designated) form. Cite the code section to *United States Code Annotated* (*e.g.*, 28 U.S.C.A. § 1404(a) (West 1993).). Be sure to check the supplement to see if the section has been added or amended since the publication of the main volume. If the current version appears in the supplement, cite the supplement appropriately. Assume that your citation will appear in a court document or legal memorandum, not in a law review article.

Unless otherwise instructed, write your answers on the answer sheet provided in Part 4 of these exercises.

PROBLEM #	CITATION
1 155 206 322 421 533	2 U.S.C.A. § 262
2 156 207 323 422 534	3 U.S.C.A. § 8
3 157 208 324 423 535	5 U.S.C.A. § 705

PROBLEM #	CITATION
4 158 209 325 424 536	5 U.S.C.A. § 2951
5 159 210 326 425 537	5 U.S.C.A. § 8912
6 160 211 327 426 538	7 U.S.C.A. § 941
7 161 212 328 427 539	7 U.S.C.A. § 1621
8 162 213 329 428 540	7 U.S.C.A. § 2619
9 163 214 330 429 541	8 U.S.C.A. § 1258
10 164 215 331 430 542	10 U.S.C.A. § 507
11 165 216 332 431 543	10 U.S.C.A. § 850
12 166 217 333 432 544	10 U.S.C.A. § 1168
13 167 218 334 433 545	10 U.S.C.A. § 2541
14 168 219 335 434 546	11 U.S.C.A. § 324
15 169 220 336 435 547	11 U.S.C.A. § 509
16 170 221 337 436 548	11 U.S.C.A. § 553
17 171 222 338 437 549	11 U.S.C.A. § 1122
18 172 223 339 438 550	12 U.S.C.A. § 1729
19 173 224 340 439 551	12 U.S.C.A. § 1814
20 174 225 341 440 552	12 U.S.C.A. § 2183
21 175 226 342 441 553	15 U.S.C.A. § 64
22 176 227 343 442 554	15 U.S.C.A. § 382
23 177 228 344 443 555	15 U.S.C.A. § 1001
24 178 229 345 444 556	15 U.S.C.A. § 2303
25 179 230 346 445 557	16 U.S.C.A. § 457
26 180 231 347 446 558	16 U.S.C.A. § 820
27 181 232 348 447 559	16 U.S.C.A. § 1860
28 182 233 349 448 560	17 U.S.C.A. § 407
29 183 234 350 449 561	18 U.S.C.A. § 111
30 184 235 351 450 562	18 U.S.C.A. § 498
31 185 236 352 451 563	18 U.S.C.A. § 1302
32 186 237 353 452 564	18 U.S.C.A. § 2276
33 187 238 354 453 565	18 U.S.C.A. § 3107
34 188 239 355 454 566	18 U.S.C.A. § 3691
35 189 240 356 455 567	19 U.S.C.A. § 1323
36 190 241 357 456 568	19 U.S.C.A. § 2391
37 191 242 358 457 569	20 U.S.C.A. § 804
38 192 243 359 458 570	21 U.S.C.A. § 351
39 193 244 360 459 571	21 U.S.C.A. § 957
40 194 245 361 460 572	23 U.S.C.A. § 113
41 195 246 362 461 573	25 U.S.C.A. § 476
42 196 247 363 462 574	26 U.S.C.A. § 32
43 197 248 364 463 575	26 U.S.C.A. § 74
44 198 249 365 464 576	42 U.S.C.A. § 1986
45 199 250 366 465 577	26 U.S.C.A. § 318
46 200 251 367 466 578	26 U.S.C.A. § 441
47 101 252 368 467 579	26 U.S.C.A. § 513
48 102 253 369 468 580	26 U.S.C.A. § 960
49 103 254 370 469 581	26 U.S.C.A. § 1055
50 104 255 371 470 582	26 U.S.C.A. § 2206
51 105 256 372 471 583	28 U.S.C.A. § 1351
52 106 257 373 472 584	28 U.S.C.A. § 1335

PROBLEM #	CITATION
53 107 258 374 473 585	26 U.S.C.A. § 6214
54 108 259 375 474 586	26 U.S.C.A. § 7421
55 109 260 376 475 587	28 U.S.C.A. § 1392
56 110 261 377 476 588	28 U.S.C.A. § 2678
57 111 262 378 477 589	29 U.S.C.A. § 153
58 112 263 379 478 590	29 U.S.C.A. § 180
59 113 264 380 479 591	29 U.S.C.A. § 528
60 114 265 381 480 592	30 U.S.C.A. § 83
61 115 266 382 481 593	31 U.S.C.A. § 9105
62 116 267 383 482 594	33 U.S.C.A. § 386
63 117 268 384 483 595	33 U.S.C.A. § 591
64 118 269 385 484 596	33 U.S.C.A. § 1227
65 119 270 386 485 597	33 U.S.C.A. § 1507
66 120 271 387 486 598	35 U.S.C.A. § 33
67 121 272 388 487 599	35 U.S.C.A. § 141
68 122 273 389 488 600	35 U.S.C.A. § 363
69 123 274 390 489 501	37 U.S.C.A. § 308
70 124 275 391 490 502	42 U.S.C.A. § 1101
71 125 276 392 491 503	42 U.S.C.A. § 1306
72 126 277 393 492 504	39 U.S.C.A. § 407
73 127 278 394 493 505	40 U.S.C.A. § 601
74 128 279 395 494 506	42 U.S.C.A. § 1201
75 129 280 396 495 507	42 U.S.C.A. § 6901
76 130 281 397 496 508	42 U.S.C.A. § 8311
77 131 282 398 497 509	43 U.S.C.A. § 322
78 132 283 399 498 510	44 U.S.C.A. § 517
79 133 284 400 499 511	45 U.S.C.A. § 34
80 134 285 301 500 512	45 U.S.C.A. § 723
81 135 286 302 401 513	41 U.S.C.A. § 11
82 136 287 303 402 514	5 U.S.C.A. § 559
83 137 288 304 403 515	5 U.S.C.A. § 2108
84 138 289 305 404 516	5 U.S.C.A. § 8343
85 139 290 306 405 517	6 U.S.C.A. § 6
86 140 291 307 406 518	7 U.S.C.A. § 154
87 141 292 308 407 519	7 U.S.C.A. § 949
88 142 293 309 408 520	7 U.S.C.A. § 1854
89 143 294 310 409 521	7 U.S.C.A. § 2619
90 144 295 311 410 522	10 U.S.C.A. § 514
91 145 296 312 411 523	10 U.S.C.A. § 935
92 146 297 313 412 524	10 U.S.C.A. § 1371
93 147 298 314 413 525	11 U.S.C.A. § 329
94 148 299 315 414 526	11 U.S.C.A. § 508
95 149 300 316 415 527	12 U.S.C.A. § 1468
96 150 201 317 416 528	17 U.S.C.A. § 402
97 151 202 318 417 529	18 U.S.C.A. § 211
98 152 203 319 418 530	18 U.S.C.A. § 1161
99 153 204 320 419 531	18 U.S.C.A. § 2421
100 154 205 321 420 532	20 U.S.C.A. § 129

CITATION EXERCISE 33
STATE STATUTES (I)

A. INTRODUCTION

1. State Statutes

State legislatures enact state statutes. These statutes are published in the same pattern as federal laws—in (1) slip form and session laws (chronologically) and (2) statutory (subject) compilations. They are frequently cited in legal writing.

2. *Bluebook* Table T.1

The state portion of *Bluebook* Table T.1 ("United States Jurisdictions") provides useful information about the statutory compilations and session laws for every state. This table also provides the abbreviation of the various compilations and session laws for use in *Bluebook* citations.

3. Typeface Conventions

As you will see in the next exercise, statutory compilations are cited in ordinary roman type in documents submitted to courts and in legal memoranda. *See Bluebook* Practitioners' Note P.1(h). Thus, a citation to West's *Wisconsin Statutes Annotated* would appear as follows:

[Example 1] Wis. Stat. Ann. § x (West 19xx).

In law review footnotes, the name of the statutory compilation appears in large and small capital letters.

[Example 2] WIS. STAT. ANN. § x (West 19xx).

In contrast, session laws always appear in ordinary roman type:

[Example 3] 19xx Wis. Laws xxx.

B. INSTRUCTIONS FOR COMPLETING THIS EXERCISE

To complete this exercise, you will need to consult *Bluebook* Table T.1 to determine information about the statutory compilation(s) and session laws for the state jurisdiction listed with your problem number below. Assume that the information requested below will appear in a document submitted to a court or in a legal memorandum. For your answer to this exercise, state the following.

(a) the name(s) of the statutory compilation(s) for the jurisdiction (*e.g.*, Wisconsin Statutes (1975 & biannually); West's Wisconsin Statutes Annotated);

(b) the *Bluebook* citation form(s) listed for the statutory compilation(s) stated for your answer in (a), above (*e.g.*, Wis. Stat. § x (19xx); Wis. Stat. Ann. § x (West 19xx));

(c) the session laws available for the jurisdiction (*e.g.*, Laws of Wisconsin; West's Wisconsin Legislative Service); and

(d) the *Bluebook* citation form(s) listed for the session laws stated for your answer in (c), above (*e.g.*, 19xx Wis. Laws xxx; 19xx Wis. Legis. Serv. xxx (West)).

Unless otherwise instructed, write your answers on the answer sheet provided in Part 4 of these exercises.

PROBLEM #	JURISDICTION
1 126 292 348 459 513	Idaho
2 127 293 349 460 514	Miss.
3 128 294 350 461 515	N.C.
4 129 295 351 462 516	N.M.
5 130 296 352 463 517	N.C.
6 131 297 353 464 518	S C.
7 132 298 354 465 519	Tenn.
8 133 299 355 466 520	Utah
9 134 300 356 467 521	Vt.
10 135 201 357 468 522	W. Va.
11 136 202 358 469 523	Wyo.
12 137 203 359 470 524	Ala.
13 138 204 360 471 525	Ariz.
14 139 205 361 472 526	Ark.
15 140 206 362 473 527	Colo.
16 141 207 363 474 528	Idaho
17 142 208 364 475 529	Miss.
18 143 209 365 476 530	S.C.
19 144 210 366 477 531	N.M.
20 145 211 367 478 532	N.C.
21 146 212 368 479 533	S.C.
22 147 213 369 480 534	Tenn.
23 148 214 370 481 535	Utah
24 149 215 371 482 536	Fla.
25 150 216 372 483 537	W. Va.
26 151 217 373 484 538	Wyo.
27 152 218 374 485 539	Ala.
28 153 219 375 486 540	Ariz.
29 154 220 376 487 541	Ark.
30 155 221 377 488 542	Colo.
31 156 222 378 489 543	Idaho
32 157 223 379 490 544	Miss.
33 158 224 380 491 545	Utah

PROBLEM #	JURISDICTION
34 159 225 381 492 546	N.M.
35 160 226 382 493 547	N.C.
36 161 227 383 494 548	S.C.
37 162 228 384 495 549	Tenn.
38 163 229 385 496 550	Utah
39 164 230 386 497 551	Vt.
40 165 231 387 498 552	W. Va.
41 166 232 388 499 553	Wyo.
42 167 233 389 500 554	Ala.
43 168 234 390 401 555	Ariz.
44 169 235 391 402 556	Ark.
45 170 236 392 403 557	Miss.
46 171 237 393 404 558	Tenn.
47 172 238 394 405 559	N.M.
48 173 239 395 406 560	N.C.
49 174 240 396 407 561	S.C.
50 175 241 397 408 562	Tenn.
51 176 242 398 409 563	Utah
52 177 243 399 410 564	Vt.
53 178 244 400 411 565	W. Va.
54 179 245 301 412 566	Wyo.
55 180 246 302 413 567	Ala.
56 181 247 303 414 568	Ariz.
57 182 248 304 415 569	Ark.
58 183 249 305 416 570	Colo.
59 184 250 306 417 571	Idaho
60 185 251 307 418 572	Miss.
61 186 252 308 419 573	S.C.
62 187 253 309 420 574	N.M.
63 188 254 310 421 575	N.C.
64 189 255 311 422 576	S.C.
65 190 256 312 423 577	Tenn.
66 191 257 313 424 578	Utah
67 192 258 314 425 579	Vt.
68 193 259 315 426 580	W. Va.
69 194 260 316 427 581	Wyo.
70 195 261 317 428 582	Okla.
71 196 262 318 429 583	Ariz.
72 197 263 319 430 584	Ark.
73 198 264 320 431 585	Colo.
74 199 265 321 432 586	Idaho
75 200 266 322 433 587	Miss.
76 101 267 323 434 588	N.M.
77 102 268 324 435 589	N.C.
78 103 269 325 436 590	S.C.
79 104 270 326 437 591	Tenn.
80 105 271 327 438 592	Utah
81 106 272 328 439 593	Vt.
82 107 273 329 440 594	W. Va.
83 108 274 330 441 595	Wyo.

PROBLEM #	JURISDICTION
84 109 275 331 442 596	Ala.
85 110 276 332 443 597	Ariz.
86 111 277 333 444 598	Ark.
87 112 278 334 445 599	Colo.
88 113 279 335 446 600	Idaho
89 114 280 336 447 501	Miss.
90 115 281 337 448 502	N.M.
91 116 282 338 449 503	N.C.
92 117 283 339 450 504	S.C.
93 118 284 340 451 505	Tenn.
94 119 285 341 452 506	Utah
95 120 286 342 453 507	Vt.
96 121 287 343 454 508	W. Va.
97 122 288 344 455 509	Wyo.
98 123 289 345 456 510	Ala.
99 124 290 346 457 511	Ariz.
100 125 291 347 458 512	Ark.

CITATION EXERCISE 34
STATE STATUTES (II)

A. INTRODUCTION

1. Citing State Statutory Codes

Citations of state statutes follow the same basic rules that were outlined for federal statutes.

(a) Sources to Cite

In general, cite state statutes to the current official code (if available) or to a current unofficial code, session laws, legislative advance sheets, or other available sources. Cite codified provisions by section numbers (title or chapter designations are also used when necessary to identify the particular section), but session laws usually are cited by page number. Follow the abbreviations and include the publisher, editor, or compiler as provided in *Bluebook* Table T.1. Note also that the official version is preferred source when multiple sources are available. *See Bluebook* Table T.1.

[**Example 1**] Wis. Stat. Ann. § 230.40 (West 1987).

When a code contains separate parts or sections identified by distinct subject-matter titles, that subject-matter title is included in the name of the code, such as the California Business & Professions Code in the following citation:

[**Example 2**] Cal. Bus. & Prof. Code § 4980 (West 1990).

The various abbreviations of the subject-matter codes are set forth in Table T.1 (*see infra* Citation Exercise 35).

(b) Date and Other Parenthetical Information

For codified state statutes, give (1) the year that appears on the spine of the volume, (2) the year that appears on the title page, or (3) the latest copyright year, in that order of preference. If the volume is a "replacement" of an earlier edition, the date of the replacement volume is used, not the year of the original. If the date on the spine or title page spans more than one year, all years are included in the citation (*e.g.*, 1998-1999). *Bluebook* Rule 12.3.2.

Some state codifications are in looseleaf form. In citing those codifications, use (1) the year on the page on which the material is printed or (2) the year on the first page of the subdivision within which the cited material appears, if any, in that order of preference (in lieu of the dates stated above). *Bluebook* Rule 12.3.2.

Additional information indicated parenthetically can include repeals, amendments, and prior history. *See Bluebook* Rules 12.6.1-.3 & 12.7.

(c) *Electronic Sources for Statutes*

Some law libraries will not have the statutory collections of all fifty states. Thus, as a practical matter, they will be available only online or in some other electronic format, such as CD-ROM. When an electronic source for statutes is cited, the database should be identified (*e.g.*, WESTLAW, LEXIS, West CD-ROM, etc.) and its currency (*e.g.*, through all 1998 legislation, etc.) should be indicated instead of the year of the code. Also include the publisher, editor, or compiler for unofficial sources (*e.g.*, McKinney, West, Deering, etc.). *See Bluebook* Rule 12.5(a).

[**Example 3**] Wis. Stat. Ann. § 240.10 (West, WESTLAW through 1997 Act 67).

[**Example 4**] Wis. Stat. § 240.10 (LEXIS through 1997 Act 60).

2. State Statutory Supplements

When the material cited appears in a supplement, that fact should be indicated in the citation:

[**Example 5**] Wis. Stat. Ann. § 240.10 (West Supp. 1997).

3. Typeface Conventions

As shown in the above examples, statutory compilations are cited in ordinary roman type in documents submitted to courts and in legal memoranda. *See Bluebook* Practitioners' Note P.1(h). In law review footnotes, the name of the statutory compilation appears in large and small capital letters:

[**Example 6**] WIS. STAT. ANN. § 230.40 (West 1987).

B. INSTRUCTIONS FOR COMPLETING THIS EXERCISE

Find the state statutory provision listed with your problem number below in an available compilation of the statutes of that state. If the provision is no longer included in the statutory compilation or the statutes of the relevant state are unavailable, complete a different problem. For your answer to this exercise, state the following:

(a) the title of the state statutory set you used to find the statute (*e.g.*, Vermont Statutes Annotated);

(b) the year that appears on the spine of the volume you used, or the year that appears on the title page, or the latest copyright year—in that order of preference (*e.g.*, 1998). If the volume is a replacement, reissue, or republication of an earlier edition, use the year of the replacement, reissued, or republished volume rather than the original. After stating the year, indicate parenthetically which source for the year you used (*e.g.*, 1998 (date on the spine of the volume)); and also indicate parenthetically that a replacement, reissued, or republished volume was used (*e.g.*, 1998 (date on the spine of the reissued volume)); however, if you are citing a looseleaf codification, state (1) the year on the page on which the material is printed or (2) the year on the first page of the subdivision within which the cited material appears, if any, in that order of preference, (in lieu of the dates stated above); and

(c) the citation of the statutory provision in *Bluebook* (or another designated) form; assume that your citation will appear in a court document or legal memorandum, not in a law review article.

Unless otherwise instructed, write your answers on the answer sheet provided in Part 4 of these exercises.

PROBLEM #	**STATUTORY PROVISION**
1 157 240 329 411 516	Code of Alabama § 9-11-153
2 158 241 330 412 517	Arizona Revised Statutes § 3-203
3 159 242 331 413 518	Arkansas Code Annotated § 16-19-407
4 160 243 332 414 519	Colorado Revised Statutes § 8-42-202
5 161 244 333 415 520	Hawaii Revised Statutes § 25-4
6 162 245 334 416 521	Idaho Code § 15-5-303
7 163 246 335 417 522	Mississippi Code Annotated § 9-9-31
8 164 247 336 418 523	Revised Statutes of Nebraska § 17-951
9 165 248 337 419 524	New Hampshire Revised Statutes Annotated § 103:14
10 166 249 338 420 525	New Mexico Statutes Annotated § 3-2-1
11 167 250 339 421 526	General Statutes of North Carolina § 31-12
12 168 251 340 422 527	North Dakota Century Code § 10-27-08
13 169 252 341 423 528	Oregon Revised Statutes § 192.420
14 170 253 342 424 529	Code of Laws of South Carolina § 5-7-20
15 171 254 343 425 530	Tennessee Code Annotated § 2-4-102
16 172 255 344 426 531	Utah Code Annotated § 10-8-59
17 173 256 345 427 532	Vermont Statutes Annotated tit. 8, § 2230
18 174 257 346 428 533	Code of Virginia Annotated § 35.1-13
19 175 258 347 429 534	West Virginia Code § 7-5-3
20 176 259 348 430 535	Wyoming Statutes Annotated § 11-30-112
21 177 260 349 431 536	Code of Alabama § 6-5-284
22 178 261 350 432 537	Arizona Revised Statutes Annotated § 13-1504
23 179 262 351 433 538	Ark. Code Ann. § 15-74-304
24 180 263 352 434 539	Colorado Revised Statutes § 12-36-127
25 181 264 353 435 540	Hawaii Revised Statutes § 605-2
26 182 265 354 436 541	Idaho Code § 22-701
27 183 266 355 437 542	Mississippi Code Annotated § 11-19-7
28 184 267 356 438 543	Revised Statutes of Nebraska § 32-1406
29 185 268 357 439 544	New Hampshire Revised Statutes Annotated § 402:39
30 186 269 358 440 545	New Mexico Statutes Annotated § 3-28-20
31 187 270 359 441 546	General Statutes of North Carolina § 43-14
32 188 271 360 442 547	North Dakota Century Code § 23-16-08
33 189 272 361 443 548	Oregon Revised Statutes § 308.545

PROBLEM #	STATUTORY PROVISION
34 190 273 362 444 549	Code of Laws of South Carolina § 7-9-20
35 191 274 363 445 550	Tennessee Code Annotated § 8-19-417
36 192 275 364 446 551	Utah Code Annotated § 16-6-92
37 193 276 365 447 552	Vermont Statutes Annotated tit. 9, § 4513
38 194 277 366 448 553	Code of Virginia Annotated § 8.2-314
39 195 278 367 449 554	West Virginia Code § 11-15A-13
40 196 279 368 450 555	Wyoming Statutes Annotated § 17-1-111
41 197 280 369 451 556	Code of Alabama § 11-94-4
42 198 281 370 452 557	Arizona Revised Statutes Annotated § 20-448
43 199 282 371 453 558	Arkansas Code Annotated § 6-13-105
44 200 283 372 454 559	Colorado Revised Statutes § 22-31-119
45 101 284 373 455 560	Hawaii Revised Statutes § 143-10
46 102 285 374 456 561	Idaho Code § 31-3508
47 103 286 375 457 562	Mississippi Code Annotated § 11-53-45
48 104 287 376 458 563	Revised Statutes of Nebraska § 71-186
49 105 288 377 459 564	New Hampshire Revised Statutes Annotated § 422:23
50 106 289 378 460 565	New Mexico Statutes Annotated § 7-1-51
51 107 290 379 461 566	General Statutes of North Carolina § 115C-307
52 108 291 380 462 567	North Dakota Century Code § 30-26-22
53 109 292 381 463 568	Oregon Revised Statutes § 419.750
54 110 293 382 464 569	Code of Laws of South Carolina § 8-11-10
55 111 294 383 465 570	Tennessee Code Annotated § 16-5-112
56 112 295 384 466 571	Utah Code Annotated § 31A-22-611
57 113 296 385 467 572	Vermont Statutes Annotated tit. 10, § 394
58 114 297 386 468 573	Code of Virginia Annotated § 14.1-122.1
59 115 298 387 469 574	West Virginia Code § 16-5-12
60 116 299 388 470 575	Wyoming Statutes Annotated § 7-3-204
61 117 300 389 471 576	Code of Alabama § 25-5-12
62 118 201 390 472 577	Arizona Revised Statutes Annotated § 31-475
63 119 202 391 473 578	Arkansas Code Annotated § 5-54-121
64 120 203 392 474 579	Colorado Revised Statutes § 24-35-207
65 121 204 393 475 580	Hawaii Revised Statutes § 208-6
66 122 205 394 476 581	Idaho Code § 37-123
67 123 206 395 477 582	Mississippi Code Annotated § 19-5-51
68 124 207 396 478 583	Revised Statutes of Nebraska § 76-215
69 125 208 397 479 584	New Hampshire Revised Statutes Annotated § 539:6
70 126 209 398 480 585	New Mexico Statutes Annotated § 13-4-1
71 127 210 399 481 586	General Statutes of North Carolina § 122C-57
72 128 211 400 482 587	North Dakota Century Code § 39-03-11
73 129 212 301 483 588	Oregon Revised Statutes § 561.520
74 130 213 302 484 589	Code of Laws of South Carolina § 11-15-520
75 131 214 303 485 590	Tennessee Code Annotated § 30-1-104
76 132 215 304 486 591	Utah Code Annotated § 54-7-22
77 133 216 305 487 592	Vermont Statutes Annotated tit. 24, § 1061
78 134 217 306 488 593	Code of Virginia Annotated § 18.2-53.1
79 135 218 307 489 594	West Virginia Code § 17-22-14
80 136 219 308 490 595	Wyoming Statutes Annotated § 35-11-1205
81 137 220 309 491 596	Code of Alabama § 37-9-7
82 138 221 310 492 597	Arizona Revised Statutes Annotated § 44-2362
83 139 222 311 493 598	Arkansas Code Annotated § 14-316-102

PROBLEM #	**STATUTORY PROVISION**
84 140 223 312 494 599	Colorado Revised Statutes § 34-29-129
85 141 224 313 495 600	Hawaii Revised Statutes § 297-23
86 142 225 314 496 501	Idaho Code § 58-138
87 143 226 315 497 502	Mississippi Code Annotated § 23-3-11
88 144 227 316 498 503	Revised Statutes of Nebraska § 83-372
89 145 228 317 499 504	New Hampshire Revised Statutes Annotated § 490:5
90 146 229 318 500 505	New Mexico Statutes Annotated § 22-10-7
91 147 230 319 401 506	General Statutes of North Carolina § 131E-95
92 148 231 320 402 507	North Dakota Century Code § 54-30-21
93 149 232 321 403 508	Oregon Revised Statutes § 677.095
94 150 233 322 404 509	Code of Laws of South Carolina § 14-19-50
95 151 234 323 405 510	Tennessee Code Annotated § 39-1-202
96 152 235 324 406 511	Utah Code Annotated § 63-9-17
97 153 236 325 407 512	Vermont Statutes Annotated tit. 26, § 1897
98 154 237 326 408 513	Code of Virginia Annotated § 23-32
99 155 238 327 409 514	West Virginia Code § 19-20-5
100 156 239 328 410 515	Wyoming Statutes Annotated § 39-3-103

CITATION EXERCISE 35
STATE STATUTES (III)

A. INTRODUCTION

1. Citing "Subject-Matter" State Statutory Compilations

Some state statutory compilations (*e.g.*, in New York, California, Maryland, Texas, etc.) are organized by individually designated "subject codes" (or "compiled laws") rather than by titles, chapters, or volume numbers. In addition to the *Bluebook* rules set out in the preceding exercise, the appropriate subject-matter code should be included in the citation of those types of codes. The various abbreviations of the subject-matter codes are set forth in *Bluebook* Table T.1. The following are examples of citations to subject-mater codes:

[Example 1] Tex. Fam. Code Ann. § 160.102 (West 1996).
[Example 2] N.Y. Lab. Law § 133 (McKinney 1986).

2. Special Note on Uniform State Laws

The National Conference of Commissioners of Uniform State Laws is responsible for encouraging the drafting and adoption of uniform state legislation on a variety of subjects. Research on a particular uniform law can be greatly aided by consulting West's *Uniform Laws Annotated*. It provides citations to relevant periodical literature, official comments, and digests of state and federal decisions interpreting or citing particular provisions of a uniform law. Deviations in particular states from the text of a uniform law are also noted. It is kept current by pocket parts, which also contain a "Table of Jurisdictions Wherein Act Has Been Adopted."

In general, uniform acts are cited as separate codes. The Uniform Commercial Code should be abbreviated to U.C.C. A citation to West's *Uniform Laws Annotated* (U.L.A.) may be given. Use the year the act was last amended in the citation (even if the cited section was not amended at that time.) *Bluebook* Rule 12.8.4. The following are examples of the citation of uniform acts:

[Example 3] U.C.C. § 2-719 (1977).
[Example 4] Uniform Parentage Act § 10 (1973).
[Example 5] Uniform Parentage Act § 10, 9A U.L.A. 600-01 (1973).

When a uniform act is cited as the law of a particular state, however, it should be cited as a state statute. *Bluebook* Rule 12.8.4.

[Example 6] Colo. Rev. Stat. § 4-8-401 (1973).

3. Typeface Conventions

As shown in the above examples, statutory compilations and uniform laws are cited in ordinary roman type in documents submitted to courts and in legal memoranda. *See Bluebook* Practitioners' Note P.1(h). In law review footnotes, the name of the statutory compilation and uniform law appears in large and small capital letters:

> **[Example 7]** TEX. FAM. CODE ANN. § 160.102 (West 1996).
> **[Example 8]** N.Y. LAB. LAW § 133 (McKinney 1986).
> **[Example 9]** UNIFORM PARENTAGE ACT § 10, 9A U.L.A. 600-01 (1973).

See Bluebook Rule 12.8.5.

B. INSTRUCTIONS FOR COMPLETING THIS EXERCISE

Find the state statutory provision listed with your problem number below in an appropriate compilation of the statutes of that state. **If it is available, use West's *Annotated California Codes*.** If the provision is no longer included in the statutory compilation, complete a different problem. For your answer to this exercise, state the following:

(a) the year that appears on the spine of the volume you used, or the year that appears on the title page, or the latest copyright year—in that order of preference (*e.g.*, 1998). If the volume is a replacement, reissue, or republication of an earlier edition, use the year of the replacement, reissued, or republished volume rather than the original. After stating the year, indicate parenthetically which source for the year you used (*e.g.*, 1998 (date on the spine of the volume)); and also indicate parenthetically that a replacement, reissued, or republished volume was used (*e.g.*, 1998 (date on the spine of the reissued volume)); and

(b) the citation of the statutory provision in *Bluebook* (or another designated) form; assume that your citation will appear in a court document or legal memorandum, not in a law review article.

Unless otherwise instructed, write your answers on the answer sheet provided in Part 4 of these exercises.

PROBLEM #	CALIFORNIA STATUTORY PROVISION
1 157 240 329 411 516	Business and Professions Code § 107
2 158 241 330 412 517	Civil Procedure Code § 13
3 159 242 331 413 518	Insurance Code § 11512
4 160 243 332 414 519	Civil Code § 1559
5 161 244 333 415 520	Welfare and Institutions Code § 1764
6 162 245 334 416 521	Public Utilities Code § 12134
7 163 246 335 417 522	Welfare and Institutions Code § 726
8 164 247 336 418 523	Public Resources Code § 2533

PROBLEM #	CALIFORNIA STATUTORY PROVISION
9 165 248 337 419 524	Government Code § 820
10 166 249 338 420 525	Civil Procedure Code § 393
11 167 250 339 421 526	Penal Code § 154
12 168 251 340 422 527	Civil Code § 1185
13 169 252 341 423 528	Business and Professions Code § 2746
14 170 253 342 424 529	Penal Code § 310
15 171 254 343 425 530	Penal Code § 602
16 172 255 344 426 531	Labor Code § 3601
17 173 256 345 427 532	Business and Professions Code § 2746
18 174 257 346 428 533	Vehicle Code § 21355
19 175 258 347 429 534	Public Utilities Code § 2705
20 176 259 348 430 535	Water Code § 2752
21 177 260 349 431 536	Penal Code § 999i
22 178 261 350 432 537	Civil Procedure Code § 474
23 179 262 351 433 538	Vehicle Code § 10655
24 180 263 352 434 539	Civil Procedure Code § 602
25 181 264 353 435 540	Government Code § 6518
26 182 265 354 436 541	Probate Code § 1203
27 183 266 355 437 542	Insurance Code § 10170
28 184 267 356 438 543	Penal Code § 802
29 185 268 357 439 544	Harbors and Navigation Code § 661
30 186 269 358 440 545	Unemployment Insurance Code § 9261
31 187 270 359 441 546	Education Code § 16082
32 188 271 360 442 547	Penal Code § 1252
33 189 272 361 443 548	Civil Procedure Code § 435
34 190 273 362 444 549	Revenue and Taxation Code § 7309
35 191 274 363 445 550	Civil Code § 1810.20
36 192 275 364 446 551	Civil Procedure Code § 531
37 193 276 365 447 552	Revenue and Taxation Code § 3705
38 194 277 366 448 553	Labor Code § 4652
39 195 278 367 449 554	Vehicle Code § 550
40 196 279 368 450 555	Civil Procedure Code § 670
41 197 280 369 451 556	Penal Code § 1100
42 198 281 370 452 557	Public Contract Code § 20416
43 199 282 371 453 558	Civil Code § 1723
44 200 283 372 454 559	Streets and Highways Code § 820
45 101 284 373 455 560	Public Contract Code § 20863
46 102 285 374 456 561	Military and Veterans Code § 721
47 103 286 375 457 562	Business and Professions Code § 2055
48 104 287 376 458 563	Labor Code § 1177
49 105 288 377 459 564	Evidence Code § 351
50 106 289 378 460 565	Penal Code § 397
51 107 290 379 461 566	Harbors and Navigation Code § 306
52 108 291 380 462 567	Civil Procedure Code § 651
53 109 292 381 463 568	Welfare and Institutions Code § 327
54 110 293 382 464 569	Vehicle Code § 24002
55 111 294 383 465 570	Public Resources Code § 5101
56 112 295 384 466 571	Penal Code § 4101
57 113 296 385 467 572	Evidence Code § 720
58 114 297 386 468 573	Insurance Code § 1220

PROBLEM #	CALIFORNIA STATUTORY PROVISION
59 115 298 387 469 574	Civil Code § 1957
60 116 299 388 470 575	Public Contract Code § 10783
61 117 300 389 471 576	Evidence Code § 1271
62 118 201 390 472 577	Corporations Code § 317
63 119 202 391 473 578	Revenue and Taxation Code § 1638
64 120 203 392 474 579	Welfare and Institutions Code § 11254
65 121 204 393 475 580	Streets & Highways § 31551
66 122 205 394 476 581	Revenue and Taxation Code § 11934
67 123 206 395 477 582	Public Utilities Code § 30930
68 124 207 396 478 583	Civil Procedure Code § 1859
69 125 208 397 479 584	Civil Code § 2273
70 126 209 398 480 585	Penal Code § 1466
71 127 210 399 481 586	Labor Code § 1733
72 128 211 400 482 587	Evidence Code § 940
73 129 212 301 483 588	Welfare and Institutions Code § 6251
74 130 213 302 484 589	Insurance Code § 620
75 131 214 303 485 590	Civil Procedure Code § 738
76 132 215 304 486 591	Evidence Code § 125
77 133 216 305 487 592	Food and Agricultural Code § 62094
78 134 217 306 488 593	Civil Procedure Code § 912
79 135 218 307 489 594	Harbors and Navigation Code § 5891
80 136 219 308 490 595	Penal Code § 12083
81 137 220 309 491 596	Labor Code § 6511
82 138 221 310 492 597	Evidence Code § 450
83 139 222 311 493 598	Streets and Highways Code § 6446
84 140 223 312 494 599	Public Resources Code § 19532
85 141 224 313 495 600	Civil Procedure Code § 1211
86 142 225 314 496 501	Vehicle Code § 40308
87 143 226 315 497 502	Penal Code § 4500
88 144 227 316 498 503	Public Contract Code § 10371
89 145 228 317 499 504	Evidence Code § 767
90 146 229 318 500 505	Business and Professions Code § 6062
91 147 230 319 401 506	Health & Safety § 2835
92 148 231 320 402 507	Education Code § 228
93 149 232 321 403 508	Corporations Code § 12627
94 150 233 322 404 509	Evidence Code § 1293
95 151 234 323 405 510	Government Code § 11044
96 152 235 324 406 511	Evidence Code § 970
97 153 236 325 407 512	Business and Professions Code § 7030
98 154 237 326 408 513	Welfare and Institutions Code § 4705
99 155 238 327 409 514	Government Code § 14841
100 156 239 328 410 515	Streets and Highways Code § 8324

CITATION EXERCISE 36
CONSTITUTIONS

A. INTRODUCTION

1. Federal and State Constitutions

In the United States, constitutions are the most basic written source of law. The text of the U.S. Constitution is conveniently included in volumes of the *United States Code Annotated* and *United States Code Service*—privately published statutory compilations of federal statutes (codes). Both of these compilations have extensive historical notes, annotations of judicial decisions, and other useful references related to federal constitutional provisions.

State constitutions establish the power and responsibilities of each branch of a state government. They also establish the relationship of the state government to local governmental units within a state. In addition, they guarantee individual liberties. State constitutions are usually included in state statutory compilations.

2. Citing the U.S. Constitution and State Constitutions

According to Rule 11 of *The Bluebook*, the U.S. Constitution should be cited as follows:

(1) Cite the U.S. Constitution by **article**, **section**, and, if appropriate, by **clause**. Abbreviate "United States" to "U.S." and "Constitution" to "Const." Abbreviate "Article" to "art.," "Section" to "§," "Sections" to "§§," and "Clause" to "cl." Do not capitalize "art." or "cl."

(2) Cite **amendments** to the U.S. Constitution by **roman number**. Abbreviate "Amendment" to "amend." Do not capitalize "amend." *Bluebook* Table T.16 ("Subdivisions").

(3) Cite constitutional provisions currently in force without a date.
Bluebook Rule 11.

The following are examples of *Bluebook* citations of the U.S. Constitution:

[**Example 1**] U.S. Const. art. III, § 3, cl. 1.
[**Example 2**] U.S. Const. amend. V.

State constitutions are cited in the same manner:

[**Example 3**] W. Va. Const. art. 7, § 4.

3. Typeface Conventions

As shown in the above examples, constitutions are cited in ordinary roman type in documents submitted to courts and in legal memoranda. *See Bluebook* Practitioners' Note P.1(h). In law review footnotes, the name of the constitution appears in large and small capital letters:

[Example 4] U.S. CONST. art. III, § 3, cl. 1.
[Example 5] U.S. CONST. amend. V.
[Example 6] W. VA. CONST. art. 7, § 4.

See Bluebook Rule 11.

B. INSTRUCTIONS FOR COMPLETING THIS EXERCISE

This exercise requires you to find and cite the federal constitutional provision that governs the subject matter listed with your problem number below. Use any available source containing an indexed text or topical division of the U.S. Constitution, such as the *United States Code Annotated* or the *United States Code Service*.

For your answer to this exercise, cite the provision in *Bluebook* (or another designated) form. Include the clause in your citation, if appropriate. If the subject matter listed with your problem number is governed by more than one provision of the U.S. Constitution, you may cite any one of them; assume that your citation will appear in a court document or legal memorandum, not in a law review article.

Unless otherwise instructed, write your answer on the answer sheet provided in Part 4 of these exercises.

PROBLEM #	SUBJECT
1 177 262 385 498 509	Right to bear arms
2 178 263 386 499 510	Qualifications of senators
3 179 264 387 500 511	Quartering soldiers
4 180 265 388 401 512	President of the Senate
5 181 266 389 402 513	Full Faith and Credit
6 182 267 390 403 514	Unreasonable searches
7 183 268 391 404 515	Runaway slaves
8 184 269 392 405 516	Cruel punishments
9 185 270 393 406 517	Admission of new states
10 186 271 394 407 518	Bail
11 187 272 395 408 519	Privileges and immunities
12 188 273 396 409 520	Original jurisdiction of Supreme Court
13 189 274 397 410 521	Punishment of treason
14 190 275 398 411 522	Powers reserved to states
15 191 276 399 412 523	Income tax
16 192 277 400 413 524	Women suffrage
17 193 278 301 414 525	Power of Congress to tax

PROBLEM #	SUBJECT
18 194 279 302 415 526	Post Offices
19 195 280 303 416 527	Patents
20 196 281 304 417 528	Unreasonable seizures
21 197 282 305 418 529	Copyrights
22 198 283 306 419 530	Naturalization
23 199 284 307 420 531	Postal roads
24 200 285 308 421 532	Bankruptcy
25 101 286 309 422 533	Habeas corpus
26 102 287 310 423 534	Congress' power to borrow
27 103 288 311 424 535	Bill of attainder
28 104 289 312 425 536	Repeal of 18th Amendment
29 105 290 313 426 537	Coinage
30 106 291 314 427 538	Ex post facto laws
31 107 292 315 428 539	Commander in Chief
32 108 293 316 429 540	Titles of nobility
33 109 294 317 430 541	Weights and measures
34 110 295 318 431 542	Restriction of suits against states
35 111 296 319 432 543	Slavery prohibited
36 112 297 320 433 544	Counterfeiting
37 113 298 321 434 545	Preference of ports
38 114 299 322 435 546	Amendment of the Constitution
39 115 300 323 436 547	Delivery of fugitives
40 116 201 324 437 548	Just compensation for taking
41 117 202 325 438 549	18-year-old voting
42 118 203 326 439 550	Provision for a Navy
43 119 204 327 440 551	Regulation of commerce with Indians
44 120 205 328 441 552	Letters of Marque and Reprisal
45 121 206 329 442 553	Presents from foreign states
46 122 207 330 443 554	Tax on exports from states
47 123 208 331 444 555	Establishment of religion
48 124 209 332 445 556	Supremacy Clause
49 125 210 333 446 557	Freedom of the press
50 126 211 334 447 558	Pardons
51 127 212 335 448 559	Petitioning for redress
52 128 213 336 449 560	Legislative power vested in Congress
53 129 214 337 450 561	Right to assemble peaceably
54 130 215 338 451 562	Freedom of speech
55 131 216 339 452 563	Probable cause for warrants
56 132 217 340 453 564	Unusual punishments
57 133 218 341 454 565	Trial by jury—$20
58 134 219 342 455 566	Speedy and public trial
59 135 220 343 456 567	President—oath of office
60 136 221 344 457 568	Double jeopardy
61 137 222 345 458 569	Excessive fines
62 138 223 346 459 570	Confrontation of witnesses
63 139 224 347 460 571	Equal protection of laws
64 140 225 348 461 572	Involuntary servitude abolished
65 141 226 349 462 573	Free exercise of religion
66 142 227 350 463 574	President's power to make treaties
67 143 228 351 464 575	Right to assistance of counsel

PROBLEM #	**SUBJECT**
68 144 229 352 465 576	Commerce clause
69 145 230 353 466 577	President's duty to receive ambassadors
70 146 231 354 467 578	Right to assistance of counsel
71 147 232 355 468 579	Commerce clause
72 148 233 356 469 580	President's duty to receive ambassadors
73 149 234 357 470 581	Witness against oneself
74 150 235 358 471 582	President—at least 35 years old
75 151 236 359 472 583	Nomination of ambassadors
76 152 237 360 473 584	Republican form of government
77 153 238 361 474 585	Debts of the Confederacy not to be paid
78 154 239 362 475 586	Right to vote—race not to disqualify
79 155 240 363 476 587	Death of President (amendment)
80 156 241 364 477 588	Impartial jury in criminal trials
81 157 242 365 478 589	Representatives—at least 25 years old
82 158 243 366 479 590	House of Representatives sole power to impeach
83 159 244 367 480 591	Senators—at least 30 years old
84 160 245 368 481 592	Treason—two witnesses
85 161 246 369 482 593	President's State of the Union address
86 162 247 370 483 594	States prohibited from laying tonnage duties
87 163 248 371 484 595	Revenue bills originate in the House of Representatives
88 164 249 372 485 596	Expulsion of a member from Congress
89 165 250 373 486 597	Senators—citizen for 9 years
90 166 251 374 487 598	Representatives—citizen for 7 years
91 167 252 375 488 599	Senate's sole power to try impeachments
92 168 253 376 489 600	Habeas corpus may be suspended during rebellions
93 169 254 377 490 501	Congress' power to make all "necessary and proper" laws
94 170 255 378 491 502	Two-thirds vote for impeachment
95 171 256 379 492 503	Congress' power to declare war
96 172 257 380 493 504	President limited to two terms
97 173 258 381 494 505	Poll tax prohibited as a qualification of electors
98 174 259 382 495 506	Voting shall not be denied on account of sex
99 175 260 383 496 507	Slavery prohibited
100 176 261 384 497 508	Debts prior to adoption of the Constitution valid

CITATION EXERCISE 37
TREATIES

A. INTRODUCTION

1. Treaties and Other International Agreements

The United States is a party to numerous treaties and international agreements. The U.S. Constitution provides that the President has the authority to make "treaties" with the advice and consent of Congress and two-thirds approval by the Senate. U.S. Const. art. II, § 2, cl. 2. Under Article VI of the Constitution, treaties made under the authority of the United States are declared the supreme law of the land, and state laws inconsistent with such treaties are invalid. In contrast to treaties, "international agreements" or "executive agreements" are entered into under the President's own constitutional power. Also classified in this same way are those agreements entered into by the President based upon authority granted to the President by an act of Congress.

Before 1950, treaties and international agreements were officially published in *United States Statutes at Large* (Stat.). Since 1950, those agreements have been officially published in *United States Treaties and Other International Agreements* (U.S.T.).

The State Department also has published treaties and other international agreements in several series: *Treaty Series* (T.S., to 1945), *Treaties and Other International Act Series* (T.I.A.S., 1945 to date), and *Executive Agreement Series* (E.A.S., to 1945).

Other sources for international agreements include the *League of Nations Treaty Series* (L.N.T.S., 1920-1945), the *United Nations Treaty Series* (U.N.T.S., 1945 to date), the *Pan American Union Treaty Series* (Pan-Am. T.S.), and the *European Treaty Series* (Europ. T.S.).

2. First Citation of Bilateral and Multilateral Treaties with the United States as a Party

Bluebook Rule 20.4.5 governs the **first citation** of a bilateral or a multilateral treaty with the United States as a party. Slightly different rules govern subsequent citations (see below). Cite such treaties as follows:

(1) Designate the **form of agreement** (*e.g.*, Treaty, Convention, etc.) based on the first designation given on the title page of the agreement; do not use multiple designations (*e.g.*, Treaty, not "Treaty and Protocol");

(2) Designate the **subject-matter** by using the description that is provided as part of the title of the agreement (*e.g.*, Treaty on Extradition); *Bluebook* Rule 20.4(a) provides that the subject matter or the agreement form may be given first (*e.g.*, Extradition Treaty);

(3) Provide the exact **signing date**(s) (*e.g.*, May 22, 1980); for agreements between two parties, the first and last signing dates should be given (*e.g.*, May 22-June 4, 1980); for agreements between more than two parties that are not signed on a single date, the date on which the agreement was opened for signature, approved, or adopted should be given in italics (*e.g.*, *opened for signature* Sept. 9, 1998); consult Table T.12 ("Months") for proper abbreviation of the month; when it is of particular significance, an additional date can be added parenthetically (*e.g.*, the date that the agreement entered into force);

(4) Give the **parties to agreement** when there are two parties; otherwise, they need not be given (*e.g.*, U.S.-Spain); consult Table T.10 "Geographical Terms") for abbreviations for the parties;

(5) Give the **part or subdivision cited**, if any (*e.g.*, art. I, para. 4); *see Bluebook* Rules 3.4 ("Sections and Paragraphs") and 3.5 ("Appended Material");

(6) When the **agreement is between the United States and only one other party**, cite to **one of the following sources** (in order of preference):

(a) *United States Treaties and Other International Agreements* (U.S.T.) or *United States Statutes at Large* (Stat.);

(b) *Treaties and Other International Act Series* (T.I.A.S.) or Treaty Series (T.S.) or *Executive Agreement Series* (E.A.S.);

(c) Senate Treaty Documents or Senate Executive Documents;

(d) Department of State Bulletin;

(e) Department of State Press Releases; or

(f) Unofficial sources (when the agreement has not appeared in one of the above). *Bluebook* Rule 20.4.5(a)(i).

(7) When the **agreement is between the United States and three or more parties**, cite to one of the above listed sources and one of the following intergovernmental sources:

(a) *League of Nations Treaty Series* (L.N.T.S.);

(b) the *United Nations Treaty Series* (U.N.T.S.);

(c) the *Pan American Union Treaty Series* (Pan-Am. T.S.); or

(d) the *European Treaty Series* (Europ. T.S.), if therein; *see Bluebook* Rule 20.4.5(a)(ii).

If these official citations are not available, cite to one unofficial treaty source, with a preference given to *International Legal Materials*; *see Bluebook* Rule 20.4.5(c) ("Unofficial treaty sources").

3. Subsequent Citation of Bilateral and Multilateral Treaties with the United States as a Party

When the name of a treaty is very lengthy or it is known by a popular name, Rule 20.4(b) permits the use of a shortened or popular name in **subsequent citations**. *See Bluebook* Rules 20.4(b) & 4.2(b) (hereinafter short form citations).

4. Examples of *Bluebook* Citations

The following are examples of typical *Bluebook* citations of treaties to which the United States is a party:

[Example 1] Extradition Treaty, May 29, 1970, U.S.-Spain, 22 U.S.T. 737.

> In the above example, a bilateral treaty between the United States and Spain is cited; in addition, United States is abbreviated according to *Bluebook* Table T.10.

[Example 2] Geneva Convention for the Amelioration of the Condition of the Wounded and Sick Armed Forces in the Field, Aug. 12, 1949, 6 U.S.T. 3114, 75 U.N.T.S. 31 (hereinafter Geneva Convention).

> In the above example, the United States is a party to a multilateral convention; in Examples 1 and 2, above, no specific part or provision of the agreement is cited; in addition, August is abbreviated according to *Bluebook* Table T.12.

[Example 3] Treaty of Peace, Friendship, Limits, and Settlement, May 30, 1848, U.S.-Mex., 9 Stat. 922.

> Here, because the treaty was entered into before 1950, the *United States Statutes at Large* is cited; in addition, United States and Mexico are abbreviated according to *Bluebook* Table T.10.

[Example 4] Geneva Convention, Aug. 12, 1949, art 50, 6 U.S.T. 3114, 3196, 75 U.N.T.S. 31, 62.

> Here, a shortened form is used in a subsequent citation, and a specific article of the Geneva Convention is cited; compare the first citation of this Convention in Example 2, above.

5. Citation of Treaties When the United States is Not a Party

When the United States is not a party to the cited agreement, consult *Bluebook* Rule 20.4.5(b).

6. Typeface Conventions

Citations of treaties in court documents, legal memoranda, and law review articles all have the same typeface, as illustrated in the examples above.

B. INSTRUCTIONS FOR COMPLETING THIS EXERCISE

Find the treaty or other international agreement cited to *United States Treaties and Other International Agreements* (U.S.T.) listed with your problem number below. For your answer to this exercise, state the following:

    (a) the form of agreement (*e.g.*, Treaty, Convention, etc.) based on the first designation given on the title page of the agreement;

    (b) the subject of the cited agreement (*e.g.*, Outer Space Mining);

    (c) the exact date(s) of signing (*e.g.*, Aug. 15, 1998);

    (d) the parties to the agreement (*e.g.*, United States-Colombia); and

    (e) the citation of the agreement in *Bluebook* (or another designated) form.

    Unless otherwise instructed, write your answer on the answer sheet provided in Part 4 of these exercises.

PROBLEM #	CITATION
1 112 225 345 470 502	1 U.S.T. 760
2 113 226 346 471 503	2 U.S.T. 13
3 114 227 347 472 504	2 U.S.T. 1554
4 115 228 348 473 505	3 U.S.T. 379
5 116 229 349 474 506	28 U.S.T. 437
6 117 230 350 475 507	3 U.S.T. 3767
7 118 231 351 476 508	4 U.S.T. 939
8 119 232 352 477 509	30 U.S.T. 757
9 120 233 353 478 510	5 U.S.T. 453
10 121 234 354 479 511	5 U.S.T. 2010
11 122 235 355 480 512	5 U.S.T. 2143
12 123 236 356 481 513	6 U.S.T. 507
13 124 237 357 482 514	6 U.S.T. 2023
14 125 238 358 483 515	6 U.S.T. 2843
15 126 239 359 484 516	6 U.S.T. 5715
16 127 240 360 485 517	7 U.S.T. 161
17 128 241 361 486 518	7 U.S.T. 2234
18 129 242 362 487 519	7 U.S.T. 2383
19 130 243 363 488 520	32 U.S.T. 3747
20 131 244 364 489 521	8 U.S.T. 2447
21 132 245 365 490 522	9 U.S.T. 131
22 133 246 366 491 523	10 U.S.T. 1
23 134 247 367 492 524	10 U.S.T. 2087
24 135 248 368 493 525	10 U.S.T. 3014
25 136 249 369 494 526	29 U.S.T. 4183
26 137 250 370 495 527	11 U.S.T. 1330
27 138 251 371 496 528	29 U.S.T. 2975
28 139 252 372 497 529	12 U.S.T. 1390
29 140 253 373 498 530	12 U.S.T. 3181
30 141 254 374 499 531	27 U.S.T. 2019
31 142 255 375 500 532	13 U.S.T. 1227
32 143 256 376 401 533	13 U.S.T. 2711
33 144 257 377 402 534	14 U.S.T. 251
34 145 258 378 403 535	14 U.S.T. 1547
35 146 259 379 404 536	26 U.S.T. 687
36 147 260 380 405 537	15 U.S.T. 1982
37 148 261 381 406 538	29 U.S.T. 501
38 149 262 382 407 539	16 U.S.T. 1183
39 150 263 383 408 540	17 U.S.T. 570

PROBLEM #	CITATION
40 151 264 384 409 541	17 U.S.T. 1412
41 152 265 385 410 542	18 U.S.T. 384
42 153 266 386 411 543	18 U.S.T. 1257
43 154 267 387 412 544	18 U.S.T. 2503
44 155 268 388 413 545	19 U.S.T. 4568
45 156 269 389 414 546	19 U.S.T. 5836
46 157 270 390 415 547	19 U.S.T. 7809
47 158 271 391 416 548	20 U.S.T. 334
48 159 272 392 417 549	28 U.S.T. 2167
49 160 273 393 418 550	20 U.S.T. 3017
50 161 274 394 419 551	21 U.S.T. 403
51 162 275 395 420 552	28 U.S.T. 8877
52 163 276 396 421 553	21 U.S.T. 2495
53 164 277 397 422 554	28 U.S.T. 259
54 165 278 398 423 555	2 U.S.T. 383
55 166 279 399 424 556	2 U.S.T. 1599
56 167 280 400 425 557	3 U.S.T. 530
57 168 281 301 426 558	3 U.S.T. 2927
58 169 282 302 427 559	3 U.S.T. 3942
59 170 283 303 428 560	4 U.S.T. 116
60 171 284 304 429 561	4 U.S.T. 1563
61 172 285 305 430 562	5 U.S.T. 317
62 173 286 306 431 563	5 U.S.T. 1387
63 174 287 307 432 564	5 U.S.T. 2263
64 175 288 308 433 565	28 U.S.T. 5471
65 176 289 309 434 566	6 U.S.T. 2721
66 177 290 310 435 567	6 U.S.T. 2897
67 178 291 311 436 568	6 U.S.T. 5739
68 179 292 312 437 569	28 U.S.T. 3694
69 180 293 313 438 570	7 U.S.T. 2047
70 181 294 314 439 571	7 U.S.T. 3467
71 182 295 315 440 572	33 U.S.T. 1971
72 183 296 316 441 573	8 U.S.T. 2343
73 184 297 317 442 574	9 U.S.T. 601
74 185 298 318 443 575	10 U.S.T. 13
75 186 299 319 444 576	10 U.S.T. 1237
76 187 300 320 445 577	25 U.S.T. 3090
77 188 201 321 446 578	27 U.S.T. 4039
78 189 202 322 447 579	11 U.S.T. 1401
79 190 203 323 448 580	12 U.S.T. 1127
80 191 204 324 449 581	12 U.S.T. 1703
81 192 205 325 450 582	12 U.S.T. 3081
82 193 206 326 451 583	13 U.S.T. 97
83 194 207 327 452 584	13 U.S.T. 2452
84 195 208 328 453 585	27 U.S.T. 2353
85 196 209 329 454 586	14 U.S.T. 397
86 197 210 330 455 587	14 U.S.T. 2222
87 198 211 331 456 588	15 U.S.T. 153
88 199 212 332 457 589	15 U.S.T. 1439
89 200 213 333 458 590	27 U.S.T. 975

PROBLEM #	**CITATION**
90 101 214 334 459 591	26 U.S.T. 2905
91 102 215 335 460 592	26 U.S.T. 1674
92 103 216 336 461 593	17 U.S.T. 2171
93 104 217 337 462 594	18 U.S.T. 558
94 105 218 338 463 595	18 U.S.T. 1268
95 106 219 339 464 596	18 U.S.T. 2510
96 107 220 340 465 597	19 U.S.T. 5211
97 108 221 341 466 598	19 U.S.T. 5900
98 109 222 342 467 599	23 U.S.T. 3501
99 110 223 343 468 600	26 U.S.T. 880
100 111 224 344 469 501	20 U.S.T. 2720

CITATION EXERCISE 38
LEGISLATIVE HISTORY

A. INTRODUCTION

1. Legislative History

The legislative process generates various sources that can be consulted to determine the "intent" of legislative bodies. Legislative history includes proposed bills, testimony presented at hearings, committee reports, legislative debates, etc. Federal legislative histories can be found by consulting West's *United States Code Congressional and Administrative News* (U.S.C.C.A.N.), the Congressional Information Service (C.I.S.), compiled legislative histories for particular statutes, and other sources. Legislative history of state legislation, however, is often difficult to obtain because debates or hearings are rarely published.

2. Citing Legislative History

Bluebook Rule 13 provides detailed rules for citing legislative history. The following are the basic rules for (a) federal bills, (b) congressional committee hearings, (c) congressional committee reports, and (d) congressional debates.

(a) Federal Bills

Many proposed bills are never enacted into law. Unenacted federal bills are cited by the following:
 (1) the **name of the bill**, if relevant;
 (2) the **abbreviated name of the house of Congress** (*e.g.*, S. or H.R.);
 (3) the **bill number**;
 (4) the **number of the Congress** (*e.g.*, 101st Cong., 102d Cong., etc.)
 (5) the **section** of the bill, if relevant; and
 (6) the **year** of publication.
Bluebook Rule 13.2(a).

Enacted bills should ordinarily be cited as statutes (*see supra* Citation Exercise 31). However, when they are used to document a legislative history, enacted bills should be cited in the same manner as unenacted bills. *Bluebook* Rule 13.2(b) (also providing that the fact of enactment should be noted parenthetically unless that fact is otherwise clear from the context).

Consider the following examples of typical citations of bills:

[Example 1] Child Labor Deterrence Act of 1993, H.R. 1397, 103d Cong., 1st Sess. (1993).

[Example 2] S. 717, 95th Cong. (1977) (enacted).

(b) Congressional Hearings

Congressional committee hearings are cited by the following:

(1) the **full subject-matter title** as it appears on the cover;

(2) the **bill number**, if any;

(3) the **subcommittee name**, if any, (which may be abbreviated pursuant to *Bluebook* Tables T.6 and T.10);

(4) the **committee name** (which may be abbreviated pursuant to *Bluebook* Tables T.6 and T.10);

(5) the **number of the Congress** (*e.g.*, 101st Cong.)

(6) the **page number(s)** on which the cited material appears, if any; and

(7) the **year** of publication.

Bluebook Rule 13.3.

Consider the following example of a typical citation of a congressional hearing:

[Example 3] *The Preference System: Hearing Before the Subcomm. on Immigration and Refugee Policy of the Senate Comm. on the Judiciary*, 97th Cong. 12 (1982).

(c) Congressional Committee Reports

Congressional committee reports are cited by the following:

(1) the House or Senate **report number**, with the **number of the Congress** connected by a hyphen to the number of the report (*e.g.*, S. Rep. No. 95-185, H.R. Rep. No. 95-263, etc.);

(2) the **part or page number(s)** where the cited material appears, if any;

(3) the **year** of publication; and

(4) the **parallel citation to the permanent edition of West's** *United States Code Congressional and Administrative News* (U.S.C.C.A.N.) (whenever possible) (*e.g.*, 1962 U.S.C.C.A.N. 2844 or 1962 U.S.C.C.A.N. 2844, 2846).

Bluebook Rule 13.4(a); *see also Bluebook* Rules 13.4(b) (titles and authors) & 13.4(c) (unnumbered federal documents and committee prints).

Consider the following examples of typical citations of congressional committee reports:

[Example 4] H.R. Rep. No. 100-390, at 2 (1962), *reprinted in* 1962 U.S.C.C.A.N. 2137, 2138.

[Example 5] S. Rep. No. 103-57, at 9-10 (1993), *reprinted in* 1993 U.S.C.C.A.N. 1802, 1810-11.

[Example 6] H.R. Conf. Rep. No. 94-655 (1977), *reprinted in* 1977 U.S.C.C.A.N. 3485.

(d) Congressional Debates

Modern congressional debates (after 1873) are cited to the *Congressional Record*. The daily edition of the *Congressional Record* should be cited only when the material has not yet appeared in the bound edition. *Bluebook* Rule 13.5.

Consider the following examples of typical citations of the *Congressional Record*:

[Example 7] 111 Cong. Rec. 19,379 (1965).

[Example 8] 136 Cong. Rec. H10959 (daily ed. Oct. 22, 1990) (remarks of Rep. Dingell).

3. Typeface Conventions

Citations of bills and hearings in court documents, legal memoranda, and law review articles all have the same roman typeface. In law reviews, congressional committee reports and debates are shown in large and small capital letters:

[Example 9] H.R. REP. NO. 100-390, at 2 (1962), *reprinted in* 1962 U.S.C.C.A.N. 2137, 2138.

[Example 10] 111 CONG. REC. 19,379 (1965).

B. INSTRUCTIONS FOR COMPLETING THIS EXERCISE

West's *United States Code Congressional and Administrative News* (U.S.C.C.A.N.) reprints the text of enacted federal statutes and selected legislative history for those statutes. To complete this exercise, find the committee report related to the statute listed with your problem number below in the appropriate volume of *United States Code Congressional and Administrative News*. For your information, the committee report listed below relates to the statute in the *United States Statutes at Large* cited in Citation Exercise 31, above.

For your answer to this exercise, cite the committee report in *Bluebook* (or another designated) form; **include a parallel citation to *United States Code Congressional and Administrative News*.**

Unless otherwise instructed, write your answer on the answer sheet provided in Part 4 of these exercises.

PROBLEM #	COMMITTEE REPORT AND STATUTE
1 158 255 328 453 572	H.R. Rep. No. 88-1703 — Housing Act of 1964
2 159 256 329 454 573	S. Rep. No. 89-1479 — Oil Pollution of the Sea (1966)
3 160 257 330 455 574	H.R. Rep. No. 90-805 — Age Discrimination in Employment (1967)
4 161 258 331 456 575	H.R. Rep. No. 88-1538 — Wilderness Act (1964)
5 162 259 332 457 576	H.R. Rep. No. 91-699 — Committee on Opportunities for Spanish Speaking People (1969)
6 163 260 333 458 577	S. Rep. No. 91-1080 — Merchant Marine Act of 1970
7 164 261 334 459 578	S. Rep. No. 92-437 — Revenue Act of 1971
8 165 262 335 460 579	S. Rep. No. 95-1260 — Ocean Shipping Act of 1978
9 166 263 336 461 580	S. Rep. No. 92-988 — Vietnam Era Veterans' Readjustment Assistance Act of 1972
10 167 264 337 462 581	H.R. Rep. No. 93-659 — Comprehensive Employment and Training Act of 1973
11 168 265 338 463 582	H.R. Rep. No. 89-1651 — Foreign Assistance Act of 1966
12 169 266 339 464 583	S. Rep. No. 93-127 — Employee Retirement Income Security Act of 1974
13 170 267 340 465 584	S. Rep. No. 94-168 — Handicapped Children's Education (1975)
14 171 268 341 466 585	S. Rep. No. 90-801 — Postal Revenue and Federal Salary Act of 1967
15 172 269 342 467 586	H.R. Rep. No. 94-1476 — Copyrights Act (1976)
16 173 270 343 468 587	H.R. Rep. No. 90-1585 — Housing and Urban Development Act of 1968
17 174 271 344 469 588	H.R. Rep. No. 95-240 — International Development and Food Assistance (1977)
18 175 272 345 470 589	H.R. Rep. No. 91-951 — Middle Income Student Assistance Act (1978)
19 176 273 346 571 590	S. Rep. No. 91-546 — Federal Contested Election Act (1969)
20 177 274 347 472 591	S. Rep. No. 96-230 — Bankruptcy (Student Loans) (1979)
21 178 275 348 473 592	H.R. Rep. No. 96-45 — Lotteries (Transportation of Materials to Foreign Countries) (1979)
22 179 276 349 474 593	H.R. Rep. No. 91-1193 — Newspaper Preservation Act (1970)
23 180 277 350 475 594	H.R. Rep. No. 96-115 — Disqualification of Former Government Employees and Officers (1979)
24 181 278 351 476 595	S. Rep. No. 95-1243 — Suspension of Duties on Metal Waste and Scrap (1978)
25 182 279 352 477 596	H.R. Rep. No. 92-379 — Emergency Loan Guarantee Act (1971)
26 183 280 353 478 597	H.R. Rep. No. 95-1 — Small Business Act (1977)
27 184 281 354 479 598	S. Rep. No. 95-354 — Federal Rules of Criminal Procedure Amendments (1977)
28 185 282 355 480 599	S. Rep. No. 92-724 — Ports and Waterways Safety Act of 1972
29 186 283 356 481 600	H.R. Rep. No. 89-439 — Voting Rights Act of 1965
30 187 284 357 482 501	S. Rep. No. 92-102 — Emergency Medical Services Systems Amendments of 1979
31 188 285 358 483 502	S. Rep. No. 92-835 — Consumer Product Safety Act (1972)
32 189 286 359 484 503	H.R. Rep. No. 85-277 — Social Security Act (Disability Determination) (1957)
33 190 287 360 485 504	H.R. Rep. No. 86-1715 — Vessels (Construction Subsidy) (1960)
34 191 288 361 486 505	H.R. Rep. No. 93-227 — Health Programs Extension Act of 1973
35 192 289 362 487 506	S. Rep. No. 86-730 — National Banking Laws (Clarification) (1959)
36 193 290 363 488 507	S. Rep. No. 85-1625 — Temporary Unemployment Compensation (1958)

PROBLEM #	COMMITTEE REPORT AND STATUTE
37 194 291 364 489 508	S. Rep. No. 93-906 — Colorado River Basin Salinity Control Act (1974)
38 195 292 365 490 509	S. Rep. No. 87-1221 — Public Debt Limit Act (1962)
39 196 293 366 491 510	S. Rep. No. 88-239 — Lead-Zinc Producers (1963)
40 197 294 367 492 511	H.R. Rep. No. 94-340 — Energy Policy and Conservation Act (1975)
41 198 295 368 493 512	H.R. Rep. No. 96-510 — Energy Policy and Conservation Act (Amendment) (1979)
42 199 296 369 494 513	S. Rep. No. 96-182 — Pipeline Safety Act of 1979
43 200 297 370 495 514	H.R. Rep. No. 94-439 — Electric and Hybrid Vehicle Research (1976)
44 101 298 371 496 515	S. Rep. No. 96-169 — Export Administration Act of 1979
45 102 299 372 497 516	H.R. Rep. No. 94-390 — Speedy Trial Act Amendments of 1979
46 103 300 373 498 517	S. Rep. No. 95-166 — State Veterans' Home Assistance (1977)
47 104 201 374 499 518	S. Rep. No. 95-795 — National Consumer Cooperative Bank Act (1978)
48 105 202 375 500 519	H.R. Rep. No. 95-1211 — Airline Deregulation Act of 1978
49 106 203 376 401 520	H.R. Rep. No. 95-1558 — Tribally Controlled Community College Assistance (1978)
50 107 204 377 402 521	S. Rep. No. 95-962 — Cigarettes (Distribution and Racketeering) (1978)
51 108 205 378 403 522	H.R. Rep. No. 85-473 — St. Lawrence Seaway Development Corp. (1957)
52 109 206 379 404 523	S. Rep. No. 95-1108 — Diplomatic Relations Act (1978)
53 110 207 380 405 524	H.R. Rep. No. 86-1861 — Federal Hazardous Substances Labeling (1960)
54 111 208 381 406 525	H.R. Rep. No. 86-741 — Labor-Management Reporting Act of 1959
55 112 209 382 407 526	S. Rep. No. 88-1378 — Nurse Training act of 1964
56 113 210 383 408 527	S. Rep. No. 87-1830 — District Courts (Jurisdiction) (1958)
57 114 211 384 409 528	S. Rep. No. 87-651 — Manpower Development and Training Act of 1962
58 115 212 385 410 529	H.R. Rep. No. 89-618 — National Foundation on the Arts and Humanities (1965)
59 116 213 386 411 530	S. Rep. No. 88-665 — Interstate Commerce (Seat Belts) (1963)
60 117 214 387 412 531	S. Rep. No. 95-746 — Tax Treatment Extension Act of 1977
61 118 215 388 413 532	S. Rep. No. 95-580 — Communication Act Amendments of 1978
62 119 216 389 414 533	H.R. Rep. No. 88-1002 — Airports (Federal Grants) (1964)
63 120 217 390 415 534	S. Rep. No. 89-65 — Federal Reserve Banks (Gold Reserves) (1965)
64 121 218 391 416 535	H.R. Rep. No. 89-51 — Appalachian Regional Development Act of 1965
65 122 219 392 417 536	S. Rep. No. 89-146 — Elementary and Secondary Education Act of 1965
66 123 220 393 418 537	S. Rep. No. 89-324 — Excise Tax Reduction Act of 1965
67 124 221 394 419 538	S. Rep. No. 89-1062 — Back Pay Act of 1966
68 125 222 395 420 539	H.R. Rep. No. 89-1315 — Uniform Time Act of 1966
69 126 223 396 421 540	H.R. Rep. No. 89-1348 — Small Business Act (Revolving Funds) (1966)
70 127 224 397 422 541	H.R. Rep. No. 89-1025 — Marine Resources and Engineering Development Act of 1966
71 128 225 398 423 542	H.R. Rep. No. 89-1541 — Bail Reform Act of 1966
72 129 226 399 424 543	S. Rep. No. 90-219 — Saline Water Conversion Program (1967)
73 130 227 400 425 544	H.R. Rep. No. 90-267 — Military Selective Service Act of 1967

PROBLEM #	COMMITTEE REPORT AND STATUTE
74 131 228 301 426 545	S. Rep. No. 90-294 — Mental Health Amendments of 1967
75 132 229 302 427 546	H.R. Rep. No. 90-68 — Interest Equalization Tax Extension Act of 1967
76 133 230 303 428 547	S. Rep. No. 90-1097 — Omnibus Crime Control and Safe Streets Act of 1968
77 134 231 304 429 548	S. Rep. No. 90-1317 — Postal Employees (Embezzlement) (1968)
78 135 232 305 430 549	S. Rep. No. 90-1353 — Aircraft Noise Abatement (1968)
79 136 233 306 431 550	S. Rep. No. 91-185 — Air Carriers (Ownership and Control) (1969)
80 137 234 307 432 551	H.R. Rep. No. 91-501 — Securities (Institutional Investors Study) (1969)
81 138 235 308 433 552	H.R. Rep. No. 91-466 — Educational Television and Radio Amendments of 1969
82 139 236 309 434 553	S. Rep. No. 91-534 — Naturalization (Waiting Period) (1969)
83 140 237 310 435 554	H.R. Rep. No. 91-1670 — Egg Products Inspection Act (1970)
84 141 238 311 436 555	S. Rep. No. 91-1424 — Seamen's Service Act (1970)
85 142 239 312 437 556	H.R. Rep. No. 91-1146 — Clear Air Amendments of 1970
86 143 240 313 438 557	H.R. Rep. No. 91-1554 — Federal-Aid Highway Act of 1970
87 144 241 314 439 558	H.R. Rep. No. 96-373 — Emergency Energy Conservation Act of 1979
88 145 242 315 440 559	S. Rep. No. 92-206 — Railroad Retirement (Annuities) (1971)
89 146 243 316 441 560	H.R. Rep. No. 92-351 — Health Care Benefits (Dependents) (1971)
90 147 244 317 442 561	H.R. Rep. No. 92-379 — Emergency Loan Guarantee Act of 1979
91 148 245 318 443 562	H.R. Rep. No. 92-1027 — Atomic Energy Commission (Licenses) (1972)
92 149 246 319 444 563	H.R. Rep. No. 92-554 — Education Amendments of 1972
93 150 247 320 445 564	S. Rep. No. 92-941 — Civil Defense (Extension) (1972)
94 151 248 321 446 565	S. Rep. No. 92-1003 — Juvenile Delinquency Prevention Act (1972)
95 152 249 322 447 566	S. Rep. No. 93-63 — Economic Stabilization Amendments of 1973
96 153 250 323 448 567	S. Rep. No. 93-84 — Interest Equalization Tax Extension Act of 1973
97 154 251 324 449 568	H.R. Rep. No. 93-43 — Older Americans Comprehensive Services Amendments of 1973
98 155 252 325 450 569	H.R. Rep. No. 93-249 — Crime Control Act of 1973
99 156 253 326 451 570	S. Rep. No. 93-418 — Federal Prisoners (Extension of Confinement Limits) (1973)
100 157 254 327 452 571	H.R. Rep. No. 93-680 — Federal Water Pollution Control Act (Amendments) (1973)

CITATION EXERCISE 39
ADMINISTRATIVE REGULATIONS (I)

A. INTRODUCTION

1. Federal Administrative Regulations

Proposed and final federal regulations first appear in the *Federal Register* (chronological publication). They then are published in the *Code of Federal Regulations* (organized topically). The *Code of Federal Regulations* has fifty subject titles. Each volume is revised and reissued annually on a rotational basis. Only those rules in force at the time the volume is revised are included.

2. Citing Federal Administrative Regulations

The *Federal Register* (Fed. Reg.) is cited by **volume**, **page**, and **date**. In addition, when the rule or regulation has a commonly used name, that name may be added before the volume number. When the *Federal Register* indicates where the regulation will appear in the *Code of Federal Regulations*, that information should be given parenthetically. *Bluebook* Rule 14.2(a). The following are typical citations to material in the *Federal Register*:

[Example 1] 50 Fed. Reg. 52,170 (1985).
[Example 2] Cuban Assets Control Regulations, 28 Fed. Reg. 6974 (1963) (codified as amended at 31 C.F.R. §§ 515.101-.809 (1998)).

The Code of Federal Regulations (C.F.R.) is cited by **title**, **section**, and **year**. The year of the volume is given in parentheses. In addition, when the rule or regulation has a commonly used name, that name may be added before the volume number. *Bluebook* Rule 14.2(a). Note that the section number is formed from a part number and subsection; thus, § 55.161 is subsection 161 of Part 55. The following are typical citations to regulations in the *Code of Federal Regulations*:

[Example 3] 31 C.F.R. § 515.101 (1998).
[Example 4] S.E.C. Rule 13e-1, 17 C.F.R. § 240.13e-4(f)(3) (1984).

3. Typeface Conventions

Citations of federal rules and regulations in court documents, legal memoranda, and law review articles all appear as having the same typeface (as shown above).

B. INSTRUCTIONS FOR COMPLETING THIS EXERCISE

This exercise requires you to find a federal regulation cited to the *Code of Federal Regulations* (C.F.R.). The citation consists of a title and section (*e.g.*, 29 C.F.R. § 1910.38). The decimals, however, are not ordered in the usual way. For example, § 1910.4 would appear *before* § 1910.38, and § 1910.120 would appear *after* § 1910.38. If the provision cited no longer appears in the current *C.F.R.*, complete a different problem.

For your answer to this exercise, state the citation of the provision in the *C.F.R.* in *Bluebook* (or another designated) form.

Unless otherwise instructed, write your answer on the answer sheet provided in Part 4 of these exercises.

PROBLEM #	**C.F.R. CITATION**
1 126 292 348 459 513	50 C.F.R. § 16.11
2 127 293 349 460 514	49 C.F.R. § 1045.3
3 128 294 350 461 515	48 C.F.R. § 814.403
4 129 295 351 462 516	47 C.F.R. § 15.6
5 130 296 352 463 517	46 C.F.R. § 174.045
6 131 297 353 464 518	45 C.F.R. § 500.2
7 132 298 354 465 519	44 C.F.R. § 12.6
8 133 299 355 466 520	43 C.F.R. § 11.15
9 134 300 356 467 521	42 C.F.R. § 53.111
10 135 201 357 468 522	40 C.F.R. § 58.20
11 136 202 358 469 523	40 C.F.R. § 166.2
12 137 203 359 470 524	39 C.F.R. § 265.6
13 138 204 360 471 525	38 C.F.R. § 4.10
14 139 205 361 472 526	37 C.F.R. § 10.6
15 140 206 362 473 527	36 C.F.R. § 7.75
16 141 207 363 474 528	35 C.F.R. § 61.123
17 142 208 364 475 529	34 C.F.R. § 300.124
18 143 209 365 476 530	33 C.F.R. § 23.10
19 144 210 366 477 531	32 C.F.R. § 634.4
20 145 211 367 478 532	31 C.F.R. § 2.4
21 146 212 368 479 533	30 C.F.R. § 218.100
22 147 213 369 480 534	29 C.F.R. § 408.10
23 148 214 370 481 535	28 C.F.R. § 14.8
24 149 215 371 482 536	27 C.F.R. § 19.133
25 150 216 372 483 537	25 C.F.R. § 38.10
26 151 217 373 484 538	24 C.F.R. § 27.15
27 152 218 374 485 539	24 C.F.R. § 3280.303
28 153 219 375 486 540	23 C.F.R. § 190.3
29 154 220 376 487 541	22 C.F.R. § 501.6
30 155 221 377 488 542	21 C.F.R. § 514.11
31 156 222 378 489 543	21 C.F.R. § 176.170
32 157 223 379 490 544	20 C.F.R. § 216.5
33 158 224 380 491 545	19 C.F.R. § 143.11
34 159 225 381 492 546	18 C.F.R. § 286.101

PROBLEM #	*C.F.R.* CITATION
35 160 226 382 493 547	17 C.F.R. § 17.04
36 161 227 383 494 548	16 C.F.R. § 15.122
37 162 228 384 495 549	15 C.F.R. § 19.24
38 163 229 385 496 550	14 C.F.R. § 25.23
39 164 230 386 497 551	13 C.F.R. § 107.2
40 165 231 387 498 552	12 C.F.R. § 26.4
41 166 232 388 499 553	11 C.F.R. § 103.3
42 167 233 389 500 554	10 C.F.R. § 456.103
43 168 234 390 401 555	9 C.F.R. § 91.25
44 169 235 391 402 556	8 C.F.R. § 101.2
45 170 236 392 403 557	7 C.F.R. § 1002.5
46 171 237 393 404 558	7 C.F.R. § 1924.3
47 172 238 394 405 559	5 C.F.R. § 1205.2
48 173 239 395 406 560	5 C.F.R. § 430.102
49 174 240 396 407 561	4 C.F.R. § 105.3
50 175 241 397 408 562	1 C.F.R. § 302.5
51 176 242 398 409 563	50 C.F.R. § 281.2
52 177 243 399 410 564	49 C.F.R. § 190.203
53 178 244 400 411 565	48 C.F.R. § 1801.102
54 179 245 301 412 566	47 C.F.R. § 65.100
55 180 246 302 413 567	46 C.F.R. § 287.3
56 181 247 303 414 568	45 C.F.R. § 205.10
57 182 248 304 415 569	44 C.F.R. § 205.7
58 183 249 305 416 570	43 C.F.R. § 4710.2
59 184 250 306 417 571	42 C.F.R. § 38.5
60 185 251 307 418 572	40 C.F.R. § 247.101
61 186 252 308 419 573	40 C.F.R. § 436.20
62 187 253 309 420 574	39 C.F.R. § 778.1
63 188 254 310 421 575	38 C.F.R. § 21.130
64 189 255 311 422 576	37 C.F.R. § 404.4
65 190 256 312 423 577	36 C.F.R. § 504.7
66 191 257 313 424 578	35 C.F.R. § 103.1
67 192 258 314 425 579	34 C.F.R. § 201.33
68 193 259 315 426 580	33 C.F.R. § 203.85
69 194 260 316 427 581	32 C.F.R. § 705.2
70 195 261 317 428 582	31 C.F.R. § 339.2
71 196 262 318 429 583	30 C.F.R. § 779.18
72 197 263 319 430 584	29 C.F.R. § 519.13
73 198 264 320 431 585	28 C.F.R. § 42.104
74 199 265 321 432 586	27 C.F.R. § 240.132
75 200 266 322 433 587	25 C.F.R. § 135.6
76 101 267 323 434 588	24 C.F.R. § 511.33
77 102 268 324 435 589	24 C.F.R. § 880.209
78 103 269 325 436 590	23 C.F.R. § 637.207
79 104 270 326 437 591	22 C.F.R. § 101.2
80 105 271 327 438 592	21 C.F.R. § 1302.06
81 106 272 328 439 593	21 C.F.R. § 201.56
82 107 273 329 440 594	20 C.F.R. § 636.2
83 108 274 330 441 595	19 C.F.R. § 210.22
84 109 275 331 442 596	18 C.F.R. § 156.1

PROBLEM #	*C.F.R.* CITATION
85 110 276 332 443 597	17 C.F.R. § 250.5
86 111 277 333 444 598	16 C.F.R. § 1018.15
87 112 278 334 445 599	15 C.F.R. § 904.108
88 113 279 335 446 600	14 C.F.R. § 75.13
89 114 280 336 447 501	13 C.F.R. § 316.14
90 115 281 337 448 502	12 C.F.R. § 205.3
91 116 282 338 449 503	11 C.F.R. § 113.3
92 117 283 339 450 504	10 C.F.R. § 960.1
93 118 284 340 451 505	9 C.F.R. § 313.16
94 119 285 341 452 506	8 C.F.R. § 215.3
95 120 286 342 453 507	7 C.F.R. § 356.2
96 121 287 343 454 508	7 C.F.R. § 1064.17
97 122 288 344 455 509	5 C.F.R. § 1320.3
98 123 289 345 456 510	5 C.F.R. § 870.202
99 124 290 346 457 511	4 C.F.R. § 407.40
100 125 291 347 458 512	1 C.F.R. § 315.103

ADMINISTRATIVE REGULATIONS (II)

A. INTRODUCTION

1. State Administrative Regulations

Several states now officially codify and publish state administrative regulations in sets similar to the *Code of Federal Regulations*. In other states, each agency issues its own regulations, which are generally available from that agency and possibly in local law libraries.

2. Citing State Administrative Regulations

State administrative rules and regulations are cited in a manner similar to federal administrative regulations. *See* Citation Exercise 39 *supra* & Table T.1. (listing state administrative compilations and administrative registers).

3. Typeface Conventions

Some state administrative compilations appear in large and small capital letters in law review footnotes (*e.g.*, N.M. ADMIN. CODE, WIS. ADMIN. CODE, etc.). These state administrative compilations appear in ordinary roman type in citations in court documents and legal memoranda. *See Bluebook* Practitioners' Note P.1(h).

B. INSTRUCTIONS FOR COMPLETING THIS EXERCISE

This exercise requires you to consult *Bluebook* Table T.1 for the purpose of determining information about the administrative compilation and register for the state listed with your problem number below.

For your answer to this exercise, state the following:

(a) the name of the administrative compilation for the state (*e.g.*, *California Code of Regulations*);

(b) the *Bluebook* citation form of the administrative compilation listed in (a), above (*e.g.*, Cal. Code Regs. tit. x, § x (19xx);

(c) the name of the administrative register for the state (*e.g.*, *California Regulatory Notice Register*); and

(d) the *Bluebook* citation form of the administrative register listed in (c), above (*e.g.*, Cal. Regulatory Notice Reg.).

Unless otherwise instructed, write your answer on the answer sheet provided in Part 4 of these exercises.

PROBLEM #	JURISDICTION
1 126 292 348 459 513	Ill.
2 127 293 349 460 514	Minn.
3 128 294 350 461 515	N.C.
4 129 295 351 462 516	N.M.
5 130 296 352 463 517	N.C.
6 131 297 353 464 518	S.D.
7 132 298 354 465 519	Tenn.
8 133 299 355 466 520	Utah
9 134 300 356 467 521	Vt.
10 135 201 357 468 522	Fla.
11 136 202 358 469 523	Ariz.
12 137 203 359 470 524	Mich.
13 138 204 360 471 525	Ariz.
14 139 205 361 472 526	Mont.
15 140 206 362 473 527	Colo.
16 141 207 363 474 528	Ill.
17 142 208 364 475 529	Minn.
18 143 209 365 476 530	S.D.
19 144 210 366 477 531	N.M.
20 145 211 367 478 532	N.C.
21 146 212 368 479 533	S.D.
22 147 213 369 480 534	Tenn.
23 148 214 370 481 535	Utah
24 149 215 371 482 536	Fla.
25 150 216 372 483 537	Fla.
26 151 217 373 484 538	Ariz.
27 152 218 374 485 539	Mich.
28 153 219 375 486 540	Ariz.
29 154 220 376 487 541	Mont.
30 155 221 377 488 542	Colo.
31 156 222 378 489 543	Ill.
32 157 223 379 490 544	Minn.
33 158 224 380 491 545	Utah
34 159 225 381 492 546	N.M.
35 160 226 382 493 547	N.C.
36 161 227 383 494 548	S.D.
37 162 228 384 495 549	Tenn.
38 163 229 385 496 550	Utah
39 164 230 386 497 551	Vt.
40 165 231 387 498 552	Fla.
41 166 232 388 499 553	Ariz.
42 167 233 389 500 554	Mich.
43 168 234 390 401 555	Ariz.
44 169 235 391 402 556	Mont.
45 170 236 392 403 557	Minn.
46 171 237 393 404 558	Tenn.
47 172 238 394 405 559	N.M.
48 173 239 395 406 560	N.C.
49 174 240 396 407 561	S.D.
50 175 241 397 408 562	Tenn.

PROBLEM #	JURISDICTION
51 176 242 398 409 563	Utah
52 177 243 399 410 564	Vt.
53 178 244 400 411 565	Fla.
54 179 245 301 412 566	Ariz.
55 180 246 302 413 567	Mich.
56 181 247 303 414 568	Ariz.
57 182 248 304 415 569	Mont.
58 183 249 305 416 570	Colo.
59 184 250 306 417 571	Ill.
60 185 251 307 418 572	Minn.
61 186 252 308 419 573	S.D.
62 187 253 309 420 574	N.M.
63 188 254 310 421 575	N.C.
64 189 255 311 422 576	S.D.
65 190 256 312 423 577	Tenn.
66 191 257 313 424 578	Utah
67 192 258 314 425 579	Vt.
68 193 259 315 426 580	Fla.
69 194 260 316 427 581	Ariz.
70 195 261 317 428 582	Okla.
71 196 262 318 429 583	Ariz.
72 197 263 319 430 584	Mont.
73 198 264 320 431 585	Colo.
74 199 265 321 432 586	Ill.
75 200 266 322 433 587	Minn.
76 101 267 323 434 588	N.M.
77 102 268 324 435 589	N.C.
78 103 269 325 436 590	S.D.
79 104 270 326 437 591	Tenn.
80 105 271 327 438 592	Utah
81 106 272 328 439 593	Vt.
82 107 273 329 440 594	Fla.
83 108 274 330 441 595	Ariz.
84 109 275 331 442 596	Mich.
85 110 276 332 443 597	Ariz.
86 111 277 333 444 598	Mont.
87 112 278 334 445 599	Colo.
88 113 279 335 446 600	Ill.
89 114 280 336 447 501	Minn.
90 115 281 337 448 502	N.M.
91 116 282 338 449 503	N.C.
92 117 283 339 450 504	S.D.
93 118 284 340 451 505	Tenn.
94 119 285 341 452 506	Utah
95 120 286 342 453 507	Vt.
96 121 287 343 454 508	Fla.
97 122 288 344 455 509	Ariz.
98 123 289 345 456 510	Mich.
99 124 290 346 457 511	Ariz.
100 125 291 347 458 512	Mont.

PART 4

ANSWER SHEETS

CITATION EXERCISE 1
DICTIONARIES

Your Name _____

Your Professor's or Instructor's Name _____

Your Assigned Section (if applicable) _____

Your Assigned Problem Number _____

Self-Reassigned Problem Number (if applicable) _____

    (a) State the title of the legal dictionary used for this exercise:

    (b) State the author's full name; if none is listed, simply state "None listed" as your answer:

    (c) State the copyright date of the dictionary that you used:

    (d) State the edition of the dictionary if it is not the first edition:

    (e) the editor's full name, if any is listed (*e.g.*, William S. Anderson); and

    (f) Cite the dictionary in proper *Bluebook* (or another designated) form:

NOTES ON CITATION EXERCISE 1

♠* Be sure to use a **legal dictionary** to complete this exercise.

♠* The instructions indicate that you are to assume that the above citation will appear in a court document or legal memorandum, not in a law review article; thus, you should <u>underscore</u> (italicize) the title of the dictionary (*e.g.*, <u>Black's Law Dictionary</u>).

♠* Do not indicate the edition in the citation if it is the first edition.

♠* Use 2d ed. (**not** 2nd ed.), 3d ed. (**not** 3rd ed.), 4th ed., etc. in the citation. *See Bluebook* Rule 15.7(a) for examples of this format. Also, do not use the following form in a *Bluebook* citation: 4th ed. or $4^{\underline{th}}$ ed.

♠* Remember that *Black's* and *Ballentine's* are cited using a special form. *See Bluebook* Rule 15.7 (no author or editor given).

♠* Citations in these exercises should appear as citation sentences. *See Bluebook* Rule 1.1 & Practitioners' Notes P.2. A citation sentence begins with a capital letter and ends with a period. Thus, be sure to include a period at the end of your citations in these exercises.

♠* The instructions indicate that you should include in your citation the specific page(s) where the definition can be found; multiple pages should be cited by giving inclusive page numbers, separated by a hyphen (*e.g.*, 35-36); if the pages cited consist of three or more numbers, the last two digits should be retained; the remaining repetitious digit(s) should be dropped (*e.g.*, 173-74 or 1135-36).

CITATION EXERCISE 2
LEGAL ENCYCLOPEDIAS (I)

Your Name _____

Your Professor's or Instructor's Name _____

Your Assigned Section (if applicable) _____

Your Assigned Problem Number _____

Self-Reassigned Problem Number (if applicable) _____

    (a) State the volume number of the *Am. Jur. 2d* volume in which you found the topic and section:

    (b) State the copyright date of the *Am. Jur. 2d* volume in which you found this topic and section (*e.g.*, 1999):

    (c) Cite the section of the encyclopedia in proper *Bluebook* (or another designated) form:

Notes on Citation Exercise 2

♦* The instructions indicate that you are to assume that the above citation will appear in a court document or legal memorandum, not in a law review article; thus, you underscore (italicize) the topic (*e.g.*, Public Utilities) in the citation.

♦* Remember that legal encyclopedias such *as American Jurisprudence Second* and *Corpus Juris Secundum* are cited using a special form. *See Bluebook* Rule 15.7(a) (requiring a special form for a few frequently cited works). Be sure to include (1) the volume number at the beginning of the citation and (2) the copyright date of the volume in a parenthetical at the end of the citation. Abbreviate "and" to "&" when that word is included the name of the topic.

♦* Citations in these exercises should appear as citation sentences. *See Bluebook* Rule 1.1 & Practitioners' Notes P.2. A citation sentence begins with a capital letter and ends with a period. Thus, be sure to include a period at the end of your citations in these exercises.

CITATION EXERCISE 3
LEGAL ENCYCLOPEDIAS (II)

Your Name _____

Your Professor's or Instructor's Name _____

Your Assigned Section (if applicable) _____

Your Assigned Problem Number _____

Self-Reassigned Problem Number (if applicable) _____

(a) State the volume number of the *C.J.S.* volume in which you found the title and section:

(b) State the copyright date of the *C.J.S.* volume in which you found this title and section (*e.g.*, 1999):

(c) Cite the section of the encyclopedia in proper *Bluebook* (or another designated) form:

NOTES ON CITATION EXERCISE 3

♠* The instructions indicate that you are to assume that the above citation will appear in a court document or legal memorandum, not in a law review article; thus, you should <u>underscore</u> (italicize) the title (*e.g.*, <u>Public Utilities</u>).

♠* Remember that legal encyclopedias such *as American Jurisprudence Second* and *Corpus Juris Secundum* are cited using a special form. *See Bluebook* Rule 15.7(a) (requiring a special form for a few frequently cited works). Be sure to include (1) the volume number at the beginning of the citation and (2) the copyright date of the volume in a parenthetical at the end of the citation. Abbreviate "and" to "&" when that word is included the name of the title.

♠* Citations in these exercises should appear as citation sentences. *See Bluebook* Rule 1.1 & Practitioners' Notes P.2. A citation sentence begins with a capital letter and ends with a period. Thus, be sure to include a period at the end of your citations in these exercises.

CITATION EXERCISE 4
TEXTS AND TREATISES

Your Name _____

Your Professor's or Instructor's Name _____

Your Assigned Section (if applicable) _____

Your Assigned Problem Number _____

Self-Reassigned Problem Number (if applicable) _____

    (a) State the volume number of the text or treatise (if there is more than one) (*e.g.*, 3, 9A, etc.):

    (b) State the full name(s) of the author(s) as stated on the title page of the text or treatise (*e.g.*, Homer H. Clark, Jr.):

    (c) State the title of the book (*e.g.*, The Law of Domestic Relations in the United States):

    (d) State the edition of the text or treatise (if other than the first) (*e.g.*, second edition):

    (e) State the copyright date of the text or treatise (*e.g.*, 1988):

    (f) State the citation of the text or treatise in *Bluebook* (or another designated) form; **include a specific ("pinpoint") reference to the designated section or page in your citation.** Assume that your citation will appear in a court document or legal memorandum, not in a law review article (*e.g.*, Homer H. Clark, Jr., <u>The Law of Domestic Relations in the United States</u> § 13.6 (2d ed. 1988):

NOTES ON CITATION EXERCISE 4

♠* Be sure to use the **designated edition** of the text or treatise.

♠* Remember that works with three or more authors are cited using the first plus et al. (*e.g.*, Roger A. Cunningham, William D. Stoebuck, & Dale A. Whitman = Roger A. Cunningham et al.).

♠* Note that "et" does **not** have a period after it, but "al." does; nor is "et al." capitalized.

♠* The instructions indicate that you are to assume that the above citation will appear in a court document or legal memorandum, not in a law review article; thus, you should underscore (italicize) the title of the text or treatise (*e.g.*, Civil Procedure); the remainder of the citation should appear in ordinary roman typeface.

♠* When a text or treatise is organized by consecutively numbered sections, the relevant section(s) should be cited. *See Bluebook* Rule 3.4. When a section is cited, the relevant page number(s) may be added (*e.g.*, § 52, at 102) when it would facilitate finding the specific matter cited within the section. Multiple sections are indicated by double section signs (*e.g.*, §§ 33-35); give inclusive numbers; *et seq.* should not be used. *See Bluebook* Rules 3.4 & 3.4(a).

♠* Be careful to apply the rule concerning inclusive page numbers if you are citing more than one page. Cite multiple pages by giving inclusive page numbers, separated by a hyphen (*e.g.*, 35-36); if the pages cited consist of three or more numbers, you should retain the last two digits and drop the repetitious digit(s) (*e.g.*, 173-74 or 1135-36).

♠* Do not indicate the edition if it is the first; use 2d ed. (**not** 2nd ed.), 3d ed. (**not** 3rd ed.), 4th ed., etc. *See Bluebook* Rule 15.7(a) for examples of this format. Also, do not use the following form in a *Bluebook* citation: 4th ed. or $4^{\underline{th}}$ ed.

♠* Citations in these exercises should appear as citation sentences. *See Bluebook* Rule 1.1 & Practitioners' Notes P.2. A citation sentence begins with a capital letter and ends with a period. Thus, be sure to include a period at the end of your citations in these exercises.

CITATION EXERCISE 5
LEGAL PERIODICALS (I)

Your Name _____

Your Professor's or Instructor's Name _____

Your Assigned Section (if applicable) _____

Your Assigned Problem Number _____

Self-Reassigned Problem Number (if applicable) _____

     For your answer to this exercise, state the proper abbreviations of the names of the periodicals listed with your problem number. You should assume that your citation will appear in a court document or legal memorandum, not in a law review article.

    (a) First Periodical Title

       (i) Full title of the periodical:

       (ii) Abbreviation:

    (b) Second Periodical Title:

       (i) Full title of the periodical:

       (ii) Abbreviation:

Notes on Citation Exercise 5

♠* Remember that when a periodical is not specifically listed in *Bluebook* Table T.13, you should look up each word of the title. The table provides abbreviations for many of the words that are commonly used in periodical names. Geographical words in the name of the periodical should be abbreviated as provided in *Bluebook* Table T.10. Follow the specific directions given at the beginning of Table T.13 for articles and prepositions appearing in the name.

♠* **Be extra careful about spacing in abbreviations of periodicals.** *See Bluebook* Rule 6.1(a) and the various *Bluebook* Tables, especially Table T.13. Recall that Rule 6.1(a) specifically provides that when names of periodicals are abbreviated, all adjacent single capital letters must be closed up (*i.e.*, no space between the capital letters). For example, Yale L.J. is **not** written as Yale L. J. However, when one or more of the capital letters in the abbreviation stands for the name of a geographic or institutional entity, *Bluebook* Rule 6.1(a) provides that the capital letters referring to that entity must be set off from other adjacent single capital letters with a space. For example, Fla. St. U. L. Rev. is **not** written as Fla. St. U.L. Rev. Recall also that under *Bluebook* Rule 6.1(a), single capital letters should not be closed up with longer abbreviations (*e.g.*, Fordham Urb. L.J., **not** Fordham Urb.L.J.).

♠* The instructions indicate that you are to assume that the above citation will appear in a court document or legal memorandum, not in a law review article; thus, **the abbreviated names of the periodicals should appear in ordinary roman typeface**. In contrast, the typeface used in *Bluebook* Table T.13 is the typeface used in law review footnotes. Periodical names appear in large and small capital letters in law review footnote citations.

CITATION EXERCISE 6
LEGAL PERIODICALS (II)

Your Name _____

Your Professor's or Instructor's Name _____

Your Assigned Section (if applicable) _____

Your Assigned Problem Number _____

Self-Reassigned Problem Number (if applicable) _____

For your answer to this exercise, cite the article listed with your problem number in proper *Bluebook* (or another designated) form; assume that your citation will appear in a court document or legal memorandum, not in a law review article.

Full Citation of the Article:

NOTES ON CITATION EXERCISE 6

✷ Be sure to use the appropriate spacing in the abbreviation of the name of the periodical (*see supra* Citation Exercise 5).

✷ The instructions indicate that you are to assume that the above citation will appear in a court document or legal memorandum, not in a law review article; thus, the title of the article should be underscored (italicized) (*e.g.*, Trademarked Generic Words).

✷ Titles of periodical articles should be capitalized according to *Bluebook* Rule 8. Thus, the capitalization of the title in your citation may differ from the actual capitalization of the title of the article in the periodical. Rule 8 provides that the initial word, the word immediately following a colon, and all other words in the title should be capitalized; however, articles, conjunctions, and prepositions of four or fewer letters should not be capitalized (*e.g.*, The Locus of Sovereignty: Judicial Review, Legislative Supremacy, and Federalism in the Constitutional Traditions of Canada and the United States). *See Bluebook* Rule 8.

✷ A comma should be used after the name of the author(s) and after title of the article (*e.g.*, Ralph H. Folsom & Larry L. Teply, Trademarked Generic Words, 89 Yale L.J. 1323 (1980).

✷ Remember that articles with two authors should be cited in the order they are given in the publication, connected by an ampersand (&); articles with three or more authors should be cited to the first author only, followed by "et al." (and others).

✷ Remember that certain periodicals do not have volume numbers. If the volume is paginated consecutively throughout the entire volume, you should use the year of publication as the volume number and omit the year designation at the end of the citation (*e.g.*, Calvin R. Massey, The Locus of Sovereignty: Judicial Review, Legislative Supremacy, and Federalism in the Constitutional Traditions of Canada and the United States, 1990 Duke L.J. 1229). *See Bluebook* Rules 3.2(a) & 16.2.

✷ Several periodicals paginate each *issue* separately. In this situation, you should cite the periodical by the date or period of publication and omit the year designation at the end of the citation (*e.g.*, Gene H. Wood, *The Child as Witness*, 6 Fam. Advoc., Spring 1984, at 14.). *See Bluebook* Rule 16.3 ("Nonconsecutively Paginated Journals and Magazines").

✷ Citations in these exercises should appear as citation sentences. *See Bluebook* Rule 1.1 & Practitioners' Notes P.2. A citation sentence begins with a capital letter and ends with a period. Thus, be sure to include a period at the end of your citations in these exercises.

CITATION EXERCISE 7
A.L.R. ANNOTATIONS

Your Name _____

Your Professor's or Instructor's Name _____

Your Assigned Section (if applicable) _____

Your Assigned Problem Number _____

Self-Reassigned Problem Number (if applicable) _____

(a) State the full name of the author of the annotation, if any:

(b) State the full title of the annotation exactly as it is given at the beginning of the annotation:

(c) State the copyright date of the volume:

(d) Cite the annotation in *Bluebook* (or another designated) form; assume that your citation will appear in a court document or legal memorandum, not in a law review article:

♠* Be sure to use the correct series (*A.L.R.4th*, *A.L.R.5th*, or *A.L.R. Federal*) to complete this exercise.

♠* Degree designations (such as J.D., LL.B., LL.M., etc.) should be omitted when you cite the author's name (*e.g.*, Christopher Hall, **not** Christopher Hall, J.D.).

♠* You must include the word, Annotation, in the citation after the author's name; if no author is listed, simply begin the citation with the word, Annotation.

♠* The instructions indicate that you are to assume that the above citation will appear in a court document or legal memorandum, not in a law review article; thus, you should <u>underscore</u> (italicize) the title of the annotation (*e.g.*, <u>Nonuse of Seatbelts as Reducing Amount of Damages Recoverable</u>).

♠* Titles of annotations should be capitalized according to *Bluebook* Rule 8. Thus, the capitalization of the title of the annotation will usually differ from the actual capitalization of the published title. Recall that Rule 8 provides that the initial word, the word immediately following a colon, and all other words in the title should be capitalized; however, articles, conjunctions, and prepositions of four or fewer letters should not be capitalized.

♠* **Be especially careful about spacing.** For example, A.L.R.4th is **not** written as A.L.R. 4th. *See Bluebook* Rule 6.1(a).

♠* In law review footnotes, the abbreviated name of the particular annotation appears in large and small capital letters (*e.g.*, 65 A.L.R.5TH), but in the above citation, the name should appear in ordinary roman typeface (*e.g.*, 65 A.L.R.5th).

♠* *Bluebook* form uses 2d rather than 2nd and 3d rather than 3rd. Do not use the following form in a *Bluebook* citation: A.L.R.4ᵗʰ or A.L.R.4ᵗʰ.

♠* Citations in these exercises should appear as citation sentences. *See Bluebook* Rule 1.1 & Practitioners' Notes P.2. A citation sentence begins with a capital letter and ends with a period. Thus, be sure to include a period at the end of your citations in these exercises.

CITATION EXERCISE 8
RESTATEMENTS OF THE LAW

Your Name _____

Your Professor's or Instructor's Name _____

Your Assigned Section (if applicable) _____

Your Assigned Problem Number _____

Self-Reassigned Problem Number (if applicable) _____

(a) State the subject with which the cited section deals (*e.g.*, the definition of an offer):

(b) State the year the Restatement Second volume was published (*e.g.*, 1979):

(c) Cite the section listed with your problem number in *Bluebook* (or another designated) form; assume that your citation will appear in a court document or legal memorandum, not in a law review article:

♠* Be sure to use the **principal volume** containing the cited section. **The appendix and other volumes accompanying the Restatements should not be used.** All of the citations below are to sections appearing in a **Restatement Second**.

♠* Be sure to include "(Second)" in the citation; otherwise, it will be taken that you are citing the first restatement rather than the second.

♠* Do not use the section title in the citation.

♠* The instructions indicate that you are to assume that the above citation will appear in a court document or legal memorandum, not in a law review article; thus, the citation should entirely be given in ordinary roman typeface.

♠* Citations in these exercises should appear as citation sentences. *See Bluebook* Rule 1.1 & Practitioners' Notes P.2. A citation sentence begins with a capital letter and ends with a period. Thus, be sure to include a period at the end of your citations in these exercises.

CITATION EXERCISE 9
CASE NAMES: ABBREVIATIONS

Your Name _____

Your Professor's or Instructor's Name _____

Your Assigned Section (if applicable) _____

Your Assigned Problem Number _____

Self-Reassigned Problem Number (if applicable) _____

      In the space provided, indicate the unabbreviated words listed with your problem number and then give the proper abbreviation for each. Your answers should appear as follows:

(a) Educational = Educ.
(b) American Samoa = Am. Sam.
(c) Uzbekistan = Uzb.
(d) On the information of = ex rel.
(e) Roads = Rds.
(f) Savings = Sav.

(a) _____ = _____

(b) _____ = _____

(c) _____ = _____

(d) _____ = _____

(e) _____ = _____

(f) _____ = _____

♦※ *Bluebook* Table T.6 ("Case Names") lists required abbreviations for approximately 120 words that typically appear in case names. These abbreviations must be used **as long as they are not the first word of the name of a party or a relator.** *Bluebook* Rules 10.2.1(c) & 10.2.2.

♦※ *Bluebook* Table T.10 ("Geographical Terms") lists required abbreviations for U.S. states, cities, and territories, Australian states, Canadian provinces, foreign countries, and foreign regions. These abbreviations are used **unless the geographical unit itself is a named party.** *Bluebook* Rule 10.2.2.

♦※ "Petition of," "matter of," or "application of," and similar expressions should be abbreviated to "*In re*" in all case citations. *Bluebook* Rule 10.2.1(b).

♦※ "On relation of," "for the use of," "on behalf of," "on the information of," "by," and similar expressions should be shortened to "*ex rel.*" in all case citations. *Bluebook* Rule 10.2.1(b).

♦※ **Watch for plurals of words listed in Table T.6.** Plurals of words listed in Table T.6 are formed by adding the letter "s" to the abbreviation (*e.g.*, Manufacturers = Mfrs. or Administrators = Adm'rs)—**unless otherwise indicated in the table** (*e.g.*, Laborator[y, ies] = Lab.).

CASE NAMES: INCLUSIONS AND DELETIONS (I)

Your Name _____

Your Professor's or Instructor's Name _____

Your Assigned Section (if applicable) _____

Your Assigned Problem Number _____

Self-Reassigned Problem Number (if applicable) _____

(a) (1) State the full title of the case as it is stated in the reporter at the beginning of the reported case; **you should omit obviously irrelevant portions of the case title if the title is a lengthy one:**

(2) State the proper citation of the case name using *Bluebook* (or another designated) form; **do not give a full citation of the case**; assume that the case name is going to appear in a **citation sentence or clause**, not as a grammatical part of a textual sentence:

(b) (1) State the full title of the case as it is stated in the reporter at the beginning of the reported case; **you should omit obviously irrelevant portions of the case title if the title is a lengthy one:**

(2) State the proper citation of the case name using *Bluebook* (or another designated) form; **do not give a full citation of the case**; assume that the case name is going to appear in a **citation sentence or clause**, not as a grammatical part of a textual sentence:

(c) (1) State the full title of the case as it is stated in the reporter at the beginning of the reported case; **you should omit obviously irrelevant portions of the case title if the title is a lengthy one**:

(2) State the proper citation of the case name using *Bluebook* (or another designated) form; **do not give a full citation of the case**; assume that the case name is going to appear in a **citation sentence or clause**, not as a grammatical part of a textual sentence:

(d) (1) State the full title of the case as it is stated in the reporter at the beginning of the reported case; **you should omit obviously irrelevant portions of the case title if the title is a lengthy one**:

(2) State the proper citation of the case name using *Bluebook* (or another designated) form; **do not give a full citation of the case**; assume that the case name is going to appear in a **citation sentence or clause**, not as a grammatical part of a textual sentence:

(e) (1) State the full title of the case as it is stated in the reporter at the beginning of the reported case; **you should omit obviously irrelevant portions of the case title if the title is a lengthy one**:

(2) State the proper citation of the case name using *Bluebook* (or another designated) form; **do not give a full citation of the case**; assume that the case name is going to appear in a **citation sentence or clause**, not as a grammatical part of a textual sentence:

(f) (1) State the full title of the case as it is stated in the reporter at the beginning of the reported case; **you should omit obviously irrelevant portions of the case title if the title is a lengthy one**:

(2) State the proper citation of the case name using *Bluebook* (or another designated) form; **do not give a full citation of the case**; assume that the case name is going to appear in a **citation sentence or clause**, not as a grammatical part of a textual sentence:

NOTES ON CITATION EXERCISE 10

☑ TERMS DESCRIBING A PARTY ALREADY NAMED

✸ Terms describing a party already named, such as defendant, appellant, warden, superintendent, etc., should be omitted. *Bluebook* Rule 10.2.1(e).

☑ GIVEN NAMES AND INITIALS OF INDIVIDUALS

✸ Do not omit a part of a surname consisting of more than one word (*e.g.*, Garcilaso de la Vega, Von Der Linden, etc.). *Bluebook* Rule 10.2(g).

✸ Given names or initials of individuals should be omitted (*e.g.*, a party listed in the reporter as "Jane S. Smith" would be cited as "Smith"). *Bluebook* Rule 10.2.1(g). However, given names and initials of individuals should be retained in the citation (1) when the party's surname has been abbreviated in the report (*e.g.*, Jane S., J.S., or J.S.S.): (2) when they are part of the name of a business firm (*e.g.*, Jane S. Smith Construction Co.); and (3) when they are part of a foreign name and the name is **entirely** in a foreign language or when the given names follow a foreign surname (*e.g.*, Le Bup Thi Dao, Chom Cho Ha, etc.). *Bluebook* Rule 10.2.1(g).

☑ WORDS INDICATING MULTIPLE PARTIES

✸ Words indicating multiple parties, such as *et al.* (and others), *et ux.* (and wife), and *et vir.* (and husband), should be omitted. *Bluebook* Rule 10.2.1(a).

☑ ALTERNATIVE NAMES FOR A PARTY

✸ Alternative names for a party should be omitted. *Bluebook* Rule 10.2.1(a).

☑ CONSOLIDATION OF TWO OR MORE ACTIONS

✸ When the case is a consolidation of two or more actions, only the first listed case should be cited. *Bluebook* Rule 10.2.1(a).

☑ ADDITIONAL PARTIES ON EACH SIDE OF THE CASE

✒ All parties other than the first listed on each side of the case should be omitted, except the first-listed "relator" should be included in the citation. *Bluebook* Rule 10.2.1(a).

☑ PARTNERSHIP NAMES

✒ No portion of a partnership name should be omitted. *Bluebook* Rule 10.2.1(a).

☑ BUSINESS FIRM DESIGNATIONS

✒ Business firm designations like Incorporated or Inc., Limited or Ltd., National Association or N.A., Federal Savings Bank or F.S.B., Socidad Anonima or S.A., Aktiengesellchaft or A.G., etc. should be omitted when "the [cited] name also contains words such as 'Ass'n,' 'Bros.,' 'Co.,' 'Corp.,' and 'R.R.,' clearly indicating that the party is a business firm." *Bluebook* Rule 10.2.1(h).

☑ COMMISSIONER OF INTERNAL REVENUE AS A PARTY

✒ When the cited party name is "Commissioner of Internal Revenue," only "Commissioner" should be used as the name of the party. *Bluebook* Rule 10.2.1(j).

✒ Commissioner of Internal Revenue should be dropped entirely if it follows the actual name of the Commissioner because it describes a party already named.

☑ ABBREVIATIONS

✒ The following eight words should always be abbreviated **unless** they are the **first word** of a party's name, including a relator: And = &; Association = Ass'n; Brothers = Bros.; Company = Co.; Corporation = Corp.; Incorporated = Inc.; Limited = Ltd.; and Number = No. *Bluebook* Rule 10.2.1(c).

✒ Some governmental agencies, boards, commissions, businesses, and private organizations are commonly referred to in spoken language by their widely recognized initials. These initials (without periods between them) **may** be used in case names rather than their full names. *Bluebook* Rules 10.2.1(c) & 6.1(b).

✒ Table T.6 ("Case Names") lists required abbreviations for approximately 120 words that typically appear in case names. These abbreviations must be used **as long as they are not the first word of the name of a party or a relator.** *Bluebook* Rules 10.2.1(c) & 10.2.2.

✒ Watch for **plurals** of words listed in Table T.6. Plurals of words listed in Table T.6 are formed by adding the letter "s" to the abbreviation (*e.g.,* Manufacturers = Mfrs. or Administrators = Adm'rs)—**unless otherwise indicated in the table** (*e.g.,* Laborator[y, ies] = Lab.).

✒ Table T.10 ("Geographical Terms") lists required abbreviations for U.S. states, cities, and territories, Australian states, Canadian provinces, foreign countries, and foreign regions. These abbreviations are used **unless the geographical unit itself is a named party.** *Bluebook* Rule 10.2.2. *Bluebook* Rule 10.2.2 also specifically states that "United States" should **not** be abbreviated.

CITATION EXERCISE 11
CASE NAMES: INCLUSIONS AND DELETIONS (II)

Your Name _____

Your Professor's or Instructor's Name _____

Your Assigned Section (if applicable) _____

Your Assigned Problem Number _____

Self-Reassigned Problem Number (if applicable) _____

(a) (1) State the full title of the case as it is stated in the reporter at the beginning of the reported case; **you should omit obviously irrelevant portions of the case title if the title is a lengthy one**:

(2) State the proper citation of the case name using *Bluebook* (or another designated) form; **do not give a full citation of the case**; assume that the case name is going to appear in a **citation sentence or clause**, not as a grammatical part of a textual sentence:

(b) (1) State the full title of the case as it is stated in the reporter at the beginning of the reported case; **you should omit obviously irrelevant portions of the case title if the title is a lengthy one**:

(2) State the proper citation of the case name using *Bluebook* (or another designated) form; **do not give a full citation of the case**; assume that the case name is going to appear in a **citation sentence or clause**, not as a grammatical part of a textual sentence:

(c) (1) State the full title of the case as it is stated in the reporter at the beginning of the reported case; **you should omit obviously irrelevant portions of the case title if the title is a lengthy one**:

(2) State the proper citation of the case name using *Bluebook* (or another designated) form; **do not give a full citation of the case**; assume that the case name is going to appear in a **citation sentence or clause**, not as a grammatical part of a textual sentence:

(d) (1) State the full title of the case as it is stated in the reporter at the beginning of the reported case; **you should omit obviously irrelevant portions of the case title if the title is a lengthy one**:

(2) State the proper citation of the case name using *Bluebook* (or another designated) form; **do not give a full citation of the case**; assume that the case name is going to appear in a **citation sentence or clause**, not as a grammatical part of a textual sentence:

(e) (1) State the full title of the case as it is stated in the reporter at the beginning of the reported case; **you should omit obviously irrelevant portions of the case title if the title is a lengthy one**:

(2) State the proper citation of the case name using *Bluebook* (or another designated) form; **do not give a full citation of the case**; assume that the case name is going to appear in a **citation sentence or clause**, not as a grammatical part of a textual sentence:

(f) (1) State the full title of the case as it is stated in the reporter at the beginning of the reported case; **you should omit obviously irrelevant portions of the case title if the title is a lengthy one**:

(2) State the proper citation of the case name using *Bluebook* (or another designated) form; **do not give a full citation of the case**; assume that the case name is going to appear in a **citation sentence or clause**, not as a grammatical part of a textual sentence:

NOTES ON CITATION EXERCISE 11

☑ LABOR UNIONS

🖋 Labor unions are cited exactly as they appear in the official reporter, subject to the following modifications: (1) Cite only the smallest unit of the union; (2) Omit all craft and industry designations **except the first full designation**; (3) Omit all prepositional phrases of location; and (4) In lieu of citing the union name, a widely recognized abbreviation may be used. *Bluebook Rule* 10.2.1(i). No periods are used between the letters. *Bluebook* Rules 6.1(b) & 10.2.1(c).

☑ "STATE OF" AND SIMILAR PHRASES

🖋 "State of," "People of," and "Commonwealth of" should be omitted from the citation when the state, people, or commonwealth are litigating **in courts of other jurisdictions**. When the state, people, or commonwealth are litigating **in courts in their own respective jurisdictions**, cite only "State," "People," or "Commonwealth" as the party in the case name. *Bluebook* Rule 10.2.1(f).

☑ TERMS INDICATING NATIONAL OR LARGER GEOGRAPHICAL LOCATIONS

🖋 Terms indicating national or larger geographic locations should be included in the case name, except (1) when they occur in union names and (2) when "of America" follows "United States." *Bluebook* Rule 10.2.1(f).

☑ "CITY OF" AND SIMILAR PHRASES

🖋 "City of," "Town of," "Village of," "Borough of," "County of," and similar phrases should be omitted **except when they begin the name of a cited party**. *Bluebook* Rule 10.1(f).

☑ OTHER PREPOSITIONAL PHRASES OF LOCATION

🖋 Other prepositional phrases of location (*i.e.*, those of less than national geographical areas, except when they follow "City of" or similar phrases)—should be omitted **unless only one word would be left in the party's name**. *Bluebook* Rule 10.2.1(f).

☑ Geographical Words Not Introduced by a Preposition

🔥* All geographical words that are not introduced by a preposition should be retained. *Bluebook* Rule 10.2.1(f).

☑ Procedural Phrases

🔥* All procedural phrases except *ex rel.* should be omitted when adversary parties are named. *Bluebook* Rule 10.2.1(b). For purposes of this rule, "Estate of," "Succession of," "Will of," "Marriage of," and similar terms are not treated as procedural phrases and must be retained in the citation. *Bluebook* Rule 10.2.1(b).

🔥* All procedural phrases after the first one should be omitted. *Bluebook* Rule 10.2.1(b). Again, for purposes of this rule, "Estate of," "Succession of," "Will of," "Marriage of," and similar terms are not treated as procedural phrases and must be retained in the citation. *Bluebook* Rule 10.2.1(b).

☑ "The"

🔥* "The" should be omitted from citations except when. (1) it begins the name of the res in an "in rem" action; (2) "The Queen" or "The King" is the cited party; and (3) it begins the popular name of the case. *Bluebook* Rule 10.2.1(d).

☑ "In Rem" Cases

🔥* When several items are used as the title of an "in rem" action, only the first listed item or group of items should be cited. *Bluebook* Rule 10.2.1(a).

🔥* When real property is the cited party, the common street address, if available, should be used. *Bluebook* Rule 10.2.1(a).

☑ Bankruptcy and Similar Cases

🔥* When a case name contains both adversary and non-adversary parties at the beginning of the opinion, such as in many bankruptcy cases, the adversary name should be cited first; the nonadversary name should be added parenthetically, introduced by an appropriate procedural phrases, such as "*In re,*" and then followed by any other descriptive or introductory phrases, such as "Estate of " or "Interest of," if any. *Bluebook* Rule 10.2.1(a).

Remember also to check for and to apply the rules for the following (*see supra* Citation Exercises 9 & 10):

☑ Abbreviations
☑ Terms Describing a Party Already Named
☑ Given Names and Initials of Individuals
☑ Words Indicating Multiple Parties
☑ Alternative Names for a Party
☑ Consolidation of Two or More Actions
☑ Additional Parties on Each Side of the Case
☑ Partnership Names
☑ Business Firm Designations
☑ Commissioner of Internal Revenue as a Party

CITATION EXERCISE 12
U.S. SUPREME COURT DECISIONS (I)

Your Name _____

Your Professor's or Instructor's Name _____

Your Assigned Section (if applicable) _____

Your Assigned Problem Number _____

Self-Reassigned Problem Number (if applicable) _____

(a) State the full case name as it is stated in the reporter at the beginning of the opinion (*e.g.*, Montana et al. v. United States); **you may omit obviously irrelevant portions of a party's name if the full name is a lengthy one**:

(b) State the exact date of decision (*e.g.*, Feb. 22, 1979):

(c) State the proper citation of that case in *Bluebook* (or another designated) form; assume that the case name is going to appear in a **citation sentence or clause**, not as a part of a grammatical part of a textual sentence, in a **legal memorandum**; **cite the case to only *United States Reports***:

✒ Because the case name is going to appear in a **legal memorandum**, you should underscore (italicize) the case name (and any procedural phra*ses*) in your citation given in (c) above (*e.g.*, <u>Marbury v. Madison</u>). Note that the comma following the case name in the citation is not underscored (italicized). *See Bluebook* Practitioners' Note P.1(a).

✒ Citations in these exercises should appear as citation sentences. *See Bluebook* Rule 1.1 & Practitioners' Notes P.2. A citation sentence begins with a capital letter and ends with a period. Thus, be sure to include a period at the end of your citations in these exercises.

✒ Because the case name is going to appear in a **citation sentence or clause**, not as a part of a grammatical part of a textual sentence, you should use the required abbreviations in *Bluebook* Table T.6 ("Case Names"), Table T.10 ("Geographical Terms"), Rule 10.2.1(b) ("Procedural Phrases"), and Rule 10.2.1(c) ("Abbreviations"). In addition, check your citation for the following and apply the appropriate rule(s), if applicable:

- ☑ TERMS DESCRIBING A PARTY ALREADY NAMED
- ☑ GIVEN NAMES AND INITIALS OF INDIVIDUALS
- ☑ WORDS INDICATING MULTIPLE PARTIES
- ☑ ALTERNATIVE NAMES FOR A PARTY
- ☑ CONSOLIDATION OF TWO OR MORE ACTIONS
- ☑ ADDITIONAL PARTIES ON EACH SIDE OF THE CASE
- ☑ PARTNERSHIP NAMES
- ☑ BUSINESS FIRM DESIGNATIONS
- ☑ COMMISSIONER OF INTERNAL REVENUE AS A PARTY
- ☑ LABOR UNIONS
- ☑ "STATE OF" AND SIMILAR PHRASES
- ☑ TERMS INDICATING NATIONAL OR LARGER GEOGRAPHICAL LOCATIONS
- ☑ "CITY OF" AND SIMILAR PHRASES
- ☑ OTHER PREPOSITIONAL PHRASES OF LOCATION
- ☑ GEOGRAPHICAL WORDS NOT INTRODUCED BY A PREPOSITION
- ☑ PROCEDURAL PHRASES
- ☑ "THE"
- ☑ "IN REM" CASES
- ☑ BANKRUPTCY AND SIMILAR CASES

See supra Citation Exercises 9-11.

✒ When a decision is published in a reporter such as *United States Reports*, the year of decision (*e.g.*, 1999) is placed in the parentheses at the end of the citation. *Bluebook* Rule 10.5(a).

U.S. SUPREME COURT DECISIONS (II)

Your Name _____

Your Professor's or Instructor's Name _____

Your Assigned Section (if applicable) _____

Your Assigned Problem Number _____

Self-Reassigned Problem Number (if applicable) _____

(a) State the full case name as it is stated in the reporter at the beginning of the opinion (*e.g.*, Montana et al. v. United States); **you may omit obviously irrelevant portions of a party's name if the full name is a lengthy one**:

(b) State the exact date of decision (*e.g.*, Feb. 22, 1979):

(c) State the citation of the case. **For purposes of this exercise only**, cite the case to *United States Reports*, West's *Supreme Court Reporter*, and the *Lawyers' Edition* (in that order) (*e.g.*, <u>Montana v. United States</u>, 440 U.S. 147, 99 S. Ct. 970, 59 L. Ed. 2d 210 (1979). Use the appropriate volume of *Shepard's or* the "Table of Cases" in one of the U.S. Supreme Court digests to find the parallel citations. Assume that the case name is going to appear in a **citation sentence or clause**, not as a part of a grammatical part of a textual sentence, in a **legal memorandum**:

NOTES ON CITATION EXERCISE 13

🖝* Despite the *Bluebook* requirement to cite only to *United States Reports*, many lawyers include references where the opinion can also be found in all three reporters (*i.e.*, "parallel citations") for convenience of the reader. Be sure to follow the traditional order in your answer in (c), above: *United States Reports*, West's *Supreme Court Reporter*, and the *Lawyers' Edition*.

💣* Note that both "S. Ct." and "L. Ed. 2d" have spaces in the abbreviations; "U.S." does not.

💣* Citations in these exercises should appear as citation sentences. *See Bluebook* Rule 1.1 & Practitioners' Notes P.2. A citation sentence begins with a capital letter and ends with a period. Thus, be sure to include a period at the end of your citations in these exercises.

💣* Because the case name is going to appear in a **legal memorandum**, you should underscore (italicize) the case name (and any procedural phra*ses*) in your citation given in (c) above (*e.g.*, <u>Marbury v. Madison</u>). Note that the comma following the case name in the citation is not underscored (italicized). *See Bluebook* Practitioners' Note P.1(a). Furthermore, be sure to check your citation for the following and apply the appropriate rule(s), if applicable:

- ☑ ABBREVIATIONS
- ☑ TERMS DESCRIBING A PARTY ALREADY NAMED
- ☑ GIVEN NAMES AND INITIALS OF INDIVIDUALS
- ☑ WORDS INDICATING MULTIPLE PARTIES
- ☑ ALTERNATIVE NAMES FOR A PARTY
- ☑ CONSOLIDATION OF TWO OR MORE ACTIONS
- ☑ ADDITIONAL PARTIES ON EACH SIDE OF THE CASE
- ☑ PARTNERSHIP NAMES
- ☑ BUSINESS FIRM DESIGNATIONS
- ☑ COMMISSIONER OF INTERNAL REVENUE AS A PARTY
- ☑ LABOR UNIONS
- ☑ "STATE OF" AND SIMILAR PHRASES
- ☑ TERMS INDICATING NATIONAL OR LARGER GEOGRAPHICAL LOCATIONS
- ☑ "CITY OF" AND SIMILAR PHRASES
- ☑ OTHER PREPOSITIONAL PHRASES OF LOCATION
- ☑ GEOGRAPHICAL WORDS NOT INTRODUCED BY A PREPOSITION
- ☑ PROCEDURAL PHRASES
- ☑ "THE"
- ☑ "IN REM" CASES
- ☑ BANKRUPTCY AND SIMILAR CASES

See supra Citation Exercises 9-11.

💣* When a decision is published in a reporter such as *United States Reports*, West's *Supreme Court Reporter*, and the *Lawyers' Edition*, the year of decision (*e.g.*, 1999) is placed in the parentheses at the end of the citation. *Bluebook* Rule 10.5(a).

CITATION EXERCISE 14
U.S. SUPREME COURT DECISIONS (III)

Your Name _____

Your Professor's or Instructor's Name _____

Your Assigned Section (if applicable) _____

Your Assigned Problem Number _____

Self-Reassigned Problem Number (if applicable) _____

(a) State the full case name as it is stated in the reporter at the beginning of the opinion (*e.g.*, Montana et al. v. United States); **you may omit obviously irrelevant portions of a party's name if the full name is a lengthy one**:

(b) State the exact date of decision (*e.g.*, Feb. 22, 1979):

(c) State the citation of the case in *Bluebook* (or another designated) form. **Cite only to *United States Reports*** using the parallel citation to *United States Reports* provided at the beginning of the opinion in the *Supreme Court Reporter*. Assume that the case name is going to appear in a **citation sentence or clause**, not as a part of a grammatical part of a textual sentence, in a **legal memorandum**:

NOTES ON CITATION EXERCISE 14

✒* Because the case name is going to appear in a **legal memorandum**, you should underscore (italicize) the case name (and any procedural phra*ses*) in your citation given in (c) above (*e.g.*, <u>Marbury v. Madison</u>). Note that the comma following the case name in the citation is not underscored (italicized). *See Bluebook* Practitioners' Note P.1(a). Furthermore, be sure to check your citation for the following and apply the appropriate rule(s), if applicable:

☑ ABBREVIATIONS
☑ TERMS DESCRIBING A PARTY ALREADY NAMED
☑ GIVEN NAMES AND INITIALS OF INDIVIDUALS
☑ WORDS INDICATING MULTIPLE PARTIES
☑ ALTERNATIVE NAMES FOR A PARTY
☑ CONSOLIDATION OF TWO OR MORE ACTIONS
☑ ADDITIONAL PARTIES ON EACH SIDE OF THE CASE
☑ PARTNERSHIP NAMES
☑ BUSINESS FIRM DESIGNATIONS
☑ COMMISSIONER OF INTERNAL REVENUE AS A PARTY
☑ LABOR UNIONS
☑ "STATE OF" AND SIMILAR PHRASES
☑ TERMS INDICATING NATIONAL OR LARGER GEOGRAPHICAL LOCATIONS
☑ "CITY OF" AND SIMILAR PHRASES
☑ OTHER PREPOSITIONAL PHRASES OF LOCATION
☑ GEOGRAPHICAL WORDS NOT INTRODUCED BY A PREPOSITION
☑ PROCEDURAL PHRASES
☑ "THE"
☑ "IN REM" CASES
☑ BANKRUPTCY AND SIMILAR CASES

See supra Citation Exercises 9-11.

✒* When a decision is published in a reporter such as *United States Reports*, the year of decision (*e.g.*, 1999) is placed in the parentheses at the end of the citation. *Bluebook* Rule 10.5(a).

CITATION EXERCISE 15
U.S. SUPREME COURT DECISIONS (IV)

Your Name _____

Your Professor's or Instructor's Name _____

Your Assigned Section (if applicable) _____

Your Assigned Problem Number _____

Self-Reassigned Problem Number (if applicable) _____

(a) State the full case name as it is stated in the reporter at the beginning of the opinion (*e.g.*, Montana et al. v. United States); **you may omit obviously irrelevant portions of a party's name if the full name is a lengthy one**:

(b) State the exact date of decision (*e.g.*, Feb. 22, 1979);

(c) State the citation of the case. **For purposes of this exercise only, cite the case to *United States Reports*, West's *Supreme Court Reporter*, and the *Lawyers' Edition* (in that order) using the parallel citations provided at the beginning of the opinion in the *Lawyers' Edition*** (*e.g.*, Montana v. United States, 440 U.S. 147, 99 S. Ct. 970, 59 L. Ed. 2d 210 (1979).). Assume that the case name is going to appear in a **citation sentence or clause**, not as a part of a grammatical part of a textual sentence, in a **legal memorandum**:

NOTES ON CITATION EXERCISE 15

🕭* Despite the *Bluebook* requirement to cite only to *United States Reports*, many lawyers include references where the opinion can also be found in all three

245

reporters (*i.e.*, "parallel citations") for convenience of the reader. Be sure to follow the traditional order in your answer in (c), above: *United States Reports*, West's *Supreme Court Reporter*, and the *Lawyers' Edition*.

⚫ Note that both "S. Ct." and "L. Ed. 2d" have spaces in the abbreviations; "U.S." does not.

⚫ Citations in these exercises should appear as citation sentences. *See Bluebook* Rule 1.1 & Practitioners' Notes P.2. A citation sentence begins with a capital letter and ends with a period. Thus, be sure to include a period at the end of your citations in these exercises.

⚫ Because the case name is going to appear in a **legal memorandum**, you should underscore (italicize) the case name (and any procedural phra*ses*) in your citation given in (c) above (*e.g.*, Marbury v. Madison). Note that the comma following the case name in the citation is not underscored (italicized). *See Bluebook* Practitioners' Note P.1(a). Furthermore, be sure to check your citation for the following and apply the appropriate rule(s), if applicable:

- ☑ ABBREVIATIONS
- ☑ TERMS DESCRIBING A PARTY ALREADY NAMED
- ☑ GIVEN NAMES AND INITIALS OF INDIVIDUALS
- ☑ WORDS INDICATING MULTIPLE PARTIES
- ☑ ALTERNATIVE NAMES FOR A PARTY
- ☑ CONSOLIDATION OF TWO OR MORE ACTIONS
- ☑ ADDITIONAL PARTIES ON EACH SIDE OF THE CASE
- ☑ PARTNERSHIP NAMES
- ☑ BUSINESS FIRM DESIGNATIONS
- ☑ COMMISSIONER OF INTERNAL REVENUE AS A PARTY
- ☑ LABOR UNIONS
- ☑ "STATE OF" AND SIMILAR PHRASES
- ☑ TERMS INDICATING NATIONAL OR LARGER GEOGRAPHICAL LOCATIONS
- ☑ "CITY OF" AND SIMILAR PHRASES
- ☑ OTHER PREPOSITIONAL PHRASES OF LOCATION
- ☑ GEOGRAPHICAL WORDS NOT INTRODUCED BY A PREPOSITION
- ☑ PROCEDURAL PHRASES
- ☑ "THE"
- ☑ "IN REM" CASES
- ☑ BANKRUPTCY AND SIMILAR CASES

See supra Citation Exercises 9-11.

⚫ When a decision is published in a reporter such as *United States Reports*, West's *Supreme Court Reporter*, and the *Lawyers' Edition*, the year of decision (*e.g.*, 1999) is placed in the parentheses at the end of the citation. *Bluebook* Rule 10.5(a).

U.S. SUPREME COURT DECISIONS (V)

Your Name _____

Your Professor's or Instructor's Name _____

Your Assigned Section (if applicable) _____

Your Assigned Problem Number _____

Self-Reassigned Problem Number (if applicable) _____

(a)   State the full case name as it is stated in the reporter at the beginning of the opinion (*e.g.*, Montana et al. v. United States); **you may omit obviously irrelevant portions of a party's name if the full name is a lengthy one**:

(b)   State the exact date of decision (*e.g.*, Feb. 22, 1979):

(c)   State the citation in *Bluebook* (or another designated) form, **including a pinpoint reference to the quotation. Cite only to *United States Reports* based on the star paging in the *Lawyers' Edition*.** Do not give parallel citations. Assume that the case name is going to appear in a **citation sentence or clause**, not as a part of a grammatical part of a textual sentence, in a **legal memorandum**:

NOTES ON CITATION EXERCISE 16

❦* Star paging allows you to quote from the opinion in the *Lawyers' Edition* and to give a pinpoint citation to *United States Reports*. When the quoted portion of the case extends over more than one page in *United States Reports*, use inclusive page numbers covering the quotation, separated by a hyphen; retain the last two digits and delete other repetitious digits (*e.g.*, 748-49, **not** 748-749). *Bluebook* Rule 3.3(d).

    ☙ Citations in these exercises should appear as citation sentences. *See Bluebook* Rule 1.1 & Practitioners' Notes P.2. A citation sentence begins with a capital letter and ends with a period. Thus, be sure to include a period at the end of your citations in these exercises.

    ☙ Because the case name is going to appear in a **legal memorandum**, you should underscore (italicize) the case name (and any procedural phra*ses*) in your citation given in (c) above (*e.g.*, <u>Marbury v. Madison</u>). Note that the comma following the case name in the citation is not underscored (italicized). *See Bluebook* Practitioners' Note P.1(a). Furthermore, be sure to check your citation for the following and apply the appropriate rule(s), if applicable:

- ☑ ABBREVIATIONS
- ☑ TERMS DESCRIBING A PARTY ALREADY NAMED
- ☑ GIVEN NAMES AND INITIALS OF INDIVIDUALS
- ☑ WORDS INDICATING MULTIPLE PARTIES
- ☑ ALTERNATIVE NAMES FOR A PARTY
- ☑ CONSOLIDATION OF TWO OR MORE ACTIONS
- ☑ ADDITIONAL PARTIES ON EACH SIDE OF THE CASE
- ☑ PARTNERSHIP NAMES
- ☑ BUSINESS FIRM DESIGNATIONS
- ☑ COMMISSIONER OF INTERNAL REVENUE AS A PARTY
- ☑ LABOR UNIONS
- ☑ "STATE OF" AND SIMILAR PHRASES
- ☑ TERMS INDICATING NATIONAL OR LARGER GEOGRAPHICAL LOCATIONS
- ☑ "CITY OF" AND SIMILAR PHRASES
- ☑ OTHER PREPOSITIONAL PHRASES OF LOCATION
- ☑ GEOGRAPHICAL WORDS NOT INTRODUCED BY A PREPOSITION
- ☑ PROCEDURAL PHRASES
- ☑ "THE"
- ☑ "IN REM" CASES
- ☑ BANKRUPTCY AND SIMILAR CASES

See supra Citation Exercises 9-11.

    ☙ When a decision is published in a reporter such as *United States Reports* and the *Lawyers' Edition*, the year of decision (*e.g.*, 1999) is placed in the parentheses at the end of the citation. *Bluebook* Rule 10.5(a). However, when cases are cited to a looseleaf service, the exact date must be given. *Bluebook* Rule 10.5(b).

CITATION EXERCISE 17
U.S. COURT OF APPEALS DECISIONS
AND OTHER SPECIALIZED FEDERAL
APPELLATE COURTS

Your Name _____

Your Professor's or Instructor's Name _____

Your Assigned Section (if applicable) _____

Your Assigned Problem Number _____

Self-Reassigned Problem Number (if applicable) _____

(a) State the full case name as it is stated in the reporter at the beginning of the opinion (*e.g.*, Robert L. Butler, Petitioner-Appellant, v. John C. Burke, Warden, Wisconsin State Prison); **you may omit obviously irrelevant portions of a party's name if the full name is a lengthy one**:

(b) State the complete reference to the court exactly as it is indicated at the beginning of the opinion (*e.g.*, United States Court of Appeals, Seventh Circuit):

(c) State the exact date of decision (*e.g.*, April 15, 1966):

(d) State the citation of the case in *Bluebook* (or another designated) form. Assume that the case name is going to appear in a **citation sentence or clause**, not as a part of a grammatical part of a textual sentence, in a **legal memorandum**. For purposes of this exercise, do not indicate any subsequent history in the citation:

NOTES ON CITATION EXERCISE 17

💣 Remember to identify the year of decision and the specific circuit in the parenthetical at the end of the citation. *Bluebook* Rule 10.5(a). The abbreviation for the U.S. Courts of Appeal is "Cir." *Bluebook* Table T.7. The numbered circuits are cited as "1st Cir.," "2d Cir.," "3d Cir.," "4th Cir.," etc. The U.S. Court of Appeals for the District of Columbia Circuit (and its predecessors) is always cited as "D.C. Cir." The U.S. Court of Appeals for the Federal Circuit is always cited as "Fed. Cir." *Bluebook* Rule 10.4(a).

💣 Citations in these exercises should appear as citation sentences. *See Bluebook* Rule 1.1 & Practitioners' Notes P.2. A citation sentence begins with a capital letter and ends with a period. Thus, be sure to include a period at the end of your citations in these exercises.

💣 Because the case name is going to appear in a **legal memorandum**, you should underscore (italicize) the case name (and any procedural phras*es*) in your citation given in (d) above (*e.g.*, Butler v. Burke). Note that the comma following the case name in the citation is not underscored (italicized). *See Bluebook* Practitioners' Note P.1(a). Furthermore, be sure to check your citation for the following and apply the appropriate rule(s), if applicable:

- ☑ ABBREVIATIONS
- ☑ TERMS DESCRIBING A PARTY ALREADY NAMED
- ☑ GIVEN NAMES AND INITIALS OF INDIVIDUALS
- ☑ WORDS INDICATING MULTIPLE PARTIES
- ☑ ALTERNATIVE NAMES FOR A PARTY
- ☑ CONSOLIDATION OF TWO OR MORE ACTIONS
- ☑ ADDITIONAL PARTIES ON EACH SIDE OF THE CASE
- ☑ PARTNERSHIP NAMES
- ☑ BUSINESS FIRM DESIGNATIONS
- ☑ COMMISSIONER OF INTERNAL REVENUE AS A PARTY
- ☑ LABOR UNIONS
- ☑ "STATE OF" AND SIMILAR PHRASES
- ☑ TERMS INDICATING NATIONAL OR LARGER GEOGRAPHICAL LOCATIONS
- ☑ "CITY OF" AND SIMILAR PHRASES
- ☑ OTHER PREPOSITIONAL PHRASES OF LOCATION
- ☑ GEOGRAPHICAL WORDS NOT INTRODUCED BY A PREPOSITION
- ☑ PROCEDURAL PHRASES
- ☑ "THE"
- ☑ "IN REM" CASES
- ☑ BANKRUPTCY AND SIMILAR CASES

See supra Citation Exercises 9-11.

CITATION EXERCISE 18
FEDERAL TRIAL COURT DECISIONS (I)

Your Name _____

Your Professor's or Instructor's Name _____

Your Assigned Section (if applicable) _____

Your Assigned Problem Number _____

Self-Reassigned Problem Number (if applicable) _____

   . (a) State the full case name as it is stated in the reporter at the beginning of the opinion (*e.g.*, A. Shepard Titcomb, Plaintiff, v. Norton Company, Defendant); **you may omit obviously irrelevant portions of a party's name if the full name is a lengthy one**:

   (b) State the complete reference to the court exactly as it is indicated at the beginning of the opinion (*e.g.*, United States District Court, D. Connecticut):

   (c) State the exact date of decision (*e.g.*, Oct. 9, 1959):

   (d) State the citation of the case in *Bluebook* (or another designated) form. Assume that the case name is going to appear in a **citation sentence or clause**, not as a part of a grammatical part of a textual sentence, in a **legal memorandum**. For purposes of this exercise, do not indicate any subsequent history in the citation:

NOTES ON CITATION EXERCISE 18

   ✎* When U.S. District Court decisions are cited, the district (but not the division within the district) and the state should be indicated parenthetically in addi-

tion to the date (*e.g.*, S.D. Cal. 1999). *Bluebook* Rule 10.4(a) & Table T.1. The appropriate abbreviation for the state, if any, is listed in *Bluebook* Table T.10.

🖐* In states having only one federal district, the district is indicated by "D." (*e.g.*, D. Neb. for the District of Nebraska). When the state has more than one district, the district must be specifically indicated (*e.g.*, W.D.N.Y. for the Western District of New York).

🖐* Adjacent capitals should be closed up (W.D.N.Y.), but single capitals should not be closed up with longer abbreviations (D. Neb.). The same is true for reporter abbreviations (*e.g.*, F. Supp.). Individual numbers consisting of both numerals and ordinals (*e.g.*, 3d) are treated as single capitals (F.3d). *Bluebook* Rule 6.1(a).

🖐* Because the case name is going to appear in a **legal memorandum**, you should underscore (italicize) the case name (and any procedural phra*ses*) in your citation given in (d) above (*e.g.*, <u>Titcomb v. Norton Co.</u>). Note that the comma following the case name in the citation is not underscored (italicized). *See Bluebook* Practitioners' Note P.1(a). Furthermore, be sure to check your citation for the following and apply the appropriate rule(s), if applicable:

- ☑ ABBREVIATIONS
- ☑ TERMS DESCRIBING A PARTY ALREADY NAMED
- ☑ GIVEN NAMES AND INITIALS OF INDIVIDUALS
- ☑ WORDS INDICATING MULTIPLE PARTIES
- ☑ ALTERNATIVE NAMES FOR A PARTY
- ☑ CONSOLIDATION OF TWO OR MORE ACTIONS
- ☑ ADDITIONAL PARTIES ON EACH SIDE OF THE CASE
- ☑ PARTNERSHIP NAMES
- ☑ BUSINESS FIRM DESIGNATIONS
- ☑ COMMISSIONER OF INTERNAL REVENUE AS A PARTY
- ☑ LABOR UNIONS
- ☑ "STATE OF" AND SIMILAR PHRASES
- ☑ TERMS INDICATING NATIONAL OR LARGER GEOGRAPHICAL LOCATIONS
- ☑ "CITY OF" AND SIMILAR PHRASES
- ☑ OTHER PREPOSITIONAL PHRASES OF LOCATION
- ☑ GEOGRAPHICAL WORDS NOT INTRODUCED BY A PREPOSITION
- ☑ PROCEDURAL PHRASES
- ☑ "THE"
- ☑ "IN REM" CASES
- ☑ BANKRUPTCY AND SIMILAR CASES

See supra Citation Exercises 9-11.

CITATION EXERCISE 19
FEDERAL TRIAL COURT DECISIONS (II)

Your Name _____

Your Professor's or Instructor's Name _____

Your Assigned Section (if applicable) _____

Your Assigned Problem Number _____

Self-Reassigned Problem Number (if applicable) _____

(a) State the full case name as it is stated in the reporter at the beginning of the opinion (*e.g.*, A. Shepard Titcomb, Plaintiff, v. Norton Company, Defendant); **you may omit obviously irrelevant portions of a party's name if the full name is a lengthy one**:

(b) State the complete reference to the court exactly as it is indicated at the beginning of the opinion (*e.g.*, United States District Court, D. Connecticut):

(c) State the exact date of decision (*e.g.*, Oct. 9, 1959):

(d) State the citation of the case in *Bluebook* (or another designated) form. Assume that the case name is going to appear in a **citation sentence or clause**, not as a part of a grammatical part of a textual sentence, in a **legal memorandum**. For purposes of this exercise, do not indicate any subsequent history in the citation:

NOTES ON CITATION EXERCISE 19

♦* When U.S. District Court decisions are cited, the district (but not the division within the district) and the state should be indicated parenthetically in addi-

tion to the date (*e.g.*, S.D. Cal. 1999). *Bluebook* Rule 10.4(a) & Table T.1. The appropriate abbreviation for the state, if any, is listed in *Bluebook* Table T.10.

💣 In states having only one federal district, the district is indicated by "D." (*e.g.*, D. Neb. for the District of Nebraska). When the state has more than one district, the district must be specifically indicated (*e.g.*, W.D.N.Y. for the Western District of New York).

💣 Adjacent capitals should be closed up (W.D.N.Y.), but single capitals should not be closed up with longer abbreviations (D. Neb.). The same is true for reporter abbreviations (*e.g.*, F. Supp.). Individual numbers consisting of both numerals and ordinals (*e.g.*, 3d) are treated as single capitals (F.3d). *Bluebook* Rule 6.1(a).

💣 Because the case name is going to appear in a **legal memorandum**, you should underscore (italicize) the case name (and any procedural phra*ses*) in your citation given in (d) above (*e.g.*, <u>Titcomb v. Norton Co.</u>). Note that the comma following the case name in the citation is not underscored (italicized). *See Bluebook* Practitioners' Note P.1(a). Furthermore, be sure to check your citation for the following and apply the appropriate rule(s), if applicable:

- ☑ ABBREVIATIONS
- ☑ TERMS DESCRIBING A PARTY ALREADY NAMED
- ☑ GIVEN NAMES AND INITIALS OF INDIVIDUALS
- ☑ WORDS INDICATING MULTIPLE PARTIES
- ☑ ALTERNATIVE NAMES FOR A PARTY
- ☑ CONSOLIDATION OF TWO OR MORE ACTIONS
- ☑ ADDITIONAL PARTIES ON EACH SIDE OF THE CASE
- ☑ PARTNERSHIP NAMES
- ☑ BUSINESS FIRM DESIGNATIONS
- ☑ COMMISSIONER OF INTERNAL REVENUE AS A PARTY
- ☑ LABOR UNIONS
- ☑ "STATE OF" AND SIMILAR PHRASES
- ☑ TERMS INDICATING NATIONAL OR LARGER GEOGRAPHICAL LOCATIONS
- ☑ "CITY OF" AND SIMILAR PHRASES
- ☑ OTHER PREPOSITIONAL PHRASES OF LOCATION
- ☑ GEOGRAPHICAL WORDS NOT INTRODUCED BY A PREPOSITION
- ☑ PROCEDURAL PHRASES
- ☑ "THE"
- ☑ "IN REM" CASES
- ☑ BANKRUPTCY AND SIMILAR CASES

See supra Citation Exercises 9-11.

CITATION EXERCISE 20
FEDERAL TRIAL COURT DECISIONS (III)

Your Name _____

Your Professor's or Instructor's Name _____

Your Assigned Section (if applicable) _____

Your Assigned Problem Number _____

Self-Reassigned Problem Number (if applicable) _____

(a) State the full case name as it is stated in the reporter at the beginning of the opinion (*e.g.*, A. Shepard Titcomb, Plaintiff, v. Norton Company, Defendant); **you may omit obviously irrelevant portions of a party's name if the full name is a lengthy one**:

(b) State the complete reference to the court exactly as it is indicated at the beginning of the opinion (*e.g.*, United States District Court, D. Connecticut):

(c) State the exact date of decision (*e.g.*, Oct. 9, 1959):

(d) State the citation of the case in *Bluebook* (or another designated) form. Assume that the case name is going to appear in a **citation sentence or clause**, not as a part of a grammatical part of a textual sentence, in a **legal memorandum**. For purposes of this exercise, do not indicate any subsequent history in the citation:

NOTES ON CITATION EXERCISE 20

☛* When U.S. District Court decisions are cited, the district (but not the division within the district) and the state should be indicated parenthetically in addi-

tion to the date (*e.g.*, S.D. Cal. 1999). *Bluebook* Rule 10.4(a) & Table T.1. The appropriate abbreviation for the state, if any, is listed in *Bluebook* Table T.10.

    ♦* In states having only one federal district, the district is indicated by "D." (*e.g.*, D. Neb. for the District of Nebraska). When the state has more than one district, the district must be specifically indicated (*e.g.*, W.D.N.Y. for the Western District of New York).

    ♦* Adjacent capitals should be closed up (W.D.N.Y.), but single capitals should not be closed up with longer abbreviations (D. Neb.). The same is true for reporter abbreviations (*e.g.*, F. Supp.). Individual numbers consisting of both numerals and ordinals (*e.g.*, 3d) are treated as single capitals (F.3d). *Bluebook* Rule 6.1(a).

    ♦* Because the case name is going to appear in a **legal memorandum**, you should underscore (italicize) the case name (and any procedural phra*ses*) in your citation given in (d) above (*e.g.*, <u>Titcomb v. Norton Co.</u>). Note that the comma following the case name in the citation is not underscored (italicized). *See Bluebook* Practitioners' Note P.1(a). Furthermore, be sure to check your citation for the following and apply the appropriate rule(s), if applicable:

- ☑ ABBREVIATIONS
- ☑ TERMS DESCRIBING A PARTY ALREADY NAMED
- ☑ GIVEN NAMES AND INITIALS OF INDIVIDUALS
- ☑ WORDS INDICATING MULTIPLE PARTIES
- ☑ ALTERNATIVE NAMES FOR A PARTY
- ☑ CONSOLIDATION OF TWO OR MORE ACTIONS
- ☑ ADDITIONAL PARTIES ON EACH SIDE OF THE CASE
- ☑ PARTNERSHIP NAMES
- ☑ BUSINESS FIRM DESIGNATIONS
- ☑ COMMISSIONER OF INTERNAL REVENUE AS A PARTY
- ☑ LABOR UNIONS
- ☑ "STATE OF" AND SIMILAR PHRASES
- ☑ TERMS INDICATING NATIONAL OR LARGER GEOGRAPHICAL LOCATIONS
- ☑ "CITY OF" AND SIMILAR PHRASES
- ☑ OTHER PREPOSITIONAL PHRASES OF LOCATION
- ☑ GEOGRAPHICAL WORDS NOT INTRODUCED BY A PREPOSITION
- ☑ PROCEDURAL PHRASES
- ☑ "THE"
- ☑ "IN REM" CASES
- ☑ BANKRUPTCY AND SIMILAR CASES

See supra Citation Exercises 9-11.

CITATION EXERCISE 21
FEDERAL TRIAL COURT DECISIONS (IV)

Your Name _____

Your Professor's or Instructor's Name _____

Your Assigned Section (if applicable) _____

Your Assigned Problem Number _____

Self-Reassigned Problem Number (if applicable) _____

(a) State the full case name as it is stated in the reporter at the beginning of the opinion (*e.g.*, Backus v. The Marengo); **you may omit obviously irrelevant portions of a party's name if the full name is a lengthy one:**

(b) State the complete reference to the court exactly as it is indicated at the beginning of the opinion (*e.g.*, United States District Court, D. Connecticut, etc.):

(c) State the exact date of decision (*e.g.*, July 11, 1849, May 1878, or June Term, 1857):

(d) State the citation of the case in *Bluebook* (or another designated) form. Assume that the case name is going to appear in a **citation sentence or clause**, not as a part of a grammatical part of a textual sentence, in a **legal memorandum**. For purposes of this exercise, do not indicate any subsequent history in the citation:

NOTES ON CITATION EXERCISE 21

♣* In citing cases in West's *Federal Cases* in *Bluebook* form, be sure to include the Federal Case Number at the end of the citation in a separate parenthetical. Numbers over 10,000 have a comma before the last three digits.

♦* When U.S. District Court or U.S. Circuit Court decisions are cited, the district (but not the division within the district) and the state should be indicated parenthetically in addition to the date. *Bluebook* Rule 10.4(a) & Table T.1. The appropriate abbreviation for the state, if any, is listed in *Bluebook* Table T.10.

♦* In states having only one federal district, the district is indicated by "D." When the state has more than one district, the district must be specifically indicated (*e.g.*, S.D.N.Y.).

♦* Adjacent capitals should be closed up (C.C.S.D.N.Y. or D.S.C.), but single capitals should not be closed up with longer abbreviations. The same is true for reporter abbreviations (*e.g.*, F. Cas.). *Bluebook* Rule 6.1(a).

♦* Because the case name is going to appear in a **legal memorandum**, you should underscore (italicize) the case name (and any procedural phra*ses*) in your citation given in (d) above (*e.g.*, The Aslesund). Note that the comma following the case name in the citation is not underscored (italicized). *See Bluebook* Practitioners' Note P.1(a). Furthermore, be sure to check your citation for the following and apply the appropriate rule(s), if applicable:

☑ ABBREVIATIONS
☑ TERMS DESCRIBING A PARTY ALREADY NAMED
☑ GIVEN NAMES AND INITIALS OF INDIVIDUALS
☑ WORDS INDICATING MULTIPLE PARTIES
☑ ALTERNATIVE NAMES FOR A PARTY
☑ CONSOLIDATION OF TWO OR MORE ACTIONS
☑ ADDITIONAL PARTIES ON EACH SIDE OF THE CASE
☑ PARTNERSHIP NAMES
☑ BUSINESS FIRM DESIGNATIONS
☑ COMMISSIONER OF INTERNAL REVENUE AS A PARTY
☑ LABOR UNIONS
☑ "STATE OF" AND SIMILAR PHRASES
☑ TERMS INDICATING NATIONAL OR LARGER GEOGRAPHICAL LOCATIONS
☑ "CITY OF" AND SIMILAR PHRASES
☑ OTHER PREPOSITIONAL PHRASES OF LOCATION
☑ GEOGRAPHICAL WORDS NOT INTRODUCED BY A PREPOSITION
☑ PROCEDURAL PHRASES
☑ "THE"
☑ "IN REM" CASES
☑ BANKRUPTCY AND SIMILAR CASES

See supra Citation Exercises 9-11.

CITATION EXERCISE 22
STATE COURT DECISIONS (I)

Your Name _____

Your Professor's or Instructor's Name _____

Your Assigned Section (if applicable) _____

Your Assigned Problem Number _____

Self-Reassigned Problem Number (if applicable) _____

    (a) Jurisdiction: _____

State the name of the highest court in that jurisdiction:

    (b) Jurisdiction: _____

State (i) the name **and** *Bluebook* abbreviation of the modern jurisdiction-named reports for the highest court in that jurisdiction and (ii) the date, if any, those reports ceased to be published (*e.g.*, Alabama Reports, Ala., ceased 1976; Arizona Reports, Ariz., to date; Iowa Reports, Iowa (no abbreviation), ceased 1968; etc.):

    (c) Jurisdiction: _____

State the name **and** the *Bluebook* abbreviation of the West regional reporter covering that jurisdiction (*e.g.*, Southern Reporter, So., So. 2d;):

    (d) Jurisdiction: _____

State the name **and** the *Bluebook* abbreviation, if any, of the **earliest** nominative reporter of the highest court for that jurisdiction (*e.g.*, Coleman's Cases, Cole. Cas.; Harrington, e.g., 1 Del. (1 Harr.); Kirby, not abbreviated, etc.):

NOTES ON CITATION EXERCISE 22

☙✳ Be sure to provide all the information requested for each answer.

CITATION EXERCISE 23
STATE COURT DECISIONS (II)

Your Name _____

Your Professor's or Instructor's Name _____

Your Assigned Section (if applicable) _____

Your Assigned Problem Number _____

Self-Reassigned Problem Number (if applicable) _____

(a) State the full name of the case as it is stated in the reporter at the beginning of the opinion (*e.g.*, Kenneth Lee Benoit, Appellant, v. Commonwealth of Kentucky, Appellee); **you may omit obviously irrelevant portions of a party's name if the full name is a lengthy one**:

(b) State the full designation of the court as it is stated in the reporter at the beginning of the opinion (*e.g.*, Court of Appeals of Kentucky):

(c) State the exact date of decision (*e.g.*, May 6, 1966):

(d) State the citation of the case in *Bluebook* (or another designated) form. Assume that the case name is going to appear in a **citation sentence or clause**, not as a part of a grammatical part of a textual sentence, in a **legal memorandum**. For purposes of this exercise, do not indicate any subsequent history in the citation. **Also assume that you are citing the case in a document that WILL be submitted to a state court in the jurisdiction from which the case arises**:

NOTES ON CITATION EXERCISE 23

❧* Remember that you are to assume that you are citing the case in a document that **WILL** be submitted to a state court in the jurisdiction from which the case arises. Thus, **you must include both the official reporter citation (if available) and the parallel West reporter citation(s) in your citation for this exercise.** *See Bluebook* Rule 10.3.1 & Practitioners' Note P.3.

    ✹* The abbreviated name of the court, including its geographic jurisdiction, should be included in the parenthetical with the date. You can determine the abbreviation of the geographic jurisdiction and the court (if any) by consulting the appropriate entry in *Bluebook* Table T.1. This information appears immediately after the name of the court (*e.g.*, **Supreme Judicial Court** (Me.)). However, when the highest court of a jurisdiction is cited, the abbreviated name of the court should be omitted. Furthermore, when the abbreviated name of one of the reporters cited (*e.g.*, Me.) unambiguously indicates the geographic jurisdiction, the geographic jurisdiction should also be omitted.

    ✹* Because the case name is going to appear in a **legal memorandum**, you should underscore (italicize) the case name (and any procedural phra*ses*) in your citation given in (d) above (*e.g.*, <u>Benoit v. Commonwealth</u>). Note that the comma following the case name in the citation is not underscored (italicized). *See Bluebook* Practitioners' Note P.1(a). Furthermore, be sure to check your citation for the following and apply the appropriate rule(s), if applicable:

- ☑ ABBREVIATIONS
- ☑ TERMS DESCRIBING A PARTY ALREADY NAMED
- ☑ GIVEN NAMES AND INITIALS OF INDIVIDUALS
- ☑ WORDS INDICATING MULTIPLE PARTIES
- ☑ ALTERNATIVE NAMES FOR A PARTY
- ☑ CONSOLIDATION OF TWO OR MORE ACTIONS
- ☑ ADDITIONAL PARTIES ON EACH SIDE OF THE CASE
- ☑ PARTNERSHIP NAMES
- ☑ BUSINESS FIRM DESIGNATIONS
- ☑ COMMISSIONER OF INTERNAL REVENUE AS A PARTY
- ☑ LABOR UNIONS
- ☑ "STATE OF" AND SIMILAR PHRASES
- ☑ TERMS INDICATING NATIONAL OR LARGER GEOGRAPHICAL LOCATIONS
- ☑ "CITY OF" AND SIMILAR PHRASES
- ☑ OTHER PREPOSITIONAL PHRASES OF LOCATION
- ☑ GEOGRAPHICAL WORDS NOT INTRODUCED BY A PREPOSITION
- ☑ PROCEDURAL PHRASES
- ☑ "THE"
- ☑ "IN REM" CASES

See supra Citation Exercises 9-11.

CITATION EXERCISE 24
STATE COURT DECISIONS (III)

Your Name _____

Your Professor's or Instructor's Name _____

Your Assigned Section (if applicable) _____

Your Assigned Problem Number _____

Self-Reassigned Problem Number (if applicable) _____

(a) State the full name of the case as it is stated in the reporter at the beginning of the opinion (*e.g.*, Kenneth Lee Benoit, Appellant, v. Commonwealth of Kentucky, Appellee); **you may omit obviously irrelevant portions of a party's name if the full name is a lengthy one**:

(b) State the full designation of the court as it is stated in the reporter at the beginning of the opinion (*e.g.*, Court of Appeals of Kentucky):

(c) State the exact date of decision (*e.g.*, May 6, 1966):

(d) State the citation of the case in *Bluebook* (or another designated) form. Assume that the case name is going to appear in a **citation sentence or clause**, not as a part of a grammatical part of a textual sentence, in a **legal memorandum**. For purposes of this exercise, do not indicate any subsequent history in the citation. **Also assume that you are citing the case in a document that will NOT be submitted to a state court in the jurisdiction from which the case arises**:

NOTES ON CITATION EXERCISE 24

✒※ Remember that you are to assume that you are citing the case in a document that will **NOT** be submitted to a state court in the jurisdiction from which the case arises. Thus, **only the relevant regional reporter should be cited in your citation for this exercise.** *See Bluebook* Rule 10.3.1 & Practitioners' Note P.3.

💣* The abbreviated name of the court, including its geographic jurisdiction, should be included in the parenthetical with the date. You can determine the abbreviation of the geographic jurisdiction and the court (if any) by consulting the appropriate entry in *Bluebook* Table T.1. This information appears immediately after the name of the court (*e.g.,* **Supreme Judicial Court** (Me.)). However, when the highest court of a jurisdiction is cited, the abbreviated name of the court should be omitted. Furthermore, when the abbreviated name of the reporter (*e.g.,* Me.) unambiguously indicates the geographic jurisdiction, the geographic jurisdiction should also be omitted. **However, the geographic jurisdiction must be included in the parenthetical in the citation for this exercise because the citation to West's regional reporter will not clearly indicate the jurisdiction.**

💣* Because the case name is going to appear in a **legal memorandum**, you should underscore (italicize) the case name (and any procedural phra*ses*) in your citation given in (d) above (*e.g.,* <u>Benoit v. Commonwealth</u>). Note that the comma following the case name in the citation is not underscored (italicized). *See Bluebook* Practitioners' Note P.1(a). Furthermore, be sure to check your citation for the following and apply the appropriate rule(s), if applicable:

- ☑ ABBREVIATIONS
- ☑ TERMS DESCRIBING A PARTY ALREADY NAMED
- ☑ GIVEN NAMES AND INITIALS OF INDIVIDUALS
- ☑ WORDS INDICATING MULTIPLE PARTIES
- ☑ ALTERNATIVE NAMES FOR A PARTY
- ☑ CONSOLIDATION OF TWO OR MORE ACTIONS
- ☑ ADDITIONAL PARTIES ON EACH SIDE OF THE CASE
- ☑ PARTNERSHIP NAMES
- ☑ BUSINESS FIRM DESIGNATIONS
- ☑ COMMISSIONER OF INTERNAL REVENUE AS A PARTY
- ☑ LABOR UNIONS
- ☑ "STATE OF" AND SIMILAR PHRASES
- ☑ TERMS INDICATING NATIONAL OR LARGER GEOGRAPHICAL LOCATIONS
- ☑ "CITY OF" AND SIMILAR PHRASES
- ☑ OTHER PREPOSITIONAL PHRASES OF LOCATION
- ☑ GEOGRAPHICAL WORDS NOT INTRODUCED BY A PREPOSITION
- ☑ PROCEDURAL PHRASES
- ☑ "THE"
- ☑ "IN REM" CASES

See supra Citation Exercises 9-11.

CITATION EXERCISE 25
STATE COURT DECISIONS (IV)

Your Name _____

Your Professor's or Instructor's Name _____

Your Assigned Section (if applicable) _____

Your Assigned Problem Number _____

Self-Reassigned Problem Number (if applicable) _____

(a) State the full name of the case as it is stated in the reporter at the beginning of the opinion (*e.g.*, State of North Dakota, Plaintiff and Appellant, v. Leonard Wayne Burckhard, Defendant and Appellee); **you may omit obviously irrelevant portions of a party's name if the full name is a lengthy one**:

(b) State the full designation of the court as it is stated in the reporter at the beginning of the opinion (*e.g.*, Supreme Court of North Dakota):

(c) State the public domain citation (*e.g.*, 1998 ND App 8):

(d) State the citation of the case in *Bluebook* (or another designated) form, including the parallel West citation. Assume that the case name is going to appear in a **citation sentence or clause**, not as a part of a grammatical part of a textual sentence, in a **legal memorandum**. For purposes of this exercise, do not indicate any subsequent history in the citation:

Notes on Citation Exercise 25

✒* Remember that you must include the public domain citation in your citation if you are following *Bluebook* rules. You are also asked to include a parallel West citation in your citation for (e), above.

✒* Do not include the abbreviated name of the court, including its geographic jurisdiction, nor the date in a parenthetical that normally appears at the end of the citation in your citation for (e), above, when that information is readily apparent from the reporter(s) cited. *See Bluebook* Rule 10.3.1(b).

✒* Because the case name is going to appear in a **legal memorandum**, you should underscore (italicize) the case name (and any procedural phra*ses*) in your citation given in (e) above (*e.g.*, <u>State v. Burckhard</u>). Note that the comma following the case name in the citation is not underscored (italicized). *See Bluebook* Practitioners' Note P.1(a). Furthermore, be sure to check your citation for the following and apply the appropriate rule(s), if applicable:

- ☑ Abbreviations
- ☑ Terms Describing a Party Already Named
- ☑ Given Names and Initials of Individuals
- ☑ Words Indicating Multiple Parties
- ☑ Alternative Names for a Party
- ☑ Consolidation of Two or More Actions
- ☑ Additional Parties on Each Side of the Case
- ☑ Partnership Names
- ☑ Business Firm Designations
- ☑ Commissioner of Internal Revenue as a Party
- ☑ Labor Unions
- ☑ "State of" and Similar Phrases
- ☑ Terms Indicating National or Larger Geographical Locations
- ☑ "City of" and Similar Phrases
- ☑ Other Prepositional Phrases of Location
- ☑ Geographical Words Not Introduced by a Preposition
- ☑ Procedural Phrases
- ☑ "The"
- ☑ "In Rem" Cases

See supra Citation Exercises 9-11.

CITATION EXERCISE 26
STATE COURT DECISIONS (V)

Your Name _____

Your Professor's or Instructor's Name _____

Your Assigned Section (if applicable) _____

Your Assigned Problem Number _____

Self-Reassigned Problem Number (if applicable) _____

FIRST CASE:

(a) State the full name of the **first case** as it is stated in the reporter at the beginning of the opinion (*e.g.*, Ashland Oil & Refining Company, Appellant, v. State of New York, Respondent); **you may omit obviously irrelevant portions of a party's name if the full name is a lengthy one:**

(b) State the full designation of the court for the **first case** as it is stated in the reporter at the beginning of the opinion (*e.g.*, New York Court of Appeals):

(c) State the exact date of decision for the **first case** (*e.g.*, April 23, 1970):

(d) State the citation of the **first case** in *Bluebook* (or another designated) form. Assume that the case name is going to appear in a **citation sentence or clause**, not as a part of a grammatical part of a textual sentence, in a **legal memorandum**. For purposes of this exercise, do not indicate any subsequent history in the citation. **Also assume that you are citing the case in a document that WILL be submitted to a New York state court:**

(e) State the citation of the **first case** in *Bluebook* (or another designated) form, but **assuming that you are citing the case in a document that will NOT be submitted to a New York state court.**. Assume also that the case name is going to appear in a **citation sentence or clause**, not as a part of a grammatical part of a textual sentence. For purposes of this exercise, do not indicate any subsequent history in the citation:

SECOND CASE:

(a) State the full name of the **second case** as it is stated in the reporter at the beginning of the opinion:

(b) State the full designation of the court for the **second case** as it is stated in the reporter at the beginning of the opinion:

(c) State the exact date of decision for the **second case**:

(d) State the citation of the **second case** in *Bluebook* (or another designated) form. Assume that the case name is going to appear in a **citation sentence or clause**, not as a part of a grammatical part of a textual sentence, in a **legal memorandum**. For purposes of this exercise, do not indicate any subsequent history in the citation. **Also assume that you are citing the case in a document that WILL be submitted to a New York state court:**

(e) State the citation of the **second case** in *Bluebook* (or another designated) form, but **assuming that you are citing the case in a document that will NOT be submitted to a New York state court.**. Assume also that the case name is going to appear in a **citation sentence or clause**, not as a part of a grammatical part of a textual sentence. For purposes of this exercise, do not indicate any subsequent history in the citation:

THIRD CASE:

(a) State the full name of the **third case** as it is stated in the reporter at the beginning of the opinion:

(b) State the full designation of the court for the **third case** as it is stated in the reporter at the beginning of the opinion:

(c) State the exact date of decision for the **third case**:

(d) State the citation of the **third case** in *Bluebook* (or another designated) form. Assume that the case name is going to appear in a **citation sentence or clause**, not as a part of a grammatical part of a textual sentence, in a **legal memorandum**. For purposes of this exercise, do not indicate any subsequent history in the citation. **Also assume that you are citing the case in a document that WILL be submitted to a New York state court**:

(e) State the citation of the **third case** in *Bluebook* (or another designated) form, but **assuming that you are citing the case in a document that will NOT be submitted to a New York state court.**. Assume also that the case name is going to appear in a **citation sentence or clause**, not as a part of a grammatical part of a textual sentence. For purposes of this exercise, do not indicate any subsequent history in the citation:

🌶 *The Bluebook* has special rules for citing New York cases. *See Bluebook* Table T.1 ("United States Jurisdictions, New York"). How each of the above cases will be cited depends on whether or not you are citing the case in a document that will or will not be submitted to a New York state court. In addition, you must take into account whether the reporter information sufficiently identifies the court, including its geographic jurisdiction. Finally, you must take into account the position of the court in the New York state court system.

🌶 Because the case name is going to appear in a **legal memorandum**, you should underscore (italicize) the case name (and any procedural phra*ses*) in your citation given in (e) above (*e.g.*, Ashland Oil & Ref. Co. v. State). Note that the comma following the case name in the citation is not underscored (italicized). *See Bluebook* Practitioners' Note P.1(a). Furthermore, be sure to check your citation for the following and apply the appropriate rule(s), if applicable:

- ☑ ABBREVIATIONS
- ☑ TERMS DESCRIBING A PARTY ALREADY NAMED
- ☑ GIVEN NAMES AND INITIALS OF INDIVIDUALS
- ☑ WORDS INDICATING MULTIPLE PARTIES
- ☑ ALTERNATIVE NAMES FOR A PARTY
- ☑ CONSOLIDATION OF TWO OR MORE ACTIONS
- ☑ ADDITIONAL PARTIES ON EACH SIDE OF THE CASE
- ☑ PARTNERSHIP NAMES
- ☑ BUSINESS FIRM DESIGNATIONS
- ☑ COMMISSIONER OF INTERNAL REVENUE AS A PARTY
- ☑ LABOR UNIONS
- ☑ "STATE OF" AND SIMILAR PHRASES
- ☑ TERMS INDICATING NATIONAL OR LARGER GEOGRAPHICAL LOCATIONS
- ☑ "CITY OF" AND SIMILAR PHRASES
- ☑ OTHER PREPOSITIONAL PHRASES OF LOCATION
- ☑ GEOGRAPHICAL WORDS NOT INTRODUCED BY A PREPOSITION
- ☑ PROCEDURAL PHRASES
- ☑ "THE"
- ☑ "IN REM" CASES

See supra Citation Exercises 9-11.

CITATION EXERCISE 27
CITING STATE COURT DECISIONS (VI)

Your Name _____

Your Professor's or Instructor's Name _____

Your Assigned Section (if applicable) _____

Your Assigned Problem Number _____

Self-Reassigned Problem Number (if applicable) _____

FIRST CASE:

(a) State the full name of the **first case** as it is stated in the reporter at the beginning of the opinion (*e.g.*, Opan M. Hansford, Plaintiff, Cross-Defendant and Appellant, v. Ben Lassar, Defendant, Cross-Complainant and Respondent); **you may omit obviously irrelevant portions of a party's name if the full name is a lengthy one**:

(b) State the full designation of the court for **first case** as it is stated in the reporter at the beginning of the opinion (*e.g.*, California Supreme Court):

(c) State the exact date of decision for the **first case** (*e.g.*, Dec. 1, 1975):

(d) State the citation of the **first case** in *Bluebook* (or another designated) form. Assume that the case name is going to appear in a **citation sentence or clause**, not as a part of a grammatical part of a textual sentence. For purposes of this exercise, do not indicate any subsequent history in the citation. **Also assume that you are citing the case in a document that WILL be submitted to a California state court:**

(e) State the citation of the **first case** in *Bluebook* (or another designated) form. Assume that the case name is going to appear in a **citation sentence or clause**, not as a part of a grammatical part of a textual sentence. For purposes of this exercise, do not indicate any subsequent history in the citation. **Also assume that you are citing the case in a document that will NOT be submitted to a California state court**:

SECOND CASE:

(a) State the full name of the **second case** as it is stated in the reporter at the beginning of the opinion (*e.g.*, Opan M. Hansford, Plaintiff, Cross-Defendant and Appellant, v. Ben Lassar, Defendant, Cross-Complainant and Respondent); **you may omit obviously irrelevant portions of a party's name if the full name is a lengthy one**:

(b) State the full designation of the court for **second case** as it is stated in the reporter at the beginning of the opinion (*e.g.*, California Supreme Court):

(c) State the exact date of decision for the **second case** (*e.g.*, Dec. 1, 1975):

(d) State the citation of the **second case** in *Bluebook* (or another designated) form. Assume that the case name is going to appear in a **citation sentence or clause**, not as a part of a grammatical part of a textual sentence. For purposes of this exercise, do not indicate any subsequent history in the citations. **Also assume that you are citing the case in a document that WILL be submitted to a California state court**:

(e) State the citation of the **second case** in *Bluebook* (or another designated) form. Assume that the case name is going to appear in a **citation sentence or clause**, not as a part of a grammatical part of a textual sentence. For purposes of this exercise, do not indicate any subsequent history in the citation. **Also assume that you are citing the case in a document that will NOT be submitted to a California state court**:

♦* *The Bluebook* has special rules for citing California cases. *See Bluebook* Table T.1 ("United States Jurisdictions, California"). How each of the above cases will be cited depends on whether or not you are citing the case in a document that will or will not be submitted to a California state court. In addition, you must take into account whether the reporter information sufficiently identifies the court, including its geographic jurisdiction. Finally, you must take into account the position of the court in the California state court system.

♦* Because the case name is going to appear in a **legal memorandum**, you should underscore (italicize) the case name (and any procedural phra*ses*) in your citation given in (e) above (*e.g.*, Hansford v. Lassar). Note that the comma following the case name in the citation is not underscored (italicized). *See Bluebook* Practitioners' Note P.1(a). Furthermore, be sure to check your citation for the following and apply the appropriate rule(s), if applicable:

- ☑ ABBREVIATIONS
- ☑ TERMS DESCRIBING A PARTY ALREADY NAMED
- ☑ GIVEN NAMES AND INITIALS OF INDIVIDUALS
- ☑ WORDS INDICATING MULTIPLE PARTIES
- ☑ ALTERNATIVE NAMES FOR A PARTY
- ☑ CONSOLIDATION OF TWO OR MORE ACTIONS
- ☑ ADDITIONAL PARTIES ON EACH SIDE OF THE CASE
- ☑ PARTNERSHIP NAMES
- ☑ BUSINESS FIRM DESIGNATIONS
- ☑ COMMISSIONER OF INTERNAL REVENUE AS A PARTY
- ☑ LABOR UNIONS
- ☑ "STATE OF" AND SIMILAR PHRASES
- ☑ TERMS INDICATING NATIONAL OR LARGER GEOGRAPHICAL LOCATIONS
- ☑ "CITY OF" AND SIMILAR PHRASES
- ☑ OTHER PREPOSITIONAL PHRASES OF LOCATION
- ☑ GEOGRAPHICAL WORDS NOT INTRODUCED BY A PREPOSITION
- ☑ PROCEDURAL PHRASES
- ☑ "THE"
- ☑ "IN REM" CASES

See supra Citation Exercises 9-11.

CITATION EXERCISE 28
UNREPORTED CASES AVAILABLE ON ELECTRONIC DATABASES: WESTLAW

Your Name _____

Your Professor's or Instructor's Name _____

Your Assigned Section (if applicable) _____

Your Assigned Problem Number _____

Self-Reassigned Problem Number (if applicable) _____

(a) State the full name of the case as it is stated at the beginning of the opinion (*e.g.*, Michael W. Stout, Plaintiff, v. Louis W. Sullivan, M.D., Secretary of the Department of Health and Human Services, Defendant); **you may omit obviously irrelevant portions of a party's name if the full name is a lengthy one**:

(b) State the docket number(s) exactly as listed (*e.g.*, No. 89-0828-CV-W-3):

(c) State the complete reference to the court exactly as it is indicated at the beginning of the opinion (*e.g.*, United States District Court, W.D. Missouri, Western Division):

(d) State the exact date of the most recent major disposition (*e.g.*, April 16, 1990):

(e) State the citation of the case in *Bluebook* (or another designated) form. Assume that the case name is going to appear in a **citation sentence or clause**, not as a part of a grammatical part of a textual sentence, in a **legal memorandum**. For purposes of this exercise, do not indicate any subsequent history in the citation:

NOTES ON CITATION EXERCISE 28

☛* Use the **full date** of the most recent major disposition of the action (usually the date of decision) in the citation; however, **abbreviate the month pursuant to *Bluebook* Table T.12.**

☛* Remember to include the docket number in the citation of the case.

☛* Because the case name is going to appear in a **legal memorandum**, you should underscore (italicize) the case name (and any procedural phra*ses*) in your citation given in (e) above (*e.g.*, Stout v. Sullivan). Note that the comma following the case name in the citation is not underscored (italicized). *See Bluebook* Practitioners' Note P.1(a). Furthermore, be sure to check your citation for the following and apply the appropriate rule(s), if applicable:

☑ ABBREVIATIONS
☑ TERMS DESCRIBING A PARTY ALREADY NAMED
☑ GIVEN NAMES AND INITIALS OF INDIVIDUALS
☑ WORDS INDICATING MULTIPLE PARTIES
☑ ALTERNATIVE NAMES FOR A PARTY
☑ CONSOLIDATION OF TWO OR MORE ACTIONS
☑ ADDITIONAL PARTIES ON EACH SIDE OF THE CASE
☑ PARTNERSHIP NAMES
☑ BUSINESS FIRM DESIGNATIONS
☑ COMMISSIONER OF INTERNAL REVENUE AS A PARTY
☑ LABOR UNIONS
☑ "STATE OF" AND SIMILAR PHRASES
☑ TERMS INDICATING NATIONAL OR LARGER GEOGRAPHICAL LOCATIONS
☑ "CITY OF" AND SIMILAR PHRASES
☑ OTHER PREPOSITIONAL PHRASES OF LOCATION
☑ GEOGRAPHICAL WORDS NOT INTRODUCED BY A PREPOSITION
☑ PROCEDURAL PHRASES
☑ "THE"
☑ "IN REM" CASES

See supra Citation Exercises 9-11

CITATION EXERCISE 29
UNREPORTED CASES AVAILABLE ON ELECTRONIC DATABASES: LEXIS

Your Name _____

Your Professor's or Instructor's Name _____

Your Assigned Section (if applicable) _____

Your Assigned Problem Number _____

Self-Reassigned Problem Number (if applicable) _____

(a) State the full name of the case as it is stated at the beginning of the opinion (*e.g.*, Michael W. Stout, Plaintiff, v. Louis W. Sullivan, M.D., Secretary of the Department of Health and Human Services, Defendant); **you may omit obviously irrelevant portions of a party's name if the full name is a lengthy one:**

(b) State the docket number(s) exactly as listed (*e.g.*, No. 89-0828-CV-W-3):

(c) State the complete reference to the court exactly as it is indicated at the beginning of the opinion (*e.g.*, United States District Court for the Northern District of Illinois, Eastern Division):

(d) State the full date of the most recent major disposition of the action (usually the date of decision) (*e.g.*, November 2, 1992):

(e) State the citation of the case in *Bluebook* (or another designated) form. Assume that the case name is going to appear in a **citation sentence or clause**, not as a part of a grammatical part of a textual sentence. For purposes of this exercise, do not indicate any subsequent history in the citation.

NOTES ON CITATION EXERCISE 29

✎* Use the **full date** of the most recent major disposition of the action (usually the date of decision) in the citation; however, **abbreviate the month pursuant to *Bluebook* Table T.12.**

✎* Remember to include the docket number in the citation of the case.

✎* Because the case name is going to appear in a **legal memorandum**, you should underscore (italicize) the case name (and any procedural phra*ses*) in your citation given in (e) above (*e.g.*, Stout v. Sullivan). Note that the comma following the case name in the citation is not underscored (italicized). *See Bluebook* Practitioners' Note P.1(a). **When necessary, abbreviate "versus," "vs." or "against" to "v." in the case name.** Furthermore, be sure to check your citation for the following and apply the appropriate rule(s), if applicable:

- ☑ ABBREVIATIONS
- ☑ TERMS DESCRIBING A PARTY ALREADY NAMED
- ☑ GIVEN NAMES AND INITIALS OF INDIVIDUALS
- ☑ WORDS INDICATING MULTIPLE PARTIES
- ☑ ALTERNATIVE NAMES FOR A PARTY
- ☑ CONSOLIDATION OF TWO OR MORE ACTIONS
- ☑ ADDITIONAL PARTIES ON EACH SIDE OF THE CASE
- ☑ PARTNERSHIP NAMES
- ☑ BUSINESS FIRM DESIGNATIONS
- ☑ COMMISSIONER OF INTERNAL REVENUE AS A PARTY
- ☑ LABOR UNIONS
- ☑ "STATE OF" AND SIMILAR PHRASES
- ☑ TERMS INDICATING NATIONAL OR LARGER GEOGRAPHICAL LOCATIONS
- ☑ "CITY OF" AND SIMILAR PHRASES
- ☑ OTHER PREPOSITIONAL PHRASES OF LOCATION
- ☑ GEOGRAPHICAL WORDS NOT INTRODUCED BY A PREPOSITION
- ☑ PROCEDURAL PHRASES
- ☑ "THE"
- ☑ "IN REM" CASES

See supra Citation Exercises 9-11.

CITATION EXERCISE 30
SUBSEQUENT HISTORY IN CASE CITATIONS

Your Name _____

Your Professor's or Instructor's Name _____

Your Assigned Section (if applicable) _____

Your Assigned Problem Number _____

Self-Reassigned Problem Number (if applicable) _____

(a) Find the case that you are shepardizing in the relevant reporter. **For the case that you are shepardizing**, state the full case name as it is stated in the reporter at the beginning of the opinion (*e.g.*, The State, Respondent, v. Russell Collins, Appellant); **you may omit obviously irrelevant portions of a party's name if the full name is a lengthy one**:

(b) **For the case that you are shepardizing**, state the complete reference to the court exactly as it is indicated at the beginning of the opinion (*e.g.*, Supreme Court of South Carolina):

(c) **For the case that you are shepardizing**, state the exact date of decision (*e.g.*, Jan. 5, 1998):

(d) Find the relevant entry for the case that you are shepardizing in the appropriate volume(s) of *Shepard's Citations*. State the entry or entries in *Shepard's Citations* indicating the subsequent history (*e.g.*, US cert den in 383 US 952, v134 CaR 774, r528 F2d 745) for the case that you are shepardizing; do not, however, include the history on remand or a denial of a rehearing; if there is no subsequent history, answer "none":

(e) For any **subsequent history** listed in (d), if any, state the following information:

(i) the full case name as it is stated in the reporter at the beginning of the opinion; **you may omit obviously irrelevant portions of a party's name if the full name is a lengthy one**; (you will need to consult the reporter to find this information.):

(ii) the exact date of decision; (you will need to consult the reporter to find this information.):

(f) State the citation of the case in *Bluebook* (or another designated) form. Indicate any relevant subsequent history in the citation. For purposes of this exercise, do not show the history on remand or a denial of a rehearing in the citation; however, **do show denials or dismissals of certiorari**. Unless otherwise instructed, if you are citing a state court case, assume that you are citing it in a document that **WILL** be submitted to a state court in the jurisdiction from which the case arises. Use *Shepard's Citations* to find any missing parallel citations. **For U.S. Supreme Court actions, cite only *United States Reports*** (when relevant):

* **When the name of a case differs in prior or subsequent history, both case names must be given in the citation; however, the second name should not be given when the parties' names are merely reversed or when the difference occurs in a citation to a denial of review by writ of certiorari or a rehearing.** *Bluebook* Rule 10.7.2. A different name in subsequent history is introduced by "*sub nom.*"

* **The year of decision is included only with the *last* cited decision when a case with several decisions in the *same* year is cited.** However, if the exact date of decision is required for either case by *Bluebook* Rule 10.5 (for all unreported cases, all cases cited to newspapers, periodicals, and looseleaf services), you should include both dates. *Bluebook* Rule 10.5(c).

* Remember that the history of a case on remand and any denial of a rehearing should be omitted unless it is particularly relevant.

* Be sure to underscore (italicize) the explanatory phrases (e.g., aff'd, cert. denied, etc.). Consult *Bluebook* Table T.9 ("Explanatory Phrases").

* The sixteenth edition of the *Bluebook* provides that denials of certiorari or similar discretionary denials of review should be omitted "unless the decision is less than two years old or the denial is particularly relevant." *Bluebook* Rule 10.7. **However, for purposes of this exercise, you have been instructed to show denials or dismissals of certiorari.**

* Remember that you are to assume that you are citing a state court case in a document that **WILL** be submitted to a state court in the jurisdiction from which the case arises. Thus, **you must include both the official reporter citation (if available) and the parallel West reporter citation(s) in your citation for this exercise if you are citing a state court case.** *See Bluebook* Rule 10.3.1 & Practitioners' Note P.3.

* The abbreviated name of the court, including its geographic jurisdiction, should be included in the parenthetical with the date. You can determine the abbreviation of the geographic jurisdiction and the court (if any) by consulting the appropriate entry in *Bluebook* Table T.1. This information appears immediately after the name of the court (*e.g.*, **Supreme Judicial Court** (Me.)). However, when the highest court of a jurisdiction is cited, the abbreviated name of the court should be omitted. Furthermore, when the abbreviated name of one of the reporters cited (*e.g.*, Me.) unambiguously indicates the geographic jurisdiction, the geographic jurisdiction should also be omitted.

* If you are citing a **Texas** court for this exercise, be certain to examine the discussion in *Bluebook* Table T.1 concerning identification of Texas Courts of Appeals and writ history.

* Because the case name is going to appear in a **legal memorandum,** you should underscore (italicize) the case name (and any procedural phra*ses*) in your citation given in (e) above (*e.g.*, Stout v. Sullivan). Note that the comma following the case name in the citation is not underscored (italicized). *See Bluebook* Practitioners' Note P.1(a). Furthermore, be sure to check your citation for the following and apply the appropriate rule(s), if applicable:

- ☑ ABBREVIATIONS
- ☑ TERMS DESCRIBING A PARTY ALREADY NAMED
- ☑ GIVEN NAMES AND INITIALS OF INDIVIDUALS
- ☑ WORDS INDICATING MULTIPLE PARTIES
- ☑ ALTERNATIVE NAMES FOR A PARTY
- ☑ CONSOLIDATION OF TWO OR MORE ACTIONS
- ☑ ADDITIONAL PARTIES ON EACH SIDE OF THE CASE
- ☑ PARTNERSHIP NAMES
- ☑ BUSINESS FIRM DESIGNATIONS
- ☑ COMMISSIONER OF INTERNAL REVENUE AS A PARTY
- ☑ LABOR UNIONS
- ☑ "STATE OF" AND SIMILAR PHRASES
- ☑ TERMS INDICATING NATIONAL OR LARGER GEOGRAPHICAL LOCATIONS
- ☑ "CITY OF" AND SIMILAR PHRASES
- ☑ OTHER PREPOSITIONAL PHRASES OF LOCATION
- ☑ GEOGRAPHICAL WORDS NOT INTRODUCED BY A PREPOSITION
- ☑ PROCEDURAL PHRASES
- ☑ "THE"
- ☑ "IN REM" CASES

See supra Citation Exercises 9-11.

CITATION EXERCISE 31
FEDERAL STATUTES (I)

Your Name _____

Your Professor's or Instructor's Name _____

Your Assigned Section (if applicable) _____

Your Assigned Problem Number _____

Self-Reassigned Problem Number (if applicable) _____

State the citation of the statutory provision in *Bluebook* (or another designated) form. However, for purposes of this exercise, you should **omit** any reference the location where the statutory provision has been or will be codified in the *United States Code*:

♦* Be sure to use the official or popular name of the statute (*e.g.*, Employee Polygraph Protection Act of 1988) at the beginning of the citation; if a statute does not have an official or popular name, use the full date of enactment (*e.g.*, Act of Aug. 12, 1958). *See Bluebook* Rule 12.4(a). Abbreviate months in the full date according to *Bluebook* Table T.12 if you are using *Bluebook* form.

♦* For statutes enacted before 1957, use the chapter number (*e.g.*, ch. 42) in the citation.

♦* For statutes enacted after 1957, use the public law number (*e.g.*, Pub. L. No. 85-623) in the citation.

♦* Statutes in the *United States Statutes at Large* are cited by volume number and page number on which the act begins; the abbreviated designation for the *United States Statutes at Large* is Stat. *See Bluebook* Table T.1.

♦* The year of enactment (*e.g.*, 1998) should be given parenthetically at the end of the citation; however, the year of enactment should be omitted when it appears as part of the name of the statute; *see Bluebook* Rule 12.4(d).

CITATION EXERCISE 32
FEDERAL STATUTES (II)

Your Name _____

Your Professor's or Instructor's Name _____

Your Assigned Section (if applicable) _____

Your Assigned Problem Number _____

Self-Reassigned Problem Number (if applicable) _____

    (a) State the copyright date of the volume of West's *United States Code Annotated* that you used (located on the page following the title page of the volume):

    (b) State the citation of the code section in *Bluebook* (or another designated) form. Cite the code section to *United States Code Annotated* (*e.g.*, 28 U.S.C.A. § 1404(a) (West 1993).). Be sure to check the supplement to see if the section has been added or amended since the publication of the main volume. If the current version appears in the supplement, cite the supplement appropriately. Assume that your citation will appear in a court document or legal memorandum, not in a law review article:

NOTES ON CITATION EXERCISE 32

&* Cite West's *United States Code Annotated* by title number, the abbreviated title of the publication (U.S.C.A.), section number, and date. Include the publisher's name (West) in the parenthetical with the date when you are citing unofficial versions of the *Code* such as West's *United States Code Annotated*. *See Bluebook* Table T.1.

&* Give the name and original section number only if the statute is commonly cited in that manner or if the information would otherwise help in identifying the provision. *Bluebook* Rules 12.2 and 12.3.

&* The *United States Code Annotated* and the *United States Code Service* are kept up to date by pocket parts and replacement volumes. Be sure to check pocket part for the latest version of the statute. The supplementary material in these publications is cited as follows: 35 U.S.C.A. § 42 (West 1994 & Supp. 1998). or 22 U.S.C.A. § 6321 (West Supp. 1998).

CITATION EXERCISE 33
STATE STATUTES (I)

Your Name _____

Your Professor's or Instructor's Name _____

Your Assigned Section (if applicable) _____

Your Assigned Problem Number _____

Self-Reassigned Problem Number (if applicable) _____

(a) List the name(s) of the statutory compilation(s) for the jurisdiction listed with your problem number (*e.g.*, Wisconsin Statutes (1975 & biannually); West's Wisconsin Statutes Annotated):

(b) List the citation form(s) listed for the statutory compilation(s) stated for your answer in (a), above (*e.g.*, Wis. Stat. § x (19xx); Wis. Stat. Ann. § x (West 19xx)):

(c) State the session laws available for the jurisdiction listed with your problem number (*e.g.*, Laws of Wisconsin; West's Wisconsin Legislative Service):

(d) State the *Bluebook* citation form(s) listed for the session laws stated for your answer in (c), above (*e.g.*, 19xx Wis. Laws xxx; 19xx Wis. Legis. Serv. xxx (West)):

NOTES ON CITATION EXERCISE 33

♦* Be sure to provide all the information requested for each answer.

CITATION EXERCISE 34
STATE STATUTES (II)

Your Name _____

Your Professor's or Instructor's Name _____

Your Assigned Section (if applicable) _____

Your Assigned Problem Number _____

Self-Reassigned Problem Number (if applicable) _____

(a) State the title of the state statutory set you used to find the statute (*e.g.*, Vermont Statutes Annotated):

(b) State the year that appears on the spine of the volume you used, or the year that appears on the title page, or the latest copyright year—in that order of preference (*e.g.*, 1998). If the volume is a replacement, reissue, or republication of an earlier edition, use the year of the replacement, reissued, or republished volume rather than the original. After stating the year, indicate parenthetically which source for the year you used (*e.g.*, 1998 (date on the spine of the volume)); and also indicate parenthetically that a replacement, reissued, or republished volume was used (*e.g.*, 1998 (date on the spine of the reissued volume)). However, if you are citing a looseleaf codification, state (1) the year on the page on which the material is printed or (2) the year on the first page of the subdivision within which the cited material appears, if any, in that order of preference, (in lieu of the dates stated above):

(c) State the citation of the statutory provision in *Bluebook* (or another designated) form; assume that your citation will appear in a court document or legal memorandum, not in a law review article:

NOTES ON CITATION EXERCISE 34

♠* Be sure to follow the abbreviations and include the publisher, editor, or compiler as provided in *Bluebook* Table T.1 The official version is the preferred source when multiple sources are available.

♠* For citations of codified state statutes, give (1) the year that appears on the spine of the volume, (2) the year that appears on the title page, or (3) the latest copyright year, in that order of preference. If the volume is a "replacement" of an earlier edition, the date of the replacement volume is used, not the year of the original. If the date on the spine or title page spans more than one year, all years are given (*e.g.*, 1998-1999). *Bluebook* Rule 12.3.2. **Be careful to provide all the information requested in (b), above.**

♠* Some state codifications are in looseleaf form. In citing those codifications, use (1) the year on the page on which the material is printed or (2) the year on the first page of the subdivision within which the cited material appears, if any, in that order of preference (in lieu of the dates stated above). *Bluebook* Rule 12.3.2.

STATE STATUTES (III)

Your Name _____

Your Professor's or Instructor's Name _____

Your Assigned Section (if applicable) _____

Your Assigned Problem Number _____

Self-Reassigned Problem Number (if applicable) _____

(a) State the year that appears on the spine of the volume you used, or the year that appears on the title page, or the latest copyright year—in that order of preference (*e.g.*, 1998). If the volume is a replacement, reissue, or republication of an earlier edition, use the year of the replacement, reissued, or republished volume rather than the original. After stating the year, indicate parenthetically which source for the year you used (*e.g.*, 1998 (date on the spine of the volume)); and also indicate parenthetically that a replacement, reissued, or republished volume was used (*e.g.*, 1998 (date on the spine of the reissued volume)). If you are citing a looseleaf codification, state (1) the date on the page on which the material is printed or (2) the date on the first page of the subdivision within which the cited material appears, if any, in that order of preference, (in lieu of the dates stated above):

(b) State the citation of the statutory provision in *Bluebook* (or another designated) form; assume that your citation will appear in a court document or legal memorandum, not in a law review article:

✍ Be sure to follow the abbreviations and include the publisher, editor, or compiler as provided in *Bluebook* Table T.1 Be sure to include the appropriate subject-matter code in your citation. **The various abbreviations of the subject-matter codes are set forth in *Bluebook* Table T.1.** The official version is the preferred source when multiple sources are available.

✍ For citations of codified state statutes, give (1) the year that appears on the spine of the volume, (2) the year that appears on the title page, or (3) the latest copyright year, in that order of preference. If the volume is a "replacement" of an earlier edition, the date of the replacement volume is used, not the year of the original. If the date on the spine or title page spans more than one year, all years are given (*e.g.*, 1998-1999). *Bluebook* Rule 12.3.2. **Be careful to provide all the information requested in (a), above.**

✍ Some state codifications are in looseleaf form. In citing those codifications, use (1) the date on the page on which the material is printed or (2) the date on the first page of the subdivision within which the cited material appears, if any, in that order of preference (in lieu of the dates stated above). *Bluebook* Rule 12.3.2.

CITATION EXERCISE 36
CONSTITUTIONS

Your Name _____

Your Professor's or Instructor's Name _____

Your Assigned Section (if applicable) _____

Your Assigned Problem Number _____

Self-Reassigned Problem Number (if applicable) _____

State the citation of the constitutional provision in *Bluebook* (or another designated) form. Include the clause in your citation, if appropriate. If the subject matter listed with your problem number is governed by more than one provision of the U.S. Constitution, you may cite any one of them; assume that your citation will appear in a court document or legal memorandum, not in a law review article:

NOTES ON CITATION EXERCISE 36

♦✳ Cite the U.S. Constitution by article, section, and, if appropriate, by clause.

♦✳ Cite amendments to the U.S. Constitution by **roman number**.

♦✳ Remember to abbreviate "United States" to "U.S." and "Constitution" to "Const." There is no space between the "U." and "S." *Bluebook* Table T.1.

♦✳ Remember to abbreviate "Article" to "art.," "Section" to "§," "Sections" to "§§," and "Clause" to "cl." **Do not capitalize "art." or "cl."**

♦✳ Remember to abbreviate "Amendment" to "amend." **Do not capitalize "amend."** *Bluebook* Table T.16 ("Subdivisions").

♦✳ Cite constitutional provisions currently in force without a date. *Bluebook* Rule 11.

CITATION EXERCISE 37
TREATIES

Your Name _____

Your Professor's or Instructor's Name _____

Your Assigned Section (if applicable) _____

Your Assigned Problem Number _____

Self-Reassigned Problem Number (if applicable) _____

(a) State the form of agreement (*e.g.*, Treaty, Convention, etc.) based on the first designation given on the title page of the agreement:

(b) State the subject of the cited agreement (*e.g.*, Outer Space Mining):

(c) State the exact date(s) of signing (*e.g.*, Aug. 15, 1998):

(d) State the parties to the agreement (*e.g.*, United States-Colombia):

(e) State the citation of the agreement in *Bluebook* (or another designated) form:

♠* Cite the agreement by its form and subject matter. *Bluebook* Rule 20.4.1(a) provides that the subject matter or the agreement form may be given first (*e.g.*, Extradition Treaty or Treaty on Extradition);

♠* With regard to the form of agreement (*e.g.*, Treaty, Convention, etc.), use the **first** designation given on the title page of the agreement; do not use multiple designations (*e.g.*, Treaty, **not** "Treaty and Protocol").

♠* With regard to the subject matter of the agreement, designate the subject-matter by using the description that is provided as part of the title of the agreement. When the name of a treaty is very lengthy or it is known by a popular name, *Bluebook* Rule 20.4.1(b) permits the use of a shortened or popular name in **subsequent citations**. *See Bluebook* Rules 20.4.1(b) & 4.2(b)

♠* Remember to use the exact **signing date**(s). The dates will vary depending on the number of parties: (1) for agreements between two parties, the first and last signing dates should be given; or (2) for agreements between more than two parties that are not signed on a single date, the date on which the agreement was opened for signature, approved, or adopted should be given in italics (*e.g.*, *opened for signature* Sept. 9, 1998)

♠* Consult Table T.12 ("Months") for proper abbreviation of the month for the date used in the citation; when it is of particular significance, an additional date can be added parenthetically (*e.g.*, the date that the agreement entered into force).

♠* When there are two parties, give the parties to agreement (*e.g.*, United States-Spain); otherwise, they need not be given.

♠* When parties to the agreement are given in the citation, be sure to consult Table T.10 ("Geographical Terms") for abbreviations for the parties.

♠* When the **agreement is between the United States and only one other party**, cite to **one of the following sources** (in order of preference): (a) *United States Treaties and Other International Agreements* (U.S.T.) or *United States Statutes at Large* (Stat.); (b) *Treaties and Other International Act Series* (T.I.A.S.) or Treaty Series (T.S.) or *Executive Agreement Series* (E.A.S.); (c) Senate Treaty Documents or Senate Executive Documents; (d) Department of State Bulletin; (e) Department of State Press Releases; or (f) unofficial sources (when the agreement has not appeared in one of the above). *Bluebook* Rule 20.4.5(a)(i).

CITATION EXERCISE 38
LEGISLATIVE HISTORY

Your Name _____

Your Professor's or Instructor's Name _____

Your Assigned Section (if applicable) _____

Your Assigned Problem Number _____

Self-Reassigned Problem Number (if applicable) _____

State the citation of the committee report in *Bluebook* (or another designated) form; include a parallel citation to *United States Code Congressional and Administrative News*:

NOTES ON CITATION EXERCISE 38

♦※ Remember to use the House or Senate report number in the citation; connect the number of the Congress with a hyphen to the number of the report (*e.g.,* S. Rep. No. 95-185, H.R. Rep. No. 95-263, etc.);

♦※ Be sure to provide the parallel citation to the permanent edition of West's *United States Code Congressional and Administrative News* in your citation.

♦※ The abbreviation of West's *United States Code Congressional and Administrative News* is U.S.C.C.A.N.

♦※ *Bluebook* Rule 3.2(a) provides that when a volume number is not given and the volume is readily identifiable by year, you should use the year of the volume (*e.g.,* 1962 U.S.C.C.A.N. 2844). Thus, when you are citing West's *United States Code Congressional and Administrative News*, do not give the year at the end of the citation.

CITATION EXERCISE 39
ADMINISTRATIVE REGULATIONS (I)

Your Name _____

Your Professor's or Instructor's Name _____

Your Assigned Section (if applicable) _____

Your Assigned Problem Number _____

Self-Reassigned Problem Number (if applicable) _____

     State the citation of the provision in the *C.F.R.* in *Bluebook* (or another designated) form:

♠* The Code of Federal Regulations (C.F.R.) is cited by title, section, and year. The date of the volume is given in parentheses. The section number is formed from a part number and subsection; thus, § 55.161 is subsection 161 of Part 55.

♠* When the rule or regulation has a commonly used name, that name may be added before the volume number. *Bluebook* Rule 14.2(a). However, none of the provisions used for this exercise have a commonly used name.

CITATION EXERCISE 40
ADMINISTRATIVE REGULATIONS (II)

Your Name _____

Your Professor's or Instructor's Name _____

Your Assigned Section (if applicable) _____

Your Assigned Problem Number _____

Self-Reassigned Problem Number (if applicable) _____

(a) State the name of the administrative compilation for the state (*e.g., California Code of Regulations*):

(b) State the *Bluebook* citation form of the administrative compilation listed in (a), above (*e.g.,* Cal. Code Regs. tit. x, § x (19xx):

(c) State the name of the administrative register for the state (*e.g., California Regulatory Notice Register*):

(d) State the *Bluebook* citation form of the administrative register listed in (c), above (*e.g.,* Cal. Regulatory Notice Reg.):

Notes on Citation Exercise 40

🔴* Be sure to provide all the information requested for each answer.

Notes

Notes

Notes

Notes

Notes

Notes

Notes

Notes

Notes

Notes